# CONSUMER BEHAVIOUR AND DIGITAL TRANSFORMATION

This comprehensive textbook explores how technological developments and emerging technologies impact on, and engage with, consumer behaviour and decision making globally. The book will enable readers to develop a coherent understanding of the basic underpinnings of consumer behaviour as they relate to individual and group-oriented consumption decisions, offering insight into how consumer behaviour, contemporary real-life situations, and digital technology are inextricably linked.

Key learning objectives, exercises and activities, boxed examples and analytical frameworks facilitate and enrich students' learning. Each chapter includes 'pause, plan, and practice (PPP)' activities, as well as real-life case studies exploring digital consumption, digital consumer experiences, and digital trends across industries, from global companies such as Nike and McDonald's to the digital transformation of SMEs. Combining a thorough examination of traditional theory with a fresh approach to the impact of digital transformation on consumer behaviour, this textbook should be core reading for advanced undergraduate and postgraduate students studying Consumer Behaviour, Consumer Psychology, Customer Experience Management, and Digital Marketing.

This book will be accompanied by online resources for the use of instructors, including PowerPoint slides and a test bank.

**Ayantunji Gbadamosi** is an Associate Professor in Marketing and Co-chair of the Research Ethics Committee at Royal Docks School of Business and Law, University of East London, UK.

# Business and Digital Transformation

Digital technologies are transforming societies across the globe, the effects of which are yet to be fully understood. In the business world, technological disruption brings an array of challenges and opportunities for organizations, management and the workplace.

This series of textbooks provides a student-centred library to analyse, explore and critique the evolutionary effects of technology on the business world. Each book in the series takes the perspective of a key business discipline and examines the transformational potential of digital technology, aided by real world cases and examples.

With contributions from expert scholars across the globe, the books in this series enable critical thinking students to excel in their studies of the new digital business environment.

**Strategic Digital Transformation**
A Results-Driven Approach
*Edited by Alex Fenton, Gordon Fletcher and Marie Griffiths*

**Hospitality Management and Digital Transformation**
Balancing Efficiency, Agility and Guest Experience in the Era of Disruption
*Richard Busulwa, Nina Evans, Aaron Oh and Moon Kang*

**Digital Transformation in Accounting**
*Richard Busulwa and Nina Evans*

**Demand-Driven Business Strategy**
Digital Transformation and Business Model Innovation
*Cor Molenaar*

**Navigating Digital Transformation in Management**
*Richard Busulwa*

**Smart Business and Digital Transformation**
An Industry 4.0 Perspective
*Sándor Gyula Nagy and Tamás Stukovszky*

**Data Analytics and Digital Transformation**
*Erik Beulen and Marla A. Dans*

**Consumer Behaviour and Digital Transformation**
*Ayantunji Gbadamosi*

For more information about this series, please visit www.routledge.com/Routledge-New-Directions-in-Public-Relations--Communication-Research/book-series/BAD

# Consumer Behaviour and Digital Transformation

Ayantunji Gbadamosi

LONDON AND NEW YORK

Designed cover image: solarseven

First published 2024
by Routledge
4 Park Square, Milton Park, Abingdon, Oxon OX14 4RN

and by Routledge
605 Third Avenue, New York, NY 10158

*Routledge is an imprint of the Taylor & Francis Group, an informa business*

© 2024 Ayantunji Gbadamosi

The right of Ayantunji Gbadamosi to be identified as author of this work has been asserted in accordance with sections 77 and 78 of the Copyright, Designs and Patents Act 1988.

All rights reserved. No part of this book may be reprinted or reproduced or utilised in any form or by any electronic, mechanical, or other means, now known or hereafter invented, including photocopying and recording, or in any information storage or retrieval system, without permission in writing from the publishers.

*Trademark notice*: Product or corporate names may be trademarks or registered trademarks, and are used only for identification and explanation without intent to infringe.

*British Library Cataloguing-in-Publication Data*
A catalogue record for this book is available from the British Library

*Library of Congress Cataloging-in-Publication Data*
Names: Gbadamosi, Ayantunji, author.
Title: Consumer behaviour and digital transformation / Ayantunji Gbadamosi.
Description: Abingdon, Oxon ; New York, NY : Routledge, 2024. |
Series: Business and digital transformation |
Includes bibliographical references and index. |
Identifiers: LCCN 2023039118 (print) | LCCN 2023039119 (ebook) |
ISBN 9781032149752 (hardback) | ISBN 9781032149769 (paperback) |
ISBN 9781003242031 (ebook)
Subjects: LCSH: Consumer behavior. | Electronic commerce. | Internet marketing.
Classification: LCC HF5415.32 .G33 2024 (print) |
LCC HF5415.32 (ebook) | DDC 658.8/342–dc23/eng/20230824
LC record available at https://lccn.loc.gov/2023039118
LC ebook record available at https://lccn.loc.gov/2023039119

ISBN: 9781032149752 (hbk)
ISBN: 9781032149769 (pbk)
ISBN: 9781003242031 (ebk)

DOI: 10.4324/9781003242031

Typeset in Sabon
by Newgen Publishing UK

Access the Support Material: www.routledge.com/9781032149769

*The book is dedicated to the loving memory of my parents:
Isaac Olajire Kazeem (I.O.K.) Gbadamosi
&
Deborah Abike Gbadamosi*

# Contents

| | |
|---|---|
| *Preface* | *ix* |
| *Acknowledgements* | *xiii* |
| *About the Author* | *xiv* |
| *List of Figures* | *xvi* |
| *List of Tables* | *xviii* |

**PART 1  TECHNOLOGY AND THE CONTEMPORARY CONSUMER BEHAVIOUR: AN INTRODUCTION**    1

1 Consumer Behaviour: Discussing the Boundaries and Introducing the Digital Consumer    3
  Case Study: Meeting Consumers' Needs in a Digital Age: Amazon Leads the Way    22

2 Ethics and Contemporary Issues in Consumer Behaviour    28
  Case Study: The European Union's Agenda for SMEs and the Quest for Sustainable Consumption    49

3 Consumer Decision-making Processes    56
  Case Study: PayPal and Digital Transformation in the Consumer Decision-making Process    74

**PART 2  DIGITAL TRANSFORMATION IN THE SOCIO-CULTURAL IMPACTS ON CONSUMPTION**    81

4 Impact of Culture and Sub-culture on Consumer Decisions    83
  Case Study: McDonald's in the Middle East: How Businesses are Connecting the World of Consumer Culture    107

| | | |
|---|---|---|
| 5 | Reference Groups, Social Class, and Consumer Behaviour | 113 |
| | Case Study: Clubhouse: The Hub for Valuable Conversations | 133 |

## PART 3  DIGITAL TRANSFORMATION AND THE PSYCHOLOGICAL INFLUENCES ON CONSUMER BEHAVIOUR — 141

| | | |
|---|---|---|
| 6 | Consumer Perception – Beauty in the Eyes of the Beholder | 143 |
| | Case Study: Product Positioning for Unique Experiences at Nike | 164 |
| 7 | Impact of Learning and Memory on Consumer Behaviour | 170 |
| | Case Study: Consumers' Digital Experience at Barclays Bank | 188 |
| 8 | Attitude Formation and Change in Consumer Behaviour | 192 |
| | Case Study: Campaigning to Curb Obesity – Is the World Losing the Battle? | 214 |
| 9 | Consumer Motivation | 219 |
| | Case Study: The Drive for Ferrari Cars | 233 |
| 10 | Consumer Personality and The Self | 238 |
| | Case Study: Extending the Self on Social Media | 255 |

## PART 4  EXPLORING CREATIVITY AND INNOVATION IN HOW TECHNOLOGY IMPACTS CONSUMER BEHAVIOUR — 261

| | | |
|---|---|---|
| 11 | Technology, Diffusion of Innovation, and Consumer Behaviour | 263 |
| | Case Study: Samsung: How Technology Rules the World | 282 |
| 12 | Contemporary Consumer Research | 287 |
| | Case Study: Big Data and Consumer Research in British Supermarkets | 319 |
| 13 | Consumer Behaviour and Technology: A Look into the Future | 325 |
| | Case Study: Small is Beautiful: Can Technology be the Missing Link for SMEs in Consumer-focused Marketing? | 341 |

*Index* — *349*

# Preface

Digital transformation, as demonstrated by the significant increase in the use of digital technologies by consumers and businesses, is a notable part of the recent marketing environment. While this has been part of our lives for some time and increasing gradually over the years, the experience of the COVID-19 pandemic has increased the rate at which consumers use digital processes in their consumption dynamics. As noted by the United Nations on its website, 57% of UN member states have communicated details about the global pandemic on their national portals as at 25 March 2020, while this number had increased to 86% totalling 167 countries by 8 April 2020 (UN, 2020). This is symptomatic of the significant use of digital technologies for guidance on social distancing, lockdowns, and other related issues during the period. As we now operate in the post-COVID new normal era, the use of digital technology among consumers has increased significantly with a number of over 5 billion Internet users. So, this new reality has come to stay.

Meanwhile, over the years, consumer behaviour has been widely acknowledged as a key area of marketing, cutting across consumers' interactions with organisations of all sizes and touching on a range of issues from social to psychological, and from in-country to cross-country regions. Consequently, the dramatic changes regarding the relevance of digital technology, and other changes in the dynamic marketing environment in relation to consumption, now imply that there is a compelling need to rearticulate the terrain of the discourse of consumer behaviour. So, attention should now focus on a thorough study of contemporary consumer behaviour concerning purchases, where and why consumers make them, and how they spend their financial resources in their various value-oriented transactions with reference to the prevailing digital landscape. This is the palpable gap addressed by this proposed book.

## SCOPE OF THE BOOK

### Objectives

*Consumer Behaviour and Digital Transformation* seeks to achieve two broad objectives:

1. Enable students develop a coherent understanding of basic underpinnings of consumer behaviour as they relate to individual and group-oriented consumption decisions.
2. Provide readers with a basic insight into how consumer behaviour concepts may be applicable to contemporary real-life situations with specific reference to developments around digital technology vis-à-vis people's consumption dynamics.

Using a series of text boxes, this text includes original cutting-edge resources that showcase developments in multicultural contexts charting new directions for learning and teaching of the subject in a contemporary space.

In more specific terms and in relation to the prevalent digitalisation in consumption in recent times, the text aims to:

1. Highlight the individual aspects of consumers from perception to motivation, personality, learning, the self, and attitude.
2. Discuss consumer behaviour in the context of cultural and social settings to cover family, social class, culture, sub-culture, and how these factors interrelate to influence consumption issues.
3. Explore and explain customer relationships, consumer misbehaviour, and organisation buying behaviour and their implications for the formation of a sound marketing strategy.
4. Examine consumer decision-making processes through the use of relevant models, from a discussion of diffusion of innovations, ethnicity, and contemporary issues in consumer behaviour including social networks and evolving virtual relationships.

### The Target Audience

The book is intended to be a detailed pedagogical material for students, instructors, and practitioners in the field.

The primary target audience includes both undergraduate and postgraduate students studying Consumer Behaviour at institutions of higher learning. Emphatically, it is intended that readers on taught programmes and research students will find the book very useful as a good companion for their various relevant academic activities. The secondary target audience of the book consists of practitioners, who will find the book invaluable reference material and a source of information needed to operate within the complexity of the prevailing marketing environment.

## FEATURES OF THE BOOK

The key emphasis of this text is on technological developments as they impact upon consumer behaviour and decision making. This text makes a cutting-edge and distinct contribution to the existing discourse in consumer behaviour literature in the relevant context. Such an undertaking would, however, not exclude the need to feature the usual various pedagogical elements that make it suitable for the target audience – both UG and PG students.

### Summary of Key Ideas

The book will be structured in such a way that the key learning objectives are outlined at the beginning of every chapter to give students a clear indication of what the chapter contains, and each of the chapters ends with the summary of key ideas discussed. This is meant to serve as a way of gauging the extent to which the objectives set at the beginning of the chapter have been achieved as well as recapping the learning outcomes.

### Style of Writing

In view of the target audience, a multicultural audience, the book is written in basic but clear English language in a conversational style. This is to ensure that the communication is simplified without jeopardising the expected academic rigour/excellence. The aim is to produce an *easy-to-read* and *easy-to-follow* text that fulfills the learning experience of a multicultural student audience.

### Illustrations, Diagrams, and Case Studies

Apart from setting out the key issues both at the beginning and at the end of the chapters, each chapter will be supported with various 'real life' illustrations, exercises, group activities, boxed examples, and analytical frameworks to facilitate and enrich students' learning. Specifically, each chapter begins with a 'Digital Box' which discusses contemporary consumer behaviour issues as related to digital technology. Each of these comes with questions and tasks for discussion. Moreover, another boxed exercise titled *Pause, Plan, and Practice* (PPP) for a discussion of topics relevant to the content of the chapter is provided for each of the chapters. Furthermore, each chapter features a short contemporary real-world case study that primarily focuses on consumer behaviour problem-solving scenarios with relevant questions to discuss the issues addressed in the chapter.

### Discussion Questions

There are five discussion questions at the end of each chapter. Apart from enabling students to assess their own understanding of the topic covered, the questions will constitute an excellent 'test bank' to support learning, teaching, and assessments.

## Support Material

The book is accompanied by PowerPoint slides, answers to the case studies, boxed exercises, and Tutorial activities. Also featured are instructions for further reading. All these are meant to assist students and tutors to have the necessary materials that will ease their use of the book.

## REFERENCE

UN (2020). Digital technologies critical in facing COVID-19 pandemic, United Nations, New York, 15 April 2020, https://www.un.org/development/desa/en/news/policy/digital-technologies-critical-in-facing-covid-19-pandemic.html (accessed 7 July 2020).

# Acknowledgements

Clearly, I have received incredible support from many people in various ways concerning this project. I would like to especially thank the team at Routledge who supported the project from proposal to the final stage: Sophia Levine, Emma Morley, Rachel Cronin, and Rupert Spurrier. Evidently, their expertise and dedication to the project are noteworthy and significant in the successful completion of this work. Their professionalism has proved useful and made the publishing of *Consumer Behaviour and Digital Transformation* a reality.

I am greatly indebted to my family, my wife, Sarah Remilekun Gbadamosi, and my children (Miracle, Favour, and Joy) for their encouragement, support, and understanding. Indeed, there are many others who have supported me in various other ways towards making this book a reality, including authors whose publications are used and cited, our students whose passion and interest in Consumer Behaviour as a subject impelled some of the ideas discussed in the book, and others whom I have not explicitly mentioned, I think of you and thank you, nevertheless. Above all, it is notable that the motivation, empowerment, and vehemence for this book came from God for which I am forever grateful. This served as the bone, tendon, and ligaments of the entire project without which it would have been impossible.

*Dr Ayantunji Gbadamosi*
*Associate Professor in Marketing & Co-chair,*
*School Research Ethics Committee*
*Royal Docks School of Business and Law*
*University of East London, UK*

# About the Author

Dr Ayantunji Gbadamosi (BSc (Hons), MSc, PhD, FCIM, FCMI, SFHEA, CMBE) is an Associate Professor in Marketing, and a Co-chair for the School Research Ethics Committee at the Royal Docks School of Business and Law, University of East London, UK. He once served as the Research Coordinator and The Chair of the Research and Knowledge Exchange Committee in the school. He received his PhD from the University of Salford, UK and has taught marketing courses at various institutions including the University of Lagos (Nigeria), University of Salford (UK), Manchester Metropolitan University (UK), Liverpool Hope University (UK), and various professional bodies. Dr 'Tunji' Gbadamosi has over 120 publications – he has authored/edited 11 other books, as well as journal articles, chapters in edited books, edited books, conference papers, and case studies – and his papers have been published in a variety of refereed journals. Dr Gbadamosi is an editorial board member of several journals. At the time of publication, apart from the supervision of several undergraduate and Master students, he has been a part of the success story of 80 doctoral students through his roles as a supervisor, an examiner, and a chair of viva voces. In this, he has supervised 15 PhD students to timely completion, served as an examiner for 42 research degree examinations, and chaired 23 doctoral examinations. He has also served as the Programme chair of the Academy of African Business Development (AABD) conferences from May 2016 to May 2022 and served as the conference Chair for the same conference hosted at the University of East London in May

2023. His past and current external examiner roles include those at Lancaster University, Regent's University London, Northampton University, the University of Westminster, the University of Chester, and the University of Suffolk. His research interests lie in Consumer Behaviour, SME Marketing, Marketing to Children, and Marketing Communications. His paper won the EMERALD Best paper award at the International Academy of African Business Development (IAABD) conference [which rebranded to Academy of African Business Development (AABD)] in 2014. He is listed in *Who's Who in the World*.

# Figures

| | | |
|---|---|---|
| 1.1 | Consumer behaviour and marketing mix in a digital environment | 6 |
| 1.2 | Business markets | 9 |
| 1.3 | Interdisciplinary nature of consumer behaviour and the digital age | 12 |
| 2.1 | Consumer segments based on interest and enthusiasm towards green and sustainable consumption | 32 |
| 2.2 | Consumer segments based on unfavourable attitudes to sustainability | 33 |
| 2.3 | Criteria for selecting a brand ambassador | 34 |
| 2.4 | Digitalisation and consumers' rights | 44 |
| 3.1 | Online consumer decision making process | 59 |
| 3.2 | Major influences on the consumer decision making process in a digital age | 60 |
| 3.3 | Decision models | 70 |
| 3.4 | Situational and enduring involvement | 72 |
| 4.1 | Movement of cultural meaning | 92 |
| 5.1 | Digital transformation and the family buying roles | 119 |
| 5.2 | Socialisation agents | 120 |
| 5.3 | An example of a family life cycle model | 123 |
| 5.4 | Characteristics of a brand community | 128 |
| 6.1 | Consumers' senses | 144 |
| 6.2 | Strategies for catching consumers' attention | 146 |
| 6.3 | Consumer motivation for showrooming | 154 |
| 6.4 | Perceptual map for the automobile industry | 158 |
| 6.5 | Perceptual map for logistics companies | 159 |
| 6.6 | Some common risks associated with purchases | 160 |

| | | |
|---|---|---:|
| 7.1 | Five-stage information processing process and memory | 175 |
| 7.2 | Elements of learning | 178 |
| 7.3 | 4c's typology of digital consumers | 183 |
| 7.4 | Associative network | 185 |
| 8.1 | Three elements of attitudes | 196 |
| 8.2 | Hierarchy of effects | 197 |
| 8.3 | Balanced theory | 198 |
| 8.4 | Elements of the Theory of Reasoned Action (TRA) model and illustrative questions | 201 |
| 8.5 | Elements of the Theory of Planned Behaviour (TPB) model and illustrative questions | 202 |
| 8.6 | Attitude towards the ad model | 202 |
| 8.7 | Functions of attitudes | 206 |
| 8.8 | Consumers' rights and privacy | 208 |
| 8.9 | Liquid and solid consumption | 209 |
| 8.10 | Marketing communications model | 210 |
| 9.1 | Abraham Maslow's Hierarchy of Needs | 222 |
| 9.2 | Motivation for joining social media | 230 |
| 10.1 | Six elements of brand identity | 243 |
| 10.2 | Five brand personality dimensions | 244 |
| 11.1 | Three types of innovation | 267 |
| 11.2 | Diffusion of innovation (category of adopters) | 269 |
| 12.1 | Research brief and proposal | 292 |
| 12.2 | The marketing research process in a digital age | 295 |
| 12.3 | Types of research design | 297 |
| 12.4 | Examples of internal and external secondary sources of data | 298 |
| 12.5 | The attributes of a good focus group moderator | 303 |
| 12.6 | Sampling methods | 304 |
| 12.7 | Grounded theory data analysis process | 310 |
| 12.8 | Content of a consumer research report | 311 |
| 12.9 | Common ethical issues in consumer research | 316 |
| 13.1 | Classification of artificial intelligence (AI) | 329 |
| 13.2 | Segmentation, targeting, and positioning (STP) | 332 |

# Tables

| | | |
|---|---|---|
| 1.1 | Distinguishing characteristics of organisational purchases | 11 |
| 1.2 | Number of Internet users worldwide: 2005–2022 | 17 |
| 1.3 | Comparing traditional consumption patterns and consumption in the digital age | 19 |
| 2.1 | Reasons for purchasing counterfeit products | 39 |
| 4.1 | Religions and their dynamics | 97 |
| 5.1 | Types of reference groups | 114 |
| 8.1 | Multi-attribute model and house purchase in Greater London | 200 |
| 9.1 | Most popular reasons for Internet users worldwide to use social media as of 3rd quarter 2022 | 231 |
| 10.1 | Consumer self: Illustrations and examples | 247 |
| 10.2 | Lifestyle segmentation | 250 |
| 12.1 | A summary of positivist and phenomenological paradigms | 294 |
| 12.2 | Types of observational studies | 299 |
| 12.3 | Different views on focus group composition | 302 |
| 12.4 | Different types of samples in consumer research | 305 |
| 12.5 | Various types of questions for consumer research questionnaires | 306 |

## PART 1

# TECHNOLOGY AND THE CONTEMPORARY CONSUMER BEHAVIOUR

## AN INTRODUCTION

# CHAPTER 1

# Consumer Behaviour

## Discussing the Boundaries and Introducing the Digital Consumer

**LEARNING OBJECTIVES**

After reading this chapter, you should be able to:

- Explain consumer behaviour in relation to the associated concepts and define its boundaries;
- Discuss the justifications for the study of consumer behaviour;
- Explain the similarities and differences between organisational and consumer transactions;
- Explain the mediating role of technology in the interdisciplinary influences on consumer behaviour;
- Discuss the emergence of the digital consumer.

**INTRODUCTION**

Our daily endeavours are characterised by consumption. The toiletries we use, our range of clothing acquired to fit occasions and circumstances, the cars we drive, the food we eat, and the restaurants we patronise are all examples that depict the reality of day-to-day consumption. Similarly, our banking transactions, the services of our hairdressers, and our choice of music all constitute part of what illustrate our value-oriented transactions. Some are frequently acquired while others are bought infrequently by the nature of the product or our extent of usage. Accordingly, our interaction with various brands such as Apple, Barclays, British Airways, Colgate, Gucci, and numerous others continue to form part of our daily lives. It is therefore very important to have an understanding of how things work in these various consumption scenarios. Meanwhile, the direction of marketing theory and practice is changing by the day with the notable example of the increase in usage of technology by all stakeholders in the consumption system. The proliferation of digital activities in consumption has reached an all-time high and is still growing. This can be attributed to growing consumer knowledge in the use and dynamics of technology and many other changes we see and experience in the socio-cultural system of the marketing environment. An example of the latter is the COVID-19 pandemic, which made online transactions almost second to none in terms of how needs are met as nations moved in and out of lockdowns. Therefore, it is logical to have an in-depth understanding of *consumer behaviour in a digital age*, as is the focus of this book. This chapter sets the scene for the discussion. It presents and clarifies the concepts that underpin consumer behaviour and explains the link between them. The chapter also explains the reasons for studying this discipline, as well as its interdisciplinary nature. The differences between organisational and consumer transactions are explained with illustrations, most of which revolve around digitalisation. The chapter ends with the discussion of the emergence of the digital consumer.

## CONSUMER BEHAVIOUR: EXAMINING THE CONCEPTS AND DEFINING THE BOUNDARIES

The very nature of consumer behaviour from both theoretical and practical standpoints makes it a special phenomenon. Lawyers, engineers, students, politicians, and people from various other walks of life are all consumers. Hence, it is ubiquitous and has wide implications in various societies – developing and developed countries. Meanwhile, it is important for us to know the fundamental framework of the subject. So, we are confronted with some questions.

- What is consumer behaviour?
- What are the concepts that underpin its system?
- How is the discussion around it influenced by advancement in technology?

Before addressing these questions in more depth, let us pause for a moment and reflect on the meaning of a consumer, and the fundamental foci of contemporary marketing – value creation, value delivery, and value co-creation. Basically, consumers may be defined as those that acquire goods or services for self-gratification such as for personal consumption or as gifts for others. Hence, those purchases other than for resale or use in businesses will be positioned into this. Even though there may be many definitions of behaviour, depending on the context of usage, Levitis et al. (2009) define it as follows: '… the internally coordinated responses (actions or inactions) of whole living organisms (individuals or groups) to internal and/or external stimuli'. This is fairly telling, has wide-ranging areas of application, and could be used as a template to address the issues of what consumers do, how they do them, and why they take those courses of action, which is the focus of this book.

Contemporary thoughts on marketing emphasise that consumers and other stakeholders in marketing transactions are interested in weighing what they expend, such as money and time, with what they derive from transactions, like social acceptance and comfort. This explanation depicts the term 'value'. So, consumers are expected to be keenly interested in ensuring that the outcome is not negative. Ultimately, the study of consumer behaviour in this day and age is a significant part of contemporary marketing as it revolves around the notion of value, which could be conceptualised in different ways based on the work of Zeithaml (1988). It shows that value could be defined differently such as: *whatever the consumer wants from a market offering, the quality the consumer gets from the price they pay, low price*, or *simply what they get for what they sacrifice*. Meanwhile the notion of value co-creation centres on the acknowledgement that the consumer is a key contributor to value-creation and delivery activities. So, the consumer is actively involved in the value system associated with marketing such that they 'voice' their contributions in various ways to ensure that the outcome will result in a pleasant experience. More often than not, marketers such as banks, hospitality businesses, supermarkets, and automobile organisations to mention but a few, invite comments and reviews from consumers of their products and services. This is meant to serve as input into the organisations' strategic management towards ensuring a sound marketing system in which consumers will be satisfied, the business will be profitable and sustainable, and other relevant stakeholders will also derive their relevant value from the transactions.

Having provided a sketch of the link between consumers, consumer behaviour, and marketing, we can now consider those questions posed earlier. To define consumer behaviour, we will examine two of the existing definitions. The first is from Solomon (2020), who defines the term as '...the study of the processes involved when individuals or groups select, purchase, use, or dispose of products, services, ideas, or experiences to satisfy needs and desires'. Meanwhile, a closely related definition offered by Schiffman and Wisenblit (2019: 32) defines it as 'the study of consumers' choices during searching, evaluating, purchasing, and using products and services that they believe would satisfy their needs'. A critical look at these two definitions will see a common pattern that indicates a point of convergence between the two. So, it is logical to infer from these definitions that consumer behaviour is:

- A process;
- A phenomenon that revolves around decisions;
- About consumer value-oriented transactions;
- Not limited to the act of purchase alone but also other activities that precede and follow this;
- About consumptions issues relating to individuals and/or group contexts.

By and large, the key concepts that underpin consumer behaviour are many since the scope of consumer behaviour itself is wide. Hence, concepts such as marketing, marketing-mix, needs, wants, value, preferences, convenience, brands, satisfaction, decision, and choices are prominently relevant to the discourse on the subject. These are depicted in Figure 1.1 below. The argument here is not to suggest that these are the only factors that are relevant to consumer behaviour. Indeed, there are many, as demonstrated in the scope of this book and the chapters covered. However, these are selected to illustrate how consumer behaviour is linked to the marketing mix elements

**6** TECHNOLOGY AND CONTEMPORARY CONSUMER BEHAVIOUR: AN INTRODUCTION

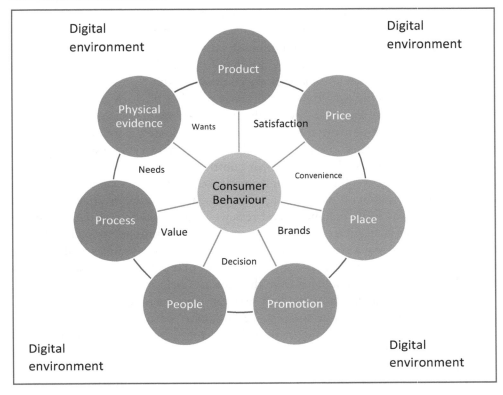

**FIGURE 1.1** Consumer behaviour and marketing mix in a digital environment

towards achieving the stated objectives. Most importantly, the figure also illustrates that all of these concepts are now closely embedded within the wider digital environment in which virtually every element in the system is influenced by the advancement in technology. This is evident from a number of examples all around us such as the increasing use of smartphones, mobile apps, e-readers, MP3s, and tablets to mention but a few.

Analysing and explaining the impact of the digital environment on how consumer behaviour is defined is a useful endeavour. Interestingly, there is a claim that e-shoppers tend to act differently when compared to the behaviour of traditional shoppers because the key focus of the former is on utilitarian and functional interests in relation to their transactions (Dennis et al., 2009). So, our knowledge of consumer behaviour will be limited if we rely unduly on the traditional viewpoint on the subject. Clearly, advancement in technology now infiltrates the consumer behaviour system. So, if we examine inferences made from the definitions of consumer behaviour above, it is sensible to concur that the development in technology is very much evident in the process of consumer behaviour, and the decisions involved are also primed by digital provisions. Similarly, digital technology opportunities now facilitate how businesses create and deliver value to the consumer and how the latter also co-create value with business organisations. Consumers' craving for convenience and the unprecedented growth of the world of technology now introduce a radical shift to consumers' affairs at the pre-purchase stages, during the purchase, and during the post-purchase evaluations and actions. Moreover, the increasing usage of the Internet for making orders and communicating with business organisations, and the proliferation of the use of social media such as X, LinkedIn, Facebook, and YouTube to connect and share marketplace information as consumers, are proof that digitisation is as useful to consumption activities of individuals as to group and socially embedded consumption decisions.

## JUSTIFICATIONS FOR THE STUDY OF CONSUMER BEHAVIOUR

Now that we have an understanding of what consumer behaviour is, it is also important to know why it is worth studying. So, why do we need to study consumer behaviour? From a wider perspective, the study of the subject is useful for all stakeholders. The consumers themselves, the marketers, society, students, governments, and other agencies such as non-governmental organisations, all have one reason or another that justifies why it is important for them to know the dynamics of consumer behaviour. Some of these are highlighted below.

## MARKETERS

The notion of value co-creation between marketers and the consumer will require having a sound understanding of consumer behaviour. Businesses operate within a dynamic marketing environment in which all factors and actors are characterised by incessant changes. For example, there have been significant changes in relation to the nature of consumers' needs and demand for market offerings in recent years. Examples of this include the increasing interest in the use of self-service technologies (SSTs) and the transition from 'brick-and-mortar' (instore) transactions to 'click-and mortar' (online) which shows consumers' taste for a whole new level of experiences that point to the prevalence of virtual stores (Pine and Gilmore, 1998; Manganari et al., 2011). According to Manganari et al. (2011) this also implies that marketers will have to strike a balance between providing enabling opportunities to consumers to navigate their website and ensuring that they are involved and excited in the online store. So, the knowledge of consumer behaviour is a necessary condition to having an effective marketing strategy in place and succeeding in the competitive marketing climate.

## THE CONSUMER

The knowledge of consumer behaviour brings consumers to the consciousness of factors and forces responsible for their actions and the impact these have on other stakeholders. In the categorisation of consumers in relation to their unfavourable attitude to sustainability, one of the segments identified by Emery (2012) is described as 'The ignorant' which portrays those consumers who lack adequate knowledge of the issue and will not know the impact of their actions on others (Gbadamosi, 2019). This knowledge gap could stand in the way of consumers embracing this issue. Understanding the intricacies of consumption will put the consumers on the path of apposite responsibility in relation to how they engage in their value-oriented transactions. As indicated by Elgaaïed-Gambier (2016) in a study on understanding consumers' reactions to overpackaging, consumers can take or modify actions at the stages of the purchase such as buying in bulk to avoid excessively packaged products.

## GOVERNMENT

Government intervention in the marketplace system, especially in terms of policy formulation and implementation on many fronts as related to consumption, is a crucial part of the society. Bos et al.'s (2013) paper on understanding consumer acceptance of intervention strategies for heathy food choices presents issues around intervention on obesity concerns and stimulating low-calorie food choices. The society has been battling to address a plethora of issues over the years including drugs, sustainability, sale of counterfeit products, debt, and alcohol consumption. The role of government and government agencies will be paramount in how these consumption-related issues are addressed. Consequently, having adequate knowledge of the internal and external factors that propel these types of consumption will give government the tools needed. This also aligns with the view of Stamminger et al. (2019), which pinpoints the relevance of designing appropriate policies that will stand the test of time, as it is possible to set a mismatch policy that will ultimately miss the target.

## OTHER STAKEHOLDERS

Apart from government, marketers, and the consumer, there are various other stakeholders with roles and activities linked to the consumption system. These include non-government organisations (NGOs) and other societal members. A relevant example here is in the social marketing activities of NGOs. Social marketing is essentially about changing attitudes to a course of action or phenomenon. Accordingly, it is expected that these organisations will need to be aware of factors influencing the behaviour they are interested in changing. This is needed to be sure that the proposed intervention will address the problem. NGOs that are interested in encouraging smokers to quit will find it very useful to know the factors that motivate the target group to start the habit in the first place and the influences that reinforce it.

## ORGANISATIONAL VS CONSUMER TRANSACTIONS

The notions of marketing exchange and value co-creation in marketing systems are not applicable to ultimate consumers, which is often termed Business-to-Consumer (B2C), alone. Businesses also engage in transactions of goods and services with other

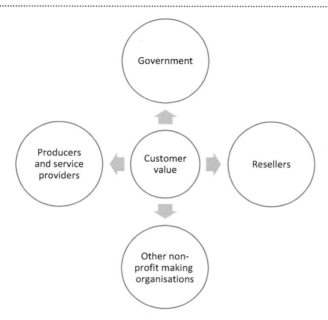

**FIGURE 1.2** Business markets

businesses, and these are notably described as Business-to-Business (B2B) transactions. Many examples of this abound all around us. Supermarkets buy stock from their suppliers, universities purchase computers and books in order to be able to satisfy the growing student population in their educational system, property developers also engage the services of insurance firms to cover their risks, and there is a plethora of other transactions that take place between firms. Figure 1.2 shows the categories of these various markets.

> **PAUSE, PLAN, AND PRACTICE: ORGANISATIONAL AND PERSONAL TRANSACTIONS FOR COVID-19 PERSONAL PROTECTIVE EQUIPMENT (PPE)**
>
> The latter part of December 2019 witnessed the outbreak of a novel coronavirus in China which was named COVID-19 by the World Health Organization (WHO) on 11 February 2019. It is now a global pandemic with significant impacts on virtually all walks of life, such that it is now a common saying that the world now operates under 'new normal' conditions based on the radical changes to things all over the world including consumption. Meanwhile, one of the things that caught the attention of the world is the purchase and use of personal protective equipment (PPE). Given that the virus has claimed many lives all over the world, PPE is considered an essential item. Governments have to order these from various sources and make them available to various health and social care workers. Similarly, there is a need for individuals to use a face mask, a type of personal protective equipment, for protection as they interact with various other people in public places such as on buses, in supermarkets, and other communal places. Consequently, various

> types of these face masks are being sold and distributed widely at the retail level to ensure easy access to individual consumers. This provides a good illustration of the difference between organisational and personal consumption.
>
> **REFERENCES**
>
> McAleer, M. (2020). Prevention is better than the cure: Risk management of COVID-19. *Journal of Risk and Financial Management*, 13(3), 1–5.
>
> WHO (2020), WHO Coronavirus Disease (COVID-19) Dashboard, https://covid19.who.int/ (Accessed 28 May 2020).
>
> **Question/Task:** Give another illustration of this distinction for two market offerings – one for a physical product and the other for a service.

Essentially, the common issue to both B2C and B2B transactions is that they involve value creation, delivery, and co-creation, and ultimately satisfaction of the customer, but there are some notable differences between the two. It is important to provide an explanation of the differences between the two at this stage of the book, after which attention will be focused on issues around transactions involving the ultimate consumers. In the organisational business system, the key distinguishing factors are as presented in Table 1.1.

The recent trends in technological development have not eluded the B2B transaction system. One of the areas where this becomes apparent is in the growth of the Internet of Things (IoT). We can tease out a meaningful explanation from the viewpoint of Akhtar et al. (2017), who show the term as covering devices that have network connectivity and the capability to receive and send data in relation to other connected devices. In complementing this perspective, it is also described as the use of sensors, actuators, as well as data communication technology made into physical objects that allows those objects to be coordinated, tracked, and controlled across a data network or the network (McKinsey Global Institute, 2013). These apply to several issues in organisational purchases that will drive changes in relation to the buying process, buying situations, and buying centres to achieve efficiency and effectiveness (Osmonbekov and Johnston, 2018). Examples of this include automated forklift and automated storage systems that facilitate the use of just-in-time (JIT) delivery.

Moreover, the issue of buyer-seller relationships in the organisational buying system is considered especially relevant in B2B. This is closely linked to the relatively smaller number of buyers and the high volume of demand involved. A good number of studies have emphasised the paramount nature of relationship management and its relevance to success in B2B transactions. One of these publications is that of Nicholls and Huybrechts (2016), which concludes that parties involved with different levels of

TABLE 1.1 Distinguishing characteristics of organisational purchases

| | Distinguishing Factors of Organisational Purchases | Further Descriptors |
|---|---|---|
| 1 | Nature of the product | The products involved are relatively technical and complex. Sophisticated equipment being used and bought by manufacturing firms for transforming inputs into outputs provides an example of the level of complexity and technicality associated with the organisation product. |
| 2 | Nature of the demand | The market is relatively smaller than the consumer market and their demand tends to be derived from the demand made for their own market offerings. For example, the demand of construction companies for building materials will be dependent on how may contracts they have to work on, while materials and parts needed by automobile companies such as batteries, wheels, and electrical fittings will be a function of the demand level for their vehicles from their various markets. |
| 3 | Reciprocal transactions | The businesses involved in the transaction tend to engage in reciprocal transactions in which case the buyer may also be the seller to the other party in future subsequent transactions. For instance, universities that buy their computer systems from computer firms could also offer consultancy services to them in a reciprocal transaction at a later stage. |
| 4 | Buying process and participants | In view of the nature of the product and complexity of the purchase, firms tend to rely on the services of their trained professional buyers and the specific contributions of the members of the decision-making unit (DMU), also known as the buying centre. |
| 5 | Buying criteria | The buying organisations tend to adopt economic and technical criteria in their purchase decisions. Given the nature of the product or service involved, decision makers in organisational purchases tend to apply more rational and systematic criteria in their evaluation of available alternatives. |

Source: Adapted from Gbadamosi (2020)

power may collaborate effectively in such a way that the weaker partner would not have to compromise its own logics.

By and large, as shown in Table 1.1, there are interesting differences between organisational purchases and purchases for ultimate consumption. Nevertheless, attention will be focused on buyers outside of the B2B context, who buy for personal use.

## THE MEDIATING ROLE OF TECHNOLOGY IN THE INTERDISCIPLINARY INFLUENCES ON CONSUMER BEHAVIOUR

Consumer behaviour is multidisciplinary in nature as it borrows from various other disciplines to offer insights into peoples' consumption dynamics. These other disciplines include the following:

- Economics;
- Anthropology;
- Sociology;
- Psychology;
- Neuroscience;
- History;
- Geography.

This section of the chapter features the discussion of how the contributions of these disciplines have been mediated by technological advancement. This is illustrated in Figure 1.3.

### Economics

The fundamental focus of economics as a discipline revolves around demand for goods and services and how this relates to consumption of households and society. A good number of issues associated with consumer behaviour emerged from Economics. One

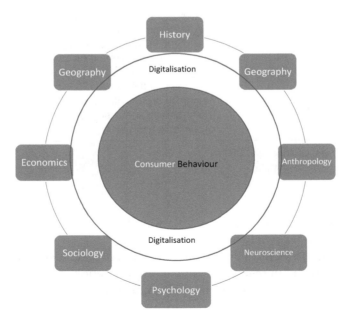

**FIGURE 1.3** Interdisciplinary nature of consumer behaviour and the digital age

of these is the notion of life-cycle theory, which is linked to the traditional utility model that describes consumption and saving behaviour in relation to the life cycle (Xiao et al., 2011). Similarly, issues around consumer socialisation and financial behaviour have a well-established foundation in Economics. The research contributions of many authors, including a Nobel laureate (Modigilani) and other co-researchers on the life-cycle hypothesis and the work of Friedman (1957), known as the permanent income model, are notably relevant to consumer behaviour. They suggest that consumers behave in a way that indicates they know their life-time permanent income. Closely related to these are the issues of relationship between economic cycles and household financial behaviour, the place of uncertainty in consumption and saving, as well as the role of consumer confidence in fostering economic activity (Kłopocka, 2017). If we reflect on these issues closely, it becomes obvious that they have experienced changes in one form or another due to digitalisation. Consequently, the digital presence in Economics as a discipline transfers to the changes we experience in consumer behaviour in the digital age.

## Anthropology

As a discipline, anthropology explores the dynamics of people, products, and the society in relation to their values, beliefs, and practices. Wagner-Tsukamoto and Tadajewski (2006) indicate that cultural anthropology views problem-solving behaviour from the practical thinking perspective, which is reminiscent of a handyman using available tools they possess while reflecting on ways they could use them to accomplish or appropriately complete the current task. In another paper on anthropology and consumer research within the context of green consumer behaviour, they state that cultural anthropology holds that consumer cognition is not optimal and departs from the argument which holds that the consumer is an information seeker who is rational (Tadajewski and Wagner-Tsukamoto, 2006). Hence, in what appears to be a summary of these perspectives, it is stated that, in this approach, the consumer shows preference for acting rather than reflecting on the phenomena in question (Hull et al., 1988).

## Sociology

The British Sociological Association provides detail on the origin of sociology on its website. As stated in this source, which traces the source of the discipline to the 18th and 19th centuries, the name sociology was given by Auguste Comte to the field of study offering the highest level of scientific explanation concerning the laws of human society. Essentially, it offers insight into social institutions and relationships of different forms among people (BSA, nd). This gives people the opportunity to learn the values, norms, and behavioural patterns of a particular society to which they belong, in a process known as socialisation (Özmete, 2009; Xiao et al., 2011). As stated by Schlaile et al. (2018: 563), '…in general, consumption is a phenomenon which is deeply embedded in a social context'. So, the issues of reference groups, formal and informal group formation, status and prestige, social class classification, and many other related factors used in the explication of consumer behaviour have their root in sociological principles.

## Psychology

Psychology is clearly a core aspect of consumer behaviour, as demonstrated by the topics that feature in consumer behaviour. It basically focusses on human mental processes. The discourse of perception, personality, self-concept, motivation, and learning are among the key topics that link consumer behaviour to psychology. As an example of this context, perception indicates how consumers see, organise, and interpret marketplace stimuli such as making sense of the new price or packaging of an existing product and interpreting the content of the marketing communication messages of specific brands. Moreover, the synthesis of concepts like drive, needs, wants, and goals explain consumer motivation. The usefulness of studies around motivational research such as those championed by Sigmund Freud and Ernest Dichter is enduring as they offer insight into what pattern consumer behaviour follows. In fact, from a more specific viewpoint, authors like Griskevicius et al., (2006); Saad et al. (2009); Cohen and Bernard (2013); Griskevicius and Kenrick (2013); and Saad (2013) highlight the advantages of conceptualising consumer behaviour from the evolutionary psychology perspective, which further emphasises the bond between these two disciplines.

## Neuroscience

One of the notable scholarship movements in marketing revolves around the claim that traditional methods of eliciting data from consumers in the marketing research process are proving inadequate. Accordingly, one of the routes out of this challenge has been identified as the use of neuroscience for making sense of consumer behaviour, which introduces neuromarketing as a subject. While neuroscience is about the study of the way the human brain works, the term 'neuromarketing' emerged from the combination of the words 'neuro' and 'marketing' and started appearing organically from around 2002 (Morin, 2011). It is about using technology to measure the activity of the brain in relation to the effect of marketing stimuli such as marketing communication messages (Hussein, 2019). This has proved useful over the years in solving numerous consumer behaviour issues, especially as the brain is responsible for all our consumption-related activities (Morin, 2011). Some of the tools used in achieving this purpose include functional magnetic resonance imaging (fMRI), positron emission tomography (PET), Electroencephalography (EEG), event-related potential (ERP), and eye-tracking.

## History

Having an appreciation of the historical contexts of issues is an important part of how they could be developed towards achieving effectiveness. As stated in the literature, while sociologists are interested in abstraction and generalisation, historians tend to be more interested in context (Laslett and Brenner, 1989). It is therefore understandable that Schmidt and Garcia (2010) state that people are 'backpackers' over time as they convey the remains of what they have from one place to another, which indicates that it is sensible to gather historical narratives by exploring documents. Accordingly, history plays a crucial role in the explanation of consumer behaviour as it links consumption issues such as products, services, marketing communications messages, and other marketing stimuli to changes in society over time.

## Geography

Geography focusses on the study of places, the atmosphere, and human activities that relate to them as well as the interaction of culture with the natural environment (National Geographic Society, nd). This applies to a good number of areas in consumer behaviour such as market segmentation and demographic studies. For instance, this knowledge is useful for explaining why consumption patterns of consumers in Canada might be different from those exhibited by consumers based in China and why consumers in Peru may buy differently from their counterparts in Pakistan. Hence, businesses and consumer researchers gain insight from geography to strengthen postulations made in Consumer Behaviour as a discipline.

There are many intellectually stimulating arguments concerning consumer behaviour as a field of study. Some of these feature in publications such as Jacoby (1976); Sheth (1982); Belk and Pollay (1985); Holbrook (1987); Kernan (1995); and Deighton (2007). Nevertheless, if we view it from a wider sense, it is logical to state that consumer behaviour is greatly diverse, as shown in the exemplar disciplines described above. It is noteworthy that each of these disciplinary foci is also dynamic and changes in relation to changes in society and technology (See Figure 1.3), which in turn result in changes in consumer behaviour (Peighambari et al., 2016). Perhaps a good way to explain the scenario is to state that consumer behaviour lies midway within these disciplines highlighted above (Engel et al., 1968; Foxall, 1974). Ultimately, the role of the marketers in co-creating value with consumers in relation to their needs and wants is greatly facilitated by knowledge obtained from these various disciplines.

## THE EMERGENCE OF THE DIGITAL CONSUMER

Emphatically, consumption has been part of human existence from the beginning, as we are all consumers of one product or another. One useful historical account of consumption is given by Szmigin and Piacentini (2018), in which early consumption is described as that which took place when people engaged in self-production of items needed to survive. They also explain that the term *consumere* was first used in Latin in the 12th century, while the Europeans were involved in importation of spices from the East in the 15th century. Other notable events and changes associated with consumption also took place afterwards. However, radical changes in the technological dimension of the marketing environment have introduced digital features into what products we buy, how we buy them, where we buy, and how often we do so. It has not been like that all along.

There have been notable shifts in the digital environment that paved the way for the emergence of the digital consumer. This is the consumer who prefers to sit at home, has the opportunities to compare options online, and receives the ordered products rather than having to wait endlessly in a queue to be served. This consumer prefers reading e-books to carrying several voluminous publications around and cherishes e-banking activities as opposed to sticking to the traditional banking system that necessitates a physical presence for virtually all transactions. This consumer also chooses paying utility bills electronically over other conventional modes and shifts his or her taste of music and movies to digitally operated options. These are just examples of several ways by which we can describe a digital consumer and illustrate how things change in that direction.

As indicated by Helberger et al. (2013), we now see considerable increase in our needs for personal development, information, communication, social interaction, and entertainment, which are being addressed by businesses supplying digital content. As explained by these authors, numerous business models have now emerged due to digitalisation as consumers can now select between 'on-demand' provision, 'near-on demand', on-demand downloading, webcasting, streaming, in-app purchases, cloud-computing, and many more. Similarly, the discussion of the virtual self, how an avatar conveys people's feelings, preferences, and personality, as well as how social media plays a major role in the construction of the self, are moving to the centre stage of consumption (Chang et al., 2018). The relevance of digitalisation is also noticeable in the health sector, as reported by Fox and Connolly (2018) in their paper on mobile health (m-health) technology adoption across generations. They emphasise that m-health can foster proactiveness among older adult patients and lessen the associated financial burden. Hence, there is now a paradigm shift on the discourse of this subject by reasons of these developments. This is evident in the pattern of usage of the Internet all over the world, as demonstrated in Table 1.2, which shows a significant yearly increase from 2005 to 2022 and the pattern still continues in that direction to the present date.

Tracing the specific beginning of when digital technology found its way into the dynamics of consumption is not an easy undertaking, as there are different phases. However, we can make reference to useful contributions that pinpoint specific historical landmarks around this phenomenon. Let us start from the discussion of the evolution of web technologies presented by Spivack (2007), which shows the following phases in the trend of web technological developments:

- PC Era – 1980–1990;
- Web 1.0 – 1990–2000;
- Web 2.0 – 2000–2010;
- Web 3.0 – 2010–2020;
- Web 4.0 – 2020–2030.

TABLE 1.2 Number of Internet users worldwide: 2005–2022

| Year | 2005 | 2006 | 2007 | 2008 | 2009 | 2010 | 2011 | 2012 | 2013 | 2014 | 2015 | 2016 | 2017 | 2018 | 2019 | 2020 | 2021 | 2022 |
|---|---|---|---|---|---|---|---|---|---|---|---|---|---|---|---|---|---|---|
| Number of users in millions | 1023 | 1147 | 1367 | 1545 | 1772 | 1981 | 2174 | 2387 | 2562 | 2750 | 2954 | 3217 | 3444 | 3729 | 4119 | 4585 | 4901 | 5300 |

**Source**: Adapted from Statista (2023)

In view of this perspective, perhaps, one could argue that digital consumption seems to have started in the 1980s–1990s and grown progressively up to the current era. From a different but closely related account, it is noted that the swift growth of the Internet could be traced to the 1990s, which leads to the development of e-commerce (Valvi et al., 2013). We can see the point of convergence in these claims.

The scope and opportunities are reasonably broad, as even young consumers and the underage are prominently represented in the digital consumption process. Available records show that smartphones are widely available among teens as 95% of them have access to such devices, which explains why up to 45% of them indicate that they are online engaging in one activity or another 'almost constantly' (Anderson and Jiang, 2018). It will be useful to present the distinction about categorisation of digital consumers based on the generational cohort of people, as cited in Hanlon (2019). This classification identifies two consumer groups, namely *digital natives* and *digital immigrants*. Digital natives are identified as those whose birth falls within the digital era that is characterised by the wide availability of digital technologies such as smartphones and tablets. Consequently, they demonstrate notable competence in the use of digital technologies. Going by this contention, these consumers are habituated to the use of social media like X, YouTube, Instagram, and several others. Conversely, consumers categorised as digital immigrants are those who were born at periods outside this digital era. However, there is a noteworthy criticism of this typology. This is mainly on the classification overlap as there may be some consumers outside of the digital native who are very versed in the use of technology, while some in the segment may not be as enthusiastically keen about technology as others in that segment.

Moreover, Tim et al. (2017) explain that social media is functioning differently for disaster response. For instance, it facilitates a swift exchange of information, such as enabling those affected by the disaster to easily reach community and neighbours for emotional and other support needed (Pyle et al., 2019). All of these result in a large quantity of data that result in the notion of big data, which companies could explore deeply through analytical tools and techniques that they could use to satisfy consumers in the competitive marketplace where they operate. To summarise the shift in consumption patterns, Table 1.2 highlights some of the differences between consumption in traditional and digital contexts.

## SUMMARY

Consumption is ubiquitous as all humans are consumers of goods and services in one way or another. Hence, consumption takes place everywhere. A number of concepts that are linked to consumer behaviour include needs, wants, satisfaction, decisions, value, convenience, and brands. They constitute part of the definition of the term either directly or indirectly. Ultimately, consumer behaviour could be explained as a process, which revolves around consumers' value-oriented decisions made by individuals or groups at various stages of the consumption process. Evidently, contemporary consumer behaviour is not only linked to the marketing-mix but also emphasises the

**TABLE 1.3** Comparing traditional consumption patterns and consumption in the digital age

| | Contexts | Traditional Consumption | Consumption in a Digital Age |
|---|---|---|---|
| 1 | Information access | Consumer access to information is limited to traditional communication modes. | Consumer access to information has expanded astronomically as it is possible to receive useful information from online product reviews and virtual communities. |
| 2 | Consumer power | Consumer power is limited. | The consumer is more powerful in relation to the increased rate of access to information. Examples includes access to information to compare prices, power to choose what to be exposed to, and what to avoid in TV digital programmes through recorders, and consumer activism. |
| 3 | Marketing communications | Most of the traditional communication modes such as TV, radio, newspapers are not amenable (or very weak) to allowing consumer response due to their inflexibility. | Consumers are able to respond to marketing communication messages through new media/e-communication modes. It is a dialogue and not monologue as is the case in traditional communication systems. |
| 4 | Needs | Even though consumers' needs are numerous under this consumption system, they are limited to the traditional consumption pattern. | Consumers' access to information in this new age and digital innovations expose them to different consumption contexts. These prompt needs for different new products that were not in existence several years ago. |
| 5 | Search | Consumers are limited to traditional methods of search like a visit to the shopping mall, High Street, or perusing magazines. | Consumers' search online for information about products and product items to buy. |
| 6 | Evaluation of alternatives | This involves physical access to the items or through traditional marketing communication tools such as magazines and newspapers. The process is rather laborious and will restrict the options that consumers could review as well as the extent to which it could be done. | Opportunities associated with consumption in the digital age facilitate evaluation of alternatives as consumers could move between websites and compare/evaluate available options. |

*(Continued)*

**TABLE 1.3** (Continued)

| | Contexts | Traditional Consumption | Consumption in a Digital Age |
|---|---|---|---|
| 7 | Decision making and selection | Decision making is influenced by the fixed store schedules. | Decision making is handled expeditiously as facilitated by the available digital measures. |
| 8 | Post-purchase evaluation | There are very limited means through which consumers' post-purchase evaluation could be communicated. | Although paper-based evaluation is still being used, the adoption of digital means to collect data from customers about satisfaction after a transaction is now widespread. |
| 9 | Rental | Rental agreements will have to take place physically in the store. | The availability of digital means for handling rental transactions introduces convenience to how consumers rent cars, properties, music, and various other products. |
| 10 | Price | The price could be relatively high due to the expenses linked to the physical facilities needed. | The price will most likely be relatively low as online transactions tend to eliminate or reduce some costs, which ultimately could result in lower prices for consumers. |

**Source**: Adapted from Gbadamosi and Sharma (2019); Hanlon (2019); Schiffman et al. (2010)

notion of value co-creation between marketers and the consumer. This explains why the study of consumer behaviour is considered important from various standpoints including those of consumers, marketers, government, and other stakeholders. Although marketing transactions could be done in relation to organisational or individual purchases, the focus in this book relates to the latter in which goods and services are bought for personal gratification. Meanwhile, Consumer Behaviour as a discipline borrows ideas, concepts, and principles from various other disciplines such as sociology, economics, psychology, and history. Given the significant change to consumption patterns in recent times, in which virtually everything has gone digital, the role of technology mediates the contributions of these disciplines to consumer behaviour. A critical review of the dynamic marketing environment, which shows significant development in the world of technology and the emergence of the digital consumer, is now imperative to study consumer behaviour in a digital age.

---

**DIGITAL BOX: 'TAP AND GO': EXPERIENCING THE WORLD OF CONTACTLESS PAYMENT**

Whether consumers are interested in having a meal at a local restaurant, buying medicine at the Pharmacy, paying for services received at the post office, or in other consumption scenarios, they are mainly interested in having satisfaction from these transactions. This is when it could be said that they have received value in the transactions. Interestingly, many factors determine consumers' satisfaction. One of the most prominent among these factors in recent years is the consumers' need for convenience. The acknowledgement of this led to a number of innovations, including the introduction of 'Contactless payments' systems, which are one of the great gains associated with digital marketing in relation to consumption. Essentially, it is a payment mode through the use of credit, debit, smartcard, or other relevant devices which involves using radio frequency identification (RFID) and near-field communication (NFC) technology. It allows consumers to pay for items to the limit of £100 without having to enter their Personal Identity Number (PIN). All they need to do is hold the card near a payment terminal from where the transaction will be registered. Even though only a handful of marketers used it at its early stage in the 1990s when it was introduced, it is now very popular among consumers in the UK, US, Canada, China, Australia, and several other countries. Google, Apple, Visa, American Express, and many other brands have now embraced the technology in various ways. Since it reduces the amount of time a consumer will need to handle cash and touch communal surfaces, its usage has been even higher during the global pandemic, with a record 150% increase in overall usage between March 2019 and June 2020 in the United States alone. Given the wide impact of the pandemic, it is logical to infer that the increase in usage applies to most other countries as well. This is only one example of how the consumption system has changed in the digital age.

**QUESTIONS:**

Reflect on your most recent experience of using the contactless payment system. What products did you buy? How would you rate the experience compared to your purchase of a similar or related product prior to the introduction of contactless payment systems? As a consumer, what are your predictions about this system for the near future?

**Sources:**

Cavaglieri, C. (2020), Contactless cards, *Which?*, https://www.which.co.uk/money/banking/banking-security-and-new-ways-to-pay/ways-to-pay/contactless-cards-ah1q15s797hb - Which? (accessed 23 November 2020).

Jones, A. (nd). The history of contactless payments, Global Payments Integrated, www.globalpaymentsintegrated.com/en-us/blog/2020/09/15/the-history-of-contactless-payments (accessed 23 November 2020).

Kagan, J., & Anderson, S. (2020), Contactless payment, Investopedia, 29 May 2020, www.investopedia.com/terms/c/contactless-payment.asp (accessed 30 November 2020).

## END OF CHAPTER DISCUSSION QUESTIONS

1. Consider the key concepts/elements that underpin consumer behaviour and attempt to define the term in your own words with reference to these concepts. Compare this definition with the one provided by another member of your class. What are the key points of similarities and differences and why? Illustrate how the definition could include the notion of group consumption.

2. Discuss the relevance of the knowledge of consumer behaviour to the following:
   a. a multinational marketer of fashion items;
   b. a government agency with a focus on encouraging and managing recycling;
   c. an NGO working on social marketing on family planning;
   d. a teenage consumer.
3. Select any three disciplines and discuss their contributions to the knowledge of consumer behaviour. Use contemporary examples to illustrate the given viewpoints.
4. Reflect on your personal experience as a consumer and select any two products and two service offerings. Discuss how your consumption experience of these products and services has changed from the conventional pattern to the consumption system in a digital age.
5. How would you discuss the differences between organisational buyers and ultimate consumers? How have the developments in the world of technology influenced transactions within these contexts in recent times?

### Case Study: Meeting Consumers' Needs in a Digital Age: Amazon Leads the Way

To many people around the world, the story of contemporary consumption would be incomplete without due reference to Amazon as a brand or, as others would prefer to call it, Amazon.com. It is a global brand that has a strong link to several other international brands. When considering it from a revenue perspective, Amazon, as an Internet-based organisation, is notably the biggest in the world. To reflect on its modest beginning in the year 1994, its commencement was engrained in selling books online. This decision by Jeff Bezos, the founder of the organisation, was informed by market research that showed selling books online was a logical strategic direction at the time. Statistically, the customer base of the company kept increasing, reached 180,000 by December 1996, and grew to 1,000,000 in 1997, when revenues reached $148 million. A year later, this revenue figure increased significantly to $610 million. This indicates the popularity of its online business mode among consumers. The convenience of being able to order these books online and have them delivered to a specified location attracted consumers to this iconic brand. At this stage, consumers' perception of value was already becoming favourable towards online transactions. Meanwhile, this success is nowhere near what is associated with the current operation of the business, which involves the sales of numerous types of product including electronics, toys, fashion items, movies, housewares, and several others.

Among the key developments that turned Amazon into a household name was the introduction of its Kindle e-readers in 2007. This is a low-cost, market-leading, hand-held tablet e-book reader. It is a sleek device designed to allow consumers to read in comfort. Whether they are going camping, travelling, or staying in several other places of their choice, they do not need to worry about the stress associated with carrying many books to read at any one time. Many factors attracted various consumers to the device. Some are drawn to the fact that it lasts for hours, thereby giving them the opportunity to stay out longer and still have the pleasure of reading their favourite books; some are quite keen about its waterproof feature; while many others crave it because of its audible capacity. This explains why Amazon presents these and other features in different versions of this product in order to address the varying needs of different consumer segments. This is a major addition to the book market such that it constituted a significant part of the sales of all Android-operated tablets. The sustained trend of success in all these prompted the company to launch Amazon publishing in 2011. This is mainly about the company developing and publishing its own titles. Clearly, Amazon indicates that having an understanding of consumer behaviour is key to succeeding in the marketplace.

A lot has changed at Amazon since the inception of the company three decades ago, as an online retailer. In 2019, apart from the launch of HD and 3D music streaming with Dolby Atmos, the company began to show Premier League football games on Prime video. Similarly, the business has also grown in its offerings of web services such that its cloud computing is not only widely acclaimed by consumers as fit-for-purpose but ranked third among the big names alongside Microsoft and Oracle, in this service. All these are indications that Amazon is receptive to the changing needs of its customers. It follows the revolution in the world of consumption and marketing in a digital age. So, it is not surprising that Forbes highlights it as one of the top 10 brands considered to be most valuable in the world in 2020. Consequently, while the annual gross profit for the year 2022 was $225.152b, its e-commerce sales worldwide for the year 2023 are projected to be around $746.22 billion. Meanwhile, CNN reports its profits for the first quarter ending 31 March 2023 to be $3.2 billion. This is also a reflection of the general increase in the preference for online consumer behaviour in various parts of the world.

Amazon works closely in partnership with other organisations. Among these are various social media networks such that an activity on these platforms will simply redirect the customer to Amazon product pages. This serves as a form of marketing communication for Amazon. An example of this is the Snapchat visual search tool, which works with scanning and camera systems. In one form or another, social media such as X, Instagram, Facebook, and YouTube are linked to Amazon to bring a whole new life of consumption patterns for the consumer. For example, the company currently has 1.7 million followers on Instagram while those following it on X and Facebook are 3 million and 28.3 million, respectively. This highlights the emergence of a new consumption pattern where consumers operate within a multifaceted online system.

At the mention of Amazon Prime to the consumer, a number of things come to mind. On its basic level, one may see it as a discount-oriented scheme in which those who hold an account can have a discount for the services they receive. However, Amazon is very keen to distinguish it from the mainstream discount membership offered by other businesses such as supermarkets. Yes, it does offer customer savings, but the consumer will also have access to contents such as movies, music, and eBooks. Apart from this, the company realises that one of the key factors that underpin consumer value revolves around convenience and time. Hence, it makes this part of the benefits for its Prime community such that it offers faster shipping to ensure delivery of the products ordered in under two days. In 2018, approximately 100 million people joined the scheme, which also resulted in significant revenue for the company. With all these and the foreseeable upward trend in online consumer transactions, Amazon is arguably at the forefront of the contemporary marketing system.

**Sources:**

Albane (2019). Amazon's marketing strategy: 5 ways to win on social, Talkwalker, 16 April 2019, www.talkwalker.com/blog/amazon-marketing-strategy (accessed 18 December 2019).

Amazon (nd). Kindle Paperwhite | Waterproof, 6" High-Resolution Display www.amazon.co.uk/dp/B07747FR44?tag=googhydr-21&ref=pd_sl_4s1f4ymfv4_e&th=1 (accessed 20 December 2020).

Grabham, D. (2020). What to expect from Amazon in 2020, Pocket.lint, www.pocket-lint.com/gadgets/news/amazon/150526-what-to-expect-from-amazon-in-2020 (accessed 18 December 2020).

Hall, M. (nd). Amazon.com: American company: Britannica, www.britannica.com/topic/Amazoncom (accessed 18 December 2020).

Hur, K. (2023). Amazon posts $3.2 billion profit as it goes through multiple rounds of layoffs, CNN, 27 April 2023, edition.cnn.com/2023/04/27/tech/amazon-earnings/index.html (accessed 10 July 2023).

McFadden, C. (2019). A very brief history of Amazon: The everything store, *Interesting Engineering*, interestingengineering.com/a-very-brief-history-of-amazon-the-everything-store (accessed 16 December 2020).

Pluimer–Amazonpov, L. (2020). Why 2020 could be the year Amazon becomes unstoppable, *Fast Company*, 1 October 2010, www.fastcompany.com/90450240/why-2020-could-be-the-year-amazon-becomes-unstoppable (accessed 18 December 2020).`

Stroud, S. (2022). Amazon and social media: How does Amazon use it? Giraffe Social Media, 15 December 2022, giraffesocialmedia.co.uk/how-do-amazon-use-social-media/#:~:text=Facebook%20%20Amazon.com%2029m%20likes%3B%20Prime%20Video%20UK,1.9m%20followers%3B%20Amazon%20Help%20387.7k%20followers%3B%20%26%20more.

www.forbes.com/the-worlds-most-valuable-brands/#1ffd1250119c (accessed 10 July 2023).

Yuen, M. (2023). Amazon annual revenue breakdown by segment in 2023, Insider Intelligence, 6 January 2023, www.insiderintelligence.com/insights/amazon-revenue/ (accessed 10 July 2023).

## CASE STUDY QUESTIONS

1. Based on your personal experience and the information available from the case study, highlight the success factors on Amazon and discuss how these are linked to the emergence of the digital consumer.
2. What evidence can be teased out from the Amazon case that justifies and emphasises the need to study consumer behaviour?
3. To what extent can you argue that Amazon is positioned to serve both the B2C and B2B consumer behaviour scenarios? Cite examples to support your position.
4. How can Amazon Prime, as a market offering to consumers, be used to explain the notion of customer value?

## REFERENCES

Akhtar, P., Khan, Z., Tarba, S., & Jayawickrama, U. (2017). The Internet of things, dynamic data and information processing capabilities, and operational agility. *Technological Forecasting and Social Change*, http://dx.doi.org/10.1016/j.techfore.2017.04.023 (accessed, 01 December 2023).

Anderson, M., & Jiang, J. (2018). Teens, social media & technology 2018, Pew Research Centre, 31 May 2018, www.pewresearch.org/internet/2018/05/31/teens-social-media-technology-2018/#:~:text=There%20are%20some%20differences%20in,41%25) (accessed, 22 November 2020).

Belk, R. W., & Pollay, R. W. (1985). Images of ourselves: The good life in twentieth century advertising. *Journal of Consumer Research*, 11(March), 887–897.

Bos, C., Van der Lans, I. A., Van Rijnsoever, F. J., & Van Trijp, H. C. (2013). Understanding consumer acceptance of intervention strategies for healthy food choices: A qualitative study. *BMC Public Health*, 13(1), 1073.

British Sociological Association (nd). What is Sociology: 19th century origin, www.britsoc.co.uk/what-is-sociology/origins-of-sociology/ (accessed, 24 November 2020).

Chang, J., Ren, H., & Yang, Q. (2018). A virtual gender asylum? The social media profile picture, young Chinese women's self-empowerment, and the emergence of a Chinese digital feminism. *International Journal of Cultural Studies*, 21(3), 325–340.

Cohen, J. B., & Bernard, H. R. (2013). Evolutionary psychology and consumer behavior: A constructive critique. *Journal of Consumer Psychology*, 23(3), 387–399.

Deighton, J. (2007). From the editor: The territory of consumer research: Walking the fences. *Journal of Consumer Research*, 34(October), 279–282.

Dichter, E. (1964). *Handbook of Consumer Motivations*. New York: McGraw-Hill.

Dennis, C., Merrilees, B., Jayawardhena, C., & Wright, L. T. (2009). E-consumer behaviour. *European Journal of Marketing*, 43(9/10), 1121–1139.

Elgaaïed-Gambier, L. (2016). Who buys overpackaged grocery products and why? Understanding consumers' reactions to overpackaging in the food sector. *Journal of Business Ethics*, 135(4), 683–698.

Emery, B. (2012). *Sustainable Marketing*. Harlow: Pearson Education Ltd.

Engel, J. F., Blackwell, R. D., & Miniard, P. W. (1968). *Consumer Behavior*. New York: Holt, Rinehart and Winston.

Fox, G., & Connolly, R. (2018). Mobile health technology adoption across generations: Narrowing the digital divide. *Information Systems Journal*, 28(6), 995–1019.

Foxall, G. R. (1974). Sociology and the study of Consumer Behavior. *The American Journal of Economics and Sociology*, 33(2), 127–135.

Friedman, M. (1957). *A Theory of the Consumption Function*. Princeton and Oxford: Princeton University Press.

Gbadamosi, A. (2019). Marketing ethics, green, and sustainable marketing, in Gbadamosi, A. (ed.), *Contemporary Issues in Marketing*, London: SAGE, pp.185–218.

Gbadamosi, A. (2020). Buyer behaviour in the 21st century: Implications for SME marketing, in Nwankwo, S. and Gbadamosi, A. (eds) *Entrepreneurship Marketing: Principles and Practice of SME Marketing*, 2nd edition, Oxfordshire: Routledge, pp.72–96.

Gbadamosi, A., & Sharma, A. (2019). The contemporary consumer, in Gbadamosi, A. (ed.) *Contemporary Issues in Marketing*, London: SAGE, pp.121–154.

Griskevicius, V., & Kenrick, D. T. (2013). Fundamental motives: How evolutionary needs influence consumer behavior. *Journal of Consumer Psychology*, 23, 372–386.

Griskevicius, V., Goldstein, N. J., Mortensen, C. R., Cialdini, R. B., & Kenrick, D. T. (2006). Going along versus going alone: When fundamental motives facilitate strategic (non)conformity. *Journal of Personality and Social Psychology*, 91, 281–294.

Hanlon, A. (2019). *Digital Marketing: Strategic Planning and Integration*, London: SAGE.

Helberger, N., Loos, M. M., Guibault, L., Mak, C., & Pessers, L. (2013). Digital content contracts for consumers. *Journal of Consumer Policy*, 36(1), 37–57.

Holbrook, M. B. (1987). What is consumer research? *Journal of Consumer Research*, 14(June), 128–132.

Hull, A., Wilkins, A., & Baddeley, A. (1988). Cognitive psychology and the wiring of plugs, in Gruneberg, M. M., Morris, P. E., & Sykes, R. N. (eds), *Practical Aspects of Memory: Current Research and Issues*, Chichester: Wiley, pp. 514–518.

Hussein, N. H. (2019). Neuromarketing, in Gbadamosi, A. (ed.), *Contemporary Issues in Marketing*, London: SAGE.

Jacoby, J. (1976). Consumer research: Telling it like it is, in *Advances in Consumer Research*, Vol. 3, (ed.) Beverlee B. Anderson, Ann Arbor, MI: Association for Consumer Research, pp. 1–11.

Kernan, J. B. (1995). Declaring a discipline: Reflections on ACR's Silver Anniversary, in *Advances in Consumer Research*, Vol. 22, (ed.) Frank R. Kardes and Mita Sujan, Provo, UT: Association for Consumer Research, pp. 553–560.

Kłopocka, A. M. (2017). Does consumer confidence forecast household saving and borrowing behavior? Evidence for Poland. *Social Indicators Research*, 133(2), 693–717.

Laslett, B., & Brenner, J. (1989). Gender and social reproduction: Historical perspectives. *Annual Review of Sociology*, 15, 381–404.

Levitis, D. A., Lidicker, W. Z., & Freund, G. (2009). Behavioural biologists don't agree on what constitutes behaviour. *Animal Behaviour*, 78, 103–110.

Manganari, E. E., Siomkos, G. J., Rigopoulou, I. D., & Vrechopoulos, A. P. (2011). Virtual store layout effects on consumer behaviour. *Internet Research*, 21(3), 326–346.

McKinsey Global Institute (2013). Disruptive technologies: Advances that will transform life, business, and the global economy, available at: McKinsey.com (accessed 17 May 2015).

Morin, C. (2011). Neuromarketing: The new science of consumer behavior. *Society*, 48(2), 131–135.

National Geographic Society (nd). What is geography?, www.nationalgeographic.org/education/what-is-geography/ (accessed, 25 November 2020).

Nicholls, A., & Huybrechts, B. (2016). Sustaining inter-organizational relationships across institutional logics and power asymmetries: The case of fair trade. *Journal of Business Ethics*, 135(4), 699–714.

Osmonbekov, T., & Johnston, W. J. (2018). Adoption of the Internet of Things technologies in business procurement: Impact on organizational buying behavior. *Journal of Business & Industrial Marketing*.

Özmete, E. (2009). Parent and adolescent interaction in television advertisement as consumer socialization agents. *Education*, 129(3), 372–381.

Peighambari, K., Sattari, S., Kordestani, A., & Oghazi, P. (2016). Consumer behavior research: A synthesis of the recent literature. *Sage Open*, 6(2), 2158244016645638.

Pine, B. J. III, & Gilmore, J. H. (1998). Welcome to the experience economy, *Harvard Business Review*, 76(4), 97–105.

Pyle, A. S., Morgoch, M. L., & Boatwright, B. C. (2019). SnowedOut Atlanta: Examining digital emergence on Facebook during a crisis. *Journal of Contingencies and Crisis Management*, 27(4), 414–422.

Saad, G. (2013). Evolutionary consumption. *Journal of Consumer Psychology*, 23, 351–371.

Saad, G., Eba, A., & Sejean, R. (2009). Sex differences when searching for a mate: A process-tracing approach. *Journal of Behavioral Decision Making*, 22, 171–190.

Schiffman, L. G., & Wisenblit, J. (2019). *Consumer Behaviour*, 12th edn. Essex: Pearson Education Limited.

Schiffman, L. G., Kanuk, L. L., & Wisenblit, J. (2010). *Consumer Behaviour*, 10th edn., New Jersey: Pearson Education Inc.

Schlaile, M. P., Klein, K., & Böck, W. (2018). From bounded morality to consumer social responsibility: A transdisciplinary approach to socially responsible consumption and its obstacles. *Journal of Business Ethics*, 149(3), 561–588.

Schmidt, M. A., & Garcia. T. M. F. B. (2010). History from children's perspectives: Learning to read and write historical accounts using family sources. *Education*, 38(3), 289–299.

Sheth, J. N. (1982). Consumer behavior: Surpluses and shortages, in *Advances in Consumer Research*, Vol. 9, (ed.) Andrew Mitchell, Ann Arbor, MI: Association for Consumer Research, pp. 13–16.

Solomon, M. R. (2020). *Consumer Behaviour: Buying, Having, and Being*, 13th edn. Essex: Pearson Education Limited.

Spivack (2007). How the WebOS evolves? Nova Spivack blog posting, 9 February 2007, www.novaspivack.com/technology/how-the-webos-evolves (accessed 25 November 2020).

Stamminger, R., Schmitz, A., & Hook, I. (2019). Why consumers in Europe do not use energy efficient automatic dishwashers to clean their dishes? *Energy Efficiency*, 12(3), 567–583.

Statista (2023). Number of Internet users worldwide from 2005 to 2022, www.statista.com/statistics/273018/number-of-internet-users-worldwide/ (accessed 10 July 2023).

Szmigin, I., & Piacentini, M. (2018). *Consumer Behaviour*, 2nd edn, Oxford: Oxford University Press.

Tadajewski, M., & Wagner-Tsukamoto, S. (2006). Anthropology and consumer research: Qualitative insights into green consumer behavior. *Qualitative Market Research: An International Journal*, 9(1), 8–25.

Tim, Y., Pan, S. L., Ractham, P., & Kaewkitipong, L. (2017). Digitally enabled disaster response: The emergence of social media as boundary objects in a flooding disaster. *Information Systems Journal*, 27(2), 197–232.

Valvi, A. C., Frangos, C. C., & Frangos, C. C. (2013). Online and mobile customer behaviour: A critical evaluation of grounded theory studies. *Behaviour and Information Technology*, 32(7), 655–667.

Wagner-Tsukamoto, S., & Tadajewski, M. (2006). Cognitive anthropology and the problem-solving behaviour of green consumers. *Journal of Consumer Behaviour: An International Research Review*, 5(3), 235–244.

Xiao, J. J., Ford, M. W., & Kim, J. (2011). Consumer financial behavior: An interdisciplinary review of selected theories and research. *Family and Consumer Sciences Research Journal*, 39(4), 399–414.

Zeithaml, V. (1988). Consumer perception of price, quality and value: A means-end model and synthesis of evidence. *Journal of Marketing*, 52(3), 2–22.

# CHAPTER 2

# Ethics and Contemporary Issues in Consumer Behaviour

................................................

**LEARNING OBJECTIVES**

After reading this chapter, you should be able to:

- Explain the main ethical issues associated with consumer behaviour;
- Discuss green and sustainable marketing in relation to sustainable consumption;
- Discuss consumer misbehaviour incorporating counterfeiting, cyberbullying, compulsive consumption, addictive consumption, digital protection, and security;
- Critically explain environmentalism, consumerism and consumer protection, and protest communities;
- Discuss the issues of brand ambassadors, hero-villain in marketing, and trolling.

**INTRODUCTION**

The prevalence of digital transformation is evident in virtually every aspect of our consumption. It now touches on consumption patterns that have been used over decades as well as more contemporary types. So, an old consumer in the United Kingdom, a middle-aged consumer in China, and a young consumer in Uganda would have experienced digital transformation in one form or another as we can say for other countries of the world. This is the reality of contemporary consumer behaviour. Similarly, digital transformation also relates to the discussion of what is right and wrong in the interaction of the existing and emerging production and consumption systems. Thus, as consumers, consumer behaviour researchers and other stakeholders, we are interested in the knowledge of how digital transformation relates to marketing and consumption ethics. Accordingly, we will be examining a rich mix of these issues in this chapter. The notion of marketing ethics, green, and sustainable marketing will be discussed as well as consumer misbehaviour to include issues such

DOI: 10.4324/9781003242031-3

as counterfeiting, cyberbullying, compulsive consumption, addictive consumption, digital protection, and security. Further sub-topics that will be examined here are environmentalism, consumerism and consumer protection, and protest communities. The chapter will also cover contemporary issues such as brand ambassadors, hero-villain in marketing, and trolling.

## MARKETING ETHICS AND CONSUMER BEHAVIOUR

One of the enduring arguments around the marketplace system is the issue of ethics in relation to marketers and consumers. This is about the question of what is right and wrong in how these and other associated parties relate. One of the prominent perspectives on this is around how the rights of consumers are being betrayed by marketers in various ways. These issues relate to each of the marketing mix elements. Some of these are as follows:

- Product management;
- Unethical pricing;
- High-pressure selling;
- Unethical marketing communications;
- Marketing research;
- International marketing;
- Exploiting disadvantaged consumers.

Over the years, there have been claims that marketers' activities concerning the products and services they offer are shrouded with unethical stratagems. For example, there are claims that consumers are offered products that are unsafe while there is planned obsolescence in respect of other market offerings. Examples of this can be seen in the food industry, automobile sectors, and beauty products. Horsemeat sold to consumers instead of beef, and a deceptive claim about car emissions by Volkswagen are two of the specific examples. A closely related issue here is planned obsolescence. In this, marketers design their products to become obsolete quickly to encourage consumers to replace them prematurely. Examples include those in the consumer electronic markets such as smartphones and tablets.

## UNETHICAL PRICING

Price is one of the key elements of the marketing mix elements, and the way it is managed will depend on the success of the business and may have an impact on customer satisfaction. One of the key claims against businesses is the exploitative charges around market offerings. With this, it is often argued that marketers' charges are primarily focused on their benefits, such as profitability, without recourse to consumers' welfare. Moreover, it is argued that marketers' pricing strategies are also deceptive. In an example of this, these organisations state their prices to be vague to deceive consumers, such as presenting a pack of fruit that will normally be sold for £1 as a 'buy two for £2' or as '£1.50 before and now £1' deal. This gives an erroneous impression that there is a price-drop on the product in these cases of how the prices have been depicted.

## HIGH-PRESSURE SELLING

There have been claims that consumers are sometimes bombarded to buy products and services they do not plan to buy through undue pressure from salespeople. More often than not, we have had various salespeople either visiting at the doorstep, calling on the telephone, or sending correspondence with the intention of selling their market offerings. While the idea of selling the products to the target consumers is not specifically out of place, the undue pressure placed on consumers through the intrusion into their time and space by salespeople and luring them to buy a product they would ordinarily not buy has been described as unethical such as the 'white is purity' ad of Nivea.

## UNETHICAL MARKETING COMMUNICATIONS

Generally, marketing communications is about making a favourable mention of the product being sold. There are many developments in the world of digital communications that have extended the strategic options available to marketers beyond the traditional methods. Hence, tools like social media are helping businesses to communicate the value of their market offerings. However, it has been argued by critics that in the process of achieving this objective, marketers engage in many unethical behaviours such as exaggerating claims of what the products offer and/or depicting some people in demeaning ways. There are many examples of this that we can draw from in recent times.

## MARKETING RESEARCH

Given the need to understand the key factors that influence consumption so that marketers can plan their strategies accordingly, marketing research is at the centre of determining this. It is about collecting, analysing, and managing data that will inform these relevant decisions. Nonetheless, there have been some key criticisms on how firms go about collecting and managing this information. Some of these revolve around the questions of:

- Invasion of privacy;
- Breach of confidentiality;
- Cohesion;
- Lack of informed consent;
- Deception;
- Inducements to commit acts diminishing self-esteem;
- Breach of agreement;
- Exposure to harm.

Overall, marketing researchers are expected to guard against these highlighted and other related unethical practices and preserve respondents' rights in their quest to obtain data and conduct their research.

## INTERNATIONAL MARKETING

The major criticism levied against marketers concerning international marketing is that marketers sometimes do not widen the scope of their strategies on ethical issues in order to be commensurate with international marketing practices, when they operate at such a level. This includes cases of businesses cherry-picking when and where they adhere to ethical guidelines between the various countries where they operate. A relevant example is the sale of tobacco products in developing countries without recourse to the applicable ethical principles they follow in developed countries, such as those relating to protecting children. Publications such as BBC (2008; 2017), Madichie and Opute (2019), and Gbadamosi (2019) present these exemplar cases that show how some international marketers are oblivious to the ethical rights of consumers in these contexts.

## EXPLOITING DISADVANTAGED CONSUMERS

Consumers such as the elderly, those on low-income, the unemployed, people with disability, the homeless, and others that have relatively very little income are often described as disadvantaged consumers (Fyfe, 1994). Characteristically, some of the existing academic literature indicates that these consumers are risky to serve, unprofitable, and fickle as they are not loyal to any brand (Gbadamosi, 2009). Hence, critics have argued that, in view of these characteristics, marketers' profitability motive prompts them to ignore serving these consumers at the bottom of the pyramid. It is argued that these consumers experience poor value for money, fewer options than their 'well-to-do' counterparts, and are at a disadvantage in terms of some store locations and retail settings. These are argued by critics to be unethical factors that require actions to protect this consumer segment.

## GREEN MARKETING AND SUSTAINABLE CONSUMPTION

Hardly any topic is more relevant to every aspect of society than the notion of green marketing. Its relevance relates to the supply of goods and services. It is of concern to large corporations as much as it is to small and medium scale businesses. The main crux in the notion of green or sustainable marketing is about practising marketing in such a way that all stakeholders including consumers, employees, society, shareholders, and others benefit mutually. So, when we talk about green and sustainable marketing, it is about ensuring that businesses satisfy their customers in a manner that demonstrates environmental friendliness. On the consumer side, there are many ways environmental friendliness is being violated in the form of waste of natural resources such as food, water, and energy. The amount of food wasted annually through production and consumption processes is estimated to be approximately 1.3 billion tons, which is equivalent to around $1 trillion (WFP, 2020). So, it is understandable that one of the key targets of the United Nations' Sustainable Development Goals is to ensure that natural resources will be used and managed effectively by 2030 (WFP, 2020).

There are many typologies of consumers based on their disposition to suitability. We will be looking at two of these to illustrate the topic in this section of the book. The first is adapted from the work of Ottman and Relly (1998), Banytė et al. (2010), and Gbadamosi (2019), which is depicted in Figure 2.1. In this, we can see that consumers have different levels of interest and enthusiasm towards green and sustainable consumption.

In this typology, the consumers who are very loyal to buying and using eco-friendly products and behave strongly in conserving the environment are depicted as 'Loyal green consumers'. The study shows that the consumer segment is prepared to pay up to 40% more for environmentally friendly products compared to alternative market offerings. Meanwhile, those identified as 'Less devoted green consumers' only go as far as paying between 10% and 20% more for eco-friendly products. Meanwhile, due to their very busy schedules, they are likely to keep their lifestyle unchanged.

Consumers who are developing towards green are only willing to spend 4% more to acquire green products and only buy them occasionally. For the consumers who are described as 'Conservative consumers unwilling to change', issues around sustainability and environmental protection should be the responsibility of government.

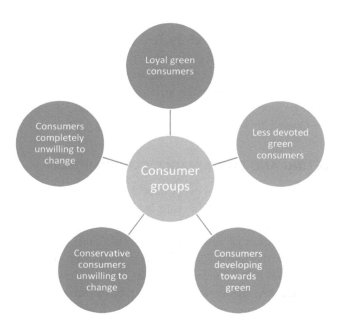

**FIGURE 2.1** Consumer segments based on interest and enthusiasm towards green and sustainable consumption

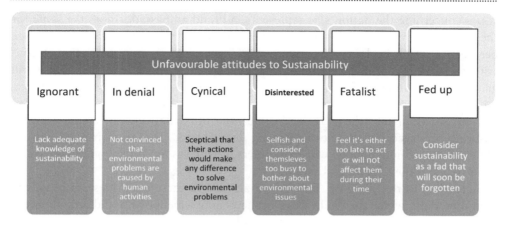

**FIGURE 2.2** Consumer segments based on unfavourable attitudes to sustainability

Hence, they are unwilling to sacrifice any more to acquire eco-friendly products but willing to buy them if the price equals the worth of alternatives. The last segment, 'Consumers completely unwilling to change', as the name suggests, are not interested in environmental issues as they do not consider them significant.

The second typology we will be discussing is more or less related to the last category of the group noted as completely unwilling to change in Figure 2.1. So, it is about the category of those that have a negative attitude to environmental issues. The reasons that underpin their negative attitude to sustainability are depicted in Figure 2.2 based on Emery (2012).

## GREENWASHING AND SUSTAINABLE CONSUMPTION

Another commonly discussed point on marketing ethics is the notion of greenwashing. It is about firms deceiving consumers about the organisations' green credentials. It takes a variety of forms, according to Ross and Deck (2011); these will include misleading visuals/graphics, misleading words, avoidance of helpful information, vagueness of claims, and exaggeration. While there are many examples of these nefarious activities in the marketing environment, the advancement in technology is strengthening consumers in how they can obtain information efficiently, report the case between consumers through word-of-mouth communications, and inform the appropriate regulatory bodies to curb the menace.

## BRAND AMBASSADORS

Whether we are at the airport, commuting, interacting with others on social media platforms, or engaging in other activities, we are exposed to images, logos, and names of several successful brands. A good number of factors and strategies are responsible for this success. Among these prominent factors that influence consumers' actions are the brand ambassadors. Just as an ambassador in a political system champions issues concerning the nation s/he represents, a brand ambassador does the same for the brand they represent. To start with the definition of the term, let us consider the perspective which explains it as anyone who is recruited by an organisation to consistently make favourable mention of its products in a personate way such that it will gain the target audiences' attention (Utami et al., 2020). As stated by these authors, a brand ambassador will be expected to be a person that consumers admire and can rely on. So, ultimately, the image and demeanour of the ambassador matter a lot for ensuring persuasion of the messages being disseminated. Due to their good personalities and good interactions with consumers, celebrities are often commissioned by firms to act as their brand ambassadors.

According to the claim of Ambroise et al. (2014), these celebrities are brands in their own right, which then indicates that their endorsement of a brand is tantamount to a co-branding strategy. Ultimately, their role is very important in triggering the purchase decisions of consumers. Schmidt and Baumgarth (2018) give a very interesting explanation of this role of ambassador, stating that a positive perception of the brand ambassador by consumers would result in a higher purchase decision for the brand involved. So, it is very important for firms to carefully consider their options before selecting a celebrity to act as their ambassador. Figure 2.3, which is adapted from the study of Ambroise et al. (2014), presents a set of criteria that marketers can use to guide their decisions on selection of brand ambassadors.

**FIGURE 2.3** Criteria for selecting a brand ambassador

> **PAUSE, PLAN, AND PRACTICE: LOUIS VUITTON AND BTS IN A GLOBAL BRAND AMBASSADOR DEAL**
>
> Selecting a brand ambassador is big business. Its relevance is applicable to physical products as well as service-oriented offerings and applies both to necessities and luxury offerings as well as other varying contexts. Although it is a luxury brand, Louis Vuitton is a popular brand known globally. It is known for top quality and respected offerings such as leathered goods, jewelleries, and accessories. This explains why in April, 2021, it chose BTS, a South Korean boy band known globally, as the ambassadors to endorse its brands. The band was launched in 2013 and its popularity has soared significantly since then. Some would be wondering why this band of seven members is doing so well and what could it add to the prestigious Louis Vuitton brand? The answers are pretty obvious. The consumers love their music and enjoy listening to their songs, the band also complements this with their impressive performances as shown in their dance steps and music videos. Similarly, BTS has a strong fan base that shows them unflinching support in various ways to project their music. This is closely linked to another point – the power of the Internet. The band has over 19 million followers on X and 23.7 million on Instagram. Interestingly, the numbers continue to grow for the group. Hence, it is understandable why its endorsement of Louis Vuitton is considered valuable to the brand.
>
> **QUESTIONS:**
>
> Identify three other popular brand ambassador deals you are aware of or have read about. Why do you think the brand have chosen these personalities or strategy? Would you have made a different choice if you are deciding for the organisation? Why? Identify one specific example where there may have been a mismatch between the chosen ambassador and the brand.
>
> **Sources:**
>
> BBC (2020). BTS: Who are they and how did they become so successful? BBC 24 March 2020, www.bbc.co.uk/newsround/45721656 (accessed 5 August 2021).
>
> Chitrakorn, K. (2021). Forget Hollywood, there's a new global brand ambassador. Business Vogue, www.voguebusiness.com/companies/forget-hollywood-new-global-luxury-brand-ambassadors-bts-blackpink (accessed 5 August 2021).
>
> Hirwany, P. (2021). BTS star addresses group's shift to making music in English: 'Language doesn't matter to us like it did in the past'. Independent, 4 August, www.independent.co.uk/arts-entertainment/music/news/bts-k-pop-music-english-b1896641.html (accessed 5 August 2021).

As shown in the figure, credibility is key to the choice in an ambassador. It is about the trustworthiness of the endorser while the attractiveness criteria relate to his or her similarity to the target audience, familiarity in the form of having knowledge through exposure, and likeability. So, the attractiveness here transcends physical appearance. The product match-up is simply about the perceived fit between the image of the celebrity and the brand he or she is endorsing. While the meaning transfer criteria is about examining the symbolic meaning that celebrity conveys to the consumer from the product/brand, the associative learning is on the cognitive connection existing between the ambassador endorsing the brand and the brand itself. Since the endorsers themselves are brands in their own right, the co-branding criteria is about how the image can be mutually beneficial on both sides.

In recent times there have been a number of changes to how brand ambassadors work to support the brand compared to how it used to be several decades before now. Prominent among these is the growing trend in online transactions and the proliferation of electronic word-of-mouth communications (eWOMs). Most of these brand ambassadors have several followers on social media with many more joining the network by the day.

## HERO-VILLAIN AND CONSUMER BEHAVIOUR

The concepts of heroes and villains, which are often discussed in the context of movies, are now becoming increasingly relevant and used in marketing contexts. In movies, we see characters, known as heroes, with determination in pursuit of goals but encountering opposition. The opposing parties are known as villains, that work to hinder the quest of the heroes (Ballantyne, 2019). We are discussing this in this chapter because of its relevance to the discussion of marketing and branding as a contemporary topic. The fundamental knowledge in marketing is about the supremacy of the consumers as the central element of marketing activities. So, in this sense, we can describe them as heroes and there could be a few factors that will be in the way of them having the desired satisfaction. Hence, in a publication titled 'every great story has a villain', it is highlighted that the illustration of a villain does not always have to be a person and may not necessarily be evil but a challenge to be overcome (Rose, 2021). This aligns with the claim of Ballantyne (2019), who also states that just as movies need villains, sports require villains and the two are significant for having a story architecture. Meanwhile, for a brand, a villain could be a competing brand.

One of the very interesting illustrations of this phenomenon is the study of Masters and Mishra (2019), in which they use the notions of vice and virtue to illustrate hero and villain labels. As stated in this study, the belief that the consumer holds about vice food is that it is tasty but could evoke some feeling of guilt, unlike virtuous food that is heathy but not fun to eat as it is not tasty. Given this background, Masters and Mishra (2019) conclude in their study that while consumers may show affinity for heathy products, they are aware that they may not taste good and may be considered as boring. So, this could be balanced out by adding a villain label that communicates fun such that it ultimately brings coherence into the scenario.

## CONSUMER MISBEHAVIOUR

The early part of this chapter highlights some grey areas where marketers' actions are under scrutiny and claims of inadequacies in how they play their roles in their quest for being profitable in the marketplace. On the other hand, there are areas where the behaviour of consumers is also outside the norm with huge ethical implications. These are described as consumer misbehaviour and explain the dark side of consumers. The view of Lee (2012) gives a detailed explanation of this phenomenon as a dysfunctional behavioural pattern exhibited by consumers for the purpose of getting unfair and unjust advantage during their transaction. Based on this perspective, it can be classified into three categories, namely:

- Distributive misbehaviour;
- Procedural misbehaviour;
- Interactional misbehaviour.

The dysfunctional consumer behaviour that prevents fair distribution of the benefits of marketing transactions such that marketers are affected and at the receiving end is distributive misbehaviour. Examples of this are financial fraud and shoplifting. The impact of this in the marketing system is significant. It was stated that around 60% of consumers have engaged in shoplifting at one time or another in their lifetime shopping experience (Klemke, 1992; De Bock and Van Kenhove, 2010). Development of digital tools has had mixed impacts on this over the years. Marketers are using various methods to curb this in the form of tagging and monitoring merchandise, but unfortunately shoplifters are also devising various means of circumventing the system. More often than not, fraudsters, like computer hackers, are violating marketers' computing systems in various ways in order to take undue advantage of the system.

Meanwhile, according to Lee (2012), those consumer behaviours that relate to their motives for selfish procedural convenience, such as wilful disobedience of rules and jumping queues, are procedural misbehaviour. We witness many examples in various places such as banking halls, airports, bus stations, hospitals, and restaurants, as well as in other places.

In this schema, interactional misbehaviour covers interpersonal actions that the sellers use unfairly such as physical abuse, threats, and verbal abuse.

Another category of consumer misbehaviour identified in the relevant academic literature (Martin and Praner, 1989; Gursoy et al., 2017) is that which irritates other customers. Examples of this include staring, smoking, having unsupervised children running around, and being noticeably drunk. Meanwhile, Gursoy et al. (2017) identify seven disruptive customer behaviours as follows:

1. Inattentive parent with naughty kids;
2. Oral abusers;
3. Outlandish requesters;
4. Hysterical shouters;
5. Poor hygiene manners;
6. Service rule breakers;
7. Ignorant customers.

In addition to these relating to services, consumers engage in other misbehaviours that relate to the tourism sector, as specifically teased out by the study of Wan et al. (2021):

- Stealing amenities from hotels;
- Stealing from airlines;
- Damaging historical buildings;
- Littering;
- Cutting queues;
- Wasting food at hotel buffets;
- Going shirtless;
- Fraudulent return of goods.

## COUNTERFEITING

Counterfeiting is one of the most common illegal transactions of recent times. The challenges associated with transactions involving counterfeit products are numerous. The scope is rather wide. Electronic gadgets, clothes, shoes, wrist watches, and a host of other products have been at the centre of these transactions, with great impacts on the economy. There are many concerning statistics on this. It is reported that the number of consumers buying counterfeit products every year is around 3 million (Bell, 2016). It has been reported that the estimated global counterfeit trade is considerable at about $653 billion, which represents approximately 7% of the total annual global world trade (Gaille, 2017; Gbadamosi, 2023).

The claim in the International Chambers of Commerce (2004) emphasises that the loss of luxury brands to these illicit transactions is estimated to be around $12 billion each year due to the demand for these counterfeit products (Bian et al., 2015), while an estimated figure of $770–$960 billion was noted for counterfeit transactions at the international level for the year 2015 (BASCAP, 2011). It is also noted that the demand for these products increases by around 12% annually (Chaudhry et al., 2009a, b; Stumpf et al., 2011). This applies on both the supply and demand sides. Considering the demand for counterfeit products shows that there are several factors responsible for this.

A key question to reflect on is 'why do consumers buy counterfeit products?'. We can tease out the answers to this question from previous publications on this topic. A very simple form of answer provided by Chaudhry and Stumpf (2011) divides the reasons into two categories, as either lack of ethical concern or a hedonic shopping experience. In this reasoning, the consumer is not bothered about the loss of revenue by the brand owners whose benefits are becoming eroded through the illicit act. The hedonic experience aspect indicates that consumers see the consumption as linked to fun, or a pleasant experience of having the brand through different and non-conventional means. From the view of Albers-Miller (1999), the significant predictors of the purchase of illicit products are:

- Product type;
- Buying situation;
- Price.

These authors noticed that consumers were able to distinguish between stolen goods and counterfeit such that in some cases, engaging in the latter is preferable to the former. The study also shows that consumers tend to be encouraged into buying the counterfeit if they experience peer pressure to do it. Meanwhile, there are further explanations; related but more detailed explications of these consumption acts are given by Stumpf et al. (2011) and Fernandes (2013), as shown in Table 2.1.

As shown in Table 2.1, there are agreements between the views of Chaudhry and Stumpf (2011) and Fernandes (2013) that a core reason for buying these products is because the consumers concerned are oblivious of the ethical implications of their actions. This self-ambiguity relates to the notion of self-concept. It indicates that the consumer buying the products lacks clarity about his or her self-concept thereby having low self-esteem. So, he or she uses consumption of counterfeit products to get acceptance from others towards boosting this low self-esteem. This is also closely related to the point that the purchase is propelled by the opinion of others (subjective norm). For example, a consumer could be motivated to buy a pirated CD or counterfeit jewellery by seeing his or her friends engage in similar purchases or being encouraged by them to do it. In most cases, the price paid for counterfeit products is less than the worth of original versions, which explains the value consciousness motivation for purchasing these products.

If we consider all these reasons for the purchase, it shows that consumers purposively engage in these purchases. However, this is not always the case. There are some cases when consumers are victims of counterfeit transactions as they were deceived into buying these products to the benefit of the dealers in these illicit transactions. This explains the claim of Staake et al. (2009) that it can be discussed from two perspectives: (1) deceptive counterfeiting (when both consumers and brand owners are victims); and (2) non-deceptive counterfeiting (in cases when the consumers are aware and make a conscious choice to purchase these items).

**TABLE 2.1** Reasons for purchasing counterfeit products

| | Author(s) | |
|---|---|---|
| | **Chaudhry and Stumpf (2011)** | **Fernandes (2013)** |
| **Reasons for Purchasing Counterfeit Products** | The product is easy to purchase<br>The product is desirable<br>The consumer considers the product as acceptable<br>The consumer making the purchase is on low-income | Lack of ethical judgement<br>Self-ambiguity<br>Subjective norm (susceptible to the opinion of others)<br>Value consciousness |

## CONSUMER MISBEHAVIOUR IN A DIGITAL AGE

Just as we witness many changes to consumer behaviour as a result of developments in the world of technology, virtually all the consumer misbehaviour acts discussed have changed in various ways for the same reason. There are now several cases of software piracy, computer virus, email fraud, auction fraud, cheque fraud, identity theft, and many other e-crimes under the new types of dysfunctional consumer behaviour. More often than not we receive deceptive email messages impersonating other parties, asking for personal details, and faking transactions. Similarly, many unscrupulous people make unsolicited approaches to consumers for the purpose of gaining access to their data and resources. There are numerous other cases on social media where many Generation Z consumers feel pressured into engaging in these unethical practices (Jacobsen and Barnes, 2020). This consumer group is heavily represented on social media like Instagram, X, Facebook, and YouTube, which explains why the study shows that half of the participants acknowledge that social media has the greatest of the influences on their consumption misbehaviour. Going by the view of Chatzidakis and Mitussis (2007) in Harris and Dumas (2009), the development in technology makes it possible for consumer dysfunctional behaviour to be done anonymously, which makes it difficult to identify those who engage in unethical behaviour.

## CYBERBULLYING

Another anomaly in consumer behaviour associated with the increase in the use of technology is cyberbullying. A review of existing literature reports that cyberbullying rates in Europe, Canada, and the USA range from between 12% and 25% and are even higher in other places (Lazuras et al., 2013). In their publication on cyberbullying and self-esteem, Patchin and Hinduja (2010) quote the 2007 publication of the Bureau of Justice statistics on school crime to show that 28% of students aged between 12 and 18 have experienced being bullied in various ways within the past 6 months, while a quarter of students in this category had that bullying experience one or twice within a month (Dinkes et al., 2007). More recently, the Office of National Statistics indicated that about 19% of children aged 10 to 15 in England and Wales had experienced some form of cyberbullying in the year ending March 2020 (ONS, 2020). So, cyberbullying is one of the developments in contemporary consumer behaviour and these statistical details that cannot be ignored in terms of scale and significance. But we need to address the question of 'what is cyberbullying?'

From a general perspective, bullying can be described as unwanted aggressive behaviour meted out to a victim repeatedly such that there is a perceived or observed power imbalance, which could be verbal, physical, relational, or some combination of these (Waasdorp and Bradshaw, 2015). Meanwhile, cyberbullying has been defined in several different ways. One perspective explains it as aggression that occurs in cyberspace with the use of contemporary information and communication technologies (ICTs) (Lazuras, 2013). This definition is also closely related to the explanation given by Calvete et al. (2010) earlier that it is deliberate, aggressive, frequently done over time, and could be perpetrated by an individual or group using electronic gadgets for the purpose of targeting their victims, who cannot easily defend themselves. So, this can take place in various ways, such as making fun of victims via email messages, online chats, and various social media platforms. Other examples can be sharing conversations about private parts of their victims online, insulting victims on social media platforms, presenting embarrassing rumours about victims, posting videos or photos of victims online, and hacking someone's gadget to impersonate them in order to share embarrassing content with others. In the practical sense, there is a high degree of similarity between cyberbullying and traditional bullying in terms of the forms it takes such as threatening, rumour spreading, exclusion, and harassment (Patchin and Hinduja, 2010).

Given that they operate in different platforms, we can tease out some differences between traditional bullying and cyberbullying. Reviewing some scholarship effort (Spears et al., 2009; Nocentini et al., 2010; Patchin and Hinduja, 2010; Berne et al., 2013; Brewer and Kerslake, 2015) on this topic reveals the following differences:

1. Cyberbullies can be anonymous as they use digital technologies;
2. There are no regulatory bodies monitoring conversations;
3. It is easier to engage in cyberbullying due to physical distance between the victim and the offender;
4. The speed at which the information is shared in cyberbullying is high;
5. The material relating to the victim shared in cyberbullying is more lasting;
6. The victim is more easily available in cyberbullying;
7. Cyberbullying has a potentially broader audience;
8. Cyberbullying is 24/7 by nature.

There is a great degree of agreement in the literature that this notoriety is often caused by a low level of self-esteem both on the side of the victim and offender and it is not exclusively the issue of the younger generation, even though it is more common among them. Brewer and Kerslake (2015) add that when there is a decrease in empathy, then there is a high probability that cyberbullying activities will increase. Some bullies perceive it as fun or think their victims deserve it, as it may even be a form of revenge (Hinduja and Patchin, 2008; Wong et al., 2014). Characteristically, bullies have been depicted as likely to be having a feeling of doing something thrilling (Psychopathy), or having a sense of entitlement, superiority, and dominance over their victims (Narcissism), or having a manipulative and cold behaviour to negatively gain control over others and/or exert influence over them (Gibb and Devereux, 2014). By and large, while there are numerous benefits associated with the increase in use of technology among consumers in recent times, cyberbullying is an example of the dark side of consumer behaviour in relation to technology. The knowledge of how it works and the impact are pointers for various stakeholders such as marketers, governments, and charity organisations to chart directions for action on how to curb the menace towards ensuring a more ethical marketing environment.

## DIGITAL PROTECTION AND SECURITY

These days, consumers' lives are connected to the Internet in a myriad of ways ranging from activities around purchases, bill payments, managing health care details, and socialising with others. In most cases, these take the form of consumers engaging in self-services like in banking transactions, supermarket self-checkouts, and a host of others. In several other cases, artificial intelligence (AI) has been introduced. A digital presence is now becoming a necessity in normal modern day business transactions. As digital transactions increase in scale due to developments in technology, one of the key concerns held by consumers revolves around digital protection.

To explain digital protection, we can look at its link to digital privacy, which is explained as the perception of consumers that their personal information may be lost and possibly used by others in the process of their digital transactions (Pavlou, 2011; Elhai et al., 2017). We can state this differently by explaining digital privacy as involving how the confidentiality of consumers' personal information kept on computer and other various digital systems of e-marketers is protected and maintaining consumers' right not to be disturbed by unsolicited information (Miller and Weckert, 2000; Hung and Wong, 2009). Exposure to risks concerning electronic data comes in various ways. Consumers use smartphone apps, tablets, wearable electronic items, and use social media platforms. As consumers become elated at the latest developments in technology, and use them in relation to their transactions with businesses, government establishment systems, and non-governmental organisations, the risks associated with their different dimensions increase and make them vulnerable to vices such as financial fraud and identify theft. The complexity associated with this phenomenon is emphasised by the links between national and international transactions in a multi-layered form. Goyens (2020) explains the link between internationalisation and digitalisation along the line of three points:

- Consumer online transactions with marketers are eased with lack of physical obstacles but also have some corresponding consumer disputes that may be partly cross-border in nature;
- Consumers are sometimes unaware that their various contracts have cross-border implications especially in relation to cases when things do not go as planned;
- Some of the products bought locally either in store or online have some form of connected features that tend to introduce extra territorial circumstances into the transactions.

In view of the devastating result of digital crimes and the sensitivity of the information involved, it is expected that effort should be made to prevent and/or mitigate their impact. According to Goyens (2020), the cooperation of key regulatory bodies in developing useful policies and procedures that will safely guide consumer protection during transactions not only across sectors by also across countries, is essential for ensuring a good enabling environment between the consumers and the marketers.

As expected, it has been shown that in the absence of any action from businesses or governments to ensure equality in how information exchange takes place in the marketplace, consumers will adopt defensive actions towards managing privacy protection (Lwin et al., 2007; Bandara et al., 2020). This is linked to the Privacy Calculus Theory (PCT), which indicates that consumers will do a risk-benefit analysis between releasing their personal information that marketers have requested, which could give them opportunities for benefits such as discounts and coupons and the risks involved like sharing such details with other parties (Li, 2012; Elhai et al., 2017). So, consumers are guided by perceived risks of their decisions about the data released online. For example, in their study on mobile banking and artificial intelligence (AI)-enabled mobile banking, Payne et al. (2018) found that security concern is one of the principal factors indicated by consumers as predictors of their adoption of AI-oriented mobile banking.

## ENVIRONMENTALISM

Concern for the environment is clearly one of the topical issues, as environmental problems continue to rise in various ways to reflect how humans have abused the planet. This is the main issue in environmentalism, which has been explained as various beliefs relating to the link between nature and humanity (Yan et al., 2015). Putting it in clear terms, natural resources such as water and timber are being abused and overused in various ways, which then indicates that a large-scale behavioural change will be needed to solve these problems (Zelezny and Schultz, 2000). Some efforts are being made in various ways to change the status quo. Yan et al. (2015) report how some consumers buy second-hand clothing instead of new ones to reduce human impact on the environment. Specifically, findings show that those engaging in the purchase of second-hand clothing tend to be more environmentally conscious than those who do not. Similarly, findings suggest that consumers even use their green credentials as a status symbol and their greenness consumption increases with their quest for green status seeking (Welsch and Kühling, 2016).

## CONSUMERISM AND PROTEST COMMUNITIES

Consumerism can be conceptualised in two ways. First, it is used as a construct to depict the act of preoccupation with acquisition and consumption of goods as prevailing in the society. In its second form, which is the focus in this segment of the chapter, is about the movement of people, consumer advocates, governments, and other stakeholders for strengthening the rights and powers of the buyers in relation to those of the sellers (Kotler, 1972; Donoghue et al., 2016; Gbadamosi, 2019). Its formal emergence is linked to 1962 when US President J. F. Kennedy introduced the 'Consumers Bill of Rights' that presents these four consumer rights: Right to be informed, right to safety, right to choose, and right to redress. Meanwhile, they have been extended to eight as shown in Figure 2.4, which is adapted from

**44** TECHNOLOGY AND CONTEMPORARY CONSUMER BEHAVIOUR: AN INTRODUCTION

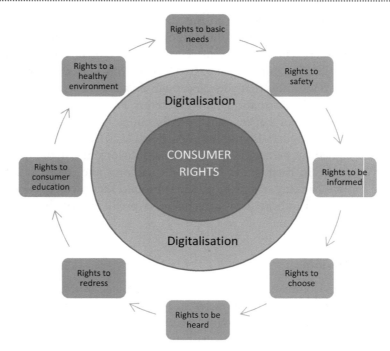

**FIGURE 2.4** Digitalisation and consumers' rights
**Source**: Consumer Rights Act 2015.

UN Guidelines for consumer protection (Consumers' Rights Act, 2015) to give a wider sense of protection to consumers in other areas in various countries. The activities of Consumers International, a charity organisation which is pioneering consumer rights, has been remarkable in various ways in this regard (Consumers International, 2016).

As shown in Figure 2.4, the way consumers go about or could approach these rights are being moderated by digital technologies. An interesting and useful contribution in this regard is seen in the publication of Kucuk (2016) titled *Consumerism in the digital age*. The author indicates that digital technologies have empowered consumers in various ways such as in the areas of their rights to choose, and rights to be heard to a great extent as they now have access to search engines and social media platforms through which the required information can be obtained, and their choices enhanced. However, there are other areas where further actions are still needed to strengthen consumers' rights. This includes the right to privacy and right to information safety as demonstrated in the increasing rate of cybercrimes.

## PROTEST COMMUNITIES

The power imbalance between marketers and consumers has been a major point of recurring discussion in recent times. As discussed in the early part of this chapter, there are many anomalies in the marketplace to the detriment of consumers and in some cases other stakeholders such as the society where businesses operate. For example, those in poor neighbourhoods indicate concerns about their environments. These have led to an increase in protest communities. In fact, as with most topics these days, this phenomenon has also gained a boost from the increase in the use of technology in various ways.

Social movements work as networks to voice their concerns and demands, which could be of different natures like political or social and can be highly integrated, loosely linked, or some variation of these (Forno, 2015). At the individual level, consumers express their dissatisfaction through word-of-mouth communication to friends, neighbours, family members, and others. They are now aided by the increased usage of technology that makes such communication faster and stronger. It is reported that consumer protesters put up websites to communicate their concerns about brands, organisations, and their offerings, and they are praised by other consumers who visit the websites and see them as crusaders (Ward and Ostrom, 2006). In several other cases, consumers come together to decide to boycott the products and services of erring businesses. There have been cases of this concerning businesses such as Starbucks, Nike, L'Oreal, and The Body Shop. By its nature, social media has played a significant role in the spread of these messages from social movements. Several examples of notable social media-related protests abound. Although it is political, the Arab Spring movement is a typical example of the speed at which technology aids a protest community (Hamelin et al., 2020), while the 'Occupy Sandy' online movement, adopted during the 2012 Hurricane Sandy in the United States for reaching the victims, demonstrated the power of network as aided by technology (Hwang and Kim, 2015).

## TROLLING

The digital age has introduced many things and enhanced several others positively and negatively. One of these contemporary phenomena in marketing is trolling. The term can be defined as positively engaging in deception communication for the purpose of causing conflict or disrupting discussion between people for amusement (Kirkwood et al., 2019). So, we can explain it as purposive, deceptive, and mischievous attempts made for the purpose of obtaining a reaction from the targeted individuals or groups, for the gain of the troll(s) and those following them with undesirable consequences for the people and the organisations involved (Golf-Papez and Veer, 2017). Trolling activities take place in different contexts such as in politics, online communities, and NGOs. It may take different forms like fabricating complaints, and generating rumours concerning the products, brands, or services of an establishment, which explains why Golf-Papez and Veer (2017) describe trolls as attention seekers.

Some trolling activities are more serious than others. Hence, there is a typology which indicates that we can have serious trolling and humourous trolling (Sanfilippo et al., 2018). According to this perspective, while the latter is just for fun and entertainment, the former has sincere ideological reason for engaging in it. In fact, when trolling first started in the 1980s, it took on harmless forms such as raising pointless questions just for the purpose of getting a reaction from others to these questions, but this has now gradually grown to the point that some trolls can be very aggressive (Cruz et al., 2018). Just like a coin, trolling can also be seen as having two sides. These are positive and negative effects. We can tease out the problems and benefits associated with it from the work of Golf-Papez and Veer (2017) based on their extensive review of relevant literature. So, the negative sides of trolling are:

- Disruption within an online community;
- Damage to property such as telephone and computer systems;
- Distress to online users;
- Harm to brand image;
- Financial loss to the organisation.

On the other hand, trolling can be beneficial in relation to these points:

- Drives traffic to the website;
- It may hold the online community together as there is an issue to focus on;
- It may give a sense of positive self-image for those who do not engage in it.

## COMPULSIVE CONSUMPTION

Consumption is fundamental to life as we are all consumers that engage in one consumption act or another to satisfy needs. Nonetheless, some consumption acts do not have the same positive impact in the lives of consumers as others, which explains the notion of compulsive consumption. Let us consider the perspective of O'Guinn and Faber (1989) to explain it. According to them we can describe compulsive consumption as engaging in chronic, repetitive purchases that constitute a primary response to negative events or feelings. Hence, we can infer that the consumer who engages in compulsive consumption is preoccupied with frequent loss of control over buying and buys those items that are not needed and not used (Mueller et al., 2011). This abnormality in consumption has been attributed to many factors including neuroticism, low self-esteem, and family breakdown such as divorce or marriage separation (Rindfleisch et al., 1997; Otero-López and Pol, 2013; Gbadamosi, 2018). So, the factors that trigger this consumption behaviour could be categorised as personal factors and social factors. Meanwhile, by the nature of this consumption behaviour, it will be associated with financial loss as these consumers will be unable to keep to budget. However, apart from this, other consequences of this consumption behaviour are family and marital discord, anxiety, frustration, time consumption, and interference with social and occupational functioning (O'Guinn and Faber, 1989; Christenson et al., 1994; Johnson and Attmann, 2009; McElroy et al., 1994; Mueller et al., 2015).

## ADDICTIVE CONSUMPTION

Addictive consumption has been a societal issue for a long time. Some consumers uncontrollably depend on certain products with varying devastating consequences. People can be addicted to any product or, just like in the case of compulsive consumption which relates to shopping, they may be addicted to an act or a process. Some of the common examples we hear of are addiction to food, drugs, and gambling. The Office of National Statistics (ONS) provides some notable statistical data on drug misuse. For the year ending March 2020, about 3.2 million people aged between 16 and 59 years were recorded to have taken a drug in England and Wales, whereas the percentage of those aged 16 to 24 was 21% (1.3 million) (ONS, 2020). While these are cited as examples, it is important to note that this concerning data about drug misuse is also noted for other age groups, and several other countries. Besides, it has been reported that premature death arising from obesity in the world is 4.7 million every year, which makes it one of the more serious health challenges (Ritchie and Roser, 2017). In a similar way, a higher gambling urge has been consistently linked to compulsive consumption with symptoms like poorer social functioning and psychological disturbances (Asharafioun et al., 2013; Loo et al., 2016), and financial loss, which could also have a multiplier effect on family structure and functioning. By and large, addictive consumption encapsulating overeating, alcoholism, and a host of other things depicts the dark side of consumer behaviour, with significant consequences not only for the individual consumers but also their social networks and society in general.

## SUMMARY

The notion of ethics is of paramount importance in consumer behaviour, and cuts across all elements of the marketing mix. As contemporary marketing introduces changes to how things are now done such as brand ambassadors, ethics become more associated with the issue of sustainable consumption. However, some consumers have unfavourable attitudes towards sustainability while some businesses engage in greenwashing. These are among the ongoing challenges in the contemporary marketing environment. Others include counterfeiting, consumer misbehaviour, compulsive consumption, and addictive consumption. They now take different forms in the current digital age, necessitating that attention will be focused on appropriate and commensurate solutions such as data protection and security, environmentalism, and consumerism and protest communities.

> **DIGITAL BOX: CYBERCRIME IN THE UK**
>
> One of the major challenges associated with the increase in technological usage is crime associated with it. Crimes of different types have now emerged online. For example, as consumers' online activities increased during the period of COVID-19, fraudsters also heightened their

game along that line. They took the opportunity of the pandemic to defraud vulnerable consumers. Generally, it is stated that serious and organised crime in the UK costs the country around £37 billion annually, of which cybercrime is inclusive. This is clearly significant. The National Crime Agency (NCA), a leading establishment in the UK, has been at the forefront of fighting these other crimes. Its website provides rich details to guide consumers against these nefarious activities. For example, it states various approaches often used by these criminals to perpetrate these frauds. These include hacking, malicious software, distributed denial of services, and phishing. As stated on the organisation's website, the criminals perpetrating these crimes could be based abroad though some are home-grown, and while the motive for this could be financial, some, especially young perpetrators, are driven by fun and the need for praise by their peers. Despite the unrelenting efforts of these criminals, the NCA provides suggestions on how consumers can help to address this menace. According to them, consumers should use a very strong password for their online transactions and avoid reusing them for multiple logins. It also advises that online users should not only install security software on their devices but should also keep that software constantly updated.

**Sources:**

NCA (nd), The threat from serious and organised crime, National Crime Agency, www.nationalcrimeagency.gov.uk/who-we-are/our-mission (accessed 2 August 2021).

**Question/Task**: Despite the effort from various stakeholders to address cybercrime, the number of cases and the associated losses are still high. What do you think are the reasons for this and what further recommendations can you make to address this problem?

## END OF CHAPTER DISCUSSION QUESTIONS

1. Discuss the main ethical issues that should be noted and addressed by multinationals as they operate in different countries.
2. What is greenwashing and why is it unethical?
3. Consumers' understanding of sustainability differs, which also explains why enthusiasm towards it varies. Identify and discuss briefly the consumer categorisation on the basis of their unfavourable attitude towards sustainability.
4. Consumer behaviours are not always positive to stakeholders in the marketplace. Discuss any four types of this consumer misbehaviour and suggest how they can be addressed.
5. Use contemporary examples to illustrate your understanding of these consumer behaviour-related terms:
    a. Counterfeiting;
    b. Environmentalism;
    c. Compulsive consumption;
    d. Cyberbullying and trolling;
    e. Consumerism and protest communities.

## Case Study: The European Union's Agenda for SMEs and the Quest for Sustainable Consumption

The European Union (EU) is a major player in the world's economy and its commitment to environmental sustainability over the years has been notably remarkable. However, the economic block also has some notable challenges concerning this laudable obligation. While some of the consumers show good intentions to tune their consumption to eco-friendly products, this is not matched by a commensurate level of action towards achieving this. Some of the reasons for this include social factors such as peer pressure, price, and convenience. In March 2020, a Eurobarometer survey concerning the attitudes of EU citizens in relation to the environment was published. It shows that two-thirds of consumers in this context acknowledge that their consumption behaviour affects the environment negatively, and that a change to their consumption pattern will be needed. In fact, 94% of the participants indicate that they hold issues about the environment as important to them personally. Based on the available indicators, the EU is committed to redeeming the environment from the looming disaster. It does so from two broad perspectives – production and consumption. The idea here is that if businesses are pursing an eco-friendly agenda and this is not supported by commensurate consumers' effort, the result will be short of what is needed. In view of this, the EU is focused on empowering consumers to be engaged in sustainable consumption by engaging in green transition. This is planned to be done through legislative processes. Part of what is done is the policy of 'polluters pay'. Similarly, the European Commission developed the European Green Deal communication in December 2019 that highlights the vision intended to achieve a climate-neutral EU by the year 2050. Besides, the vision is also about achieving greenhouse gas emissions reduction by at least 55% by the year 2030. Consequently, EU legislation directs businesses to inform consumers about the green credentials of some products being offered such as energy sources and the impact of electricity on the environment, and fuel efficiency level of tyres. In addition to these mandatory labelling systems, there are some which are voluntary for businesses, which include business use of EU ecolabels which communicate that the products and services involved are of high standards of environmental sustainability. Usually, these will cover issues such as generating less waste, making products that are repairable and durable, and upgradable.

Meanwhile, while effort is ongoing at encouraging consumers to embrace sustainable consumption, another effort is being made to boost the involvement of SMEs in encouraging this consumption behaviour. Although SMEs are typically associated with limited resources and managed in less formalised ways compared to the large corporations, their significance in Europe is huge. There are about 25 million of these businesses in the EU economy, which has about 100 million employees. Figures like these cannot be considered inconsequential. However, development in the world of technology is ubiquitous and is positioning SMEs in the EU to contribute to foster sustainable consumption among the citizens. When the European Commissioner for Internal Markets, Thierry Breton, announced the SME strategy on 10 March 2020, it was evident that these businesses will play strategic roles in boosting sustainable consumption among EU citizens. In this plan, he stresses a number of issues that the commission is focused on achieving concerning SMEs. This includes enhancing the digital innovation hub that will position SMEs to experiment with new technologies. Closely related to this is the establishment of digital crash courses for those employed by SMEs so that they can be proficient on issues like cybersecurity, artificial intelligence, and blockchain. The commission will also introduce a digital volunteers programme which will involve attracting those skilled in digital applications to share their experiences with aptitude with traditional businesses. Financially, the commission is also poised to spend not less than EUR300 million to foster Green Deal innovations.

So, ultimately, these actions and investments into SMEs are meant to give significant results from the EU twin transition to a digital and sustainable economy. Hence, they are strengthening digital transformation and fostering their contribution to sustainability. This is because digital breakthroughs will result in encouraging consumers to embrace sustainable consumption as these businesses work on making cheaper eco products, eco-friendly packaging, and many other green-related benefits. So, the impact of SMEs in the EU to bring sustainable change to Europe cannot be considered trivial. In view of their number in society, they may constitute the game changer for this important phenomenon.

**Sources:**

European Commission (2020). Communication From The Commission To The European Parliament, The Council, The European Economic And Social Committee And The Committee Of The Regions: An SME strategy for a sustainable and digital Europe, Brussels, 10.3.2020 COM(2020) 103 final, ec.europa.eu/info/sites/default/files/communication-sme-strategy-march-2020_en.pdf (retrieved on 1 August 2021).

European Commission (2021). SME strategy launched by European Commission, digital-strategy.ec.europa.eu/en/news/sme-strategy-launched-european-commission (retrieved on 1 August 2021).

European Union (nd), Climate action and the European Green Deal: Path to climate neutrality, European Union, commission.europa.eu/strategy-and-policy/priorities-2019-2024/european-green-deal/climate-action-and-green-deal_en (accessed 29 September 2023).

## CASE STUDY QUESTIONS

1. Despite the good intention to buy eco-friendly products, it is written that some EU customers do not support this with action. Explain why this is the case and what can be done to change this imbalance.
2. Do you think the legislative approach to achieving sustainable consumption such as the policy 'Polluters pay' will achieve the desired result? Give reasons for your stance.

3. The European Union (EU) is doing something to encourage SMEs to work towards contributing to sustainable consumption; in what other ways do you think SMEs could be involved in encouraging sustainable consumption?
4. How might the brand ambassador as a topic be useful in driving sustainable consumption? Give specific examples.

## REFERENCES

Albers-Miller, N. D. (1999). Consumer misbehavior: Why people buy illicit goods. *Journal of Consumer Marketing*, 16(3), 273–287.

Ambroise, L., Pantin-Sohier, G., Valette-Florence, P., & Albert, N. (2014). From endorsement to celebrity co-branding: Personality transfer. *Journal of Brand Management*, 21(4), 273–285.

Ashrafioun, L., Kostek, J., & Ziegelmeyer, E. (2013). Assessing post-cue exposure craving and its association with amount wagered in an optional betting task. *Journal of Behavioral Addictions*, 2(3), 133–137.

Ballantyne, S. (2019). Heroes and villains. Story IQ, 4 April 4 2019, storyiq.co.nz/heroes-and-villains/ (retrieved 9 July 2021).

Bandara, R., Fernando, M., & Akter, S. (2020). Managing consumer privacy concerns and defensive behaviours in the digital marketplace. *European Journal of Marketing*, 55(1), 219–246.

Banytė, J., Brazionienė, L., & Gadeikienė, A. (2010). Investigation of green consumer profile: A case of Lithuanian market of eco-friendly food products. *Economics & Management*, 15, 374–383.

BASCAP (2011). Estimating the global economic and social impacts of counterfeiting and piracy, Report by Business Action to Stop Counterfeiting and Piracy, Frontier Economics, London, available at: www.iccwbo.org/uploadedFiles/BASCAP/Pages/Global%20Impacts%20-%20Final.pdf (accessed 5 May 2011).

BBC (2008). Bannatyne takes on big tobacco. BBC, 27 June. Available at: http://news.bbc.co.uk/1/hi/programmes/this_world/7477468.stm (accessed 5 April 2018).

BBC (2017). Smoking causes one in 10 deaths worldwide, study shows. BBC, 6 April. Available at: www.bbc.co.uk/news/health-39510728 (accessed 5 April 2018).

Bell, B. (2016). What's wrong with buying fake luxury goods? BBC, 15 July, 2016, www.bbc.co.uk/news/uk-england-36782724 (accessed 28 September 2023).

Berne, S., Frisén, A., Schultze-Krumbholz, A., Scheithauer, H., Naruskov, K., Luik, P., ... & Zukauskiene, R. (2013). Cyberbullying assessment instruments: A systematic review. *Aggression and Violent Behavior*, 18(2), 320–334.

Bian, X., Haque, S., & Smith, A. (2015). Social power, product conspicuousness, and the demand for luxury brand counterfeit products. *British Journal of Social Psychology*, 54(1), 37–54.

Brewer, G., & Kerslake, J. (2015). Cyberbullying, self-esteem, empathy and loneliness. *Computers in Human Behavior*, 48, 255–260.

Calvete, E., Orue, I., Estévez, A., Villardón, L., & Padilla, P. (2010). Cyberbullying in adolescents: Modalities and aggressors' profile. *Computers in Human Behavior*, 26(5), 1128–1135.

Chaudhry, P. E., Peters, J. R., & Zimmerman, A. (2009a). Evidence of managerial response to the level of consumer complicity, pirate activity, and host country enforcement of counterfeit goods: An exploratory study. *Multinational Business Review*, 17(4), 21–44.

Chaudhry, P. E., Zimmerman, A., Peters, J. R., & Cordell, V. V. (2009b). Preserving intellectual property rights: Managerial insight into the escalating counterfeit market quandary. *Business Horizons*, 52(1), 57–66.

Chaudhry, P. E., & Stumpf, S. A. (2011). Consumer complicity with counterfeit products. *Journal of Consumer Marketing*, 28(2), 139–151.

Christenson, G. A., Faber, R. J., De Zwaan, M., Raymond, N. C., Specker, S. M., Ekern, M. D., ... & Eckert, E. D. (1994). Compulsive buying: Descriptive characteristics and psychiatric comorbidity. *The Journal of Clinical Psychiatry*, 55(1), 5–11.

Consumers International (2016). Consumer Protection: Why it Matters – A Practical Guide to United National Guidelines for Consumer Protection. Available at: www.consumersinternational.org/media/2049/un-consumer-protection-guidelines-english.pdf (accessed 26 December 2018).

Cruz, A. G. B., Seo, Y., & Rex, M. (2018). Trolling in online communities: A practice-based theoretical perspective. *The Information Society*, 34(1), 15–26.

De Bock, T., & Van Kenhove, P. (2010). Consumer ethics: The role of self-regulatory focus. *Journal of Business Ethics*, 97(2), 241–255.

Dinkes, R., Cataldi, E. F., Lin-Kelly, W., & Snyder, T. D. (2007). *Indicators of School Crime and Safety: 2007*. Washington, DC: US Department of Education; US Department of Justice, Office of Justice Programs.

Donoghue, S., Van Oordt, C., & Strydom, N. (2016). Consumers' subjective and objective consumerism knowledge and subsequent complaint behaviour concerning consumer electronics: A South African perspective. *International Journal of Consumer Studies*, 40(4), 385–399.

Elhai, J. D., Levine, J. C., & Hall, B. J. (2017). Anxiety about electronic data hacking: Predictors and relations with digital privacy protection behavior. *Internet Research*, 27(3), 631–649.

Emery, B. (2012). *Sustainable Marketing*. Harlow: Pearson Education.

Fernandes, C. (2013). Analysis of counterfeit fashion purchase behaviour in UAE. *Journal of Fashion Marketing and Management: An International Journal*, 17(1), 85–97.

Forno, F. (2015). Bringing together scattered and localized actors: Political consumerism as a tool for self-organizing anti-mafia communities. *International Journal of Consumer Studies*, 39(5), 535–543.

Fyfe, G. (1994). Life on a low income, in G. Fyfe (ed.), *Poor and Paying for It: The Price of Living on a Low Income*. Glasgow: Scottish Consumer Council/HMSO, pp.1–15.

Gaille, B. (2017). 25 remarkable counterfeit goods statistics, May 29, brandongaille.com/24 remarkable-counterfeit-goods-statistics/ (accessed 11 January 2023).

Gbadamosi, A. (2009). Cognitive dissonance: The implicit explication in low-income consumers' shopping behaviour for 'low-involvement' grocery products. *International Journal of Retail and Distribution Management*, 37(12), 1077–1095.

Gbadamosi, A. (2018). Compulsive consumption and the contemporary global consumer culture: Implication for ethnic marketing and public policy, in Rwelamila, P. D. (ed.), *Sustainable African Development and Self-Reliance*, the International Academy of African Business and Development (IAABD) Conference at University of South Africa, Durban, 16–18 May 2018.

Gbadamosi, A. (2019). Ethics and sustainable marketing, in Gbadamosi, A. (ed.) *Contemporary Issues in Marketing*, London: SAGE, pp.185–218.

Gbadamosi, A. (2023). Counterfeiting, consumerism and African business: Avenues for future research, in Amidu, M. (ed.) *Industry 4.0, Dynamic Global Business Environment, and Sustainable Development in Africa*, the Academy of African Business and Development (IAABD) Conference at the University of East London, UK, 16–20 May 2023.

Gibb, Z. G., & Devereux, P. G. (2014). Who does that anyway? Predictors and personality correlates of cyberbullying in college. *Computers in Human Behavior*, 38, 8–16.

Golf-Papez, M., & Veer, E. (2017). Don't feed the trolling: Rethinking how online trolling is being defined and combated. *Journal of Marketing Management*, 33(15–16), 1336–1354.

Goyens, M. (2020). Effective consumer protection frameworks in a global and digital world. *Journal of Consumer Policy, 43*(1), 195–207.

Gursoy, D., Cai, R. R., & Anaya, G. J. (2017). Developing a typology of disruptive customer behaviors. *International Journal of Contemporary Hospitality Management, 29*(9) 2341–2360.

Hamelin, N., Nwankwo, S., & Gbadamosi, A. (2020). Social marketing and the corruption conundrum in Morocco: An exploratory analysis. *World Development, 133*, September, 104993.

Harris, L. C., & Dumas, A. (2009). Online consumer misbehaviour: An application of neutralization theory. *Marketing Theory, 9*(4), 379–402.

Hinduja, S., & Patchin, J. W. (2008). Cyberbullying: An exploratory analysis of factors related to offending and victimization. *Deviant Behavior, 29*, 129–156. http://dx.doi.org/ 10.1080/ 01639620701457816

Hung, H., & Wong, Y. H. (2009). Information transparency and digital privacy protection: Are they mutually exclusive in the provision of e-services? *Journal of Services Marketing, 23*(3), 154–164.

Hwang, H., & Kim, K. O. (2015). Social media as a tool for social movements: The effect of social media use and social capital on intention to participate in social movements. *International Journal of Consumer Studies, 39*(5), 478–488.

International Chamber of Commerce (2004). A brief overview of counterfeiting. Retrieved 28 June 2004, from http://www.iccwbo.org/ccs/cib_bureau/overview.asp/

Jacobsen, S. L., & Barnes, N. G. (2020). Social media, Gen Z and consumer misbehavior: Instagram made me do it. *Journal of Marketing Development & Competitiveness, 14*(3), 51–58.

Johnson, T., & Attmann, J. (2009). Compulsive buying in a product specific context: Clothing. *Journal of Fashion Marketing and Management: An International Journal, 13*(3), 394–405.

Kirkwood, G. L., Payne, H. J., & Mazer, J. P. (2019). Collective trolling as a form of organizational resistance: Analysis of the #Justiceforbradswife Twitter campaign. *Communication Studies, 70*(3), 332–351.

Klemke, L. W. (1992). *The Sociology of Shoplifting: Boosters and Snitches Today*. Westport, CT: Praeger.

Kotler, P. (1972). What consumerism means to marketers. *Harvard Business Review, 50*, 48–57.

Kucuk, S. U. (2016). Consumerism in the digital age. *Journal of Consumer Affairs, 50*(3), 515–538.

Lazuras, L., Barkoukis, V., Ourda, D., & Tsorbatzoudis, H. (2013). A process model of cyberbullying in adolescence. *Computers in Human Behavior, 29*(3), 881–887.

Lee, J. (2012). An exploration of consumer misbehaviors and their influences on retail stores: An application of the theory of justice. *The Business & Management Review, 2*(2), 156.

Li, Y. (2012). Theories in online information privacy research: A critical review and an integrated framework. *Decision Support Systems, 54*, 471–481.

Loo, J. M., Shi, Y., & Pu, X. (2016). Gambling, drinking and quality of life: Evidence from Macao and Australia. *Journal of Gambling Studies, 32*, 391–407.

Lwin, M., Wirtz, J., & Williams, J. D. (2007). Consumer online privacy concerns and responses: A power–responsibility equilibrium perspective. *Journal of the Academy of Marketing Science, 35*(4), 572–585.

Madichie, N. O., & Opute, P. A. (2019). Regulatory challenges in Sub-Saharan Africa and marketing malpractices of "Big" Tobacco, in *Exploring the Dynamics of Consumerism in Developing Nations*, IGI Global, pp.101–123.

Martin, C. L., & Pranter, C. A. (1989). Compatibility management: Customer-to-customer relationships in service environments. *Journal of Services Marketing, 3*(3), 5–15.

Masters, T. M., & Mishra, A. (2019). The influence of hero and villain labels on the perception of vice and virtue products. *Journal of Consumer Psychology*, 29(3), 428–444.

McElroy, S. L., Phillips, K. A., & Keck Jr, P. E. (1994). Obsessive compulsive spectrum disorder. *The Journal of Clinical Psychiatry*, 55, 33–51.

Miller, S., & Weckert, J. (2000). Privacy, the workplace and the internet. *Journal of Business Ethics*, 28(3), 255–265.

Mueller, R. D., Wang, G. X., Liu, G., & Cui, C. C. (2015). Consumer xenocentrism in China: An exploratory study. *Asia Pacific Journal of Marketing and Logistics*, 28(1), 73–91.

Nocentini, A., Calmaestra, J., Schultze-Krumbholz, A., Scheithauer, H., Ortega, R., & Menesini, E. (2010). Cyberbullying: Labels, behaviours and definition in three European countries. *Australian Journal of Guidance and Counselling*, 20(2), 129–142.

O'Guinn, T. C., & Faber, R. J. (1989). Compulsive buying: A phenomenological exploration. *Journal of Consumer Research*, 16(2), 147–157.

ONS (2020). Drug misuse in England and Wales: Year ending March, 2020, Office for National Statistics, http://www.ons.gov.uk/peoplepopulationandcommunity/crimeandjustice/articles/drugmisuseinenglandandwales/yearendingmarch2020 (accessed 26 July 2021).

ONS (2020). Online bullying in England and Wales: Year ending March, 2020, http://www.ons.gov.uk/peoplepopulationandcommunity/crimeandjustice/bulletins/onlinebullyingingenglandandwales/yearendingmarch2020 (accessed 18 July 2021).

Otero-López, J. M., & Pol, E. V. (2013). Compulsive buying and the Five Factor Model of personality: A facet analysis. *Personality and Individual Differences*, 55(5), 585–590.

Ottman, J. A. & Reilly, W. R. (1998). *Green Marketing: Opportunity for Innovation*, 2nd edn., Prentice Hall.

Patchin, J. W., & Hinduja, S. (2010). Cyberbullying and self-esteem. *Journal of School Health*, 80(12), 614–621.

Pavlou, P. A. (2011). State of the information privacy literature: Where are we now and where should we go? *MIS Quarterly*, 35(4), 977–988.

Payne, E. M., Peltier, J. W., & Barger, V. A. (2018). Mobile banking and AI-enabled mobile banking: The differential effects of technological and non-technological factors on digital natives' perceptions and behavior. *Journal of Research in Interactive Marketing*, 12(3), 328–346.

Rindfleisch, A., Burroughs, J. E., & Denton, F. (1997). Family structure, materialism, and compulsive consumption. *Journal of Consumer Research*, 23(4), 312–325.

Ritchie, H., and Roser, M. (2017). Obesity. Published online at *OurWorldInData.org*. Retrieved from: https://ourworldindata.org/obesity

Rose, R. (2021). Who is your brand's villain? http://contentadvisory.net/who-is-your-brands-villain/ (accessed 9 July 2021).

Ross, D., & Deck Jr, D. W. (2011). Student guide to greenwashing. *B> Quest*, 1–20.

Sanfilippo, M. R., Fichman, P., & Yang, S. (2018). Multidimensionality of online trolling behaviors. *The Information Society*, 34, 27–39. doi:10.1080/01972243.2017.1391911

Schmidt, H. J., & Baumgarth, C. (2018). Strengthening internal brand equity with brand ambassador programs: Development and testing of a success factor model. *Journal of Brand Management*, 25(3), 250–265.

Spears, B., Slee, P., Owens, L., & Johnson, B. (2009). Behind the scenes and screens insights into the human dimension of covert and cyberbullying. *Zeitschrift für Psychologie/Journal of Psychology*, 217(4), 189–196.

Staake, T., Thiesse, F., & Fleisch, E. (2009). The emergence of counterfeit trade: A literature review. *European Journal of Marketing*, 43(3/4), 320–349.

Stumpf, S. A., Chaudhry, P. E., & Perretta, L. (2011). Fake: Can business staunch the flow of counterfeit products? *Journal of Business Strategy*, 32(2), 4–12.

Utami, S. P., Setyowati, N., & Mandasari, P. (2020). Celebrity brand ambassador and e-WOM as determinants of purchase intention: A survey of Indonesian celebrity cake. In *E3S Web of Conferences* (Vol. 142, p. 05001). EDP Sciences, 1–9.

Waasdorp, T. E., & Bradshaw, C. P. (2015). The overlap between cyberbullying and traditional bullying. *Journal of Adolescent Health*, *56*(5), 483–488.

Wan, L. C., Hui, M. K., & Qiu, Y. C. (2021). Tourist misbehavior: Psychological closeness to fellow consumers and informal social control. *Tourism Management*, *83*, 104258.

Ward, J. C., & Ostrom, A. L. (2006). Complaining to the masses: The role of protest framing in customer-created complaint web sites. *Journal of Consumer Research*, *33*(2), 220–230.

Welsch, H., & Kühling, J. (2016). Green status seeking and endogenous reference standards. *Environmental Economics and Policy Studies*, *18*(4), 625–643.

WFP (2020). 5 facts about food waste and hunger, World Food Programme, www.wfp.org/stories/5-facts-about-food-waste-and-hunger (accessed 28 September 2023).

Wong, D. S., Chan, H. C. O., & Cheng, C. H. (2014). Cyberbullying perpetration and victimization among adolescents in Hong Kong. *Children and Youth Services Review*, *36*, 133–140.

Yan, R. N., Bae, S. Y., & Xu, H. (2015). Second-hand clothing shopping among college students: The role of psychographic characteristics. *Young Consumers*, *16*(1), 85–98.

Zelezny, L. C., & Schultz, P. W. (2000). Promoting environmentalism. *Journal of Social Issues*, *56*(3), 365–371.

# CHAPTER 3

# Consumer Decision-making Processes

## LEARNING OBJECTIVES

After reading this chapter, you should be able to:

- Explain the consumer decision-making process and its variants in the digital context;
- Discuss how consumers' needs are varied and have changed over the years;
- Discuss how digital transformation has introduced many opportunities for consumer information search;
- Examine the consumer evaluative criteria in a digital era;
- Critically discuss consumer decision rules and decision models depicting the contemporary consumer;
- Discuss the post-purchase evaluation in relation to digital transformation;
- Explain consumer involvement and its link to the consumer decision-making process.

## INTRODUCTION

Whether we are ardent consumers of luxury brands like Lamborghini, Rolex, and Gucci, or low-income consumers that are fickle buyers, our lives as consumers are characterised by decisions on a daily basis. The food we eat, the fashion items we use, the house we live in, and a plethora of others are a function of our decisions. Similarly, we are confronted with the questions like: Which bank should we choose? Which lawyer will give us the best service? Which music would give us the most desired level of entertainment? Which university should we attend? These are examples of cases that pinpoint how our consumption behaviour is a reflection of our decisions. No doubt, decision making is an age-old phenomenon. However, its dynamics with

DOI: 10.4324/9781003242031-4

consumer behaviour attracts special interest. The interest in the topic goes beyond the decision itself. It is a process involving stages which precede the decision and last beyond it. Meanwhile, the role of digital transformation in consumer decision making raised even greater interest in the topic. Everywhere we turn this day shows evidence of digital transformation. Accordingly, we will be examining the consumer decision-making process in relation to the prevalent digital transformation. We will be discussing each of the stages in the process and how it has become transformed as a result of the ubiquity of digital technology. So, let us start by discussing an overview of consumer decision making.

## OVERVIEW OF CONSUMER DECISION MAKING

The consumer decision making process is fundamental to consumer behaviour. Over the years, before the prevalence of digitisation in marketing processes, studies have been done on the topic with wide-ranging contributions. Similarly, a number of perspectives have been documented that depict the changes in the issue due to digital transformation. Fundamentally, the consumer decision making process is known to involve the following sequential stages leading through to the purchase and afterwards as shown in the Engel-Kollat-Blackwell model (Engel et al., 1968):

- Need recognition;
- Information search;
- Evaluation of alternatives;
- Purchase act;
- Post-purchase evaluation.

As it is done in some instances, we can simply categorise these steps into three phases: The Prepurchase phase, Purchase, and Post-purchase phase of the process. While we will be examining the activities involved in each of these stages later in this chapter, it is important for us to note that there have been many changes to this process due to the advancement in technology. This has led to digital transformation in virtually all ramifications. The idea inherent in digital transformation is that modification of business approaches is required as a result of changes experienced in the technological progress, which in turn bring about changes in consumption pattens and social behaviour (Kotarba, 2018). Consumers' interest in digital processes is prompted partly due to their quest for time efficiency and convenience. From a business perspective, digital transformation means changes to many parts of the organisation. As stated by Proskurnina (2019) these changes include the following:

- Innovation in the development of products and services;
- Marketing and sales;
- Distribution channels;
- Digital interaction with customers;
- Risk optimisation;

- Intelligence information management and customer service;
- Customer relationship management.

The pressure for businesses to embrace these and other changes is understandable as consumers' taste is changing rapidly in favour of technology-oriented market offerings. Accordingly, there are some differences between the consumer decision-making process in the traditional sense and during the e-commerce era. For example, in the studies of Grewal et al. (2010), Schneider et al. (2018), and Dennis et al. (2020), it is noted that retailers have the opportunity to offer a wider range of products than in the physical store as they are not limited by space, and they tend to have a much greater control of consumers' access to their products as well as how they interact with them online through the design of their websites and digital nudging. In a study addressing the impact of digital strategies on the decision journey of the consumers, Dasgupta and Grover (2019) indicate that consumers engage in not only consuming content but also in browsing online through product categories they are attracted to, even before their desire for the product is ignited. In the view of these authors, while the stages in the decision making process have not been altered by the digital revolution, the journey in the process has changed and each of the stages is impacted by both online and offline factors. For example, they indicate that evaluation of alternative and post-purchase evaluation stages are influencing mega sales and social media. What we now see with digital transformation about the consumer decision making process indicates that there is now a shift in focus from influencing the outcome of the process to proactively influencing the process itself (Faulds et al., 2018). So, ultimately, we need to explore the differences between the traditional process and the online-oriented process. One of the noteworthy claims indicates that while the traditional process consists of stages with discrete activities with a focus on the outcome, the one related to the mobile shopping process is continuous (Faulds et al., 2018). These authors suggest that mobile shopping involves four key pillars which are:

- Consumer-retailer interconnectedness;
- Proximity-based consumer engagement;
- Consumer empowerment;
- Web-based consumer engagement.

Accordingly, these pillars influence the consumer decision making process. In a different context, Singh et al. (2016) highlight five key criteria that influence online consumption as the following:

- Personal innovativeness on information technology;
- Online reputation;
- Web quality dimension;
- Information and e-service dimension;
- Incentive and post-purchase service.

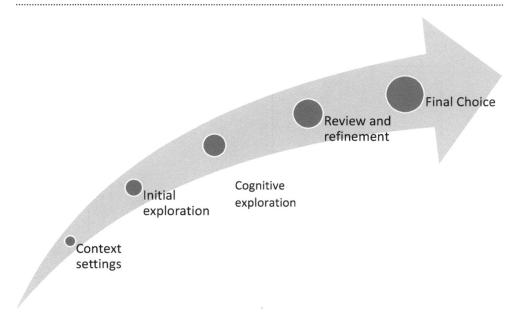

**FIGURE 3.1** Online consumer decision making process
**Source**: Adapted from Karimi et al. (2018).

It is understandable that new terms amenable to the prevalence of technology are now commonplace and constantly being used to depict the consumer decision making process. In a study that focused on how consumer archetypes impact how consumers make purchases online, Karimi et al. (2018) indicate that the old traditional stages of the consumer decision making process cannot effectively be used for online transactions. According to them, the online purchase behaviour is more dynamic and has different stages identified as:

- Context settings;
- Initial exploration;
- Cognitive exploration;
- Review and refinement;
- Final choice.

To relate to this suggested framework, you will need to picture in your mind what goes on before you hold the mouse and the computer keyboard as the context settings. These stages are clearly interconnected through to the final phase when a choice is made online. Now let us turn our attention to the stages of the conventional decision making process and see how they are linked. Figure 3.2 shows the stages but, more importantly, it emphasises all the factors that influence the activities in the stages and the decisions taken as well as the post-purchase evaluation. To adapt the framework to fit the digital age, the figure shows that every element now operates within the influence of digitalisation.

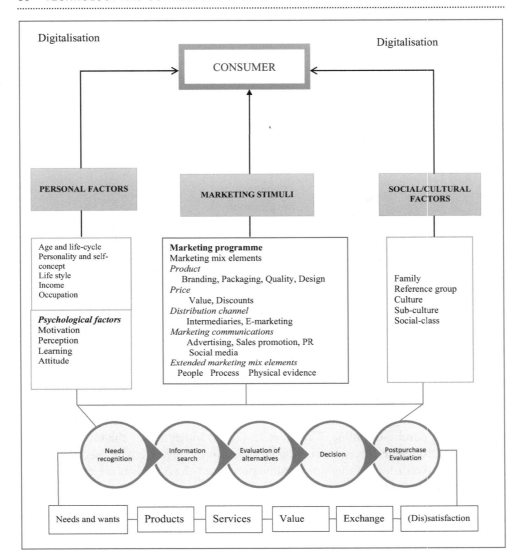

**FIGURE 3.2** Major influences on the consumer decision making process in a digital age
**Source**: Adapted from Gbadamosi (2020).

## NEED RECOGNITION

We indulge ourselves with purchases and acquire items in various contexts. Some of these are luxuries like cars, houses, and jewellery while others are trifling such as cookies, water, and table salt. One of the things common to all these purchases is that we, as consumers, go through 'a journey' towards reaching the moment of purchase. This begins with the stage of need recognition. This is the stage where the gap between the current stage and the desired stage is recognised. This is like the breakdown of an old car signalling the need for a replacement, the rumbling of the stomach indicating hunger, or the feeling of deprivation of a desirable social system due to lack of what it takes to join the group, such as fashion items. The superficial understanding of this may suggest that a need for the product arises when the old one becomes completely non-functional. Nonetheless, as stated in the examples given, this is not always the case. It may be a case of replacing an old model with a newer version. It could also be about casting an eye on a completely new area of need that was not realised in the past. The seminal work of Abraham Maslow with his hierarchy of needs indicates that consumers can even move from a level of need to higher levels of need.

The various changes we see daily in the dynamic marketing environment show that consumers' needs keep changing. One of these notable changes is the digital transformation that keeps redefining consumers' need. For instance, consumers' need for information becomes more complex with the increase in digitalisation in the marketplace. Arcia et al. (2019) cite examples of pregnant women to indicate people's need for information on health-related issues through online platforms and search engines like Google. Needs around entertainment, counselling, education, and others that in turn introduce a greater usage rate of devices like smartphones, tablets, or laptops exemplify the different dimension brought about by digital transformation. Similarly, the increasing usage of artificial intelligence (AI) is another indication of the consumers' need for convenience, which points to digital revolution that characterises the contemporary consumption system. We now hear of consumers' need for digital banking, digital books, and a host of other products and services defined by their digital presence.

## INFORMATION SEARCH

With recognition of the need, the journey to consumption has only just begun. Consumers need information on the goods and services that could fill the needs identified. Consumers would require information on various issues pertaining to the purchase. This may be product availability, quality, prices, packaging. There are many sources of information, but these could be categorised as commercial and non-commercial sources. While commercial sources relate to sources sponsored or initiated for commercial motives such as advertising messages, company websites, brochures, salespeople, and the like, other sources are not linked to the organisation and are not associated with commercial motives. Examples include friends and family members, neighbours, co-workers, government publications, NGO publications. In addition to these and similar sources, another key non-commercial source of information is one's personal experience. Consumers can reflect on their experience of prior purchase of the products or product of similar characteristics for information on the new decision case.

Considering all these together, non-commercial sources seem to be seen as having more credibility compared to commercial sources. The obvious commercial reasons associated with advertising messages, websites, and other sponsored sources of product information leads consumers to take them with a pinch of salt on some issues whereas they tend to trust their friends, co-workers, or other independent sources as they know that the opinions they offer in the information provided are free and fair-minded.

It is important to not see these two sources of information as a strict choice of choosing one over the other. They tend to be complementary in some cases. This is because a particular source may be useful for a type of information while the other could fill the gap. For example, while non-commercial sources could be very good at revealing details like service quality of a hotel and relative price-value relationship between alternatives, commercial sources would provide details about room availability. This is confirmed by Vinhas and Bowman (2019) in their study on online/offline information search patterns. They found that some customers rely on brand websites or multibrand websites primarily without combining it with recommendations from other sources, while others combine these with word-of-mouth communications from non-commercial sources like family members and friends.

Meanwhile, the increase in the use of technology has widened the opportunities available for consumer information searches. In a study that uses fashion as an example, Jones and Kang (2020) indicate that brands now have less autonomy concerning information dissemination about their brands as consumers can now have access to very detailed information, including those not previously available, to serve as input to their decisions. One of the key reasons for this is that the Internet is making it easier or less costly not only to search for information but also to share with others. The facilities of multibrand websites are becoming increasingly used in this day and age where consumers have access to information and can be linked to multiple websites. Examples of these websites are Zoopla for getting information about houses for purchase or rent, Money Supermarket for information about financial products like insurance and mortgages, and TripAdvisor for hotels, holidays, and restaurants. In a study of digital transformation in relation to search and reformation in the innovation function, Lanzolla et al. (2021) provide some useful and interesting findings. Although this is discussed in relation to business innovations, we can adapt it to explain consumer search amidst growing digital transformation. One can tease out from this seminal work that consumers can have the following cases:

- Digitalisation replaces existing competencies;
- Digitalisation overturns existing knowledge structures;
- Digitalisation complements existing competencies;
- Digitalisation reinforces existing knowledge structures.

In adapting this postulation, we can argue that, in some cases, digitalisation will replace the existing information sources that consumers use about the intended purchase, and there may be cases where digitalisation will complement the existing sources. For instance, sending an email to a friend requesting information about her opinion or experience on a holiday in some location is exploring the opportunity of the digital platform with interpersonal relationship.

## EVALUATION OF ALTERNATIVES

The plethora of sources of information discussed in the previous stage indicates that consumers will be bombarded by information concerning the planned purchase. It is very important to screen the information obtained from various sources towards reaching an optimal choice. As expected, alternative offerings will be beckoning for consumers' attention. Different sizes, shapes, colours, prices, locations, efficiency, comfort levels, and many other factors would be available in the information gathered but the resources required to buy them are limited. Besides, it is important to look at the need that prompted the consumer to go through this stage in the first place. Whatever the product to be purchased, it is important to develop the applicable evaluation criteria. The criteria that will be used to evaluate restaurants will be different from that used to select a car, while those to use for the selection of a fragrance will be different from the one used for mobile phones. An example of a selection criteria that is sometimes taken for granted but may be very significant to consumers' choice is the product or organisation's image. It is argued that, when consumers find it difficult to evaluate the quality of the product, it often results in high perceived risk (Engel, 1995; Chen-Yu and Kincade, 2001). Accordingly, product image often influences how consumers perceive product quality and how they expect it to function for the satisfaction of the need (Chen-Yu and Kincade, 2001).

While evaluating alternatives, consumers work through the *Evoke set* and *Consideration set*. The evoke set consists of brands or options known to the consumers that could satisfy the stated needs while the consideration set are specifically those alternatives that the consumer might consider buying (Solomon, 2020). So, we can state that the consideration set is a subset of the evoke set.

Just as digital transformation has had an impact on the need recognition and search for information, development in the world of technology has transformed how alternative offerings are evaluated. As stated by Verhoef et al. (2021), digital transformation, and the business model that emerged from it, have changed consumers' expectations and behaviour significantly as they now have access to several media channels. They are now more demanding, which puts businesses under pressure. Accordingly, the evaluation criteria also follow the same pattern. One of the tools for evaluation in the digital age is to examine the online reviews posted by other customers who have bought or used a product in the past. This takes the form of electronic word-of-mouth (eWOM), which is considered credible as the communicators are independent of the persuasive intent of the marketers (Shan, 2016). Most prospective lodgers in hotels would first check online reviews and ratings left by previous customers to know whether selecting the organisation will be the right choice. This is an interesting and useful point to make in that the type of evaluation model used will likely influence consumers' preferences (Tan et al., 2018). When someone leaves a positive online customer review (OCR), the impact continues in the long-run to condition how consumers evaluate through the entire decision making process (Hermandez-Ortega, 2019). In many ways, the digital transformation on both sides of the transaction ends. Apart from making firms competitive, it reduces the costs of information search and evaluation for consumers. This is a main point highlighted in the study of Kuksov and Villas-Boas (2010) that when the alternatives they have to deal with far exceed their preference, the cost involved in search and evaluation of alternatives may result in consumers not searching or not choosing at all. This is because too many alternatives would result in searches and evaluation towards reaching the most optimal choice, which may be costly. However, with the information about alternatives widely available as facilitated by Internet facilities, and in some cases the evaluation simplified through electronic platforms, these costs are significantly reduced.

## DECISION STAGE

The decision stage is the moment of reality when consumers conclude which among the alternatives evaluated will be chosen as being the best fit in relation to the need identified at the beginning of this process. As indicated in Chapter 1, while explaining and defining consumer behaviour, it is emphasised that consumption can be at either the individual or group level. When deciding as an individual on which of the products to buy after evaluation, the task is challenging but it may not be any easier when the decision is done in respect of group consumption. At the individual level, a bachelor can easily decide on the car to buy after reviewing the alternatives, but a family buying a car may need to go further, especially between the couple, checking preferences, the fit to accommodate the children, and other family circumstances. In fact, in some cases, a product to be used by an individual may be decided upon by another member of the group. An example is the decision made by the husband to buy a gift for the wife and vice versa. In many cases, mothers decide things like brand and style of products to be used by their young children, while the father may eventually decide the holiday destinations and how much they choose to spend. Similarly, we decide the types, quantity, and brand of foods to buy for our pets. Understandably, there is no hard and fast rule about who buys and decides.

## DECISION RULES

In deciding which product, service, or specific brand to choose among alternatives, the strategies used by consumers are often categorised into two rules:

- Compensatory rule;
- Non-compensatory rule.

In compensatory rule, the consumer identifies all the relevant attributes of the market offerings and weighs them. With the view that the product that has been rated low in an attribute can have strength in another, the consumer chooses the one that gives the highest weighted score. For instance, a bank may take longer to approve a loan and have more stringent conditions for the transaction but have a very low interest rate. If it has the overall positive weighting compared to others, it will be the one to be chosen.

The non-compensatory rule is different from this because the limitation of an alternative is not balanced by the positive attribute. For instance, a consumer who has been medically advised against a diet is expected to avoid it even if it is the cheapest of all the options. With reference to the views of Solomon (2020) and Schiffman et al. (2010), there are three types of non-compensatory rule. These are highlighted below:

**Lexicographic rule:** In this, the consumer selects the item that is ranked the best in relation to the single attribute that is most important to the decision maker;
**Conjunctive rule:** This is about setting a minimal level for each attribute that will constitute the cut-off below which the consumer will not be willing to go. So, any brand or option that falls below this on any of the attributes will be dropped;
**Disjunctive rule:** This involves setting the cut-off on each attribute but in this case, the consumer chooses a brand if it meets the level or exceeds on any of the attributes.

As we can see from the conjunctive and disjunctive rules, it is highly likely that the consumer will end up with many possible options after applying these rules. Hence, additional rules will be involved to resolve cases where there are ties towards arriving at the final choice (Schiffman et al., 2010).

As is the case for evaluation of alternatives, the purchase act or stage of a decision is also now significantly influenced by digital technology. It is reported that approximately 82% of adult consumers in the US relies on online customer review (OCR) to make a decision as to whether to buy a product or not (Smith and Anderson, 2016; Shin et al., 2020). As stated by these authors, this is usually the case when the buyer could see that the review is credible. We can link this to another avenue used that could help consumers at the stage of decision or purchase – the blog. The development in technology has led to a significant increase in the number of bloggers in recent years. They are involved in recording or discussing ideas, personal feelings, and opinions on a specific incident in our daily life and their influence can be crucial to each of the stages in the decision making process including the decision stage in terms of their recommendations (Hsu et al., 2013).

One of the key factors crucial to consumption in the digital context is the time element. Online purchase has the potential to save time, especially during the payment transaction (Thirumalai and Sinha, 2011; Gómez-Díaz, 2016). In most cases, the stage is done with the click of a mouse. For most purchases, gone are the days when consumers will have to wait in a very long queue to make purchases. The list of products that can be bought online keeps growing. Firms in the fashion business, those selling furniture, and others selling computer products are just examples of businesses where an order could be made online for the products to be delivered at an agreed later date. Besides, in some cases, as a way of combining the efficiency of digital marketing and social interaction, orders can be made in the stores so that the product could be delivered to the consumers later. The relevance of social factors such as friends, family members, co-workers, and associates are significant at the stage of purchase whether one is making the purchase online or offline. The interaction at the shopping mall, and exchange of information on social media platforms, are clear examples of why this factor cannot be considered irrelevant, especially by marketers formulating marketing strategies to influence consumers' action at the stage of decision.

Consumers are also driven by the issue of trust in online purchasing behaviour. In view of the different types of risks associated with online purchases, consumers' trust cannot be undermined in the process. In online transactions, the threat of fraud is real as is evident in many cases reported in the news. In a closely related example, consumers' perceived risk in online transactions may also be based on whether the product presented online will be as depicted in offline settings. Consumers may not be able to get a good idea of suitability of some products until they touch, smell, or feel them. This brings us to the relevance of showrooming and webrooming as ways by which consumers address these issues. Using the idea of Mukherjee and Chatterjee (2021), when consumers apply showrooming, they first obtain information about the products they are interested in such as price and its features in the offline settings and engage in online purchase of the item later. On the other hand is when they use webrooming, the search for market offerings online to get all the necessary details and then make the actual purchase in an offline retail setting.

If there is no trust in the process or system, it may result in consumers' deciding to exit from the website of the vendor, which is a problem not only for the online marketers but also for the consumers that may have wasted resources from the beginning of the process, such as searching for information only to abandon it at the end (Chau et al., 2007). In online purchases, it has been shown that consumers act differently based on their characteristics. For example, Fang et al. (2016) studied the role of gender and age in relation to online shopping and found that consumers are different, as some are task-focused while others are experiential buyers. As indicated in the findings of the study, when consumers are task-focused, the impact of the e-service quality offered is not significantly different between young and old consumers. Nonetheless, for consumers that are experiential, the impact of e-service quality on perceived value is significantly stronger for young consumers than older consumers. Based on their online shopping, another typology of consumers is given by Karimi et al. (2018) as:

- Maximiser;
- Satisficers.

In this perspective, the maximiser goes for the best possible option after engaging in intensive information searches but a satisficer simply goes for just enough options, as they exert reduced effort (Karimi et al, 2018). So, a number of factors combine to explain what takes place at the stage of decision and how this is done online.

## POST-PURCHASE EVALUATION

The decision journey is not deemed to be complete at the stage of decision or purchase. The stage of post-purchase evaluation is considered crucial in marketing transactions for products and services. It is the stage where the consumer compares the experience of using the market offerings with the needs which prompted the purchase and the promise made by the product or brands. When needs are met, or exceeded, the consumer is deemed satisfied. Conversely, unmet needs leave the consumer dissatisfied. There are several implications for these outcomes. A satisfied consumer would most likely repurchase the product or brand when the need arises in future and possibly becomes loyal to the offerings and the establishment. More importantly, the consumer will also most likely spread the news of the good experience to others associated with him or her in a process known as word-of-mouth (WOM) communications. On the other hand, consumers with negative experience about the market offerings or the company will also spread the news in the form of negative WOM to others.

Digital transformation has now removed the geographical limitations around how news about product purchase is spread between consumers. The wide availability of online customer reviews (OCRs) made by customers about their experiences of using specific products on various websites became very handy for most potential buyers of the products. In some cases, the presence of reviews in relation to the particular products to buy can go a long way to positively influence consumers' purchase decisions. In the study of Chen (2016), the question of whether the reviews provided online are perceived to be helpful or not to the consumer has been linked to three key factors:

- Content-based features, which is about sidedness (one-sided or two-sided);
- Source-based features, which is about the expertise of the reviewer;
- Consumers' decision context (whether the products involved are search products or experience products).

Unlike the case in one-sided reviews where the focus is on either negative or positive issues associated with the products, two-sided online reviews offer readers information on the pros and cons of the product. Meanwhile, we can gather from the literature (Nelson, 1970; Chen, 2016) that search products are those whose quality can be easily gauged through product information even without having first-hand experience, but the quality of experience goods is difficult to assess before having direct experience of its consumption. Chen (2016) found that when experts are the ones writing the reviews, consumers will take two-sided reviews to be more helpful than one-sided reviews, but the case is different for experience goods in which consumers consider one-sided reviews to be more helpful for them. Meanwhile, the same study shows that one-sided reviews and two-sided reviews will be taken to be equally helpful by consumers when the reviews are written by novices.

As reported in Smith and Anderson (2016), 82% of US adult consumers rely on OCR when buying a new product. Part of the key benefits of the Internet is not only in the speed at which consumers make their reviews known. Through this medium, consumers are able to communicate their thoughts about their product or service experience in the form of 'one-to-many' communication mode, indicating that they can reach several other Internet users globally without any geographical limitation (Lee and Cude, 2012). One of the ways by which this takes place is through social networking sites (SNS). When recommendations are given online through SNS, evidence shows that product risk, online tie strength, and perceived diagnosticity will be very significant to the decision of the consumers as to whether to accept the recommendation or not (Wang and Chang, 2013).

In a study considering which of the negative or positive reviews are more influential concerning apparel, Shin et al. (2020) found that positive review is more influential than negative review for the female participants of their study. This led them to suggest that retailers would benefit greatly if they can encourage consumers to write a review about their positive experience. This said, there are some cases of unethical practices around this whereby some marketers hide negative reviews or forge positive reviews. This can cause distrust of the firm by the consumers (Shin et al., 2020) and will have a long-run negative impact on the credibility of the organisation.

Meanwhile, one of the possible outcomes of post-purchase evaluation will be for consumers to complain of their unpleasant experiences about the product bought. Lee and Cude (2012) show that those consumers who buy their products online are more likely to complain online than their counterparts that buy offline. It is important for us to acknowledge that many factors might be responsible for consumer dissatisfaction, which could be the reasons for complaining. These could be issues such as delivery system and time. According to Park et al. (2015), while the purchase of the product may have been completed, consumers' satisfaction can still be influenced by what they experience at the delivery completion phase of the process. While the cause of service failures could be many, from the study of Kuo and Wu (2012), we can classify them into three:

- Employees' response to service delivery system failures;
- Employees' response to customer needs and requests;
- Unsolicited and unprompted employees' actions.

Concerning service offerings, Kuo and Wu (2012) note that, as we experience an increase in e-commerce, online shopping failures are unavoidable but when they happen, firms should take appropriate measures to restore satisfaction to the dissatisfied consumers, which will ultimately build and strengthen long-term relationships. One of the ways businesses foster long-term relationships in the marketplace is to allow consumers to return products purchased and considered not fit for purpose. This is particularly beneficial for online transactions where the consumers may not have had experience of the products prior to purchase. As an example in this regard, the product return rate in the United States in 2019 was stated as a whopping $309 billion, which represents approximately 8% of the sales in the retail sector (National Retail Federation, 2019; Patel et al., 2021).

**PAUSE, PLAN, AND PRACTICE: FROM ZOOPLA TO THE DREAM HOME**

The decision to purchase a house is considered very strategic. To many consumers, it is probably the most expensive purchase to be made in their lives. An acknowledgement of this is what brings about Zoopla, which is a notable property website and app introduced to help consumers in this process. After realising the need to have a house, gathering information on which type, the appropriate location, and prices is a herculean task for the consumers. Potential buyers simply visit Zoopla to gather this information as the website gives consumers specific query fields to be completed to ensure the results meet the buyers' desires. Zoopla is not only relevant for consumers' pre-purchase evaluation of the properties. Since the website is linked to estate agents representing the vendor of the properties by showing their contact details on the website, the real purchase decision is facilitated for the consumers. However, unlike less expensive and habitual products where the final purchase can be simply concluded online, the photographs of the properties shown online only help the potential buyers to shortlist the properties so that the actual viewing leading up to the purchase can be scheduled. In addition to the specific details of the properties to be bought by the consumers, Zoopla also updates visitors to their website on details about property market trends. So, it has grown to be a major force in the UK property market over the years.

**QUESTION/TASK:**

Assume you are planning to change your current accommodation. Search for a new house on Zoopla. List your criteria and compare the case of buying the house compared to the option of renting.

## DECISION SITUATIONS

We make decisions every day on consumption issues such as what to wear, the food to each, the fragrance to use, which insurance policy to take, from which company, and a host of others. Meanwhile there are differences in how these are handled. We find some more challenging than others. These variations can be seen in the categorisation of decision situations as:

- Cognitive decision model;
- Habitual decision model;
- Affective decision model.

### Cognitive Decision Model

The cognitive decision making model depicts a scenario which assumes that the consumer is rational in approaching a decision. As such she would meticulously examine the alternatives and follow a series of steps carefully leading to the best option. As

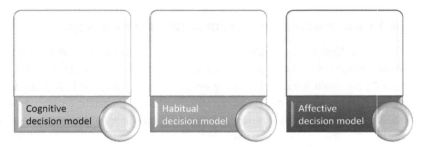

**FIGURE 3.3** Decision models

demonstrated in Figure 3.3, this decision model applies to complex decision scenarios such as buying a house or car. Similarly, choosing the services/treatment of a medical practice can also be a good example here.

## Habitual Decision Model

Differences in the products we buy and use leads us to realise that all decision scenarios do not follow the case described in the cognitive decision-making process in exactly the same way. A habitual decision scenario explains the cases in which consumers choose in routine form or out of habit and not through conscious rational thought. In most cases, for products like cookies, table salt, and bottled water, we tend to choose in ways that can be characterised as a habitual decision model. It is relevant here to explain that repetitive purchase of a particular product, service, or brand might seem to indicate that the consumer is loyal to the market offering. However, this is not always the case, as it could be out of habit and not because of any specific attachment to the product. So, a scenario like this could be a case of spurious loyalty. A typical example of this is discussed in the findings of Gbadamosi (2009) whose study shows low-income consumers' repetitive consumption of store brands disrupted by a sales promotion on manufacturers' brands. This then shows that these low-income consumers merely had spurious loyalty for the supermarket's own brand and not the sustainable loyalty that is enduring and consistent. As consumers, we often use activity biases in the habitual decision making scenario, which is also known as heuristics (Solomon, 2020). The following are just a few examples of these heuristics (rules-of-thumb) often used as teased out from Duncan (1990) and Solomon (2020):

- **Country of origin:** The place of origin of the product taken to be a signal of quality;
- **Covariations:** A belief that if certain part(s) of a product or service is good, others should be good also;
- **Brand names:** Owners or sponsors of familiar brand names will always introduce new market offerings of equivalent quality standard;
- **Stores:** Items bought from larger stores tend to be cheaper than when bought from smaller stores;

- **Prices:** Higher-priced products are of better quality than the lower-priced ones;
- **High level of advertising:** A heavily advertised product will be more expensive as the consumer is paying for the label rather than a higher quality;
- **Packaging style:** Products sold in larger-sized packaging are almost usually cheaper per unit than those sold in smaller sizes.

## Affective

Some decisions are taken that are neither cognitive nor habitual in nature. They are underpinned by emotion and known as an affective decision model. Factors such as fun, joy, excitement, and sexuality drive such decisions. The emotion associated with this decision case means that the thorough and elaborate evaluation of criteria typically associated with cognitive decision making will not apply. The fun of enjoying the company of friends and lovers could direct one's choice of restaurant and the chosen alternative may not be the most rational of available choices.

## CONSUMER INVOLVEMENT

One of the reasons for the variations in how we handle consumption decisions is the notion of involvement. It was initially discussed in the literature but became popularised in the marketing circle by Krugman (1967), who explains the term in relation to advertising.

Even though there are many definitions of the term, we will be using one of the widely cited definitions, which is the one given by Zaichowsky (1985), who defines it as the perceived relevance of an object based on the inherent need, interests, and value of the individual. We know that our investments in consumption activities vary in terms of scale and significance. Effort and resources expended to get a house will be different from what will be needed for the purchase of cookies. With reference to this definition we have adopted, it is important to also note that consumers' involvement is not only related to products. Consumers can be involved in any other goal object such as advertising, brands, media, and activities (Peter and Olson, 2005). A way of knowing this is through the results that accompany that involvement. If we take cues from the perspectives of Sadarangani and Gaur (2002), Clarke and Belk (1978), and Zaichkowsky (1985), a number of examples can be drawn on this. When consumers are involved in a product, they tend to greatly perceive differences in what constitutes the attributes, have a stronger commitment to the brand choice, and perceive high product importance. Moreover, being highly involved in purchases encourages consumers to engage in more information search and expend more time to search for information and spend more money on them. Similarly, being highly involved in advertisements makes consumers engage in counter-arguments with them.

Meanwhile, it is now evident that involvement varies. Hence, consumer involvement is often discussed as dichotomous to be high and low involvement. So, in a high-involvement scenario, the consumers' perceived risk and perceived relevance of the goal-object of such a product is high. So, the purchase is very important to

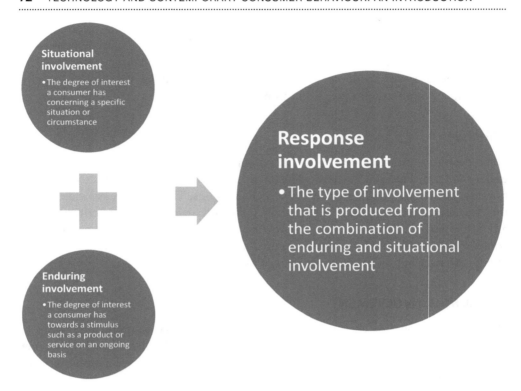

**FIGURE 3.4** Situational and enduring involvement
**Source**: Adapted from Gbadamosi, A. (2020), 'Buyer Behaviour in the 21st century: Implications for SME Marketing', in Nwankwo, S. and Gbadamosi, A. (2020), (Eds.) *'Entrepreneurship Marketing: Principles and Practice of SME Marketing'*, 2nd edition, Oxfordshire: Routledge, pp. 72–96.

the consumer, which leads him or her to do significant and extensive pre-purchase search and evaluation. Conversely, in a low-involvement situation, the perceived risk and perceived relevance of the goal-object is low. Accordingly, in this scenario, consumers engage in limited or no pre-purchase search and evaluation (Gbadamosi, 2020).

Beyond the dichotomous classification of involvement, researchers have provided further types of involvement. One of these is the classification of involvement into enduring involvement, situation involvement, and response involvement (Rothschild and Houston, 1980) as shown in Figure 3.4. According to Rothschild and Houston (1980) the response involvement captures the complexity associated with the extensiveness of behavioural processes that show the relationship a consumer has with any given goal object.

We can infer from the discussion of this topic so far that consumers' high involvement in a product, service, brand, or other goal object will be beneficial to the marketer. Accordingly, it makes sense for them to work on increasing the involvement that consumers have in their market offerings. Based on the view of Solomon (2020), these factors can be applied:

- Provide value that the customer appreciates;
- Use novel appeal;
- Use prominent stimuli;
- Invent new media to grab attention;
- Create spectacle where the message is itself a form of entertainment;
- Encourage the viewers to think about actually using the product;
- Use consumer-generated content – letting the consumer make the messages;
- Celebrity endorsement.

Similarly, Schiffman et al. (2012) highlight these other factors which align closely to the ones stated by Solomon to a great extent:

- Unusual stimuli;
- The use of sensory appeal;
- Forge relationship with the customers;
- Provide distinctive benefits to consumers;
- Celebrity endorsement.

## SUMMARY

As with other aspects of consumption, digital transformation has an impact on the consumer decision making process. The conventional decision making process brings together five stages which are: Need recognition, search for information, evaluation of alternatives, purchase decision, and post-purchase evaluation. However, as digitalisation continues to influence our consumption, many other decision making frameworks are being proposed to account for how each of these stages has been impacted upon. Having this knowledge is very important, especially as decision situations and models vary between cognitive, habitual, and affective. These also reflect in consumer involvement which could be situational or enduring.

---

**DIGITAL BOX: GOOGLE: CONSUMERS' SEARCH ENGINE**

The popularity of Google as a search engine is extraordinary with its relevance covering virtually all aspects of life. The domain name Google.com came into the limelight in 1997 when it was registered, and the company became fully founded in 1998 and has grown significantly since then over the years. It offers not only the search as a free product, but also Gmail and maps as opportunities to ease users' experience at no cost to them. Offering these products for free is possible for Google because it makes its money from advertising.

Meanwhile, as a brand, the organisation is now literarily synonymous with search as you tend to hear people say 'I will Google it'. Be it information on politics, inventions, cultural artefacts, economy, or anything else people find Google a platform for the solution to their needs. One of the common uses of Google among consumers is exploring it to obtain information about products, services, prices, availability, and many other details that facilitate their decisions. This is one of the remarkable results of advancement in technology which is a key part in the business environment. After the need recognition stage, consumers tend to visit Google web pages to search for information about the products. This puts them in the driving seat as they have access to information on a variety of products and services from various competing firms. So, the consumer decision-making process is being enhanced by digital transformation.

**QUESTION/TASK:**

Do a Google search for a potential holiday destination, flights, and the items you'll need to make it a memorable experience. Compare this process and the results in a case where online search is not involved. Discuss the differences.

**Sources:**

Google (nd) about.google, (accessed 4 October 2021).

Google (nd) about.google/how-our-business-works/ (accessed 4 October 2021).

## END OF CHAPTER DISCUSSION QUESTIONS

1. Critically discuss the relevance of the post-purchase evaluation stage in the consumer decision making process. Cite relevant examples to support your claims;
2. Discuss the conventional consumer decision making process and explain briefly how digitalisation has impacted any two of the stages;
3. Define the notion of consumer involvement. How does this influence the consumer decision making process?
4. What is the difference between a cognition decision model and the habitual decision making model? (b) Explain any two heuristic decision rules and cite some contemporary examples to support your claims;
5. A multinational company involved in the sales of confectioneries has noticed that consumers are not very passionate about its products, and this is reflected in the sales figures. Advise the management of the firm on how they can boost consumer involvement in the products.

### Case Study: PayPal and Digital Transformation in the Consumer Decision-making Process

Be it the purchase of fashion items like clothes and shoes, kitchen utensils, or services like insurance policies, and several other contexts, PayPal has made an impact in the global marketplace in terms of payment for market offerings. Its role becomes increasingly valued as digital activities continue to permeate contemporary consumption. Founded in December, 1998, it is known as a duly licensed credit institution with head office in

California, but its operations connect several millions of consumers all over the world. Statistically, PayPal facilitated transactions up to $936 billion as payment volume for year 2020 and generated $4.2 billion the same year. This is a remarkable increase from figures recorded for the previous years. It is stated on its website that the organisation currently serves over 300 million users. This is a significant milestone, but why does this number matter? It represents consumers and businesses that have gone through the consumption decision making process. They begin with need recognition. The consumer of today has numerous needs which are arguably more diverse in nature than they used to be several years before now. Digital transformation has radically changed how the consumer searches for information about the impending purchases. Opportunities of search engines have strengthened them to 'move' from one 'store' to another comparing products, prices, and terms of trade online. So, when booking holiday packages, flights, TV sets, or DIY accessories, evaluation is now easier online. As the consumer approaches the decision stage at the checkout, the role of PayPal becomes handy. Consumers shopping from millions of brands such as Nike, Argos, Netflix, and Boots find it convenient for an easy shopping experience. With the PayPal payment system, anyone that has an email address can send and receive payments conveniently, securely, and in a cost-efficient way online. With the increasing rate of online fraud, the trust that PayPal brings to the online transaction payments system continues to be an attractive factor that brings many more consumers to tow the line. It is one of the leading organisations that operates online auction websites but is also gaining popularity in other e-commerce websites. So, it has made an improvement on the existing financial solutions by offering a real-time payment system.

The role of PayPal to consumers is not only in online transactions; it also facilitates transactions when they are done in-person. Businesses operating offline such as doctors, contractors, and lawyers can conveniently receive payment through the PayPal online system. In September, 2021, the company introduced its app (Paypal App), which allows customers to receive money and pay others in a single place. With the QR code and the pay touch-free system, the only thing the consumer needs is his or her phone, and the job is done. It is a simple system which involves the consumer having to simply open the camera in their phones, scan the QR code, and get the app.

In its quest to be contemporary, PayPal scans the marketing environment to update its services to be in tune with the latest developments such that will be useful to the consumer. The experience during the global pandemic (COVID-19) lockdowns introduced many things to consumers' systems. Apart from the ease of payments with different currencies in various markets associated with the surge in online marketing, another example of how this was done is PayPal's link to crypto currency, which started in October, 2020. This caters for those consumer segments that are interested in this type of service. As stated by Dan Schulman, who is the president and CEO of the organisation, PayPal is eager to work with central banks and regulators all over the world in offering support and making meaningful contributions on how digital currencies will facilitate global finance and commerce. When considering the ease and speed of how consumers send money to themselves through PayPal, it is clear that the organisation is a key stakeholder in the contemporary marketing system. In its advance search feature, an individual can search to see the recipient of the money in the system. So, a friend that needs some money for shopping can instantly receive from his friends and family members. Even if the person does not have a PayPal account, he or she can easily open an account. Simply put, the introduction of PayPal is an interesting development to payment systems.

**Sources:**

Curry, D. (2021). PayPal revenue and usage statistics, 17 October 2021, www.businesofapps.com/data/paypal-statistics/#:~:text=PayPal%20key%20statistics%201%20PayPal%20generated%20%2421.4%20billion,4%20337%20million%20users%20and%20merchants%20use%20PayPal (accessed 31 October 2021).

Jones, C. (2021). How to create a QR code to accept touch-free payments, www.paypal.com/us/brc/article/how-to-install-a-qr-code#:~:text=How%20to%20create%20a%20QR%20code%20to%20accept,click%20QR%20Codes%20to%20generate%20your%20unique%20code (accessed 31 October 2021).

PayPal (nd). Tap into your money, www.paypal.com/uk/webapps/mpp/mobile-apps, (accessed 31 October 2021).

PayPal (2021). Introducing the new PayPal App, September, 2021, newsroom.uk.paypal-corp.com/2021-09-21-Introducing-the-New-PayPal-App (accessed 31 October 2021).

PayPal (nd). History and facts, about.pypl.com/who-we-are/history-and-facts/default.aspx (accessed 31 October 2021).

PayPal (nd). About us, www.paypal.com/uk/webapps/mpp/about (accessed 31 October 2021).

## QUESTIONS

1. Taking into consideration contemporary marketing and digital transformation, what would you say are the success factors of PayPal?
2. In a group of three or more, discuss what you can do to develop a business model that will compete against and outplace PayPal.
3. Apart from the decision stage of the consumer decision making process, do you think PayPal is relevant to any other stage? Give an explanation to support your stance.
4. Select one high-involvement product and another low-involvement product that you could buy with your PayPal account, prepare your evoke and consideration sets for each of these products. Compare and contrast the consumer decision-making process for these two items.

## REFERENCES

Arcia, A., Stonbraker, S., & Warner, E. (2019). Information needs and information-seeking processes of low-income pregnant women in relation to digital maternity education resources. *The Journal of Perinatal Education*, 28(3), 151–162.

Chau, P. Y., Hu, P. J. H., Lee, B. L., & Au, A. K. (2007). Examining customers' trust in online vendors and their dropout decisions: An empirical study. *Electronic Commerce Research and Applications*, 6(2), 171–182.

Chen, M. Y. (2016). Can two-sided messages increase the helpfulness of online reviews? *Online Information Review*, 40(3), 316–332.

Chen-Yu, H. J., & Kincade, D. H. (2001). Effects of product image at three stages of the consumer decision process for apparel products: Alternative evaluation, purchase and post-purchase. *Journal of Fashion Marketing and Management: An International Journal*, 5(1), 29–43.

Clarke, K. and Belk, R. W. (1978). The effects of product involvement and task definition on anticipated consumer effort, in Keith H. H. (ed). *Advances In Consumer Research*, Vol.5, Ann Arbor, MI: Association for Consumer Research, pp. 313–318.

Dasgupta, S., & Grover, P. (2019). Impact of digital strategies on consumer decision journey: Special. *Academy of Marketing Studies Journal*, 23(1), 1–14.

Dennis, A. R., Yuan, L., Feng, X., Webb, E., & Hsieh, C. J. (2020). Digital nudging: Numeric and semantic priming in e-commerce. *Journal of Management Information Systems*, 37(1), 39–65.

Duncan, C. P. (1990). Consumer market beliefs: A review of the literature and an agenda for future research. *ACR North American Advances*, in Goldberg, M. E., Gorn, G., and Pollay, R. W. (eds), *Advances in Consumer Research*, 729–735.

Engel, J. F., Blackwell, R. D., & Miniard, P. W. (1986). *Consumer Behavior*, 5th edn, Hinsdale, IL: Dryden.

Engel, J. F., Blackwell, R. D., & Miniard, P. W. (1995) *Consumer Behavior*, 8th edn, New York: Dryden Press.

Fang, J., Wen, C., George, B., & Prybutok, V. R. (2016). Consumer heterogeneity, perceived value, and repurchase decision-making in online shopping: The role of gender, age, and shopping motives. *Journal of Electronic Commerce Research*, 17(2), 116–131.

Faulds, D. J., Mangold, W. G., Raju, P. S., & Valsalan, S. (2018). The mobile shopping revolution: Redefining the consumer decision process. *Business Horizons*, 61(2), 323–338.

Gbadamosi, A. (2009). Cognitive dissonance: The implicit explication in low-income consumers' shopping behaviour for "low-involvement" grocery products. *International Journal of Retail & Distribution Management*, 37(12), 1077–1095.

Gbadamosi, A. (2020). Buyer behaviour in the 21st century: Implications for SME marketing, in Nwankwo, S. and Gbadamosi, A. (eds), *Entrepreneurship Marketing*, 2nd ed., pp. 72–96.

Gómez-Díaz, J. A. (2016). Reviewing a consumer decision making model in online purchasing: An ex-post fact study with a Colombian sample. *Avances en Psicología Latinoamericana*, 34(2), 273–292.

Grewal, D., Janakiraman, R., Kalyanam, K., Kannan, P. K., Ratchford, B., Song, R., & Tolerico, S. (2010). Strategic online and offline retail pricing: A review and research agenda. *Journal of Interactive Marketing*, 24, 138–154.

Hernandez-Ortega, B. (2019). Not so positive, please! Effects of online consumer reviews on evaluations during the decision-making process. *Internet Research*, 29(4), 606–637.

Hsu, C. L., Lin, J. C. C., & Chiang, H. S. (2013). The effects of blogger recommendations on customers' online shopping intentions. *Internet Research*, 23(1), 69–88.

Jones, A., & Kang, J. (2020). Media technology shifts: Exploring millennial consumers' fashion-information-seeking behaviors and motivations. *Canadian Journal of Administrative Sciences/Revue Canadienne des Sciences de l'Administration*, 37(1), 13–29.

Karimi, S., Holland, C. P., & Papamichail, K. N. (2018). The impact of consumer archetypes on online purchase decision-making processes and outcomes: A behavioural process perspective. *Journal of Business Research*, 91, 71–82.

Kotarba, M. (2018). Digital transformation of business models. *Foundations of Management*, 10(1), 123–142.

Kuksov, D., & Villas-Boas, J. M. (2010). When more alternatives lead to less choice. *Marketing Science*, 29(3), 507–524.

Kuo, Y. F., & Wu, C. M. (2012). Satisfaction and post-purchase intentions with service recovery of online shopping websites: Perspectives on perceived justice and emotions. *International Journal of Information Management*, 32(2), 127–138.

Lanzolla, G., Pesce, D., & Tucci, C. L. (2021). The digital transformation of search and recombination in the innovation function: Tensions and an integrative framework. *Journal of Product Innovation Management*, 38(1), 90–113.

Lee, S., & Cude, B. J. (2012). Consumer complaint channel choice in online and offline purchases. *International Journal of Consumer Studies*, 36(1), 90–96.

Mukherjee, S., & Chatterjee, S. (2021). Webrooming and showrooming: A multi-stage consumer decision process. *Marketing Intelligence & Planning*, 39(5), 649–669.

National Retail Federation. (2019). Consumer returns in the retail industry. Appriss Retail (January 22). Retrieved from https://appriss.com/retail/wp-content/uploads/sites/4/2020/01/ AR3019-2019-Customer-Returns-in-the-Retail-Industry.pdf

Nelson, P. (1970). Information and consumer behavior, *Journal of Political Economy*, 78(20), 311–329.

Park, I., Cho, J., & Rao, H. R. (2015). The dynamics of pre- and post-purchase service and consumer evaluation of online retailers: A comparative analysis of dissonance and disconfirmation models. *Decision Sciences*, 46(6), 1109–1140.

Patel, P. C., Baldauf, C., Karlsson, S., & Oghazi, P. (2021). The impact of free returns on online purchase behavior: Evidence from an intervention at an online retailer. *Journal of Operations Management*, 67(4), 511–555.

Peter, J. P., & Olson, J. C. (2005). *Consumer Behaviour and Marketing Strategy*, 7th ed., New York: McGraw-Hill Companies Inc.

Proskurnina, N. (2019). Purchasing decisions making in the context of digital transformation of retail. *Economics of Development*, 18(4), 11–18.

Rothschild, M. L., & Houston, M. J. (1980). Individual differences in voting behavior: Further investigations of involvement, in NA – *Advances in Consumer Research* Volume 07, (eds) Jerry C. Olson, Ann Abor, MI: Association for Consumer Research, pp. 655–658.

Sadarangani, P. H., & Gaur, S. S. (2002). Role of Emotions and the Moderating Influence of Product Involvement in Web Site Effectiveness, *Conference proceedings at ITS 14th Biennial conference, challenges and Opportunities in the Digital Century. The Role of Information and Telecommunications*, Seoul, Korea (August).

Schiffman, L., & Wisenblit, J. (2019). *Consumer Behaviour*, 12th edn, Essex: Pearson Education Limited.

Schiffman, L. G., Kanuk, L. L., & Kumar, S. R., in collaboration with Wisenblit, J. (2012). *Consumer Behaviour*, 10th edn, Essex: Pearson Education Limited.

Schneider, C., Weinmann, M., & vom Brocke, J. (2018). Digital nudging: Influencing choices by using interface design. *Communications of the ACM*, 61(7), 67–73.

Shan, Y. (2016). How credible are online product reviews? The effects of self-generated and system-generated cues on source credibility evaluation. *Computers in Human Behavior*, 55, 633–641.

Shin, E., Chung, T., & Damhorst, M. L. (2020). Are negative and positive reviews regarding apparel fit influential? *Journal of Fashion Marketing and Management: An International Journal*, 25(1), 63–79.

Singh, D. K., Kumar, A., & Dash, M. K. (2016). Using analytic hierarchy process to develop hierarchy structural model of consumer decision making in digital market. *Asian Academy of Management Journal*, 21(1), 111.

Smith, A., & Anderson, M. (2016). Online reviews, available at: http://www.pewinternet.org/2016/12/ 19/online-reviews/ (accessed 16 October 2019).

Solomon, M. R. (2020). *Consumer Behaviour: Buying, Having, and Being*, 13th edn, Essex: Pearson Education Limited.

Tan, H., Lv, X., Liu, X., & Gursoy, D. (2018). Evaluation nudge: Effect of evaluation mode of online customer reviews on consumers' preferences. *Tourism Management*, 65, 29–40.

Thirumalai, S. & Sinha, K. K. (2011). Customization of the online purchase process in electronic retailing and customer satisfaction: An online field study. *Journal of Operations Management*, 29(5), 477–487. doi: 10.1016/j.jom.2010.11.009

Verhoef, P. C., Broekhuizen, T., Bart, Y., Bhattacharya, A., Dong, J. Q., Fabian, N., & Haenlein, M. (2021). Digital transformation: A multidisciplinary reflection and research agenda. *Journal of Business Research*, 122, 889–901.

Vinhas, A. S., & Bowman, D. (2019). Online/offline information search patterns and outcomes for services. *Journal of Services Marketing*, 33(7), 753–770.

Wang, J. C., & Chang, C. H. (2013). How online social ties and product-related risks influence purchase intentions: A Facebook experiment. *Electronic Commerce Research and Applications*, 12(5), 337–346.

Zaichkowsky, J. L. (1985). Measuring the involvement construct, *Journal of Consumer Research*, 12(December), 341–352.

# PART 2

# DIGITAL TRANSFORMATION IN THE SOCIO-CULTURAL IMPACTS ON CONSUMPTION

# CHAPTER 4

# Impact of Culture and Sub-culture on Consumer Decisions

**LEARNING OBJECTIVES**

After reading this chapter, you should be able to:

- Define culture with reference to relevant illustrations;
- Critically discuss the characteristics of culture in relation to consumer behaviour;
- Analyse consumer culture and its dimensions as well as the associated relevant models;
- Clearly explain the notion of global consumer culture and how it extends the discussion of culture beyond the conventional understanding;
- Critically discuss high- and low-context cultures and apply them to consumer behaviour;
- Understand myths and rituals in relation to consumer behaviour;
- Evaluate the interrelationship of religion, spirituality, and culture in relation to consumption decisions;
- Understand the consumer subculture.

**INTRODUCTION**

The food types and eating habits, clothes and clothing patterns, music and entertainment styles, language and communication styles, and numerous other life phenomena tend to distinguish us as consumers from one another in various ways as members of different societal contexts. Members of particular societies demonstrate consistencies in behaviour that show them as sharing values, customs, and mores. As you interact with others in different social settings or hear about what they do that is unique to them, there are indications of what sets them apart. This is an underpinning explanation concerning culture. Accordingly, this reflects in our consumption decisions. From an early age as young consumers, we observe, learn, and act in various circumstances consistent with people of the society that we belong to. The celebration of Thanksgiving in the United States is well known and shared by members of the society, whereas the meaning and activities linked to the event are unlikely to be consistent with the thoughts of people in other cultural systems such as in India and the United Arab Emirates (UAE). This points to the interesting arbitrariness of culture and cultural values. Meanwhile, as with the other topics in this book, digital transformation has influenced the way culture influences consumer behaviour. This demonstrates the dynamic nature of culture as it gradually accommodates changes and development in technology in the way members of these cultural systems are influenced. In this chapter, we will first define culture and examine its characteristics and examine how it has influenced consumers in their choices in recent times.

## WHAT IS CULTURE?

Culture is an important aspect of our consumption behaviour. It is a fundamentally broad concept that covers many themes. In this book, we will define it as:

*A set of learned and shared beliefs, customs, mores, and values that pattern the attitudes and behaviour of people of a specific society.*

If we examine this definition closely, we can see the elements that constitute its building blocks as very core to the discussion of what people buy and use every day. People's beliefs are thoughts held by them about something while their values are the enduring beliefs about what is considered to be good or bad (Szmigin and Piacentini, 2018). So, they constitute key aspects of peoples' culture. Clearly, this explains why people belonging to a cultural setting would show a preference for a type of product, service, or brand compared to what their counterparts in another culture would love to buy. It is very common for people in the Western world to express emotions through the use of flowers such as for marriage proposals, Valentines, and bereavements but this is not regarded as fittingly appropriate in some other cultural contexts. Perhaps, one of the commonly identified cultural elements is the spoken language that aids communication among people.

It is important to underscore the fact that culture is learned. It is not hereditary like the skin color, height, or the nature of hair that children often get from their parents. It is adopted as a result of exposure to it. This brings us to the notions of **enculturation** and **acculturation**. While enculturation is about learning one's own culture, acculturation is about learning the culture of other people. We will discuss these further under the characteristics of culture later in the chapter. Moreover, it has to be shared by people of a setting which could be a community, city, nation, or other milieus for it to be known as culture. Interestingly, this observation can be linked to the description given by Solomon (2020) that we can simply explain it as the personality of a society. This explains why digital transformation also brings us to the discussion of a digital culture where digitisation brings people together in one form or another. As indicated by Lee (2009), the impacts of digital technologies on the music industry include the discourse around digital economy and digital culture. In their paper titled 'From Culture to Smart Culture', Fanea-Ivanovici and Pană (2020) came to the conclusion that cultural digitisation is an uneven process across nations. Hence, we can describe a nation or particular society by their e-culture level. They argue that there is a vicious cycle around this, implying that poor performance in cultural digitalisation can result in adverse consequences in relation to the well-being of the citizen as there would be larger developmental gaps between the countries. One of the leading scholars on culture, Hofstede, through a series of seminal publications on the topic (1980; 1984; 2001), indicates that we can explain differences in culture of nations through five dimensions, namely:

- Individualism;
- Masculinity;
- Power distance;
- Uncertainty avoidance;
- Long-term orientation.

These dimensions are discussed further later in the chapter.

## CHARACTERISING CULTURE

Now that we know what culture means, to have a deeper level of understanding of how it works, we will be examining its characteristics. Hence, we note here that:

- Culture is learned;
- Culture is shared;
- Culture is enduring;
- Culture is dynamic;
- Culture is arbitrary;
- Culture is purpose-driven and satisfies needs;
- Culture regulates behaviour.

### Culture is Learned

A fundamental part of culture is that it is learned. The consumers are exposed to norms, mores, and values of societies and learn to pattern their behaviour in conformity with them. A child consumer learns the consumption of market offerings of his or her culture through interaction with members of the culture such as parents, siblings, and peers. This is a typical example of enculturation, which is about learning the beliefs, mores, and values of one's own culture. Apart from the mainstream cultural issues, this learning is played out in the activities of the marketplace. A seminal paper indicates that as long as a child is able to hold a coin, they are deemed to be part of the family purchase activities (McLeod, 1974), which indicates that they begin to learn the culture in terms of what they see adults buy and consume and what they ignore. This aligns with another claim which categorises children into trolley loaders and 'pesters' (*The Snacks Magazine*, 1993, in Gelperowic and Beharrell, 1994). In this categorisation, those who are trolley loaders fill their parents' trolleys with unwanted products during shopping trips, while 'pesters' pester their parents to engage in some unwanted products. From these, we can see that the interaction of children in the marketplace is one of the key opportunities they use to learn the culture, not only of the society but that which their parents are associated with.

Meanwhile, one of the major buzzwords these days is immigration. For many reasons such as searching for greener pastures, international job transfer, and the pursuit of education qualifications, when people find themselves within two or more cultures, they tend to learn new cultural values. This is the focus of acculturation. The work of Berry (1994; 1997) gives an explanation of the various ways people manoeuvre between their home and host cultures in relation to their identities as:

- Integration;
- Separation;
- Assimilation;
- Marginalisation.

For those immigrants or sojourners who fit the integration category, they conceptualise themselves as belonging to both cultures. In this schema, Berry shows that sojourners who see themselves as high in their home cultures but low in their host culture belong to the separation category. Those in the assimilation category perceive themselves as being high in the host culture and low in their home cultures whereas those that perceive themselves as low in both home and host cultures are described as being in the marginalisation segment. In a study of clothing acculturation among Black African women in the United Kingdom, Gbadamosi (2012a) found that the women's learning of their host culture is influenced by their personal factors, religious factors, social factors, and the weather condition. Personal factors cover issues like their age, occupation, and marital status, while religious factors encapsulate their religious beliefs and the prescribed moral codes. As shown in the findings of this study, the social factors relate to the women's need for affiliation, comfort, and self-confidence while the weather condition covers an explanation around the difference between the climate of their host and home countries and the associated discomfort and constraints.

## Culture is Shared

The cultural beliefs, values, and mores will have to be shared by members of the society to be seen as clearly constituting a culture. It is the collective sharing of these that gives society the cultural position it has. As indicated by Smith and Bond (2019), any functioning group of humans such as classrooms, professional associations, families, ethnic communities, universities, nations, companies, and so on has a culture. So, culture lies primarily in the sharing of values by members and the sharing of cultural elements can distinguish one cultural group from another. Relating this to digital transformation, we can identify two generations with shared characteristics as 'digital natives' and 'digital immigrants' (Prensky, 2001). In this categorisation, 'digital natives' refers to people born in the digital age who have the knowledge and technical know-how to use all kinds of tools in different contexts (Prensky, 2001; Ou-sekou and Zaid, 2021). Conversely, 'digital immigrants' are those whose birth does not fall within this period but are interested in technologies and make the effort to take advantage of digital opportunities. Similarly, we can see another example of the usefulness of the sharing of culture through the lens of tourism. Tourists are attracted to local environments because of what the people share. As seen in Canavan (2016), people in the host culture share specific arts and crafts, festivals, language, ways of doing things, and many other factors. These and the collective sharing of beliefs are part of what attracts tourists. Canavan (2016) explains that there could be such a thing as tourism culture, which is an emergent culture from the amalgamations of the host culture and the cultures of the visitors that take place at the destination.

## Culture is Enduring

More often than not, there are historical antecedents to every culture. Some date back several decades or centuries and the beliefs, values, and behaviour patterns persist. They are linked to certain events and circumstances. Exploring the historic sites in several countries will reveal this about culture. Stonehenge in England, UK, reportedly evolved between 3000 BC and 1600 BC and is still a dazzling site of awe and amazement to visitors who troop to explore its historical significance. The pyramids in Egypt, which are noted as tombs for the Pharaohs, are over 2600 years old. Thanksgiving Day commemorated in the United States is reported to date back to the colonial period (Mark, 2020). New Year's Day in China is noted and celebrated widely, but what is probably not known by many is that it is a tradition that has historical antecedents of over 3800 years, with links to the ancient agrarian society (Travel China Guide, nd). Clearly these and several other examples indicate the enduring nature of culture cutting across many issues such as types of food eaten, the mode of greetings, religious activities, clothing and fashion, language spoken, and a host of other things.

## Culture is Dynamic

The enduring nature of culture which we have explained and experienced in various ways does not foreclose the possibility of change. One of the key characteristics of the marketing environment is dynamism, which indicates that the associated actors, factors, and influences are changing. If we look at the macro environment as an example for illustration, we discuss issues such as political factors, economic factors, technological factors, and socio-cultural factors. Generally, a change in each of these layers of the environment tends to reflect in the other layers. Changes in governments and political systems of countries introduce policies and changes to cultural systems. Similarly, changes in the economic outlook of nations are changing some of the old cultural systems. The United Arab Emirates is one of the clear examples on this. It is a federation of seven states which has grown in significance to become an important economic centre in the Middle East (BBC, 2020). It is traditionally known to be conservative with authoritarian government but is now regarded as one of the most liberal nations in the Gulf region, which accommodates several other cultures and beliefs. It used to be predominantly dependent on fishing and the pearl industry in the 1950s before the discovery of oil. However, since the commencement of its oil exports from around 1962, it has experienced significant economic and societal transformation with important tourism activities (BBC, 2020). Digital transformation is another significant development that has changed the modes of doing things in several cultures compared to how they used to operate before. A plethora of changes can be listed regarding how the change in technological factors has fine-tuned the beliefs, norms, and values of many societies. Communications through telephones and video, mobile telecommunications, the ease of travel, food preparation being eased in several ways, computer processing of documents, the availability of e-books (including this one you are reading), and many other factors are just examples of how technology has shown that cultures are indeed dynamic. Similarly, there have been shifts in various socio-cultural factors. As an example of this, women used to be traditionally financially dependent on men, but this has now changed in several contexts as women's economic power is notably stronger and, in some cases, they constitute bread winners in homes. Also, the roles of children in families are changing. In a study by Gbadamosi (2012b), it was reported that children engage in some form of decisions in family consumption activities, especially as related to routinely consumed items.

## Culture is Arbitrary

The disparity in the cultural paraphernalia of different societies is interestingly complex. If we study the cultural values of different societies, the findings will show that what is esteemed in one society is considered an aberration in another context. Culture does not follow a common logical pattern across all societies. From a very broad perspective, the study of Hofstede (1980) which we discussed above shows differences between groups of nations as compared to other groups. This is an important cue for international businesses with presence in several nations. The fast-food giants like McDonalds understand that consumers in the United States, Canada, and United Kingdom would like their menu in a way that accommodates their cultural systems; there are variations in these that should be taken into consideration when serving consumers in other places such as the Middle East. This shows why their marketing strategies such as marketing communications also vary.

## Culture is Purpose-driven and Satisfies Needs

As consumers, we have diverse needs across different areas of our lives. The food we eat, the clothes we wear, the shelter we use, our transportation means, our hair styles, ways of being entertained, and a plethora of other things all point to how our needs are met. Interestingly, there are fingerprints of culture in how these needs are met. As stated by Schiffman et al. (2010), culture exists for the purpose of satisfying the needs of people within a society and setting standards and rules. So, culture sets patterns on specific satisfiers used by consumers for meeting these needs. While ham sandwiches would be a popular meal for satisfying the need for food among many in England and Canada, repeated reports and sustained discussion shows that it would not be so accepted in places like Saudi Arabia and Iran.

## Culture Regulates Behaviour

Following the point on how culture satisfies needs, it is also relevant for us to note that it regulates how people act in various situations. With evidence all around us, we can see that the marketplace features several alternative offerings seeking consumers' attention and action. Clearly, consumers have the challenge of choosing among them. While several factors are at play to influence consumers' choices, the role of culture tends to be very significant. As children grow, their behaviour is regulated by the mores, values, and beliefs they share with experience in their society, and this tends to pattern their behaviour into old age.

## GLOBAL CONSUMER CULTURE

While culture has been explained as what differentiates one society from another, global consumer culture (GCC) introduces an interesting twist to the phenomenon. The seminal publication of Arnould and Thompson (2002) brings this phenomenon to a clearer perspective. From their perspective, we can define global consumer culture theory as a collection of theoretical perspectives that focuses on the dynamics of relationships between consumers' actions, the marketplace, and cultural meanings (Arnould and Thompson, 2002). A thorough look into the world population mix, especially in the developed world, shows that the world is **multicultural**. Global consumer culture is about redefining this such that consumers, marketers, brands, ideologies, and the societies of multiple cultures converge and interact (Kipnis et al., 2014; Demangeot et al., 2015). So, it is about global cultural integration through the adaptation of different cultural backgrounds (Earley et al., 2006). From this explanation, it can be stated that it is about global integration linked to global brands (Özsomer, 2019). It has also been described as inherently linked to American pop culture through which the United States is globally dominant with examples of offerings such as fast foods, movies, and music being at the forefront of this global integration (Rieff, 1993; Samiee, 2019).

Over the years, GCC has been influenced by three key factors as argued by (Özsomer, 2019) which are:

- Digital networked technology (DNT);
- New brands from emerging markets;
- The digitally connected bottom of the pyramid (BOP) consumers.

Given that the core focus of globalisation is about the world being a global village such that barriers are reduced between countries to achieve closer political, economic, and personal interactions (Spears et al., 2004), this will be aided by technological advancements like the use of mobile telecommunications and the Internet. Accordingly, cultural integration that is the primary focus of the GCC will be facilitated by the prevalent digital transformations that now underpin several aspects of our lives. For example, consumers in one part of the world now have access to things that people in other parts of the world experience like entertainment contents, books, and food to mention but a few. As explained by Özsomer (2019), there is an increasing number of new brands emanating from emerging markets and playing significant roles in the world economy, such as the examples of AliBaba and several other Chinese brands that are now actively part of the forces that drive the global economic system. Moreover, it is reported that consumers at the bottom of the pyramid (BOP) are engaging in dialogue both with one another and with brands as they are becoming more digitally connected, which indicates that they are being exposed to the information which could be positive or negative about a product or service. This is acknowledged by Gbadamosi (2019) in a study on consumer behaviour in contemporary developing nations, which emphasises that the changes noticed about consumption of consumers in developing nations and the brands operating in that context cannot be described as inconsequential to the global marketing system.

## CULTURE, MODELS, AND DIMENSIONS

Many attempts have been made to develop theories and models on culture to give further understanding of the phenomenon. We will review some of these in this section. Some of these are highlighted below and discussed in turn.

### Hofstede's (1980) Cultural Dimensions

- One of the enduring studies on culture that has been widely cited and read over the years is that of Hofstede (1980). These dimensions are highlighted below:
  **Individualism and Collectivism**
  Individualism is the degree to which a society places value on self-reliance, personal freedom, and personal achievement over that of the group. The United States, for example, is considered to be individualistic as activities of people in the society tend to be individual-oriented. Conversely, societies characterised by collectivism are group-oriented with actions underpinned by **selflessness**. Societies like China and Taiwan fill this latter category.
  **Masculinity**
  The degree to which a society expresses **stereotypical** male traits such as aggression. Conversely, a society with femininity traits shows dominant features of caring. Societies such as Japan and the United States place value

on control while societies like Brazil and Denmark are underpinned by feminine traits (Babin and Harris, 2018).

**Power Distance**

The power distance measures the degree of acknowledgement of the societal hierarchical order or social classes within the society. In order words, in a society with high power distance, the distinction between the superiors and subordinates is expected to be significantly pronounced. On the other hand, societies that are low in power distance tend to see themselves as equal. For example, in some societies such as the United Kingdom and United States, senior and junior colleagues address themselves by their first names, whereas in societies like Nigeria and Pakistan, they tend to use expression and demeanour that will glaringly depict the gap between ranks and positions.

**Uncertainty Avoidance**

Uncertainty avoidance is the degree to which a society avoids ambiguity or becomes uneasy with issues that are unknown. So, societies that are high in this tend to avoid taking risks and prefer to have an ordered, routine, and structured life (Babin and Harris, 2018). Considering this in a consumer behaviour context, societies that are high in uncertainty avoidance will be slower to adopt new inventions (Babin and Harris, 2018). By and large, the implications of this are that this knowledge should guide marketers in the design of their marketing strategies in terms of which products to introduce to different societies per time.

**Long-term Orientation**

The degree to which societies value giving priority to long-term benefits over short-term rewards. Societies that are high in long-term orientation tend to place a high value on thriftiness and persevere on issues compared to their counterparts that score low on long-term orientation (Kim and Oh, 2002; Babin and Harris, 2018). The principle of *guanxi* that guides Chinese businesses is principally underpinned by trust and is associated with high long-term orientation.

## Triandis' (1994) Subjective Culture and Social Behaviour

This model relates culture to social behaviour and shows that three factors affect our social behaviour, namely: Past experience, behavioural situation, and subjective culture. In this schema, the subjective culture covers issues such as categorisation, associations, values in a culture, roles, and mores. This influences consumers' attitudes towards the product, purchase affect, self-definition, habit through customs, and past experiences and referent expectations (Triandis, 1994: Lee, 2000). Based on these, four cultural syndromes were identified, which are complexity, collectivism, individualism, and tightness.

**FIGURE 4.1** Movement of cultural meaning

**Source**: Adapted from McCracken, G. (1986). Culture and consumption: A theoretical account of the structure and movement of the cultural meaning of consumer goods. *Journal of Consumer Research*, *13*(1), 71–84.

## MOVEMENT OF CULTURAL MEANING

One would wonder how a consumer exhibits cultural values in relation to his or her consumption. One of the prominent explanations for this is the notion of movement of cultural meaning. A widely cited publication on this is the work of McCracken (1986). In this, it is shown that cultural meaning moves from one place to another but also moves from a culturally constituted world to consumer products from which it then becomes transferred to the consumer (McCracken, 1986). In this postulation, as illustrated in Figure 4.1, it is shown that four key rituals, advertising, and fashion systems aid the movement. These rituals are identified as:

- Exchange rituals;
- Possession rituals;
- Groom rituals;
- Divestment rituals.

On occasions such as birthdays and special seasons like Christmas and New Year, consumers exchange gifts that serve as some form of communication to the recipients which emphasises the fact that the role of products to consumers transcends that of being merely functional and includes its symbolic values in that it connotes meaning (Gbadamosi, 2015a, b). As consumers invest in consumer goods, they claim them.

This is not only in terms of territorial ownership but also in terms of drawing out qualities given to them by marketing forces (McCracken, 1986). So, consumers flaunt and compare goods at occasions, and devote a considerable amount of time to cleaning them, which are examples of how possession rituals are demonstrated. The grooming rituals are the actions of consumers that revolve around drawing out the cultural meaning from consumer goods, even though these meanings are perishable in nature. According to McCracken (1986), these rituals are about taking special pains to ensure that the special perishable meaning associated with the products is moved to the life of the consumer, however briefly that may be. Examples of this include preparing for a 'dinner out', hair-styling services, and make-up products and services. Meanwhile, the divestment rituals relate to the disposal of goods and are exhibited by the consumer who disposes of the products and the one buying them. The purchasing consumer removes meanings that pertain to the previous owners while the consumer selling also removes meanings associated with those prodcts. For either of the consumers, it is often done to free the products of the old meaning so that new meaning moves to the new ownership system. Examples of this include removing belongings from a home which has been sold while the new buyer redecorates it, and changing some features of used cars.

## HIGH-CONTEXT AND LOW-CONTEXT CULTURES

In view of the characteristics of culture given, we now notice that there are variations between cultures. One of the ways of differentiating between societies is whether a society falls within high-context cultures or low-context cultures. These nomenclatures are often traced to the work of Hall (1976) for explaining different cultural orientations. It is an important addition to the discussion of culture as it borders on how consumers in a cultural setting act to situations in life. Based on the work of Hall (1976), the high-context culture and low-context culture are the extreme positions when countries are positioned to be on a continuum. As indicated in Kim et al. (1998), the following factors are very useful in explaining the differences between high-context and low-context cultures:

- Social orientations;
- Commitment;
- Responsibility;
- Confrontation;
- Communications;
- Dealing with new situations.

In terms of social orientation, people in the high-context culture are known to be deeply involved with one another compared to low-context cultures where there is relatively little involvement among people and they are highly individualised and fragmented (Hall, 1976; Kim et al., 1998). Linked to the notion of high involvement among members is the issue of commitment. People that are in high-context cultures tend to be highly committed to completing action chains as they feel obliged by their promise to do something. Conversely, people in low-context cultures do not ordinarily feel so bound to achieve a course of action. As indicated by Kim et al. (1998), high-context cultures are characterised by top-down decision making and those people in authority in those contexts are personally responsible for the undertakings of their subordinates. This emphasises a sense of responsibility in the high-context cultures compared to low-context cultures where responsibility is diffused (Hall, 1976).

In view of the social coherence and deep involvement of people in high-context cultures, they tend to shun direct confrontation, and some communicate indirectly on issues that could attract disagreement. This is in contrast to low-context cultures where members tend to favour direct and open confrontation as well as direct and formally recorded criticism (Czinkota and Ronkainen, 1990). In terms of communications, high-context cultures tend to be less verbal but more about being embedded within the associated physical context unlike the case in low-context cultures where communication is engrained in explicit codes including sentences and grammar; and the key focus is on the message and how it is communicated rather than the environment where the communication takes place (Onkvisit and Shaw, 1993; Kim et al., 1998). Moreover, high-context cultures and low-context cultures deal with new situations differently. The former is noted to often be creative when dealing with new situations because they are used to context-free circumstances whereas the creativity of the latter often revolves more around their old system and tends to be less creative when dealing with something new. We can tease out examples of these two contexts from the work of Kim et al. (1998) which shows the United States as a low-context culture and China and Korea as high-context cultures.

## MYTHS AND RITUALS

Myths constitute an important phenomenon that connects people of a particular society. As we grow up, we hear many tales and share these with the younger generation as well. Myth can be simply defined as a story with symbolic elements that indicate shared emotions and ideals of a culture (Solomon, 2020). The academic literature on it tends to agree that it usually shows conflict between two forces that oppose each other, and the outcome offers moral guides for people's behaviour (Szmigin and Piacentini, 2018). Marketers are disposed to incorporate these into stimuli offered to consumers. For instance, products and services are planned to reflect nostalgia, and positioned and supported by marketing communications that emphasise the same position.

## POPULAR AND POP CULTURE

One of the bonds that bind the world in various ways is pop culture, which has grown in significance over the years. Many scholars have defined it differently, especially because of its scope and dynamic nature. Here we will look at an example of this definition as given by Lee and Bai (2016). Their definition, which considers the term from a commercial standpoint, shows that pop culture is mass culture that is meant for mass consumption. They show that it is a manifest of entertainment including music, TV programs, films, literature, and sports. This explains a claim which states that pop culture conventions are global issues with huge amounts of financial capital investments for the promotion of things like films and television shows (Raphael and Lam, 2018). So, it has become a force for globalisation which drives how images, lifestyles, and cultural meanings are becoming circulated (Cruz et al., 2019). It has become a very important phenomenon that drives tourism all over the world. Similarly, it is also being used to correct wrong impressions and address negative images. For example, the study of Lee and Bai (2016), which is focused on the influence of culture on destination image, found that pop culture has been important for the weakening of a negative image previously held about South Korea through the media, fine-tuning it into a positive image. Their study indicates that the actual visitation of tourists, as a result of pop concerts, aids in giving tourists a more positive image of the country than they had previously. It is a powerful force that influences many things because it is popular, and people form their view of the world based on it, which explains why it should not just be seen as a fun-house mirror (Rehn, 2008). It has been shown that pop culture, through the media, constitutes a means of public pedagogy and people construct knowledge not only about their own stories but about those of others through media based on their experiences.

The worldwide digital presence has connected consumers to these pop cultures in various ways. A visit to YouTube as a social media platform will show millions of views of uploaded music of singers. Meanwhile, consumers now have, at a personal level, a degree of consumer involvement, which also plays an important role as shown in the example of the study of Whang et al. (2016), which indicates that the involvement of an individual with certain types of pop culture influences how he or she will perceive the destination associated with that pop culture.

## RELIGION, SPIRITUALITY, AND CULTURE

Religion has been a part of culture for many years. If we examine its definitions closely, this stance will become evident. In the view of Paloutzian (2017), religion can be conceptualised at various levels, namely: Cultural, personal, functional, or 'substantial'. Similarly, one can also explain religion to be either personal or social (Fourali, 2018; Fourali and Gbadamosi, 2021). By and large, we can state that the scope of religion is beyond an individual. Even though it can be conceptualised in various ways, we will look at one of these that specifically suits the purpose of this segment of the chapter. It has been defined as a system of meaning connected to a pattern of life, a community of faith as well as a worldview that explains the standpoint of the sacred and what ultimately matters (Schimdt et al., 1999; Donga et al., 2021). This aligns with another definition given earlier before these publications that it revolves around extra ordinary and unique experience which has a sacred dimension and is different from everyday life (Roberts, 1984). From this, four key elements are indicated as the bedrock of religion. These are:

- Beliefs;
- Rituals;
- Values;
- Community.

Evidently consumption and religion are closely linked as shown by Gbadamosi (2021a, b) and illustrated in Figure 4.1.

Meanwhile, the diversity associated with different religions, beliefs, and values is demonstrated in Table 4.1, as presented in Gbadamosi's (2021) publication *Religion and Consumer Behaviour in Developing Nations*.

From all these perspectives, one can note the distinction between sacred and profane in relation to consumption. This is clearly argued in the publication of Belk et al. (1989). In this publication, they indicate that, in some societies, the concept of sacred covers things like magic, animism, shamanism, and totemism as such communities give sacred status to elements of the natural environment that are worshipped, feared, revered, and given utmost respect (Belk et al., 1989). Clearly, what is considered sacred differs from one society to another. Cherrier (2009) offers an interesting example of how consumers can even use the behaviour at their disposal to communicate sacredness in the form of circulation of materials, which represent terminating profane consumption in favour of the emergence of sacred consumption. It has been shown that things considered sacred in contemporary western religion include gods, days, shrines, clothing, songs, and relics (Belk et al., 1989). In some other contexts, sacredness may transcend formal religion such as we can see in the examples of art, flags, national parks, museums, collections, and automobiles (Belk, et al., 1989).

Belk et al. (1989), from a meticulous review of the literature, present the following 12 properties of sacredness:

- **Hierophany**: Sacredness manifests itself and is not created by people. However, something is noted as sacred through a process that introduces a system of meaning to people which leads to societal cohesion;
- **Kratophany**: Sacred reveals tendencies of both strong avoidance and strong approach;
- **Opposition to profane**: Since profane indicates what is ordinary that relates to our day-to-day activities, sacred is distinct from this;
- **Contamination**: Unlike the usage in the medical context, this contamination means the spread of positive sacredness and not negative sacredness or evil;
- **Sacrifice**: Examples include asceticism, self-mutilation, sexual abstinence, and fasting;
- **Commitment**: This involves personal involvement and emotional attachment, among other things;
- **Objectification**: Concretising the sacred through representation in an object;
- **Ritual**: Rules of conduct guiding people on how to behave in relation to sacred objects.

**TABLE 4.1** Religions and their dynamics

| | Religion | Basic descriptor | Further comments |
|---|---|---|---|
| 1. | **African Traditional Religions (ATR)** | They can be traced back to prehistoric times. They are characterised by reliance on oral stories which have been passed down from generation to generation about gods, superhuman entities, and ancestors. | Followers acknowledge the existence of The Supreme God who created everything and other smaller gods. Although they do not have any major doctrinal teachings, their beliefs revolve around issues like the existence of deities, divination, and ancestor veneration. |
| 2 | **Atheism** | Those following this stance on religion are known as Atheists, and hold that God or gods are man-made ideas. | Adherents have no belief in God or any other gods. |
| 3 | **Baha'i** | Founded in the 19th century by Bahá'u'lláh. | Emphasises that humankind is united spiritually. |
| 4 | **Buddhism** | A way of living based on the teachings of the founder, Siddhartha Gautama. | Espouses an understanding of cause and effect through the use of practical approaches like meditation for gaining insight towards achieving enlightenment. It focuses on shaping the future through thoughts, actions, and words. |
| 5 | **Candomblé** | Can be traced back to the slave trade and originated in Brazil. | This is a combination of elements of Catholicism and some aspects of indigenous African religion and focuses on the belief in a supreme creator as well as several minor deities. It holds that everyone has their own deity that serves to protect them and guide their destiny. |
| 6 | **Christianity** | The world's biggest faith, with a focus on the teachings of Jesus Christ. | As indicated on the Christianity.org website, Christianity should not be equated with going to church, but is about having a relationship with God. It revolves around the belief that Jesus died for the sins of the world. Hence, the religion is known as 'Good News' in that trusting in Jesus Christ makes it possible for anyone to have a relationship with God. |
| 7 | **Hinduism** | A collection of faiths entrenched in the religious ideas of India. | Hinduism revolves around a belief in reincarnation. It emphasises following righteousness through spiritual practices, called yoga, and prayers which are also known as bhakti. |

*(Continued)*

**TABLE 4.1** (Continued)

| | Religion | Basic descriptor | Further comments |
|---|---|---|---|
| 8 | **Islam** | Revealed in its final form by the Prophet Muhammad, in the 7th century CE. | The followers of Islam are called Muslims and believe in only one God, translated as Allah in Arabic Language. They believe that God sent many prophets to provide direction on how to live and the final Prophet was Muhammad. They believe that there are five pillars of Islam, namely, declaration of faith that there is no other God apart from God and Mohammed is his messenger (Shahadah), praying five times daily, fasting, giving to charity, and pilgrimage to Mecca. |
| 9 | **Jainism** | An early philosophy and moral teaching that developed in the 7th to 5th century BCE in India. | The name was formed from the word 'Jina' which refers to 'victor' or 'liberator' in the spiritual context. It focuses on achieving liberation and bliss through living a life of renunciation and harmlessness. |
| 10 | **Jehovah's Witnesses** | A Christian-oriented evangelistic religious movement that originated around the 19th century in the USA. | The followers of this religion hold many of the beliefs consistent with the traditional Christian perspective but also believe in some that are unique to this religious group. They believe that Jehovah (God) is the highest form of God and the Holy Spirit is the active force of God in this world, while Jesus Christ is the agent of God who reconciles sinful humans to God. They also believe that those who accept Jehovah will be rewarded with membership of the millennial kingdom while those who do not acknowledge him will not go to Hell but become totally exterminated. |
| 11 | **Judaism** | Judaism originated in the Middle East over 3500 years ago and is about the covenant relationship of the Jewish people with God. | It revolves around the Jews and their belief that there is only one God who appointed them to be his chosen people to set an example of ethical behaviour and holiness to the world. Their religious document is called the *Torah* and their religious leaders are addressed as Rabbis. |

**TABLE 4.1** (Continued)

| | Religion | Basic descriptor | Further comments |
|---|---|---|---|
| 12 | **Mormonism** | Founded by Joseph Smith in 1830 CE in the US. It is known as The Church of Jesus Christ of Latter-day Saints. | The followers of this religion are known as Mormons, and they believe that they are Christians but with some differences to mainstream Christianity. Their church is known as Latter-day Saints or The Church of Jesus Christ. They do not acknowledge the notion of a trinity but hold the view that the Father, Son, and Holy Ghost are three distinct gods. They believe in an afterlife and that individuals can become gods. The Mormons use a 'Temple garment' which is an underwear with special religious significance that is often used by adult members for hallowed promises to God. |
| 13 | **Paganism** | A topical religious movement with a philosophical perspective on reverence for nature. | The focus of Paganism revolves around the natural world, and Pagans worship many deities. Most of them are eco-friendly thereby keenly interested in minimising damage to the natural environment. Some simply define Paganism as having no specific religion, as people in mainstream religions such as Christianity, Islam, Judaism, and Hinduism refer to people outside of them as Pagans. |
| 14 | **Rastafari** | Originated in the 1930s and has its roots in Jamaica. | It combines mysticism, Protestant Christianity, and a pan-African political consciousness. Members are called Rastas and most of them believe that Haile Selassie I, who was crowned the King of Ethiopia in 1930, is God, who came to redeem all Black people. Part of their religious rituals are prayer sessions and all-night drumming ceremonies. |
| 15 | **Santeria** | Afro-Caribbean syncretic religion that originated from Cuba. | It is not fixed on a set of beliefs but revolves around a blend of several faiths and cultures. It shows a combination of Catholicism, West Africa's Yoruba spirituality, and Caribbean tradition. |

(*Continued*)

**TABLE 4.1** (Continued)

| | Religion | Basic descriptor | Further comments |
|---|---|---|---|
| 16 | **Shinto** | Japanese traditional worldview and ritual with no specific founder. | Adherents are not expected to follow Shinto as the only religion. It focuses on the belief that there are no absolutes as the actions taken by people, whether good or bad, are assessed in relation to the context in which they take place. |
| 17 | **Sikhism** | Founded in the 15th century CE in India by Guru Nanak. | Adherents believe that there is only one God and equality among humans. They are focused on avoiding materialism, anger, covetousness and greed, lust, and pride but embracing working, praying, and giving. |
| 18 | **Spiritualism** | Originated from the USA in mid-19th century and Spiritualists hold that it is possible to communicate with the dead. | It holds that people survive the deaths of their bodies and move into a spirit world. Adherents believe that those who have died and moved to the spirit world have an interest in the lives of those that are still alive. |
| 19 | **Taoism** | Developed from several religious and philosophical customs in early China. | Taosim, which is also known as Daoism, has its philosophical root in nature worship as well as the divination of the Chinese ancestors. It holds that it is imperative for man to put his will to be in harmony with nature. |
| 20 | **Unitarianism** | A liberal religious movement with its origin in the United States. | Even though it has its origin from Jewish and Christian practices, it is open-minded to accommodate insights from other beliefs and grounded in rational enquiry as opposed to external authority. Hence, it revolves around inclusivity and is open to all races, ages, sexual orientations, and religions. |
| 21 | **Zoroastrianism** | Founded by the Iranian prophet Zoroaster. | Adherents believe in the supremacy of God, called Ahura Mazda, and are traditionally keen about protecting the natural environment as they believe that all creations should be loved and respected. |

- **Myth:** Traditional stories that are repeated through which sacredness is maintained;
- **Mystery:** The understanding associated with sacredness transcends cognitive systems but covers things like devotion, love, and fear;
- **Communitas:** Social antistructure that involves people having to shun normal status and roles for status equality;

- **Ecstasy and Flow**: The tendency to create an ecstatic experience that is out of what can be logically obtainable through anything else.

These authors (Belk, Wallendorf, and Sherry, Jr, 1989) also show that sacred consumer domains can be categorised into these six areas:

- Places;
- Times;
- Tangible things;
- Intangibles;
- Persons;
- Experiences.

This categorisation is very telling and valuable as we can see evidence of these and how consumers relate with them in various and varying ways.

## SUBCULTURES

We have learned that cultures define who we are based on values, beliefs, and norms which indicate some degree of homogeneity among us in the settings to which we belong. Meanwhile, a deeper analysis of human systems would show that people are closer in certain contexts than they are in others. For example, while British consumers are identified so because of their settlement and life dynamics in the United Kingdom as a cultural context, there are more identifiable groups within this culture. Identifying these would make it easier for marketers to provide a clearer and more targeted marketing strategy to satisfy their needs. These are known as subcultures which exist within a broader culture. A good number of factors could be used to define these subcultures such as ethnicity, age, gender, and religion. Ultimately, several useful patterns of consumption emerge from this acknowledgement. It is stated that subcultures of consumption show complex, hierarchical structures in a social setting that reflect the status differences of individual members (Schouten and McAlexander, 1995). For instance, Cronin and McCarthy (2011) studied the consumption of fast foods among the video games subculture and found the incidence of social food consumption, with implications for symbolic consumption among gamers, as a key social ritual. In demonstrating how wide the discussion of subcultures can be, Schouten and McAlexander (1995) indicate that everyday activities that we engage in such as woodworking, gardening, and fly-fishing could guide consumption and social activities and constitute subcultures of consumption.

## AGE

Age is a widely known subcultural cue in many societies that could direct marketers on which product to offer to specific age groups and the appropriate use of other marketing-mix elements. Apart from the broad categorisation of child or adult markets, some other common age-related segments used are indicated below with specific dates on age and their dates of birth as teased out from BBC (2021), Beresford Research (2023), Debczak (2019), Solomon (2020), Szmigin and Piacentini (2018).

- Generation X are those born between 1965 and 1980;
- Generation Y are those born between 1981 and 1996;
- Generation Z are those born between the late 1990s and early 2000s;
- Baby boomers are those born between 1946 and 1964;
- Silent generation are those born between 1925 and 1945;
- Teens are those aged between 13 and 18;
- Tweens are those aged between 8 and 12.

## GEOGRAPHICAL SUBCULTURE

People's cultural values and tastes could be based on their geographical locations. Hence, there can be cultural dynamics that show things like regional subculture or state subculture. Interestingly, these give an indication of the consumption of the people in such geographical locations. Many scholars have pinpointed a number of examples relating to the United States. One of these is given by Hoyer et al. (2018) that loose-fitting, brightly coloured, clothing is often associated with sunnier regions of the country like Arizona, Hawaii, and California. Meanwhile, New York was rated as the first in the United States in terms of ordering by mail order, catalogues, Internet, and telephone, while the highest number of purchases of hair growth products was associated with Philadelphia (Doublebase Media Mark Research, 2007; Schiffman et al., 2012). The United Kingdom is another interesting context with useful examples of subcultural patterns. The United Kingdom comprises England, Wales, Scotland, and Northern Ireland with some specific consumption patterns that show how marketers would be doing a better job of targeting a specific country than having a broad cultural focus of the kingdom. For Nigeria, the country is often viewed culturally as different in many layers. The Northern vs Southern regions are culturally different in terms of dressing, foods, language, and many other areas. Similarly, Nigerians in the Eastern part of the country are notably different from those in other regions in relation to beliefs, values, and mores which make it a notable subcultural context of the country. So, it is expected that business segmentation, targeting, and positioning strategies will be formulated and implemented by taking these into consideration.

## SEX-BASED SUBCULTURE

Within a wider culture, the needs and wants of people of a specific gender type make them a subculture as this indicates a consumption pattern that is fairly homogeneous among them. Many products and services indicate this in the marketplace. Things like labelling, packaging, and branding are being used by marketers in their strategic formulation to address these subcultural patterns. The knowledge and acknowledgement of this is not only prevalent among adult consumers. Boys and girls are conscious of these cues even at their early stages of life (Pennell, 1994). Clothing, shoes, hairstyles, handbags, and sanitary products are some of the market offerings that tend to provide the distinction between sex groups, as explained by Avery (2012), when a brand is associated with sex type, it may even be difficult to link it to the opposite sex. This is linked to the school of thought that perceives women and men differently, in which case the former are seen as caregivers while the latter are noted as economically valuable (Littlefield, 2010). However, this stance has been challenged to an extent in relation to the changing economic and political landscape (Borkowska, 2018). Apart from the increasing economic opportunities for women, they are also making an incursion into specific areas that have been noted as traditionally meant for men, which indicates that the notion of masculinity is changing from what it used to be (Nagel, 2017). Similarly, Lida (2005) indicates that some young men are employing feminine aesthetics to practice new masculine identities in what is termed feminisation of masculinity. So, while the sex-related subcultural segmentation is still very potent, marketers need to apply this with caution in view of its dynamic nature and its variation from one society to another.

## RACE AND ETHNIC SUBCULTURES

It is now a common saying that the world has become a global village. One of the ways this is proven is the increasing rate of multiculturalism in society, especially in the developed nations that have attracted significant immigration rates. As an example, the percentage of the non-white population in England and Wales has increased over the years (ONS, 2011) and this trend continues. Among many reasons behind this are the need for better employment, avoidance of political persecution and insecurity in their home countries, the people's desire for better living standards, and educational pursuit, among others (Makgosa, 2012). As they settle in their host countries, they still retain some elements of the cultural values from the home countries and acquire new ones from their host through the process of acculturation, and possess increasing purchasing power. This is evident in their consumption of goods and services. As expected, this has given rise to a strong subcultural system. The resultant heterogeneity indicates that the 'one size fits all' approach might be inappropriate to capture all the peculiarities of the ethnic minority market in Britain (Nwankwo and Lindridge, 1998). Thus, it is understandable why it is stated that effort should be made by actors in these multicultural marketplaces to act in favour of ensuring that all consumer segments can pursue their universal economic, cultural, and social rights in the setting. Many studies around this topic are showing interesting and valuable findings that pinpoint the usefulness of race and ethnicity as a key theme in the understanding of subculture. Gbadamosi (2015b) studied symbolic consumption and brand personification among ethnic minority teenage consumers in the UK and shows that this consumer segment uses symbolic consumption to satisfy their needs for acceptance in society. Similarly, Gbadamosi (2015b) also highlights examples of this as evident in how supermarkets in the UK are now having many dedicated shelves to stock product items specifically relating to ethnic minority groups in the country. It is logical to attribute this to the fact that the market is substantial, growing, and profitable.

A look into subcultures in the United States would show several examples that have significant implications for their consumption and the corresponding marketing strategies formulated to reach and satisfy them. Subcultural groups such as African Americans, Latino-Americans, and Asian-Americans are often identified in society as having some considerable specific consumption behaviour. For instance, it has been shown that the Hispanic American ethnic group tends to engage in online shopping more than the general market in the country (Vann, 2017). A thorough look at other societies will also give some valuable insight into subcultural groups and the implications for their consumption. Exploring such insight in detail can go a long way to differentiate between winning and losing marketers.

## RELIGION-BASED SUBCULTURE

As shown in Table 4.1, there are several religious groups in various societies. Each of these constitutes a subculture in its own right as it gives a more specific explanation of the consumption of people in religious groups. This is because they tend to have fairly homogeneous consumption needs. The beliefs of the adherents of these religions prevent them from using some products, make others selective, and keenly prescribe several others. For instance, it is noted that many Buddhists, Hindus, Sikhs, Rastafarians, and Seventh Day Adventists are vegetarians (Public Health Agency, 2007). It is useful to know that Muslims eat only Halal foods, and Jews eat only Kosher, while the two religions avoid pork products. Apart from foods, several other transactions involving products and services like clothing are patterned by the consumers' religious beliefs. Gbadamosi (2019b) presents findings showing the interaction of ethnicity and religion with reference to Pentecostalism, in which Black African women entrepreneurs are focused on value co-creation to serve members of faith-based organisations with seasoned products and offer bespoke services for them. It is noteworthy that digital transformation now aids how these religion-oriented products are made for consumers in their various locations.

> **PAUSE, PLAN, AND PRACTICE: VALENTINE'S DAY AS A RITUAL FOR CONSUMPTION**
>
> The 14th of February every year is notably an important day for lovers all over the world. Based on its historical antecedents, it is commonly known as Valentine's Day, which people use to specially show love for one another. Apart from being a day when many lovers re-echo their

commitment of love for another, many new lovers use that opportunity to propose marriage to their lovers. The ritual has been in existence for a very long time. About 1 billion cards expressing love messages between consumers are exchanged every year to celebrate this day while around 50 million roses are given out annually on Valentine's Day. Clearly, this has been a business opportunity for many supermarkets over the years as they plan to stock and sell these and other related materials for consumers on the day. Gifts used for Valentine's Day vary, the use of flowers as an expression of love is very common and a significant part of this tradition. However, other items like wrist watches, rings, clothes, and other pieces of jewellery are also commonly associated with the day. Records indicate that more than £1.4 billion was spent on the purchase of greeting cards in 2020 while around 40 million British consumers celebrated the day in 2021. The estimated spending on the day for 2022 is given to be around £1.37 billion. By and large, this aspect of global culture continues to gain momentum every year with significant implications for consumption and marketing.

**QUESTIONS:**

1. Identify any other annual rituals that have a significant implication for consumption;
2. What is your personal consumption experience around Valentine's Day? Compare this to that of your friend, are they similar or different? Why?
3. To what extent does digital transformation influence the consumption experience of Valentine rituals?

**Sources:**

Finder (2022). Valentine's Day spending statistics 2022, https://www.finder.com/uk/valentines-day-statistics (accessed 7 March 2022).

Theholidayspot (nd). Facts about Valentine's Day, theholidayspot.com/valentine/facts.htm (accessed 7 March 2022).

## SUMMARY

Culture defines who we are as a unique society. Characteristically, culture is learned, shared, enduring, arbitrary, dynamic, purpose-driven, and regulates behaviour. It has been explained with various models such as those proposed by Hofstede (1980), Trianids (1994), Hall (1976), and McCracken (1986). Essentially, they reiterate how culture differentiates one society from another such as having high-context and low-context cultures, and how culture moves from one place to another and from the culturally constituted world to consumers. The role of advertising, fashion systems, and rituals such as exchange, possession, grooming, and divestment are considered essential. As we now see digital transformation in marketing communication, the dynamics of culture and consumption have also changed. Topics like popular culture now dominate the discourse of culture. We now see how they interact with topics such as myths and rituals and subcultures in various ramifications.

**DIGITAL BOX: YOUTUBE AND DIGITAL TRANSFORMATION OF POP CULTURE**

Although popular culture dates back to several decades before then, the advent of YouTube in 2005 has transformed the dynamics of this phenomenon. The keen desire of YouTube founders was to devise a means of sharing video to make it popular in a way that is user-friendly. The rate of interaction that takes place on this platform now indicates that this objective has been achieved. Some of the videos on this platform have attracted phenomenal attention. For example, in the account of the Top 10 most viewed videos on YouTube of all time released in 2021, the musical video titled 'Despacito' which is a Spanish word for 'slowly' has over 5 billion views and has also topped the charts in over 45 countries. Following this in popularity are the musical videos titled 'See You Again' and 'Shape of You' with approximately 3.6 and 3.5 billion views, respectively. However, the popularity of these videos is behind that of the catchy kids' song titled 'Baby Shark Dance' with over 9 billion views worldwide. So, YouTube continues to be an important agent for facilitating pop culture globally.

**QUESTION/TASK:**

In a group of 3, 4, or 5, think of a video idea and what could be used to make it go viral. Ensure that its popularity breaks several boundaries like gender, ethnicity, and religion. Make a 'To do list' of this video. To make this a big project, you can execute the plan to address all the issues and steps written on the 'To-do-list'.

**Sources:**

Bennett, R. (2021). Top 10 most viewed videos on YouTube of all time, Filmora video Editor, 23 December 2021, filmora.wondershare.com/vlogger/most-viewed-youtube-videos.html (accessed 30 December 2021).

History Computer (2021), The history of YouTube, history-computer.com/the-history-of-youtube/, History Computer, 4 January 2021 (Accessed 30 December 2021)

## END OF CHAPTER DISCUSSION QUESTIONS

1. In a group of three or more, identify any three aspects of your consumption such as clothing, food, holiday packages, and beauty products. Compare them in terms of the associated cultural values. To what extent do these demonstrate the arbitrariness of culture?
2. The consumption experience of international students in their host countries is of interest to marketers of goods and services. Why should marketers pay particular attention to acculturation of this consumer segment in designing an appropriate marketing strategy for targeting them? Can acculturation be used synonymously as enculturation?
3. What are the marketing implications of the notions of exchange and possession rituals? Do you think there are gender differences in the way these rituals are practised?

IMPACT OF CULTURE AND SUB-CULTURE ON CONSUMER DECISIONS   107

4. Using Belk et al.'s (1989) framework, discuss sacredness in the form of specific places, times, and persons. What lessons can advertisers learn from this in terms of their design of strategic marketing communication messages?
5. Assume you are a new marketing manager of a multinational food company. The findings of a recently conducted marketing research indicate that your target market has three prominent subcultures which are age-based, sex-based, and religion-based. What challenges and benefits are associated with this pattern of your target market and what can be done to address the challenges?

### Case Study: McDonald's in the Middle East: How Businesses are Connecting the World of Consumer Culture

The name McDonald's is a familiar brand all over the world. It is arguably one of the indications of the global consumer culture. Its scope and significance now transcend those noted during its humble beginnings in 1940 in the United States. One of the key factors that underscore its relevance in the global food sector is the speed of service. Many consumer segments are interested in 'food on the go'. Be it in a big shopping mall or moving around the cities, having a meal quickly has been a common ritual among many people. Besides, some are interested in an environment where having a meal and socialisation become intertwined. Accordingly, McDonald's is not only focused on doing these but also doing them with the use of technology such as by using the app, the self-ordering system in the store, and several other factors communicating that it embraces digital transformation. This is consistent with its mission and values, which focus on fostering communities and serving delicious foods to make consumers feel good about eating at affordable prices in convenient locations. Overall, the organisation prides itself in offering consumers a personalised experience in a speedy manner, which emphasises sensitivity to customer needs and commitment to enhancing the customer experience. Meanwhile, one of the challenges in international marketing is the fit of the product or service to local values, customs, and beliefs. McDonald's focuses on this as it expands into different countries and contexts. It now operates in developed countries as well as developing countries and meets consumers' need for fast-food in low-context cultures and high-context cultural settings. Clearly, this involves having a critical alignment of its strategic decisions to expansions and developments.

The presence of the organisation in the Middle East is a noteworthy marketing phenomenon. The business is confronted with the challenge of maintaining its core values as an organisation and ensuring that customers in the local communities are satisfied with their experience without jeopardising their deep-rooted cultural values. One of the very fundamental issues is the composition of the food. For example, consumers in Kuwait, Qatar, Oman, and Saudi Arabia will be keen that their food is consistent with Halal provisions. It was revealed in *The Sun* Newspaper in September 2021 that a McDonald's spokesperson in the UK indicated that their trial of the Halal provision in the United Kingdom shows that it is only popular among a very small percentage of consumers. Hence, changing their operations in favour of that is not an issue of immediate priority as it will require a major strategic shift in their supply chain and kitchen operations. However, this is a big deal in the Middle East. Visitors to the company's websites in the region are reassured in the form of questions and answers that all the food offered has 100% Halal certification with a link to use to verify the authenticity of the claim that is clearly given on the website. So, relevant research into market details about the local environment becomes crucial. From results over the years covering sales, profitability, and the number of outlets in the Middle East, McDonald's has got it right!

Part of the increasing evidence of growth is the establishment of a new restaurant in Abu Dhabi's Al Dhafra area in the first quarter of 2022. This franchise, which is a product of the business partnership between McDonald's and the Al Dhafra Sports and Cultural Club, has a capacity of 30 seats and offers those services considered valuable by consumers such as McCafé, self-ordering kiosk, drive-through service, and McDelivery service. Similarly, in December 2021, McDonald's opened its 200th branch in the Kingdom of Saudi Arabia, which marked its 28th birthday in the Kingdom when considered in relation to its very first branch, which was opened on the 8 December 1993 in Riyadh. This is not surprising as consumers can see McDonald's is sensitive to their cultural values. One of these is the mode of communication. Information provided to consumers, including in the app, is given in English and Arabic. Among the key questions raised by customers in the Middle East is the question of the source of the chicken used by the fast-food giant. The company makes it clear that the products are supplied by MacFood from Malaysia that has a reputation for supplying Halal chicken and meeting the very stringent quality standard of McDonald's. So, McDonald's has shown that culture is a defining factor in consumer behaviour.

**Sources:**

Grealish, S. (2021). I'm loving it: Is McDonald's Halal? *The Sun*, 11 September 2021, www.thesun.co.uk/news/16109778/mcdonalds-halal-menu-items/ (accessed 17 January 2022).

McDonald's (nd). Our mission and values, corporate.mcdonalds.com/corpmcd/our-company/who-we-are/our-values.html (accessed 17 January 2022).

## QUESTIONS

1. What evidence is shown in the case study about the Middle East consumers that shows that culture is purpose-driven and satisfies needs?
2. The case study above indicates that McDonald's is not only focused on providing a quick meal and a friendly environment, but also on achieving this with the use of technology, such as using the app, the self-ordering system in the store, and several other factors, communicating its embrace of digital transformation. Which characteristic of culture is exemplified here?

3. The spokesperson for McDonald's in the United Kingdom indicates that there was no immediate plan to change its operations and systems in favour of Halal provision of their food in the country. Why do you think McDonald's response to the cultural system in the Middle East is different from this?
4. Identify any conceivable sub-cultural segments that McDonald's serves in the Middle East and how the company can operate to serve them better.

## REFERENCES

Arnould, E. J., & Thompson, C. J. (2005). Consumer Culture Theory (CCT): Twenty years of research. *Journal of Consumer Research*, *31*(4), 868–883.

Avery, J. (2012). Defending the markers of masculinity: Consumer resistance to brand gender-bending. *International Journal of Research in Marketing*, 29, 322–336.

Babin, B. J., & Harris, E. J. (2018). *CB8*. Boston: Cengage Learning.

BBC (2020). United Arab Emirates country profile, www.bbc.co.uk/news/world-middle-east-14703998 (accessed 14 December 2021).

BBC (2021). Millennials, baby boomers or Gen Z: Which one are you and what does it mean?, www.bbc.co.uk/bitesize/articles/zf8j92p (accessed 2 January 2022).

Belk, R. W., Wallendorf, M., & Sherry Jr, J. F. (1989). The sacred and the profane in consumer behavior: Theodicy on the odyssey. *Journal of Consumer Research*, *16*(1), 1–38.

Beresford Research (2023). Age range by generations: Generations defined by name, birth year, and ages in 2023, Beresford Research, www.beresfordresearch.com/age-range-by-generation/ (accessed 4 October 2023).

Berry, J. W. (1997). Immigration, acculturation and adaptation. *Applied Psychology: An International Review*, *46*, 5–34.

Berry, J. W. (1994) Acculturation and psychological adaptation, in *Journeys into Cross-cultural Psychology*, ed. A.-M. Bouvy, F. J. R. van de Vijver, P. Boski, and P. Schmitz, Lisse: Swets and Zeitlinger, pp. 129–141.

Borkowska, K. (2020). Approaches to studying masculinity: A nonlinear perspective of theoretical paradigms. *Men and Masculinities*, *23*(3–4), 409–424.

Canavan, B. (2016). Tourism culture: Nexus, characteristics, context and sustainability. *Tourism Management*, *53*, 229–243.

Cherrier, H. (2009). Disposal and simple living: Exploring the circulation of goods and the development of sacred consumption. *Journal of Consumer Behaviour: An International Research Review*, *8*(6), 327–339.

Cronin, J. M., & McCarthy, M. B. (2011). Fast food and fast games: An ethnographic exploration of food consumption complexity among the videogames subculture. *British Food Journal*, *113*(6), 720–743.

Cruz, A. G. B., Seo, Y., & Binay, I. (2019). Cultural globalization from the periphery: Translation practices of English-speaking K-pop fans. *Journal of Consumer Culture*, 1469540519846215.

Czinkota, M. R., & Ronkainen, I. A. (1990). *International Marketing* (2nd ed.), Hinsdale, IL: The Dryden Press.

Debczak, M. (2019). These revised guidelines redefine birth years and classifications for millennials, Gen Z, and Gen Alpha, *Mental Floss*, Dec 6, 2019. Updated: March 10, 2023, www.mentalfloss.com/article/609811/age-ranges-millennials-and-generation-z (accessed 4 October 2023).

Demangeot, C., Broderick, A. J., & Samuel Craig, C. (2015). Multicultural marketplaces: New territory for international marketing and consumer research. *International Marketing Review*, *32*(2), 118–140. https://doi.org/10.1108/IMR-01-2015-0017.

Donga, G., Shambare, R., & Djemilou, M. (2021). A critical examination of the nexus of groups, religion and consumer behaviour: A focus on developing countries, in Gbadamosi, A. and Oniku, C. A. (2021) (eds), *Religion and Consumer Behaviour in Developing Nations*. London: Cheltenham: Edward Elgar, pp. 45–75.

Doublebase Media Mark Research (2007), Doublebase Report.

Earley, P. C., Ang, S., & Tan, J.-S. (2006), *CQ: Developing Cultural Intelligence at Work*. Stanford: Stanford University Press.

Fanea-Ivanovici, M., & Pană, M. C. (2020). From Culture to Smart Culture. How digital transformations enhance citizens' well-being through better cultural accessibility and inclusion. *IEEE Access*, 8, 37988–38000.

Fourali, C. E. (2018). Lecture on ethics in selling. London Metropolitan University.

Fourali, C., & Gbadamosi, A. (2021). Religion and consumer behaviour in developing nations: A look into the future in developing nations, in Gbadamosi, A. and Oniku, C. A. (2021) (eds), *Religion and Consumer Behaviour in Developing Nations*. London: Cheltenham: Edward Elgar, pp. 199–226.

Gbadamosi, A. (2012a). Acculturation: An exploratory study of clothing consumption among Black African women in London (UK), *Journal of Fashion Marketing and Management*, 16(1), 5–20.

Gbadamosi, A. (2012b). Exploring children, family, and consumption behaviour: Empirical evidence from Nigeria, *Thunderbird International Business Review*, 54(4), 591–605.

Gbadamosi, A. (2015a). British supermarkets and multiculturalism in consumer food shopping behaviour, in *Sage Business Cases*, doi: http://dx.doi.org/10.4135/9781473928145 | Online ISBN: 9781473928145.

Gbadamosi, A. (2015b). Brand personification and symbolic consumption among ethnic minority teenage consumers: An empirical study. *Journal of Brand Management*, 22(9), 737–754.

Gbadamosi, A. (2019a). Postmodernism, ethnicity, and celebrity culture in women's symbolic consumption, *International Journal of Market Research*, doi: 10.1177/1470785319868363.

Gbadamosi, A. (2019b). Women-entrepreneurship, religiosity, and value-co-creation with ethnic consumers: Revisiting the paradox. *Journal of Strategic Marketing*, 27(4), 303–316.

Gbadamosi, A. (2021a). A critical overview of religion, culture and consumption in developing nations, in Gbadamosi, A. and Oniku, C. A. (2021) (eds), *Religion and Consumer Behaviour in Developing Nations*. London: Cheltenham: Edward Elgar, pp. 1–24.

Gbadamosi, A. (2021b). Consumption, religion, and digital marketing in developing countries, in Gbadamosi, A. and Oniku, C. A. (2021) (eds), *Religion and Consumer Behaviour in Developing Nations*. London: Cheltenham: Edward Elgar, pp. 175–198.

Gelperowic, R., & Beharrell, B. (1994). Healthy food products for children: Packaging and mothers' purchase decisions, *British Food Journal*, 96(11), 4–8.

Hall, E. T. (1976). *Beyond Culture*. New York: Anchor Press – DoubleDay.

Hofstede, G. (1980). *Culture's Consequences: International Differences in Work-related Values* (Vol. 5). London: Sage.

Hofstede, G. (1984). *Culture's Consequences: International Differences in Work-related Values* (abridged edition), 2nd edn, London: Sage.

Hofstede, G. (2001). Culture's Consequences: Comparing Values, Behaviors, Institutions and Organizations Across Nations, 2nd edn., London: Sage.

Hoyer, W. D., MacInnis, D. J., & Pieters, R. (2018). *Consumer Behaviour*, 7th edn, Boston: Cengage Learning.

Kim, D., Pan, Y., & Park, H. S. (1998). High- versus low-context culture: A comparison of Chinese, Korean, and American cultures. *Psychology & Marketing*, 15(6), 507–521.

Kim, K., & Oh, C. (2002). On distributor commitment in marketing channels for industrial products: Contrast between the United States and Japan. *Journal of International Marketing*, 10(1), 72–97.

Kipnis, E., Broderick, A. J., & Demangeot, C. (2014). Consumer multiculturation: Consequences of multi-cultural identification for brand knowledge. *Consumption Markets and Culture*, 17(3), 231–253. https://doi.org/10.1080/ 10253866.2013.778199.

Lee, J. A. (2000). Adapting Triandis's model of subjective culture and social behavior relations to consumer behavior. *Journal of Consumer Psychology*, 9(2), 117–126.

Lee, J. Y. (2009). Contesting the digital economy and culture: Digital technologies and the transformation of popular music in Korea. *Inter-Asia Cultural Studies*, 10(4), 489–506.

Lee, S., & Bai, B. (2016). Influence of popular culture on special interest tourists' destination image. *Tourism Management*, 52, 161–169.

Lida, Y. (2005). Beyond the 'feminization of masculinity': Transforming patriarchy with the 'feminine' in contemporary Japanese youth culture. *Inter-Asia Cultural Studies*, 6(1), 56–74.

Littlefield, J. (2010). Men on the hunt: Ecofeminist insight into masculinity. *Marketing Theory*, 10(1), 97–117.

Makgosa, R. (2012). Ethnic diversity in Britain: A stimulus for multicultural marketing. *Marketing Intelligence & Planning*, 30(3), 358–378.

Mark, J. J. (2020). Thanksgiving Day: A brief history, *World History Encyclopaedia*, www.worldhistory.org/article/1646/thanksgiving-day-a-brief-history/ (accessed 10 July 2023).

McCracken, G. (1986). Culture and consumption: A theoretical account of the structure and movement of the cultural meaning of consumer goods. *Journal of Consumer Research*, 13(1), 71–84.

McLeod, J. M. (1974). Commentaries on Ward, 'Consumer Socialization', *Journal of Consumer Research*, 1(September), 15–17.

Nagel, J. (2017). The continuing significance of masculinity. *Ethnic and Racial Studies*, 40(9), 1450–1459.

Nwankwo, S., & Lindridge, A. (1998). Marketing to ethnic minorities in Britain. *Journal of Marketing Practice: Applied Marketing Science*, 4, 200–216.

Onkvisit, S. and Shaw, J. J. (1993). *International Marketing: Analysis and Strategy*, 2nd edn, New York: Macmillan.

ONS (2011). Population estimates by ethnic group 2002–2009. Statistical Bulletin, 18 May 2011, http://www.statistics.gov.uk/downloads/theme_population/PEEG-statistical-bulletin.pdf (accessed 6 August 2011).

Ou-sekou, Y., & Zaid, A. (2021). Characterizing the digital culture of prospective primary school teachers. *Education Research International*, 2021.

Özsomer, A. (2019). Some recent influences on global consumer culture: Digital networked technologies, emerging market brands and bottom of the pyramid consumers. *International Marketing Review*, 36(4), 548–552.

Paloutzian, R. F. (2017). *Invitation to the Psychology of Religion*, 3rd edn, New York: Guilford Press.

Pennell, G. E. (1994). Babes in toyland: Learning an ideology of gender, in *Advances in Consumer Research*, edited by Chris T. Allen and Deborah Roedder John. Provo, UT: Association for Consumer Research.

Prensky, M. (2001). *Digital Natives, Digital Immigrants Part 1*, pp. 5, 200.

Public Health Agency (2007). Guidance on foods for religious faith. Department of Education and the Department of Health, Social Services and Public Safety, www.publichealth.hscni.net/sites/default/files/FaithsPosterA2.pdf (accessed 22 January 2022).

Raphael, J., & Lam, C. (2018). The function of hosts: Enabling fan–celebrity interactions at pop culture conventions. *Continuum*, 32(2), 173–183.

Rehn, A. (2008). Pop (culture) goes the organization: On highbrow, lowbrow and hybrids in studying popular culture within organization studies. *Organization*, 15(5), 765–783.

Rieff, D. (1993). A global culture? *World Policy Journal*, 10(4), 73–81.

Roberts, K. A. (1984). *Religion in Sociological Perspective*, Homewood, IL: Dorsey Press.

Samiee, S. (2019). Reflections on global brands, global consumer culture and globalization. *International Marketing Review*, 36(4) 536–544.

Schiffman, L. G., Kanuk, L. L., & Hansen, H. (2012). *Consumer Behaviour: A European Outlook*, 2nd edn., Harlow: Pearson Education Limited.

Schiffman, L. G., Kanuk, L. L., & Wisenblit, J. (2010). *Consumer Behaviour*, 10th edn., New Jersey: Pearson Education Inc.

Schmidt, R., Sager, G. C., Carney, G., Jackson, J. J., Zanca, K., Muller, A., & Jackson, J. (1999). *Patterns of Religion*. Belmont, CA: Wadsworth Publishing.

Schouten, J. W., & McAlexander, J. H. (1995). Subcultures of consumption: An ethnography of the new bikers. *Journal of Consumer Research*, 22(1), 43–61.

Smith, P. B., & Bond, M. H. (2019). Cultures and persons: Characterizing national and other types of cultural difference can also aid our understanding and prediction of individual variability. *Frontiers in Psychology*, *10*, 2689.

Solomon, M. R. (2020). *Consumer Behaviour: Buying, Having, and Being*, 13th edn, Essex: Pearson Education Limited.

Spears, M. C., Parker, D. F., & McDonald, M. (2004). Globalization attitudes and locus of control, *Journal of Global Business*, 15(29), 57–64.

Szmigin, I., & Piacentini, M. (2018). *Consumer Behaviour*. Oxford: Oxford University Press.

The Snacks Magazine (1993). Crunchtime for kids – Minors present major challenges, (June) 35–41.

Travel China Guide (nd). *Chinese Year History*. www.travelchinaguide.com/essential/holidays/new-year/history.htm#:~:text=Timeline%20of%20Chinese%20New%20Year%20%20%20,%20%20Chunjie%20%204%20more%20rows%20 (accessed 14 December 2021).

Triandis, H. C. (1994). *Culture and Social Behavior*. New York: McGraw-Hill.

Vann, L. (2017). Amazon opens its doors to millions of Hispanic shoppers. *Engage: Hispanic, Media Post*, 7th July, www.mediapost.com/publications/article/304033/amazon-opens-its-doors-to-millions-of-hispanic-sho.html (accessed 22 January 2022).

Ward, S. (1974), 'Consumer Socialization', *Journal of Consumer Research*, 1, (Sept), 1–14

Whang, H., Yong, S., & Ko, E. (2016). Pop culture, destination images, and visit intentions: Theory and research on travel motivations of Chinese and Russian tourists. *Journal of Business Research*, 69(2), 631–641.

# CHAPTER 5

# Reference Groups, Social Class, and Consumer Behaviour

**LEARNING OBJECTIVES**

After reading this chapter, you should be able to:

- Explain reference groups and evaluate their various types in relation to consumer behaviour;
- Understand the impact of social identity theory on consumer behaviour;
- Critically discuss family as a key influence on consumer behaviour;
- Demonstrate an understanding of consumer socialisation;
- Analyse the relevance of social classes to consumer behaviour;
- Critically discuss the emerging trend in brand community and its roles in consumption;
- Evaluate the role of opinion leaders in consumer behaviour.

**INTRODUCTION**

We are connected to many people in various circumstances. Workplaces, places of residence, family, places of worship, schools, and several other areas have proved to be good avenues for fulfilling our social needs. These associations play important roles in how we consume. Social media platforms like Facebook, Tinder, Instagram, X, and many others are examples of opportunities for social interaction that have been made possible through development in digitisation. Consumers on these platforms share stories, and exchange photographs, videos, and other content to prompt interactions from others. Reactions such as indicating likeness or commenting on the contents are commonplace. As consumers interact both offline and online, the influence of these associations is on the increase in various ways. Some associations are more applicable to certain consumer segments than others. For example, the use of the Internet and social media platforms is more common among young consumers than

DOI: 10.4324/9781003242031-7

others. Besides, there are variations in the social media preferences of those who are using them. So, one may belong to the same social groups offline but have different social media preferences. Accordingly, marketers are expected to study these patterns as they will find that knowledge useful in planning to meet the growing and ever-dynamic needs of consumers. We will be looking at issues that revolve around how social groups influence consumption in this chapter.

## REFERENCE GROUPS AND CONSUMER BEHAVIOUR

Humans are social beings who develop various connections to other people to form groups. The discomfort expressed in different ways during the Covid-19 pandemic, when social associations were significantly curtailed, is a testament to this contention. As consumers, we are linked to people in our residences, we interact with people in our places of employment, we share consumption ideas with others in places of religious worship, and we emulate others in our ethnic groups and many other contexts. These are just examples of numerous associations we keep. These various groups tend to influence our consumption decisions in various ways. This is the key focus in our discussion of reference groups. By definition, the term is used to describe a group that a consumer uses as a framework of evaluation of the fitness of consumption choices. Table 5.1 shows various types of reference groups.

During a period of enrolment on a programme and studying for a qualification, one is in the in-group of other fellow students whereas, after graduation, the status has changed from being a student to becoming an alumnus which is an 'out-group'. From

**TABLE 5.1** Types of reference groups

| | Reference Group Type | Meaning/Implications |
|---|---|---|
| 1 | In-group | A group that one is currently a member of. |
| 2 | Out-group | A group that one does not belong to. |
| 3 | Dissociative/ Avoidance group | A group one is motivated to avoid and distances himself or herself from because of their values. |
| 4 | Formal group | A group that one belongs to that has some form of structure with guidelines for the behaviour of members. |
| 5 | Informal group | Even though members of this group share many things in common, there are no hard and fast rules or formalities guiding members' behaviour. |
| 6 | Aspirational group | A group one admires and aspires to associate with. People in this group are usually those who have established themselves in their chosen career and endeavours such as sports personalities, musical artists, politicians, celebrities, and others. |
| 7 | Disclaimant group | A group of which one is presently a member but wishes to separate from. |

**Source**: Adapted from: White and Dahl (2007), Gbadamosi (2015), Szmigin and Piacentini (2022), Solomon (2020)

this, we can see that it is not all 'out-groups' that can be described as an avoidance group. An out-group may be a group that one may still join in the future but there is a negative disposition towards an avoidance or dissociative group. The findings of White and Dahl (2007) explain this further as they found that consumers exhibited a greater inclination to avoid market offerings that are associated with dissociative groups than with out-groups. Another way of explaining this is through the use of the balanced theory proposed by Heider (1946). It is stated that if one known as 'P' has a positive attitude towards someone to be known as 'O' and that person 'O' has a positive attitude towards an object denoted as (x), then 'P' will also show a positive attitude to the same object. In a subsequent publication, Heider (1958) contends that since the person 'P' favours balanced conditions, if the triad system is not balanced, the person 'P' has the following options:

(a) Change the relationship s/he has with the person 'O';
(b) Amend the relationship to the object;
(c) Make effort to change the relationship the person 'O' has with the object.

In applying this perspective to symbolic brand meaning and reference group, Hammerl et al. (2016) found that people who have a strong self-brand connection (SBR) with an in-group brand also attribute a very high symbolic meaning to such a brand, which is not the case for those who have a weak SBR with the brand of that in-group. As defined by Wei and Yu (2012), the term self-brand connection is the psychological association that an individual has with a brand. For a particular brand, this could be high for an individual while that of another person could be very low.

## SOCIAL IDENTITY THEORY

The main crux of the social identity theory is that we can conceptualise individual identity into two, namely personal and social (Wei and Yu, 2012). Personal component focuses on an individual's identity (more of this will be discussed in Chapter 10). On the other hand, social identity is that self-concept that an individual gets from their knowledge of being a member of a social group or groups as well as the value of emotional significance attached to that group (Tajfel, 1982a, b; 1986). We can link this to another relevant aspect of social interaction known as **impression management theory** which was conceptualised by Goffman (1959). It is about strategically influencing other people's view of a person through his or her appearance. So, we can illustrate it as individuals carefully operating in social interactions with props, costumes, and masks to cultivate the impression others will have concerning them (Schulz, 2015). Ultimately, it is a process of self-verification which also has three sub-process which are highlighted below (Swann, 1987):

**Selective interaction:** This is about choosing which public space to interact in that will also lead to which specific group of people the individual will interact with;

**Displaying identity cues:** This is about the displaying of certain cues such as clothing, hairstyle, cell phone, cars, or other items to people in these social settings to communicate his or her identity;

**Interaction strategies:** This is the behavioural pattern exhibited while communicating directly with other people in social settings.

Put together, as people operate in various social settings, they are encouraged by the feedback, clues, and hints they get from others about their items shown. This illustration is a way of presenting the reference group topic as an imagined audience where the individual is the actor, and the members of the social settings are the audience (Swann, 1987).

More often than not, marketers tune their strategies to get the best from consumers' association or dissociation with groups. For example, a comparative marketing communication message such as advertising might link competing products or services to dissociative groups of their target market, thereby highlighting its negative value (White and Dahl, 2007). This is because consumers tend to avoid products, services, or brands that are associated with dissociative groups (White and Dahl, 2007).

Many have argued that the use of digital technology has significantly reduced the impact of social groups on consumption as technology now encroaches on the time that people used to have together in groups. To what extent do you agree with this?

## FAMILY AND CONTEMPORARY CONSUMER BEHAVIOUR

Family, as a phenomenon, has been a fundamental part of society with huge implications for consumption. Irrespective of one's current status, he or she belongs to a particular family. To discuss the relevance of family to consumption, we will look at categorisations of family. One of the common family structures identifies three types which are:

- Nuclear family;
- Extended family;
- Stem family.

The nuclear family is the most basic of all. It consists of the couple as parents and their children in the same household. As the name indicates, the extended family structure has many more members than what is commonly associated with the nuclear family system. It consists of the nuclear family and some members of its multiple generations staying together in the same house. For example, the grandparents, cousins, uncles, and other family members staying with the family constitute an extended family. While the nuclear family is very common in developed countries in the West, extended family structure is prevalent in places like Sub-Sahara Africa, Asia, and the Middle East (Hota and Bartsch, 2019). Meanwhile, the stem family structure is different from these two and can be of three types (Hota and Bartsch, 2019). The first type has the parents and their children who are unmarried in the household but with one of these children, his or her spouse, and their children living with them. The second type is the one which consists of a couple and one young married couple that has not got children living together. The third type consists of one parent who is either divorced or widowed living together with a married child, spouse, and their children.

In the second categorisation of family structure, we have two types which are:

- Family of orientation;
- Family of procreation.

Considering consumption from the perspective of a family of orientation, it means that the consumer is being influenced by parents. Even at maturity, in some cases, consumers' decisions may be influenced by their parents and relatives, which indicates the influence of his or her family of orientation. As an example, decisions about the purchase of houses in specific locations may benefit from the wealth of experience of the parents. Meanwhile, a family of procreation is the one that one is linked to by virtue of marriage. Hence, couples are in a family of procreation, and they consume and are influenced as such when making decisions that border on their family, including addressing the children's needs.

Part of the interesting issues in family consumption dynamics is the role played by each of the couples in the household purchases. Many studies have shown that women are primarily involved in innovative purchase decision making for a good number of products such as groceries and electronic products (Burns, 1992; Hamilton, 2009). As expected, decisions are not always conflict-free between the couple or in the family as a whole including children. Many times, members of the family would have disparate needs and opinions on consumption within the budgetary constraints of the family. The wife may be very keen about the need to fulfil the family's needs for a holiday at a choice location, while the husband might think such could be sacrificed for a year in order to be able to get a new family car. Similarly, children might be interested in games and, as mentioned in the literature, one of their tactics is to simply ask and they expect the need to be met without hesitation (Gbadamosi, 2012). When such conflicts arise, they make efforts to resolve them. Four of the commonly used approaches for resolving family conflicts are given by Sheth (1974) as:

- Bargaining;
- Persuasion;
- Problem-solving;
- Politics.

When bargaining is used, the conflict is resolved by the spirit of 'give and take'. For example, a member of the family will forgo the choice of his or her desire while another pleasant offer is given to him or her as a form of resolution of the current conflict. A demand for a visit to Disney by the children could be bargained for a longer visit if it is delayed to a later date. Persuasion often involves begging to resolve the conflict (Palan and Wilkes, 1997; Gbadamosi, 2012). When they use problem-solving tactics, they search for further information about the purchase. For example, when there is conflict about which type or brand to choose and there are different views leading to the conflict, engaging in a further search for information from various other sources can provide validation and confirmation for specific alternatives among several others. The use of politics involves the coming together of some members of the family on specific decisions to make and then isolating the family members with a dissenting view or using a coalition to compel him or her to agree with the others (Sheth, 1974; Hamilton, 2009). Meanwhile, apart from resolving family conflicts associated with consumption issues, they also avoid such conflicts through the use of some other strategies as identified in the finding of the study of Hamilton (2009). One of these is to allocate budget responsibility to a member of the family which could also include the purchase of the item, while another is to be open about the financial situation of the family. Another one found in the study is to yield to the request of the children.

## FAMILY BUYING ROLES

Since family consumption revolves around a group of people whether in the form of couples without children, those with children, or another form of family structure discussed above, it involves certain roles that are played by its members. It has been established over the years that members of a household play the role of:

- Initiators;
- Influencers;
- Deciders;
- Users;
- Buyers;
- Gatekeepers.

As shown in Figure 5.1, these roles are complementary. In this, the initiator brings up the idea to buy a product or service while an influencer is someone whose views support the idea introduced by the initiator. The decider makes the decision around the purchase covering issues such as when to buy, where to buy it from, and in what quantity. The buyer does the actual purchase of the product, while the gatekeepers control the flow of information between the marketers and the family; and the users consume the product or services.

How these roles are played by members of the family tend to vary by which products or services are involved, the circumstance of purchase, and other factors. For instance, while the father could be seen as the decider in some cases because some societies typically see men as breadwinners for their home who control most of the resources, this has changed to an extent as some women are in a better position financially and the changes in socio-cultural factors indicate that women take

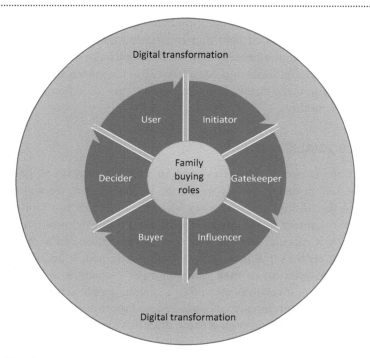

**FIGURE 5.1** Digital transformation and the family buying roles

more key decisions in home purchases than they used to several decades before now. Similarly, while the role of the purchase of household products is typically associated with women, the increasing trend of single fathers in the society indicates that this viewpoint is not generally applicable. Moreover, the role of children in families is becoming strengthened. They are no longer 'mere users' of the product and services but active participants, in some respects, in their household decisions across various other roles. For example, Gbadamosi (2012) found that children participate as decision makers in purchases of routine items like confectioneries and other 'low ticket' local refreshments and in some cases are consulted in decisions of special products. As shown in Figure 5.1, the ways these roles are played in the modern environment are influenced by digital transformation. This is one of the key reasons why children's influence in family decisions is becoming stronger as they have access to marketplace information through digital technological means (Broniarczyk and Griffin, 2014; Bertol et al. 2017). The following are three primary reasons that underpin children as consumers (Sheth et al., 1999; Bertol et al., 2017):

- They have their own preferences for products and services purchased by their parents;
- They have their own money that they use for products meant for their use;
- They influence purchases of goods and services to be shared by the family.

Interestingly, as children learn consumption behaviour and are influenced by various factors and agents as discussed below in consumer socialisation, their parents also relearn from them through a process that is called reverse socialisation (Hyatt et al., 2018). In a related study, Essiz and Mandrik (2021) reported the intergenerational influence on sustainable consumption and found that daughters exert significant influence on their mothers.

## CONSUMER SOCIALISATION

Social interactions between consumers come in a variety of ways. A primary part of this is the one maintained by family members. In this section, we will be discussing the one related to children and how they learn the act of consumption. This is the specific focus of consumer socialisation. We will refer to the definition of Ward (1974) of the term which is succinct and valuable to the explanation of the term. Using this, we can define the term as 'the process by which young people acquire skills, knowledge, and attitudes relevant to their functioning as consumers in the marketplace' (Ward, 1974: p. 2). So, it revolves around how young people acquire consumer skills in relation to attitudes, preferences as well as consumption-related knowledge (Kim et al., 2009). A major question now is 'how does this actually work?' So, the significant role of socialisation agents comes to the fore. Over the years, studies have shown that young consumers learn from these socialisation agents as shown in Figure 5.1. Clearly, the idea of learning about consumption for young consumers is a complex one and these agents offer them opportunities on these key areas as shown in extant literature (Carlson and Grossbart, 1988; Rose 1999; Hota and Bartsch, 2019):

- Participation in purchasing decisions;
- Gaining autonomy in consumption;

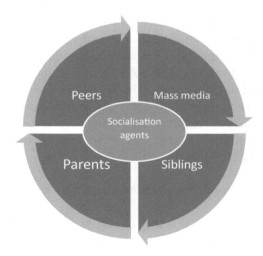

**FIGURE 5.2** Socialisation agents

- Communicating about consumption;
- Restriction of consumption in media exposure.

Over the years these socialisation agents have been identified as very influential to how young consumers develop the relevant skills in relation to consumption. Evidence shows that the social and cognitive developments of children from birth to adolescence serve as pathways for their evolution into consumers (John, 1999). As we experience changes in socio-cultural factors in the society where both parents are becoming engaged in economic activities that consume a lot of their time, children are spending considerably more time with their siblings. This is the focus of the study of Kerrane et al. (2015) whose findings show that siblings act as significant opinion leaders giving them up-to-date knowledge around consumption. This is also consistent with the findings of Gbadamosi (2015) which revolves around symbolic consumption and brand personification among ethnic minority teenagers in the UK where the young consumers see their siblings as trailblazers in relation to brands and consumers.

Parents are very close to their children, which explains their roles in their socialisation. In some cases, children follow their parents on shopping trips, discuss marketing communication messages, and engage in a series of questions and answers on consumption issues. These interactions between parents and children vary, especially in relation to age. For instance, it has been shown that between the age of 6 and 8, children are already aware of the notion of shopping (Feenstra et al, 2015; in Thaichon, 2017). At a level, some children have their own monies and are allowed to exercise their purchasing skills by their parents. They get money from gifts given to them by parents and grandparents on special occasions such as when they get good grades in their education, in some cases from family friends. With these they buy regular items (Gbadamosi, 2012), others even buy items like trainers and MP3 players. There are many studies that have been conducted on parents' role in their children's socialisation over the past years. One of them specifically shows that the communication orientation of mothers influences how adolescents make a purchase decision and influence family consumption activities (Kim et al., 2009). Consumer socialisation literature identifies four types of parents in terms of family communication patterns as follows (Baxter and Clark, 1996; Kim et al., 2009):

- **Laissez-faire parents**: Have little influence on the socialisation of their children as they have little communication with them;
- **Protective parents**: Are very keen on achieving social harmony, emphasise obedience, and restrict their children in terms of the limit of exposure they have to marketplace information;
- **Consensus parents**: Encourage autonomy for the children but are still desirous of maintaining their control as parents on children's marketplace activities;
- **Pluralistic parents**: Are devoted to issue-oriented communication and are keen for their children to have competence and skills related to consumption.

As parents use different styles to communicate with their children and adopt different practices, they tend to do this to achieve different purposes (Kim et al., 2015). Besides, it is also important to note that in some cases, there can be father-mother differences in how these are deployed (Kim et al., 2015). By and large, the nature of the family influences children's consumption behaviour. This reflects in the findings of the study of Rindfleisch et al. (1997) which shows that young adults that are from households with separated or divorced parents show higher levels of compulsive buying and materialism than those whose parents' relationship is still intact. The reason for this has been stated to be because children from divorced or separated parents have low self-esteem and use material objects to boost this aspect of their life (Holdnack, 1992).

While these are noted as primary agents, we can stretch the discussion to include a number of other related agents. While parents and siblings are involved as shown, children may also learn the act of consumption from grandparents. The general discussion of family influence as a social factor in consumption is presented in an early section of this chapter. Similarly, the reference to peers in Figure 5.1 also means that those peers could be from schools, they may be their neighbours who are playmates, and others from churches, mosques, synagogues, or other various places of religious gathering.

The mass media cover TV, radio, and other media where children can pick up cues about consumption. These are various means by which marketers make favourable mention of the goods and services they offer. Children spend a significant amount of time watching TV programmes every day with an increasing number of channels devoted to their entertainment. These are being used by marketers to promote various products. Children are also exposed to different brands as they interact in various places including in schools and playgrounds. Of late, the scope of this has become increasingly widened with the use of the Internet and social media platforms for marketing activities. It has been shown that 89% of children aged 10–15 reported that they are online every day (ONS, 2021).

The impact of these agents also vary by several factors such as age, as what influences adolescents tends to be different from what propels the consumer socialisation of other categories of children. The study of Hota and Bartsch (2019) shows that as children become older, they have more contact with extended family members and engage more in peer-group communications. For example, digital transformation has introduced social media interactions as an influence on consumption, which adds to the level of influence adolescents are exposed to compared to younger children. While children tend to use technology, especially the Internet, in relation to shopping and in some cases with the help and supervision of their parents (Thaichon and Quach, 2016; Thaichon, 2017), this will tend to be more prominent among older children. A report shows that no less than 26% of consumers in the UK engage in regular online grocery shopping (Mintel, 2014); with the developments around COVID-19, it is logical to argue that this number continues to increase. The peer communications that take place online influence consumer socialisation and purchases either directly or indirectly. As shown by Wang et al. (2012), the direct influence of this is conformity in relation to consumption issues while the indirect aspect takes place through reinforcement of product involvement. So, social media offers marketers opportunities to interact and engage with potential consumers, and foster a sense of intimacy between them and the consumers as well as forge continued relationships (Mersey et al., 2010; Wang et al., 2012).

## FAMILY LIFE CYCLE

The family life cycle (FLC) refers to the cyclical process of life stages of a family in relation to members' age, size of the family, and employment status of the head of household (Schiffman and Wisenblit, 2019). Studying the consumption pattern in relation to this will show interesting dynamics. Ultimately, the key point to note on this, is that as a family moves from one stage to another, their consumption pattern changes. For example, the purchase of baby wipes is unlikely to be a common item of purchase for couples in the post-parenthood or dissolution but will be a frequently bought item for those at the parenthood stage. Accordingly, this will help marketers in the design of appropriate marketing strategies to be sure they are of good fit for the target markets. For example, disposable income will vary between these different phases of a cycle. A great deal of scholarship effort has been done on this topic such as the work of Wells and Guba (1966) and Du and Kamakura (2006). Instead of moving in and out of various versions of this phenomenon, we will use the one in Figure 5.3 as presented, as it covers most of the salient phases in the cycle, and we will make it into an exercise where you, as the reader of this book, will be able to present alternatives based on experiences you have regarding family in various countries and societies.

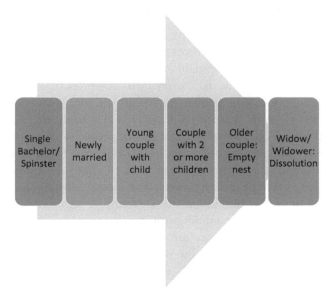

**FIGURE 5.3** An example of a family life cycle model

Pause for a moment and think of the speed of going into the supermarket and getting all you need within a short time compared to when you accompany your parents to do the shopping for the family. Apart from the differences in time, and the mode of doing the shopping, you'll probably notice some differences in the items bought such as the quantity and the types of offers you'll find attractive. Hence, while digital transformation has made the way we shop easier, the quantity and pattern of consumption will still reflect the differences between individual families. This is a part of the significance of the FLC on consumer behaviour as well as marketing theory and practice.

While the FLC illustrative diagram given here is useful to understand the concept, we need to acknowledge some salient points for extending our knowledge on the topic in relation to the present day.

The pattern might vary with culture and circumstances of life such as the following:

- Some couples might decide not to have children in the early days of their marriage and wait until they are older;
- Some are divorced and raise children as single parents;
- Some couples are in a same-sex marriage with different dynamics of family system;
- Some are widowed and are remarrying, even at old age, for many reasons like companionship;
- Some grandparents take care of some of their grandchildren on an ongoing basis;
- Some families operate a stem family system where both or one of the parents live with an older married child with his or her spouse and their children living with them.

## SOCIAL CLASSES AND CONSUMER BEHAVIOUR

We live in a world that is characterised by inequity in many ways. The society is hierarchical as some have access to resources more than others and this reflects in their consumption dynamics. This is the main crux in the discussion of social class which explains the ranking of people in the society into categories based on certain factors which include occupation, educational qualifications, and income. A seminal perspective on this was given by Warner and Lunt (1941) with the definition of the term, which states that it refers to two or more orders of people who are not only believed to be ranked by community members but are so classified to be in socially inferior or superior positions. By this, members of each of these positions have approximately comparable esteem in the community and interact socially among themselves (Sivadas, 1997). Essentially, looking at this structure, a very easy classification that will serve as the basis for understanding others is to see the society as having those who are wealthy at the top, those who are at the base of the hierarchy, and those that are in the middle often identified as the middle-class. To a great extent, this aligns with the perspective of Giddens (1973) who states that three key social elements produce a three-part model of class structuring that tends to be common in modern capitalist societies. And these are identified to be:

- Property;
- Professional skills or education;
- Manual labour.

So from these, three power points are established in the society with the upper class being known for owning property, which also leads to control of means of production, while the middle-class are people who do not own property but obtain power position in the social hierarchy through the professional skills or education they have acquired (Giddens, 1973; Aydin, 2006). According to this perspective, the lower or working class are at the bottom of the social order and only involved in manual labour in order to get subsistence wages.

Even though this classification is simple and easy to understand, the classes are often more than three as there are other classes within these with identifiable characteristics that distinguish them from others. These classifications vary from one society to another. We will look at two of these in this chapter. The first is presented by Koter and Armstrong (2018) to depict American social classes:

- Upper uppers;
- Lower uppers;
- Upper middles;
- Middle class;
- Working class;
- Upper lowers;
- Lower lowers.

The second one is that related to the United Kingdom in the 21st century, which shows the following seven social classes as proposed by Mike Savage from London School of Economics (Horton, 2015):

- Elite;
- Established middle class;
- Technical middle class;
- New affluent workers;
- Traditional working class;
- Emergent service workers;
- Precariat.

Overall, there is a common point across these two examples that is noteworthy. The hierarchies in the two societies show that consumers at the top classes are ranked higher in terms of their endowment of the social class indicators than those at the lower classes. This reflects in the consumption patterns of the classes and their response to many other issues in the society. It has been shown that consumers in the lower-class exhibit lower interest in global consumption and are less likely to be interested in high levels of cosmopolitanism (Carlson et al.,

2017; Aljukhadar et al., 2021). On the other hand, those at the upper level are more disposed to globalised consumption and benefit more from social networks associated with cosmopolitanism (Skovgaard-Smith and Poulfelt, 2018). Another related point was discussed in the publication of Bihagen (1999) titled 'How do classes make use of their income?' In this, and with reference to a body of literature including Bourdieu (1984) and Veblen (1953), it is explained that consumption can be used for social exclusion in three ways, which are:

- Snobbism;
- Transmission of tacit knowledge;
- Achieving information advantage.

When consumption is used for snobbism, consumers in the upper class show contempt for the consumption pattern of those in the lower classes. Tacit knowledge is not easy to transfer to others, but members of the higher classes might use access to resources to be able to acquire this. It is noted that members of the top class may not only have information advantage but often pass this to their children, which also enables them to become members of the class (Douglas and Isherwood, 1979; Bihagen, 1999). In their study about the middle-class, Banerjee and Duflo (2008) note that those in this class live healthier lives than the poor, tend to have steady well-paying jobs, and they run businesses but only while they are still relatively poor, and will be quite content to discontinue the business if they can find good salaried employment. So, ultimately, the purchasing power of the middle-class is very significant. In fact, it is shown that countries with a larger middle-class tend to grow faster, at least, if the class ethnic diversity is not too high (Easterly, 2001; Banerjee and Duflo, 2008).

The relationship between social class and income has been an area of interest over the years in relation to the question of which is more influential on consumer behaviour. Studies have shown that the influence of each of these varies with the nature of the product. For instance, Mihić and Čulina (2006) found that social class proved to be more influential in purchase of furniture design and theatre attendance. On the other hand, income is a better indicator of purchases of inconspicuous products that have significant expenditures such as insurance policies and alcoholic drinks.

## BRAND COMMUNITY

Consumers' social relationships also extend to products and brands as indicated in the marketing literature (Aaker, 1997; Fournier, 1998, Gbadamosi, 2015). Some parts of this relationship get them involved in being members of various brand communities where the focus is primarily on the brand. Essentially, we can explain a brand community as a specialised, non-geographically bound community that is underpinned by a structured set of social relationships that exists among users of a particular brand, and members have a common understanding that they have a shared identity

(Muniz and O'Guinn, 2001). It is a phenomenon closely linked to value co-creation in marketing. With this, the firm or business is not the only party involved in creating value or ensuring that market offerings meet the needs of the consumers. Hence, consumers are also actively involved not only as consumers that benefit from the brand but as active participants in ensuring the fit of the product or services, and brand community is one of the ways of doing that. In doing this, according to McAlexander et al. (2002), we can have four types of relationships in a brand community, which are:

- Between the customer and the brand;
- Between the customer and the brand in use;
- Between the customer and the firm;
- Between the customer and other customers.

Clearly, brand community supports the brand and the customer in a number of ways. Essentially, the spreading of word-of-mouth communication (WOM) about the brand is a key aspect of this issue. It supports relationship marketing that indicates that businesses can have a competitive advantage for maintaining long-term relationships with their customers rather than focusing on just individual transactions (Grönroos, 1989; 2000).

If we examine this perspective properly, we can provide a reasonable link to the claim of Ellemers et al. (1999), who present three components of social identification as:

- Cognitive;
- Evaluative;
- Emotional.

According to these authors, the cognitive component is about awareness of being a member of the group, while the evaluative is about negative or positive implications associated with the group, and the emotional component relates to members' involvement. From this, we can see that joining a brand community is not only in favour of the brand. It plays some role in the lives of the members also. As we now know, we live in a world connected digitally and this also plays some part in brand community, its formation, membership, and their dynamics. From our experiences of digital technology tools, we now know that you can be anywhere in the world and be in a brand community without having face-to-face interaction with members of the community. Schembri and Latimer's (2016) study on online brand communities indicates that online brand culture is constructed and co-constructed in four ways which are:

- Construction of self;
- Storytelling;
- Emotional relationships;
- Ritualistic practices.

As is the case in symbolic consumption in which consumers use their consumption to express their personality, indicate class, and express their distinctness, joining a brand community also tends to aid the consumer in identity construction, aid their storytelling and emotional bond with members as well as giving them an opportunity to participate in various rituals associated with membership of that community. Accordingly, we can explain the relationships of individuals within a brand community as comprising the relationship the person has with the brand and the relationship with members of the community, with each offering him or her some benefits such as having the opportunity to interact with other likeminded people (Dessart et al., 2015), expressing themselves and their uniqueness.

The fundamental components of the brand community are shown in Figure 5.4. Members have shared consciousness, engage in rituals and tradition, and have a sense of moral responsibility (Muniz and O'Guinn, 2001).

This kind of consciousness is about members recognising that they are connected to other members and the brand that constitutes the key focus of the setting. It is about a sense of togetherness understood and appreciated by the community members. Meanwhile, the community is run and considered ongoing through key social processes that members engage in and transmit to various contexts, such as stories about the brand and celebration of its history (Szmigin and Piacentini, 2018). This is related to the rituals and traditions as a component of the community. Moral responsibility is about the support that members of the community give to one another as a result of their love for the brand.

While the foregoing about brand community is a positive issue concerning the brand that encourages the spread of word-of-mouth communications within and outside the

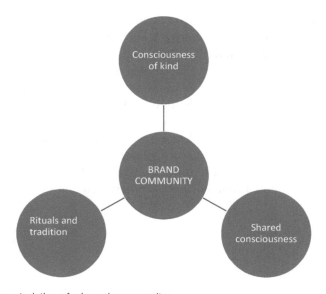

**FIGURE 5.4** Characteristics of a brand community

community, there are cases where the forming of the community is not to support the brand but to organise against a brand based on what the members think are undesirable issues concerning it. This is known as anti-brand activity which can have a serious effect on the brand. For example, some brands are accused of using child labour, while others are in the news for poor customer services, among many other alleged offences. The United Airlines case where a customer felt aggrieved that his guitar was mishandled and damaged during a trip on the airline in 2009 is a relevant example. He produced a piece of music about this which became very popular on YouTube. The negative word-of-mouth did not go unnoticed among passengers and commentators.

Meanwhile, apart from the benefits of the traditional brand communities, digital transformation implies that they even have a far wider reach and impact as members are digitally connected to several others. Examples of online brand communities are those in respect of Starbucks, Xbox, and Lego which give members opportunities to offer ideas for product development and improvement. Since a key aspect of brand communities is the word-of-mouth spread about the brand, the audience and efficiency at which this is done in online communities is far greater.

## OPINION LEADERS

As we have noticed from the beginning of this chapter, consumers' decisions are influenced by the opinions of others in many instances. This is possible because they are connected to several others in networks in the form of dyads, triads, and other groups (Cho et al., 2012). At the crossroad, this can be very handy for such individuals. One special aspect of these is the relevance of opinion leaders, who can be defined as individuals who offer an asymmetric peer effect by exerting a stronger influence on the consumption behaviour of others (Rogers, 2003; Nair et al., 2010). So, an opinion leader has a stronger influence on the consumer in relation to his or her attitude to market stimuli than the other way around. It is often considered very valuable for the diffusion of innovation and the rate of adoption of new products. We can draw a link between this and the market maven who is known to be a person that willingly searches for information about the goods and services, owns the information, and shares it with others (Litterio et al., 2017). The study of Van Eck et al. (2011) on the role of opinion leaders in innovation diffusion shows that if opinion leaders engage actively in a social network, the information about the products will spread faster and the diffusion of the information of the product item in question is faster over the network, and the percentage of adopters of the products is significantly higher when compared to social networks that do not have opinion leaders. Furthermore, they found that product diffusion is dependent on the capability of the opinion leaders to judge the quality of the product. In most cases, the intentions of businesses and brands for sponsoring marketing communication messages are laced with suspicion from the viewpoint of the consumers. Their commercial motive means that information from them may not be totally objective from the customers' point of view. Hence, consumers benefit from non-commercial sources of information such as that of an opinion leader.

The activities of opinion leaders are noticeable in respect of many products or services. The cases of doctors, lawyers, pharmacists, brokers, are some of examples of the increasing use of the role of opinion leaders in influencing what consumers choose in their transactions. In 2004, it was revealed based on industry reports that about 24% of the budget on new product commercialisation is spent on activities around opinion leaders (Cutting Edge Information, 2004). Such a level of financial commitment is understandable when considering the fact that opinion leaders play a key role in facilitating the diffusion of innovation. This is explained further in the claim that the role of opinion leaders is about having 10% of the people influencing the adoptive behaviour of the remaining 90% through word-of-mouth communications (Gladwell, 2002; Kratzer and Lettl, 2009). We can also use it to explain the link between consumer and citizen activism (Cho et al., 2015). So, an opinion leader can pull a crowd to support a particular cause of action. Essentially, the opinion leaders are in social networks through which they influence consumption and aid the spread of WOM in the diffusion of innovation. In a study of the roles of opinion leaders and lead users in the social networks of schoolchildren, findings show that children who have many direct contacts with other social networks tend to be opinion leaders (Kratzer and Lettl, 2009). With this discussion of opinion leadership so far, we can see that such roles can emerge in both formal and informal settings. Interestingly, it has been noted that informal social networks can offer a better route for a successful innovation diffusion than more formal settings (Rogers, 1976; Kratzer and Lettl, 2009).

It is important to characterise opinion leaders. Authors who have written on this have given some useful points on the characteristics of opinion leaders but some of these vary by product and the nature of the social network they belong to. We will highlight some of these as teased out from Shoham and Ruvio (2008) as follows:

- They tend to be technically competent in relation to the use of new high-tech products (Rogers, 1983; Summers, 1970);
- They are socially active (Baumgarten, 1975; Venkatraman, 1989);
- They act and feel differently by showing public individualism (Chan and Misra, 1990);
- They are conscious of their appearance, self-confident, and self-centred (Baumgarten, 1975; Summers, 1970);
- In relation to wine, they are heavier consumers of it than others (Goldsmith and Flynn 1998);
- In the fashion context, they tend to have a high need for uniqueness and attention for social comparison (Bertrandias and Goldsmith, 2006);
- They are heavy users of mass media (Rogers, 1983; Summers, 1970).

In addition to these Cho et al. (2015) also present these characteristics:

- They have higher level of education, interest in politics, social status, and are keen to achieve (Weimann, 1994);
- Early adopters that are at the forefront of social trends (Weimann, 1994);

- They are more likely to be involved in civic activities like volunteering (Shah and Scheufele, 2006);
- They exhibit a high level of gregariousness in relation to social clubs and establishments (Troldahl and Van Dam, 1965).

Understandably, opinion leadership and opinion seeking are linked. In the context of this chapter, it is about seeking opinion on consumption related issues such as what product or service to pay for, when is the appropriate time to buy them, where to buy them and how to make the purchase, from someone considered knowledgeable on the issue. People seek opinion on numerous purchases. For instance, they will seek opinion on the trends about fashion items, prices and location of houses to buy, which brand of cars to buy, which university to attend, and which insurance products to get. These are some of the examples among the plethora of transactions that involve gathering opinions before making a decision. Ultimately, when opinion seekers approach opinion leaders, he or she understands that the opinion leader has more experience concerning the product involved, has relevant information or has been exposed to such details, shows high involvement in the products, and displays innovative and explanatory behaviour (Lyons and Henderson, 2005; Van Eck et al., 2011).

---

**PAUSE, PLAN, AND PRACTICE: CONSUMER SOCIALISATION AT DISNEYLAND**

One may boldly claim that children's life is synonymous with fun. They love to play, interact, and spend. Disneyland seems to have offered them opportunities to meet these needs. As a multinational, the organisation is focused on creating and delivering value to households through its various offerings such as amusement, entertainment, hotel experience, celebration, and special occasion experience. Whether they are based in France, the United States, or the United Kingdom, the focus is to ensure that the family have a lasting experience of Disneyland. As parents spend at the park, buy merchandise, food, confectioneries, or make hotel reservations, most children are part of the experience, which helps in their socialisation. In most cases, the older children also engage in reverse socialisation. As one notices the movements in and around the parks, entertainment centres, spas, and other areas, one can see the family buying roles in action around initiating ideas of what to pay for, influencing those ideas, making decisions, directly experiencing, or using them. To many families, the experience of Disneyland is lifelong.

**QUESTION/TASK:**

Apply the family buying roles to the decision to pay for the Disneyland experience. Which circumstances would change this buying role pattern you have indicated?

## SUMMARY

Consumers are social beings, and this reflects in their various consumption activities. Individuals use some groups as a form of comparison when making consumption decisions and these reference groups can be of various types. Some of them are known as in-group, out-group, formal group, informal group, dissociative/avoidance group, aspirational group, and disclaimant group. One of the most fundamental of these is one's family, which can be conceptualised in a number of ways such as nuclear, extended, and stem family. Another conceptualisation is seen as a family of orientation and a family of procreation. One of the ways of discussing how digitalisation has influenced family and consumption activities is through the family buying roles which are initiators, influencers, deciders, users, buyers, and gatekeepers. All these are being facilitated by digital technology such as we have in consumer socialisation agents. Other evidence of the impact of social interaction of consumers on consumption comes in the form of social classes and brand community, and the role of opinion leaders.

---

**DIGITAL BOX: CONNECTING AND CONSUMING ON WHATSAPP**

Connection with social groups such as family members, co-workers, associations, standing committees, and other reference groups is improving by the day. The dimension of this offered by WhatsApp is unique, valuable, and systematic. Information sharing among members of in-groups has become easier with this platform. After creating a group, the app allows for the group to be named. Apart from the easy identification of the group, doing this also gives members a sense of belonging. In addition to the basic chat messages that can be shared by members, the app allows voice and video calls as well as instant voice messages. This implies that members of the platform can share word-of-mouth (WOM) communication about their purchase experiences such as a holiday experience, the fit of fashion items to specific needs, dissatisfaction experienced in a particular banking transaction, and many others. Some of the key points that highlight the popularity of this platform are the ease of use and the fact that it attracts no fee for making calls and sending messages to others as long as the phone is connected to the Internet. As people share videos, photos, messages, and documents with others, these are often accompanied by opinion seeking and opinion leadership on decisions associated with the transactions.

**DISCUSSION QUESTION**

Can the role of an opinion leader be practically executed through the WhatsApp platform? Explain and illustrate the (im)possibility.

**Sources:**

www.whatsapp.com/features (accessed 11 April 2022).

---

## END OF CHAPTER DISCUSSION QUESTIONS

1. Identify any one of your dissociative groups. What are the values and beliefs of the group that you find unsatisfactory? Critically explain the implication of

this for strategic marketing especially in the area of segmentation, targeting, and positioning. Explain why young adults may be interested in joining a brand community.
2. Family has been identified as a fundamental consumption unit. Critically discuss any two types of family and how they are changing in relation to contemporary family buying roles. To what extent do the type of parents in these families in terms of their communication pattern/styles influence childrens' consumption of social media content?
3. The use of social media platforms such as Facebook, Instagram, and X has been increasing in recent times. In view of this, explain how this development is facilitating consumers' use of electronic word-of-mouth (WOM) communications in the consumption of fashion products.
4. With the use of contemporary and relevant examples, discuss the role of consumer socialisation in children's brand preferences. How related is this discussion to the distinction between the in-group and out-group opinion leadership?
5. Assume you have recently heard the comments of a social critic on the radio who has downplayed the role of social class in consumption. She argued that the claim of the relevance of social class to consumption is more academic and does not hold in the practical sense. To what extent do you agree with this position?

### Case Study: Clubhouse: The Hub for Valuable Conversations

The surge in the use of technology in recent times has introduced many new pathways into our lives in ways that were unimaginable several years ago. One of these is the introduction of Clubhouse, a social audio app that gives users the opportunity to join groups spontaneously for a chat. In its design, a single virtual room of the app can allow up to 5000 participants. This gives opportunity to consumers to fulfil their social needs, exercise social powers, and share information in the form of word-of-mouth communications to various other people all over the world. It is open to all users irrespective of the social class to which they belong, and level of wealth, gender, marital status, or religion. Each member on the platform has the prerogative of a decision on who to interact with. Essentially, only a certain number of people can speak while everyone else listens. Nonetheless, one could ask to contribute to an ongoing conversation by using the raising hand feature. It has attracted the attention and interest of many celebrities who are keen to be a part of this big and global phenomenon. The likes of Mark Zuckerberg of Facebook, Oprah Winfrey, a media mogul, and Elon Musk, a billionaire technology investor, are already on the app. The opinion leadership role of these individuals and several others on the platform is noteworthy. They constitute an aspirational group for several members on the platform. Given the wide scope of the platform, it is becoming a useful avenue for building brands, and communicating about them effectively to members. Apart from the interaction on the platform, Clubhouse members also explore the associated communication opportunities to promote brands such as creating their club profiles on other social media platforms for reaching a larger audience. The increase in the reach of the platform is considerable since it was introduced in March 2020 and continues to grow.

Essentially, it allows people to gather in all ways to talk about issues and help one another through the interaction that ensues. The workability of the platform is significantly linked to the work of the moderators who ensure that things in the chat rooms flow according to plan. By virtue of their roles, they tend to be very influential. When we attend conventional meetings, we tend to move from one room to another if need be and join in an ongoing conversation. From the hallway, you could peep to see the speakers and a bit of information about the audience. This is similar to what is obtainable in the clubhouse which is a virtual environment. Within a room in the clubhouse, after minimising the room, the count of the audience members will become visible. When gauging the influence of an opinion leader, it is very relevant to check the strength and scope of their networks as the stronger these are the better his or her position of influencing others. Clubhouse functionality allows one to track member count from the user profile page.

The rules guiding the platform constitute an added advantage in that it attracts many participants as they know that the virtual environment will be safe and ideal for interaction. These regulations stipulate acceptable behaviour, for example the platform frowns at harassment of any type and does not condone discrimination, hateful behaviour and speech, the threat of violence, or trolling activities. Clubhouse is also noted for its stance against sexual exploitation, nudity, illegal activities, and several other offences.

Joining the clubhouse has already opened opportunities for many people to meet others who constitute their reference groups that have an influence on what they buy and how they buy them based on what they say in the chat rooms. Consumers can start gradually and after learning the dynamics can also host a room as an individual. The talking point could be anything like music, politics, education, or a host of other subjects. When someone is a moderator on the platform, he or she has total control on who is permitted on stage. So, being in a room makes one a member of the in-group in relation to the conversation. Nevertheless, this can change as someone could later be in a disassociate group. For example, members can unfollow any Clubhouse member from their profile page if they are in contravention of the rules. So, the influences on Clubhouse as an entity depicting social groups have consumer behaviour and marketing implications.

## QUESTIONS

1. How can membership of Clubhouse help opinion seekers in their choices of service offerings?
2. What do you think motivates celebrities joining the clubhouse to do so?
3. Illustrate the relevance of Heider's (1958) balanced theory with information from the case study.

4. As a group, think of another social media platform that will rival the likes of Clubhouse, Facebook, X, and others currently in use. Highlight the unique selling proposition (USP) of this new platform being proposed and the likely implication it will have on consumer behaviour.

**REFERENCES**

Aaker, J. L. (1997). Dimensions of brand personality. *Journal of Marketing Research*, 34(3), 347–356.

Aljukhadar, M., Boeuf, B., & Senecal, S. (2021). Does consumer ethnocentrism impact international shopping? A theory of social class divide. *Psychology & Marketing*, 38(5), 735–744.

Aydin, K. (2006). Social stratification and consumption patterns in Turkey. *Social Indicators Research*, 75(3), 463–501.

Banerjee, A. V., & Duflo, E. (2008). What is middle class about the middle classes around the world? *Journal of Economic Perspectives*, 22(2), 3–28.

Baumgarten, S. A. (1975). The innovative communicator in the diffusion research. *Journal of Marketing Research*, 12, 12–18.

Baxter, L. A., & Clark, C. L. (1996). Perceptions of family communication patterns and the enactment of family rituals. *Western Journal of Communication*, 60, 254–258.

Bertol, K. E., Broilo, P. L., Espartel, L. B., & Basso, K. (2017). Young children's influence on family consumer behavior. *Qualitative Market Research: An International Journal*. 20(4), 452–468.

Bertrandias, L., & Goldsmith, R. E. (2006). Some psychological motivations for fashion opinion leadership and fashion opinion seeking. *Journal of Fashion Marketing and Management*, 10, 25–40.

Bihagen, E. (1999). How do classes make use of their incomes? A test of two hypotheses concerning class and consumption on a Swedish data-set from 1992. *Social Indicators Research*, 47(2), 119–151.

Bourdieu, P. (1984). *Distinction – A Social Critique of the Judgement of Taste*, Paris: Les editions de minuit.

Broniarczyk, S. M., & Griffin, J. G. (2014). Decision difficulty in the age of consumer empowerment. *Journal of Consumer Psychology*, 24(4), 608–625.

Burns, D. J. (1992). Husband-wife innovative consumer decision making: Exploring. *Psychology & Marketing*, 9(3), 175–189.

Carlson, L., & Grossbart, S. (1988). Parental style and consumer socialization of children. *Journal of Consumer Research*, 15(1), 77–94.

Carlson, S., Gerhards, J., & Hans, S. (2017). Educating children in times of globalisation: Class-specific child-rearing practices and the acquisition of transnational cultural capital. *Sociology*, 51(4), 749–765.

Chan, K. K., & Misra, S. (1990). Characteristics of the opinion leader: A new dimension. *Journal of Advertising*, 19, 53–60.

Cho, J., Keum, H., & Shah, D. V. (2015). News consumers, opinion leaders, and citizen consumers: Moderators of the consumption–participation link. *Journalism & Mass Communication Quarterly*, 92(1), 161–178.

Cho, Y., Hwang, J., & Lee, D. (2012). Identification of effective opinion leaders in the diffusion of technological innovation: A social network approach. *Technological Forecasting and Social Change*, 79(1), 97–106.

Cutting Edge Information (2004). *Pharmaceutical Thought Leaders: Brand Strategies and Product Positioning*. Report No. PH64.

Dessart, L., Veloutsou, C., & Morgan-Thomas, A. (2015). Consumer engagement in online brand communities: A social media perspective. *Journal of Product & Brand Management*, 24(1), 28–42.

Douglas, M., & Isherwood, B. (1979). *The World of Goods: Towards an Anthropology of Consumption*, New York: Basic Books.

Du, R. Y., & Kamakura, W. A. (2006). Household life cycles and lifestyles in the United States. *Journal of Marketing Research*, 43(1), 121–132.

Easterly, W. (2001). The middle class consensus and economic development. *Journal of Economic Growth*, 6(4), 317–335.

Ellemers, N., Kortekaas, P., & Ouwerkerk, J. W. (1999). Self-categorisation, commitment to the group and group self-esteem as related but distinct aspects of social identity. *European Journal of Social Psychology*, 29(2/3), 371–389.

Essiz, O., & Mandrik, C. (2021). Intergenerational influence on sustainable consumer attitudes and behaviors: Roles of family communication and peer influence in environmental consumer socialization. *Psychology & Marketing*, https://doi.org/10.1002/mar.21540

Feenstra, F., Muzellec, L., de Faultrier, B., & Boulay, J. (2015). Edutainment experiences for children in retail stores, from a child's perspective. *Journal of Retailing and Consumer Services*, 26, 47–56.

Fournier, S. (1998). Consumers and their brands: Developing relationship theory in consumer research. *Journal of Consumer Research*, 24(4), 343–373.

Gbadamosi, A. (2012). Exploring children, family, and consumption behaviour: Empirical evidence from Nigeria. *Thunderbird International Business Review*, 54(4), 591–605.

Gbadamosi, A. (2015). Brand personification and symbolic consumption among ethnic teenage consumers: An empirical study. *Journal of Brand Management* 22(9), 737–759.

Giddens, A. (1973). *The Class Structure of Advanced Societies*, England: Hutchinson.

Gladwell, M. (2002). *The Tipping Point: How Little Things Can Make a Big Difference*, New York: Little Brown.

Goffman, E. (1959), *The Presentation of Self in Everyday Life*, New York, NY: Doubleday.

Goldsmith, R. E., & Flynn, L. R. (1998). Heavy wine consumption: Empirical and theoretical perspectives. *British Food Journal*, 100, 184–190.

Grönroos, C. (1989). Defining marketing: A market-oriented approach. *European Journal of Marketing*, 23(1), 52–60.

Grönroos, C. (2000). *Service Management and Marketing: A Customer Relationship Management Approach*. Chichester: John Wiley & Sons.

Hamilton, K. (2009). Consumer decision making in low-income families: The case of conflict avoidance. *Journal of Consumer Behaviour: An International Research Review*, 8(5), 252–267.

Hammerl, M., Dorner, F., Foscht, T., & Brandstätter, M. (2016). Attribution of symbolic brand meaning: The interplay of consumers, brands and reference groups. *Journal of Consumer Marketing*, 33(1), 32–40.

Heider, F. (1958). *The Psychology of Interpersonal Relations*, New York, NY: John Wiley & Sons.

Holdnack, J. A. (1992). The long-term effects of parental divorce on family relationships and the effects on adult children's self-concept. *Journal of Divorce and Remarriage*, 16, 137–155.

Horton, H. (2015). The seven social classes of 21st century Britain – Where do you fit in? *The Telegraph*, 7th December, Available at: https://www.telegraph.co.uk/news/uknews/12037247/the-seven-socialclasses-of-21st-century-britain-where-do-you-fit-in.html (accessed 17 December 2019).

Hota, M., & Bartsch, F. (2019). Consumer socialization in childhood and adolescence: Impact of psychological development and family structure. *Journal of Business Research*, *105*, 11–20.

Hyatt, C., Kerwin, S., Hoeber, L., & Sveinson, K. (2018). The reverse socialization of sport fans: How children impact their parents' sport fandom. *Journal of Sport Management*, *32*(6), 542–554.

John, D. (1999). Consumer socialization of children: A retrospective look at twenty-five years of research. *Journal of Consumer Research*, *26*(December), 183–213.

Kerrane, B., Bettany, S. M., & Kerrane, K. (2015). Siblings as socialization agents: Exploring the role of 'sibship' in the consumer socialization of children. *European Journal of Marketing*, *49*(5/6), 713–735.

Kim, C., Lee, H., & Tomiuk, M. A. (2009). Adolescents' perceptions of family communication patterns and some aspects of their consumer socialization. *Psychology & Marketing*, *26*(10), 888–907.

Kim, C., Yang, Z., & Lee, H. (2015). Parental style, parental practices, and socialization outcomes: An investigation of their linkages in the consumer socialization context. *Journal of Economic Psychology*, *49*, 15–33.

Koter, P., & Armstrong, G. (2018). *Principles of Marketing*, Global Edition, Harlow: Pearson Education Limited.

Kratzer, J., & Lettl, C. (2009). Distinctive roles of lead users and opinion leaders in the social networks of schoolchildren. *Journal of Consumer Research*, *36*(4), 646–659.

Litterio, A. M., Nantes, E. A., Larrosa, J. M., & Gómez, L. J. (2017). Marketing and social networks: A criterion for detecting opinion leaders. *European Journal of Management and Business Economics*, *26*(3), 347–366.

Lyons, B., & Henderson, K. (2005). Opinion leadership in a computer mediated environment. *Journal of Consumer Behavior*, *4*(5), 319–329.

McAlexander, J. H., Schouten, J. W., & Koenig, H. F. (2002). Building brand community. *Journal of Marketing*, *66*(1), 38–54.

Mersey, R. D., Malthouse, E. C., & Calder, B. J. (2010). Engagement with online media. *Journal of Media Business Studies*, *7*(2), 39–56.

Mihić, M., & Čulina, G. (2006). Buying behavior and consumption: Social class versus income. *Management: Journal of Contemporary Management Issues*, *11*(2), 77–92.

Mintel (2014). Online Grocery Shopping. Mintel Oxygen Reports, London.

Muniz, A. M. Jr, & O'Guinn, T. C. (2001). Brand community. *Journal of Consumer Research*, *27*(4), 412–432.

Nair, H. S., Manchanda, P., & Bhatia, T. (2010). Asymmetric social interactions in physician prescription behavior: The role of opinion leaders. *Journal of Marketing Research*, *47*(5), 883–895.

ONS (2021). Children's online behaviour in England and Wales: Year ending March 2020, Office of National Statics, 9 February 2021, www.ons.gov.uk/peoplepopulationandcommunity/crimeandjustice/bulletins/childrenonlinebehaviourinenglandandwales/yearendingmarch2020 (accessed 12 February 2022).

Palan, K. M., & Wilkes, R. E. (1997). Adolescent-parent interaction in family decision making. *Journal of Consumer Research*, *24*(September), 159–169.

Rindfleisch, A., Burroughs, J. E., & Denton, F. (1997). Family structure, materialism, and compulsive consumption. *Journal of Consumer Research*, *23*(4), 312–325.

Rogers, E. M. (1976). New product adoption and diffusion. *Journal of Consumer Research*, *2*(3), 290–301.

Rogers, E. M. (1983). *Diffusion of Innovations*. New York: The Free Press.

Rogers, E. M. (2003). *Diffusion of Innovations*, 5th ed. New York: The Free Press.

Rose, G. M. (1999). Consumer socialization, parental style, and developmental timetables in the United States and Japan. *Journal of Marketing*, 63(3), 105–118.

Schembri, S., & Latimer, L. (2016). Online brand communities: Constructing and co-constructing brand culture. *Journal of Marketing Management*, 32(7–8), 628–651.

Schiffman, L., & Wisenblit, J. (2019). *Consumer Behaviour*, 12th edn., Essex: Pearson Education Limited.

Schulz, H. M. (2015). Reference group influence in consumer role rehearsal narratives. *Qualitative Market Research: An International Journal*, 18(2), 210–229.

Shah, D. V., & Scheufele, D. A. (2006). Explicating opinion leadership: Nonpolitical dispositions, information consumption, and civic participation. *Political Communication*, 23(1), 1–22.

Sheth, J. N. (1974). A theory of family buying decisions, in Sheth, J. N. (ed.), *Models of Buyer Behavior*, pp. 17–33, New York: Harper & Row.

Sheth, J. N., Mittal, B., & Newman, B. I. (1999). *Customer Behavior: Consumer Behavior and Beyond*, Fort Worth, TX: Dryden Press.

Shoham, A., & Ruvio, A. (2008). Opinion leaders and followers: A replication and extension. *Psychology & Marketing*, 25(3), 280–297.

Sivadas, E. (1997). A preliminary examination of the continuing significance of social class to marketing: A geodemographic replication. *Journal of Consumer Marketing*, 14(6), 463–479.

Skovgaard-Smith, I., & Poulfelt, F. (2018). Imagining 'non-nationality': Cosmopolitanism as a source of identity and belonging. *Human Relations*, 71(2), 129–154.

Solomon, M. R. (2020). *Consumer Behaviour: Buying, Having, and Being*, 13th edn, Essex: Pearson Education Limited.

Summers, J. O. (1970). The identity of women's clothing fashion opinion leaders. *Journal of Marketing Research*, 7, 178–185.

Swann, W. B. (1987). Identity negotiation: Where two roads meet, *Journal of Personality and Social Psychology*, 53(6), 1038–1051.

Szmigin, I., & Piacentini, M. (2018). *Consumer Behaviour*, Oxford: Oxford University Press.

Szmigin, I., & Piacentini, M. (2022). *Consumer Behaviour*, 3rd edn., Oxford: Oxford University Press.

Tajfel, H. (1982a). Social psychology of intergroup relations. *Annual Review of Psychology*, 33, 1–39.

Tajfel, H. (ed.) (1982b). *Social Identity and Intergroup Relations*, Cambridge, UK: Cambridge University Press.

Tajfel, H. (1986). *The Social Identity Theory of Intergroup Behavior*, Chicago: Nelson.

Thaichon, P. (2017). Consumer socialization process: The role of age in children's online shopping behavior. *Journal of Retailing and Consumer Services*, 34, 38–47.

Thaichon, P., Quach, T. N. (2016). Online marketing communications and childhood's intention to consume unhealthy food. *Australasian Marketing Journal*, 24(1), 79–86.

Troldahl, V. C., & Van Dam, R. (1965) A new scale for identifying public-affairs opinion leaders. *Journalism & Mass Communication Quarterly*, 42(4), 655–657.

Van Eck, P. S., Jager, W., & Leeflang, P. S. (2011). Opinion leaders' role in innovation diffusion: A simulation study. *Journal of Product Innovation Management*, 28(2), 187–203.

Veblen, T. (1953). *The Theory of the Leisure Class*, New York: Mentor Books.

Venkatraman, M. P. (1989). Opinion leaders, adopters, and communication adopters: A role analysis. *Psychology & Marketing*, 6, 51–68.

Wang, X., Yu, C., & Wei, Y. (2012). Social media peer communication and impacts on purchase intentions: A consumer socialization framework. *Journal of Interactive Marketing*, 26(4), 198–208.

Ward, S. (1974). Consumer socialization. *Journal of Consumer Research*, *1*(2), 1–14.

Warner, W. L., & Lunt, P. S. (1941). *The Social Life of a Modern Community*, New Haven, CT: Yale University Press.

Wei, Y., & Yu, C. (2012). How do reference groups influence self-brand connections among Chinese consumers? *Journal of Advertising*, *41*(2), 39–54.

Wells, W. D. & Gubar, G. (1966). Life cycle concept in marketing research. *Journal of Marketing Research*, *15*(3), 355–363.

Weimann, G. (1994). *The Influentials: People Who Influence People*, New York: State University of New York Press.

White, K., & Dahl, D. W. (2007). Are all out-groups created equal? Consumer identity and dissociative influence. *Journal of Consumer Research*, *34*(4), 525–536.

**PART 3**

# DIGITAL TRANSFORMATION AND THE PSYCHOLOGICAL INFLUENCES ON CONSUMER BEHAVIOUR

# CHAPTER 6

# Consumer Perception – Beauty in the Eyes of the Beholder

**LEARNING OBJECTIVES**

After reading this chapter, you should be able to:

- Define consumer perception;
- Explain the consumer perceptual process;
- Critically discuss semiotics in relation to consumer perception;
- Discuss showrooming and webrooming in relation to consumer perception;
- Explain virtual reality, mixed reality, and augmented reality in relation to consumer perception;
- Discuss sensory thresholds;
- Marketing implication of consumer perception.

**INTRODUCTION**

One of the intriguing areas of consumer behaviour is consumer perception. It connects most of our consumption decisions. Whether we are interested in luxurious items like automobiles, or trifling items like cookies, our senses are key elements that underpin our perception of these offerings. All items for sale are deemed good at the price offered by the marketer and they also would hold that the outlet used for selling them and the marketing communications strategies are effective. However, the ultimate test of these lies in how the target consumers perceive these stimuli. Marketers may do all they care to present these products and services, but the primary determinant of their commercial success is in how consumers perceive them since their perception determines whether they will buy them or choose an alternative course of action. We have seen many products or service offerings that have been launched and recalled as they are at variance from customers' expectations. Meanwhile, as with virtually every aspect of our lives, our perceptions in relation to marketplace issues are being

DOI: 10.4324/9781003242031-9

influenced by technology. We will be looking at how this has impacted our exposure to marketing stimuli, how our attention is attracted to them, and how we interpret these stimuli.

## PERCEPTION: CONCEPTS AND DEFINITIONS

As consumers, we are exposed to a plethora of stimuli day-in-day-out, both offline and online. The explanation of how this works and what we do with them lies in perception. We can define the term as a process through which consumers select, organise, and interpret stimuli from the environment through the sense organs (Szmigin and Piacentini, 2018). If we examine this definition in detail, some key terms could be teased out from it that will help us to have a deeper understanding of the term. These are exposure, attention, interpretation, and sensation.

Exposure is the process of perception, and it is the stage of coming into contact physically with the stimulus. This takes place through consumers' senses which are sight, smell, sound, taste, and texture. So, these five senses produce the perception data (Lindberg et al., 2018).

**Sight** is a significant sense for the consumer. Through this, they are able to visualise market offerings in terms of colours, sizes, and other factors. Different colours communicate differently in different contexts. As products are being positioned and repositioned, marketers strategically select the colour and other features that are seen by consumers. This sensation is triggered when consumers are in the store and online exploring alternative offerings. Meanwhile, in selecting clothes, shoes, furniture, and food items, consumers tend to rely on the opportunities to **touch** the item to gauge the quality and their fitness for purpose. Similarly, the relevance of this varies from one product to another. Hence, firms operating in these businesses give room for consumers to have access to the products to gauge their quality by touching them. In food consumption, **taste** is a crucial perceptual sense. Taste perception also varies based on various factors such as culture, age, and personal circumstance. The acknowledgement of this prompts marketers into having various different ice cream flavours, tea flavours, and other food variants. **Sound** plays an important role in many transactions. A common example here is the use of music to promote goods and services. It is now commonplace that supermarkets and shopping malls play music since it is linked to moods. Using music in advertising messages is now very common, from automobiles and luxury items to groceries. So, marketers will be keen to ensure that the chosen music appeals to the right audience. In this, they tend to use

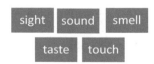

FIGURE 6.1 Consumers' senses

popular celebrities that the consumers can relate with to influence their perception. A musical piece associated with an ad can lift the mood of the target market and can bring back specific old memories in what is often called nostalgia. The importance of **smell** in perception is quite high for several market offerings. The smell takes place when one inhales chemicals from the atmosphere. Based on experience, we must have noticed that smell can be pleasant or unpleasant but either way, it communicates. The odour sends a message to the brain about the item. In the marketing context, the fragrance perceived connotes many things and can be a relevant factor in determining consumers' preference of specific products, and the extent of interaction in a particular retail setting.

The stimuli that consumers are exposed to could originate from marketers or it could be non-marketing oriented. For example, consumers are exposed to physical products in the store, brands, logos, advertising messages, the smell of food, and many others. In linking this to organic foods, it has been noted that sensory properties offer salient quality criteria in these products which comprise colour, smell, shape, taste, and texture (Beck et al., 2012; Schleenbecker and Hamm, 2013). The sources of marketing-oriented stimuli have increased significantly with the increase in the use of technology in marketing. Social media is now a platform for much marketing-oriented information which consumers are exposed to on a daily basis.

If we reflect on personal experiences, we will notice that we are exposed to numerous stimuli. For example, as you are reading this chapter of the book, if you look back at your encounters for the day, you would notice your physical encounters with brands, logos, price tags, straplines of organisations, online or offline advertising messages, and the smell of food or perfume, among very many other examples. Given this bombardment, consumers tend to manage this through various means. One of these is the use of selective exposure. What this means is that consumers pick and choose which stimulus to embrace and which to avoid. Many examples of these are readily available. In a visit to the shopping mall where various promotional flyers and banners are positioned, one is likely to be mainly drawn to the ones that relate to his or her personal needs while others will be ignored. Similarly, as perception can take on different forms and interactive roles of the human senses to trigger action, a consumer might see some dresses in the store but be drawn to touch some that he or she feels could satisfy his/her needs to gauge the fit further while others would be avoided to save time. Turning the television to specific channels for specific programmes indicates that priority is given to the chosen channel over others that are not being watched. Interestingly, even within a television programme, consumers tend to avoid commercial breaks by using such times for other things they find more valuable. This is also prevalent in the digital world. As consumers search online or explore the Internet, it is not uncommon to encounter several pop-up ads that some consumers find annoying. Following the same principle of selective exposure, they look for ways to avoid these such as using ad blocker software. In a study to examine the differences in how consumers perceive online reviews, Bae and Lee (2011) found that there is a stronger effect of online reviews on consumers' purchase intention for females compared to males. This is attributed to the selectivity theory and socialization in relation to each gender group. Based on selectivity theory, females often process information more comprehensively than males (Kempf & Palan, 2006).

Studies have shown vision is the most important sense when it comes to perceiving the environment, while the auditory experience in relation to issues such as background music and noise is also important in relation to the perception of service and consumers' intention to make the purchase (Lawless and Heymann, 2010; Hynes and Manson, 2016). In the study of Lindberg et al. (2018) on consumers' perception and behaviour in the food retail foodscape, they found that the door of the cabinet in the retail environment can be important and tune consumers' perception and behaviour. The study shows specifically that in some cases, some consumers avoid touching the door handles due to hygienic reasons. Furthermore, Liu et al. (2012) studied consumers in Austria and Japan on what determines their perception of mobile advertising. They recorded quite interesting findings on this. Although these authors studied three antecedents to the perceived value of advertising in both countries which are irritation, credibility, and infotainment, their findings only show a link between credibility, infotainment, and perceived value of advertising in both countries. In this study, infotainment refers to the degree to which the medium of advertising used offers users helpful and resourceful details (Ducoffe, 1996). The credibility factor is about the extent to which the advertising offers users trustworthy content.

## ATTENTION

Getting consumers' attention in a competitive environment is a challenge in the marketplace. In some cases, consumers practice multitasking in which attention is paid to multiple stimuli. This happens both in online and offline contexts. With the prevalence of the Internet of Things (IoT), where consumers have access to multiple devices, they tend to multitask and share attention between stimuli. A similar example can be seen in the print media where consumers manage exposure to various marketing communication messages. Nonetheless, there is a limit to how this can be

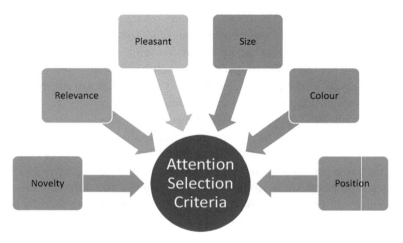

**FIGURE 6.2** Strategies for catching consumers' attention

done by the consumers. Therefore, marketers need to have strategies in place to catch the attention of the consumers. These are presented in Figure 6.2.

To grab consumers' attention, using stimuli that are different from what the target audience might expect in terms of their experience and previous exposure, in such a way that prompts curiosity, is not uncommon. This is known as adopting novelty. Getting attention can also be linked to specific consumer segments by making the stimulus relevant to them. Ad messages linked to hip-hop music targeted at teenagers will most likely lead to better attention than if they are directed at retirees. Similarly, advertising maternity products to expecting and nursing mothers will be more successful if specifically targeted at them. Engaging people that share similar characteristics with the target audience, such as children featuring in the advertisement of products meant for their age can be very useful. This shows that the stimulus is made to be relevant to them. For instance, in a study on consumers' perception of bio-based products, Sijtsema et al. (2016) found that the perception of consumers for these products is primarily based on the answer to the question of 'what's in it for me?' against the benefits of production methods of bio-based products. Hence, their perception of bio-based is more driven by consumers' personal benefits. This can come in a number of ways such as a 'feel good factor' and embracing a healthy and sustainable lifestyle.

The position of a stimulus can make a difference in how well and quickly it will be noticed. The stimuli on top will most likely generate more attention than those beneath. Marketers can make a stimulus get attention if it is presented in a pleasant way, for example via the use of humour, music, and models (Hoyer et al., 2020). Many ad messages that feature animal characters are humorous and tend to be more effective in attracting the attention of the target audience. However, it is important to carefully design the stimulus so that the humour does not override the core message about the product or brand in the ad. Celebrities in various career contexts like Cristiano Ronaldo in football, Rihanna in the music world, Gordon Ramsey in the hospitality industry, and many more feature in various ad messages to get the attention of the target audiences. In choosing this, marketers often consider many factors including the likeability of the celebrity and the possibility of getting into trouble, which could harm the brand.

The size of the stimulus in contrast with others that it competes with can explain why it attracts attention more than others. For instance, a stimulus that is bigger than others will most likely gain better attention. Marketers often pay more for more prominently displayed marketing communication messages because it is believed they get more attention compared to other stimuli that are less prominently featured. Interestingly, the same argument could be made for a relatively small stimulus. Therefore, the point here is about contrast and not necessarily only about how big the stimulus is.

The ease of processing stimuli is one of the key factors that enhance consumer attention. Hoyer et al. (2020) suggest that making the stimuli prominent could address this and can be done by making stimuli larger, longer, and more dynamic. They also emphasise that a stimulus in concrete form is more easily noticed that those considered abstract. By concrete, they mean the extent to which the stimulus can be imagined. Similarly, a stimulus can gain more prominence if it competes for attention with a limited number of other stimuli than if it is in a crowded context.

Colour is another interesting factor that aids attention. There are emotional attachments to different colours. So, using them correctly and effectively can be very rewarding in marketing for gaining attention. For instance, it has been noted that blue is associated with being calm, serene, dependable, and trustworthy while white is associated with cleanliness and purity, red goes with communicating boldness, excitement, and urgency, while green is often associated with generosity and growth, and is often used when discussing health and nature (Promolta, nd).

## INTERPRETATION

At the phase of interpretation, the consumers give meaning to the stimuli they have been exposed to. How sensory information is interpreted is usually what drives the purchase of the item promoted (Swahn et al., 2012; Lindberg et al., 2018). One of the intriguing aspects of interpretation as a stage in the perception process is its subjectivity. The way we interpret stimuli could vary based on a number of factors such as culture, personality, and personal experiences. For instance, a joke given in a context that will be found very amusing may not get the same reaction in another context. So, a particular stimulus can have different meanings to different consumers. We encounter many examples of this on a daily basis. The ad messages that strongly appeal to a wife might not have a similar reaction from the husband. Similarly, age differences might influence consumers' interpretation of stimuli, such as packaging, colour, musical themes, taste, and many others.

## GESTALT PSYCHOLOGY

Gestalt psychology has been a long-standing school of thought on the interpretation of stimuli. The term Gestalt has its origin in the German context in which it means *whole*, and the focus of Gestalt psychology is that people tend to search for patterns and meaning in the stimulus they have perceived in the environment (Szmigin and Piacentini, 2018). So, it is about interpreting meaning based on the totality of the combination of stimuli rather than just a specific stimulus. We will now discuss the common principles which depict how people interpret and organise stimuli, which are:

- Principle of similarity;
- Principle of closure;
- Figure and ground;
- Principle of proximity.

The principle of similarity indicates that consumers tend to view and interpret stimulus items that are similar in features as being together compared to those that are dissimilar. Marketers explore the benefits of this in various brand extension strategies in that consumers hold that the experience, quality, and reputation of the well-known brands will reflect in their new offerings. Virgin as a brand has various product lines that share similar names and logo such as Virgin Mobile, Virgin Trains, TV package, and Internet. Similarly, Easyjet, Easycar, Easymoney, Easystorage, Easy Internet café, and many others are different products offered by the same organisation and the use of the same name is to communicate similarities between them.

## Principle of Closure

This indicates that consumers tend to fill the gap in what they perceive as incomplete based on their experience as related to the stimuli. There are several examples of this in marketing communications messages; marketers often find this useful as it gets the consumers engaged in their messages and market offerings. The idea is that the process of figuring out the missing bits and filling it gets the consumers engaged in the stimuli.

## Figure and Ground

While perceiving stimuli, people tend to view an aspect as being dominant or prominent while others are seen as ground. The ultimate aim of the marketer is to ensure that its marketing stimuli are not subsumed into the background in relation to other parts of the stimuli the consumers are exposed to. For instance, when using humour to promote a product, it is important for marketers to ensure that the humour does not overshadow the core message.

## Principle of Proximity

People tend to visualise a set of stimuli together as being in a group when they are together compared to others that are located apart. Marketers often explore this principle by positioning complementary items together in the store so that consumers can make a selection accordingly. This is interpreted as having a package of solutions to fill needs compared to cases where the items are located apart. Supermarkets often locate bread, margarine, and butter closer together, while stationeries such as notepads, pens, and glue sticks are located in shelves that are closer together.

As we have now seen, whether we are considering it in online or offline contexts, many factors contribute to how consumers interpret the stimuli they are exposed to. It has been noted that there is a link between the perceived ease of use of technology and how the users evaluate the effort involved in the progression of using it (Davis, 1989; Bilgihan et al., 2016). In making purchases, consumers are confronted with both search attributes and experience attributes. The search attributes relate to appearance of the market offerings and can be verified before the purchase, such as the look of food. The experience attributes, on the other hand, are those that can only be verified after the usage of the product. Hence, it is important for marketers to identify these and present the appropriate attribute to the target segment, such as emphasising technological advancement when marketing durable products to the young and innovative consumer segment (Mugge et al., 2018).

## SEMIOTICS

Marketing uses symbols and signs to convey messages in relation to the products and services being offered in the marketplace. The heart shape has been a well-known symbol of love over the years. It is often used in the promotion of goods and services associated with Valentines, marriages, and love relationships. This has been used by many businesses to promote fragrances, jewellery, and clothing. This has proved useful over the years as consumers' perceptions can be very subjective. Hence, the use of signs and symbols helps consumers to be able to simplify the stimuli in relation to factors such as their past experience, cultural values, and knowledge for effective interpretation of the messages. We see examples of these in various packaging and branding activities. **Semiotics** is about how consumers link symbols, signs, and the meaning they connote (Szmigin and Piacentini, 2018). So, essentially, it is about combining the objects, the signs, and the interpretant associated with marketing communications messages. As explained by Solomon (2020), the object is the product being sold, while the sign is the sensory image representing the meaning intended and the interpretant is the term used to describe the meaning the consumer teases out from the sign.

## AUGMENTED REALITY (AR)

Technology is in almost everything we do these days. A report shows a figure of 5.22 billion mobile users in the world (wearsocial.com, 2021; Oyman et al., 2022). The development in the world of technology also influences how perception works in the business world. This comes in the use of augmented reality, virtual reality, and mixed reality. One of the examples is how retailers in the clothing business are using augmented reality interactive technology (ARIT) to allow online trials of clothes by consumers (Kim & Forsythe, 2008; Bourlakis et al., 2009). Specifically, ARIT is an image interactivity technology that comprises website features that allow firms to create and manipulate product or environment images to excite the actual experience of the user in relation to the product or environment (van Krevelen and Poelman, 2010). In the real-time mobile augmented reality (MAR) app, consumers are equipped with the resources they need to access and visualise the market offerings on their smart devices immediately in perceptible space (Qin et al., 2021). Given that it transforms physical reality by directly superimposing virtual elements into real-time environments through a screen, it creates an enhancing experience for the consumers (Javornik, 2016). This can be through video, audio, text, image, or geological information (Preece et al., 2015). Looking at the features, it is logical to indicate that the core benefit of AR is its ability to give a clear representation of a product by combining the virtual world and the real world (Heller et al., 2019; McLean and Wilson, 2019). In the words of Azuma (1997), this approach to marketing generates the illusion that the real and virtual coexist together in the same space.

So, with getting a new kitchen, the consumer can simply see how it looks having a dishwasher next to washing machines and place an oven and microwave oven at the desired places using a 3D image from the online showroom. Similarly, the sofa, dining table, and other items of furniture in a living room could be visualised before purchase. As a consumer, you can also check how a particular item would look on you by changing specific aspects such as lipstick, colour, and style. In fact, in the study of Pantano et al. (2017) which examines the use of this technology in Italy and Germany, they found it to be popular with consumers who use it to try on eyeglasses and sunglasses. There are many more examples showing the increasing use of this technology in recent times. In fact, the market for the augmented and virtual reality industry is projected to be more than $571 billion by the year 2025 (www.prnewswire.com; Oyman et al., 2022). This will give consumers the impression of how the product or service will be when the get home based on the computer-generated imagery they have seen in the store. Clearly, this can be very useful to both the consumer and the firm in the consumer decision journey from the pre-purchase to the post-purchase stage. Interestingly, as we know, the level of technological innovativeness of an 18-year-old will most likely be different from that of his/her grandparents. Huang and Liao (2015) found that the level of cognitive innovativeness of a consumer will influence the sustainable relationship they have towards using augmented reality interactive technology (ARIT). In a different study by Oyman et al. (2022), it is found that there is a positive effect of novelty seeking of consumers on their perceived augmented reality in relation to mobile applications.

To get a deeper understanding of how ARIT works, it is important to look into the broad components (aesthetics) of online retailing which, as stated in the literature (Mathwick et al., 2001; Huang and Liao, 2015), are:

- Visual appeal;
- Entertainment value.

Forming a visual appeal can be done by stimulating the internal gracefulness and picture of the body's appeal whereas the entertainment value is derived from the enjoyment associated with consumers' online shopping experience. In the study of Kim and Choo (2021) on AR as a product presentation tool, their findings show that when using AR technology consumers experience enhanced imagery in situations when they are offered utilitarian information compared to when given hedonic information.

## VIRTUAL REALITY

Virtual reality has been hailed as a new development in the marketplace and its popularity continues to grow. Businesses like IKEA, a furniture company, and Carrefour, a hypermarket, are among many companies using the technology. The estimated figure for this market for 2022 is US$209.2 billion (Statista, 2018; Meißner et al., 2020). A definition of the term as provided by the Interaction Design Foundation is relatively comprehensive and can be used in this chapter accordingly. Based on this perspective it is defined as the experience involving users being immersed in a simulated world through hardware like headsets, and software (Interaction Design Foundation, nd).

So, it is about transporting the users to 3D environments for a VR experience such as stores, museums, and other places where they are to execute explicit tasks for achieving specific objectives (Interaction Design Foundation, nd). In other words, it is a simulated or real experience in which the person perceiving it experiences telepresence (Steuer, 1992). Two key words are core to a VR system:

- Navigation;
- Interaction.

In this, navigation means the users' ability to be physically mobile in the virtually constructed space while interaction refers to the ability of the user to be able to move and select items within the virtual environment (Gutiérrez et al., 2008; Pizzi et al., 2019). With VR, businesses can have a 3D store environment simulated in a cost efficient and realistic way (Ruppert, 2011). In their study to compare shopping behaviour using virtual and pictorial representation of a store to an actual physical store, van Herpen et al. (2016) found that VR represents the behaviour in the physical store compared to a picture condition. Besides, the study shows that VR improves consumers' reaction to shelf allocation. In another study which focuses on analysing consumers' reaction to the virtual reality shopping mall, Lee and Chung (2008) present some key managerial implications that highlight the associated online competitive advantage of VR:

- VR offers compelling online sensory affluence and the customer has a better opportunity to experience a deeper value of product information and shop actively;
- Due to the convenience and enjoyment, there will be an increase in repeat visits to the VR shopping mall;
- The customers' experience in the ordinary shopping mall is different from the one in the VR shopping mall in that they are passive observers that just focus on the information given on the user interface in the ordinary shopping mall. On the other hand, they are actively involved in the VR context as they have control over the 3D visualised target products;
- Due to the increasing interest in experience in economy, there is an improvement in customer satisfaction in the VR context from the ordinary shopping mall.

## MIXED REALITY

Mixed reality (MR) has become very popular in marketing. As a way of understanding this term, it is important to acknowledge the existence of the reality-virtuality continuum. In this, the real environment which consists of real objects is at one end of the continuum while the other end is a purely virtual environment that comprises virtual objects (Milgram and Kishino, 1994; Westmattelmann et al., 2021). Accordingly, mixed reality which consists of augmented reality (AR) and augmented virtuality (AV) lies between the two ends of this continuum. The ability to combine both the real world and the virtual such that it gives the user an intuitive means of interaction is a key advantage of MR (Liu et al., 2022). In a study on the evaluation of the role of mixed reality in cognitive learning of children with autism spectrum disorder (ASD), Liu et al. (2022) indicate that it will be valuable to children that have reduced levels of cognitive development. Even though MR sounds like augmented virtuality, they are not exactly the same in that while augmented virtuality is about scenarios depicting a computer-generated world that is augmented with real conditions, mixed reality is a combination of the scenario that is real and possible with what is virtual and actual (Farshid et al., 2018). Apart from enhancing the perception of the user of the real world by superimposing generated digital data, just like in the case of AR, another motivation for developing MR systems, in general, is to leverage the current visual and spatial skills for the purpose of increasing the user's interaction capabilities (Holz et al, 2011).

## SHOWROOMING AND CONSUMER PERCEPTION

Technology has given consumers more choices in their transactions than in the past few years. One of the areas of this development is the increasing rate of showrooming. This is about consumers making an intentional visit to the offline stores prior to making a purchase online (Gensler et al., 2017; Arora and Sahney, 2018). With this approach, the consumers first gather information and seek clarifications on the items to be purchased before doing the actual purchase electronically. For example, consumers buying computers, mobile phones, cookers, and other electrical products may first come into the store to speak to a sales advisor in order to get information about the functioning of the equipment for reassurance and guidance towards knowing which alternative to buy. Quoting Statista (2016), Arora and Sahney (2018) show that the phenomenon is very popular as about 68% of shoppers in the United States have indicated that they adopt this approach. Another related phenomenon is **pseudo-showrooming** which is about going into the store intentionally to view the product and learn about it but then deciding to buy a different but related product from the seller (Gu and Tayi, 2016). This is why today's consumers are being referred to as omni-shoppers (Herrero-Crespo et al., 2021). One of the main questions that will come to mind on this approach to satisfying needs is 'why would consumers engage in the trouble of using multiple approaches before buying the products?'. An easy and logical response to this question is that such an approach gives the consumers the opportunity to reap benefits associated with both routes leading to the purchase. This is a rather broad justification for this approach. It will be helpful to go into the specific benefits identifiable with each of the two approaches. Reviewing what has been written about this topic (Flavian et al., 2016; Basak et al., 2017; Rejon-Guardia and Luna-Nevarez, 2017; Arora et al., 2022), Figure 6.3 below presents, at a glance, reasons why consumers engage in showrooming.

The convenience of buying products online is improving significantly as the development in technology increases. Apart from avoiding the long queue for payment, online purchase tends to attract a convenient return process. Meanwhile, a way of managing the process and reducing the risk of making the wrong choice, consumers do visit the

**154** DIGITAL TRANSFORMATION AND PSYCHOLOGICAL BEHAVIOUR

**FIGURE 6.3** Consumer motivation for showrooming

store ahead of the purchase to ask questions about the product and get clarification from the sales staff. Besides, as a way of encouraging online purchases, retailers often introduce special price deals for this channel of sales and often have high-quality service for online transactions. However, consumers engaging in showrooming complement these shopping benefits by fulfilling various other desirable goals. For example, they would have the opportunity to feel and touch the product in the store which is very important to some consumers and specifically important for some products. Moreover, sitting behind the computer to order the products from somewhere convenient would eliminate the possibility of social interactions they could have at the shopping mall.

One useful explanation proposed by Arora et al. (2022) shows that showrooming may not be deliberate and could be situational which can also be categorised into two factors:

- Sales-personal;
- Store-related factors.

In this schema, sales-personal factors include rude, poor, and disrespectful behaviour of the sales staff while store-related factors mean long queues in the retail store and poor product assortment (Arora et al., 2022).

More often than not, showrooming is presented negatively in that it results in what is called value co-destruction, indicating that it results in a decline in the well-being of the business because the consumer that visits the store received value but did not reciprocate through a financial transaction, rather acting as a free rider (Plé and Cáceres, 2010; Daunt and Harris, 2017). So, it is considered a key challenge to managers. However, it has been shown that multichannel retailers can benefit from it when they induce consumers for pseudo-showrooming whereby information is offered in the store to cover online exclusive products (Gu and Tayi, 2016).

## WEBROOMING: A KEY PART OF DYNAMIC CONSUMER BEHAVIOUR

As more and more consumers use technology in the purchasing process, they exhibit various interesting behavioural patterns. One of the prominent types of this is webrooming, which is another cross-channel shopping behaviour. Unlike in the case of showrooming where the consumer first visits the offline store for information before making the purchase online, webrooming involves moving in the opposite direction of this pattern. The popularity of this approach can be seen not only in the purchase of electrical and electronic products like dishwashers, TV sets, or cookers, it also applies to sales of luxury items (Shankar and Jain, 2021). Today, consumers search online and explore the reviews of products to be bought as made by previous users. This electronic word-of-mouth (eWOM) communication available online helps consumers to evaluate the products and reduce uncertainty about the product and the purchase prior to visiting the offline store for the transaction. Flavian et al. (2016) found that combining online search with offline purchase improves the pre-choice and post-purchase experience of the consumers. In webrooming, consumers make efforts to reduce or avoid risks such as product risk, financial risk, convenience risk, performance risk (Arora and Sahney, 2018), and social risk. In addition to these, consumers also favour webrooming due to risks associated with online purchasing and the distrust they have for online stores (Arora and Sahney, 2017).

In a study conducted by JNRI, about 74% of the 2000 consumers that constituted the sample in the United Kingdom and the United States practise webrooming (JNRI, 2019; Kleinlercher et al., 2020). This is a considerable figure. The challenge for businesses in this case is the free-riding behaviour of some of the consumers, they search a seller's website and make the most of the information obtained there but end up buying from another retailer (Heitz-Spahn, 2013). So, marketers are expected to have robust strategies in place in order to be able to keep webroomers engaged, not only on the information on the website but on their market offerings in order to convert the web visits to sales. It has been suggested that when operating omnichannel system, marketers should make it easy for the customers to switch seamlessly from online selling platform to offline store (Verhoef et al., 2020).

We know that it is not in all cases that searching online results in an actual purchase. In the study of Kleinlercher et al. (2020) on the antecedents of webrooming in omnichannel retailing, they found that retailers may drive webrooming behaviour among consumers who search online through the use of channel-related variables, psychographic variables, product-related variables, and shopping motivations. According to these authors, when a retailer is interested in increasing its share of webroomers, they could emphasise instore price promotions on their website.

## SENSORY THRESHOLD

Just as we have variations in different aspects of life such as our height, weight, age, and many other things, there are differences in what we can perceive. One of these is the extent to which we can pick up stimuli. This is what sensory threshold explains. It is the stage at which a stimulus will be detected by an individual. Meanwhile, absolute threshold refers to the minimum level for stimulation that can be detected by our applicable senses. This should be a key reference point for marketers in the design of marketing stimuli to ensure that they can achieve the desired objective. So, the relevant question can be like 'are the letters big or bold enough in a poster or billboard to be seen by the target audience? Is the audio message in a commercial jingle clear or loud enough to trigger consciousness of the message and the intended purpose?' A closely related phenomenon in the sensory threshold is the differential threshold, which is the stage at which the difference between two stimuli can be detected. As marketers develop new models of their offerings, the knowledge of this will be helpful to gauge if the consumers can notice the difference between the old and the new models in order to justify the new price. We can notice these in many aspects of our daily consumption, taste of a new menu at a restaurant, size and volume of new products, processing times of services in banks, hairdressing salon processing, and many others. This brings us to the notion of just noticeable difference (JND) which is the minimum difference between stimuli that can be detected by a majority of the people.

The JND is closely linked to Weber's law which states that the stronger the initial stimulus, the greater a difference will be needed for people to notice it. We can illustrate this in any areas of the marketing mix elements. If we focus on pricing as an example, we can compare price discounts offered on a range of products. While a £10 discount on a pair of shoes sold for £100 could be seen to be considerable, a discount of the same amount on an automobile sold for £10,000 will not attract a similar perception of value gain even though the same amount of money will be saved on both cases. Similarly, merely removing a stage from the loan application process of a bank such that it reduces the stages from 28 to 27 days to final decision will not be perceived as significant compared to a competing offering that uses only application leading to a decision being given on the following or same day.

Another related phenomenon is **subliminal perception**. It is about creating a stimulus below people's threshold of awareness. Why would marketers be interested in a threshold below the target consumers' awareness? This is an interesting question in that the effectiveness of the term remains nonconclusive. The core argument supporting the use of the phenomenon is that the subtle feature of such promotional messages escapes the consumers' safeguard against conventional marketing communication messages. Hence, the quick flash of the message or subtle appearance would trigger consumer action. These messages feature in several forms such as music videos, movies, and cartoons to influence subconscious behaviour. In a study by Borovac Zekan and Zekan (2022) to investigate if subliminal messages in advertising really work, their findings are quite revealing and indicate that its understanding in relation to emotion and instinct is evident. Similarly, in a study involving two experiments published in the *Journal of Applied Psychology*, Smith and Rogers (1994) also demonstrated the effectiveness of subliminal messages in TV marketing communication messages. Nonetheless, scepticism remains. The argument on the other side of the divide indicates that there is no evidence that subliminal marketing communication works (Urban and White, 1992). Despite this, many businesses have used this to promote their products and services.

## MARKETING APPLICATION OF CONSUMER PERCEPTION

Perception has been a very useful topic in consumer behaviour over the years. Examples of the commonly discussed areas of application of the topic are:

- Perceptual map;
- Positioning and repositioning;
- Perceived risks;
- Perception and the marketing mix.

A perceptual map is a tool often used by marketers to gauge the consumers' view of the relative standing of their products and services in comparison with those of their competitors. Essentially, it is a visual representation of competing brands based on consumers' perspectives in relation to the ratings of the products on the basis of the relevant attributes. Since the consumers are the ultimate judge of the fitness of the market offerings in terms of how they meet their needs, their evaluation of these products, services, or brands in relation to the relevant criteria is fundamental to the presentation of the perceptual map. We will now look at an example of a perceptual map in the automobile market.

Figure 6.4 shows a map drawn based on two dimensions, of whether the car is conservative or sporty, and price, which is presented on whether the brand is of high price or low price. So, it can be said that a Honda is more affordable than a Lexus while Nissan is more sporty than Lexus or Volkswagen. Another example shown in Figure 6.5 is hypothetical and focuses on firms/brands involving two dimensions of a range of services and prices charged by logistics companies. In this, Serv B charges more than Serv E which offers the narrowest range of services of all firms in the business, while Serv B charges more than serv G but offers a narrower range of services than the latter. Other positions on the map can be explained in a similar manner. Meanwhile, a new firm that is interested in joining the industry would be looking for gaps in the market to maximize efficiency and profit and an example of such gaps is shown in the map with the brand Serv Z, which charges the lowest in the industry.

## POSITIONING AND REPOSITIONING

Following from the discussion of the perceptual map, we can see that each product, service, or brand occupied a position in the marketplace as determined in terms of

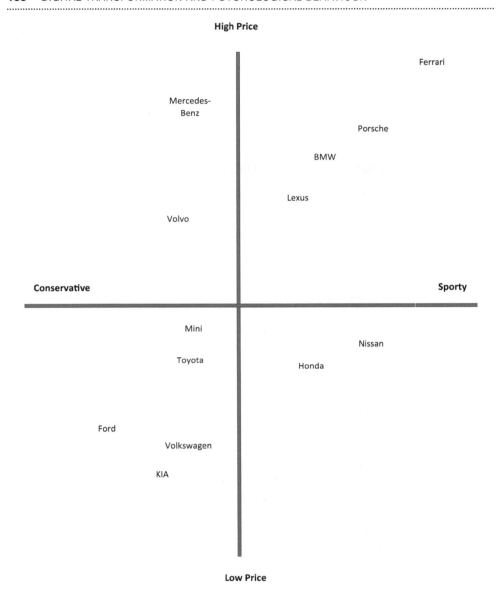

**FIGURE 6.4** Perceptual map for the automobile industry

how they are in the minds of the consumers. This is about the positioning of the product, service, or brand. The positioning map is so important that it can guide new entrants into the business to know the appropriate location for positioning the new product so that it can be seen to be addressing needs in the marketplace that remain untapped.

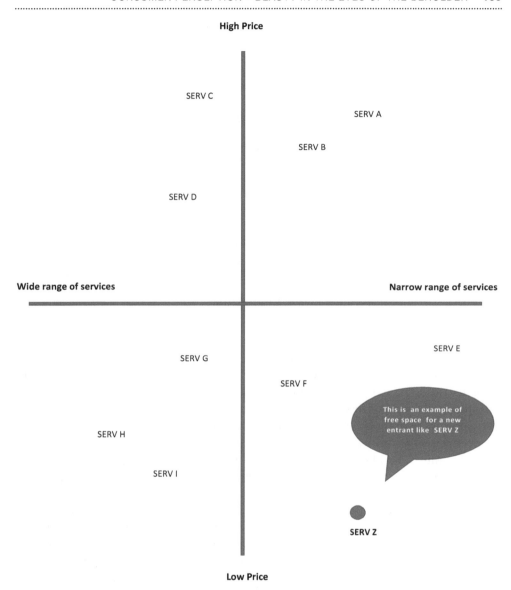

**FIGURE 6.5** Perceptual map for logistics companies

## PERCEIVED RISK

Consumers' perception about the risks associated with a product or service will influence their choices to a great extent. This tends to vary in relation to some factors such as the individual making the decision and the type of products or services involved. For example, the perceived risk of a customer who has experience of using a product and had a satisfactory experience will be far lower compared to someone buying it for

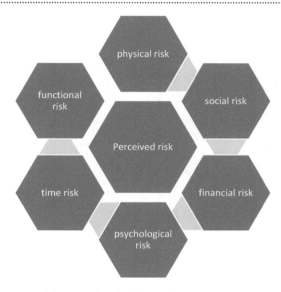

**FIGURE 6.6** Some common risks associated with purchases

the first time. Some of the commonly discussed risks associated with the purchasing of market offerings are shown in Figure 6.6.

The physical risk of a product is the likelihood of a product or service causing harm to the user. Consumers tend to gauge this between the choices available. A common example of this is the warning on a packet of cigarettes that is meant to alert consumers to the danger associated with their consumption, though the degree of effectiveness of this to trigger consumers' perceived risk associated with smoking has been limited. Food items, pharmaceutical products, chemical products, and electrical products are examples of products commonly discussed in relation to physical risk. Clarity around the usage of these products tends to help mitigate the misgivings that consumers may have about them. Financial risk is about the possibility of incurring financial loss in the transaction. It is about examining the financial investment in relation to the value of the product. We can link this to individual circumstances such as level of wealth and degree of **involvement** in a product. A billionaire is unlikely to be too bothered about the financial risk associated with the purchase of a new pair of shoes or a TV set whereas these would be a big deal to consumers in the low-income spectrum. Sometimes, we are concerned about how others will react to our products. Many decisions are driven by our consciousness of others as we discussed in Chapter 5 about reference groups. The discussion of the possibility of the product or service not being a good fit into what would be considered socially acceptable by the group one belongs to is what **social risk** addresses. The **functional risk** of a product or service is the possibility of the product or service meeting the identified needs leading to a decision. The question here is 'will it work exactly in a way that will meet the customer's expectation?' We can see many examples of this in our day-to-day consumption. One is about the lifespan of a car battery or those used to power other electrical and electronic equipment. Consumers also consider functional risk in the functional abilities of cookers, dishwashers, and refrigerators. Consumers may even be considering the option of which bank to use that will be more resilient to economic instability. The **time risk** is associated with weighing the degree of uncertainty associated with the timing of the purchase. The time value of money has been a significant discussion in economics for many years which emphasises that time is of the essence in some consumption transactions. We can look at examples of discounts and other promotional offers given by firms. When a product is offered with sales promotion packages, this often gives consumers a specific time to explore the opportunities after which the offer will be over. Consumers tend to consider the risk associated with delay in buying that product in that they will have to pay more to acquire the products or services when the offer is over. Meanwhile, conversely, some consumers tend to delay some transactions because they have expectations that some sales promotional packages will be offered later so that they can take advantage of this at the given time. Meanwhile, the notion of self-concept has been acknowledged as a key driving factor in consumption. It is about consumers' perception of self. Accordingly, the **psychological risk** addresses the issue of how consumers perceive themselves vis-à-vis their purchase decision (Szmigin and Piacentini, 2018). So, it is about gauging the extent to which consumers' decision on products or services is consistent with their self-perception. For example, consumers whose self-identity has been linked to luxury would feel unease at buying conventional or mainstream market offerings as circumstances may demand because they would perceive incongruence in this and their self-identity. Similarly, there is a psychological risk associated with the act of a consumer that prides himself or herself as a healthy-living consumer if he or she settles for an unhealthy meal as it is not consistent with their self-identity.

## PERCEPTION AND THE MARKETING MIX

The practical application of perception in marketing covers all the elements of the marketing mix. For example, the notion of perceived value, which is in relation to consumers' perception of the worth of a market offering, is an important issue in marketing. Given that this is what the customers are willing to pay, it is important for marketers to pay special attention to this. This is especially so as competition increases in the marketplace in that customer affinity and loyalty lies with the firm that offers them the value package they desire. In the same vein, as marketers offer, re-introduce, and reposition their products and services, consumers' perception becomes very important to gauge the suitability of the 'real change' when marketers claim to have modified their offerings. We tend to see this in the strategic actions of marketers when products are at the decline stage in the product life cycle (PLC). Consumers would consider whether any product modification introduced at that stage is perceived as considerable and valuable. The perceived service quality of the customer of a hotel would cover many areas such as the ease of booking online, activities at the reception, meals served in the restaurant, furniture and fittings, maintenance, and a host of others. Consumers also have a perception about the distribution outlets or means and ease of obtaining the products and various marketing communication tools used. Consumers' perception on all these and other aspects of the business can be a defining factor in relation to success or failure in the marketplace.

> **PAUSE, PLAN, AND PRACTICE: FEDEX:**
>
> FedEx is an organisation notable for excellent service in logistics. Its services are notably evident from Lagos to London, Paris to Peru, China to Chad, Japan to Jordan, and other parts of the world. It is specifically about improving people's lives by connecting them with goods, services, and ideas to create opportunities in society. The FedEx logo, which was designed in 1994 by Landor Associates, has been an enduring brand of Federal Express over the years, which resonates with the customers. The design of the logo has elements of Gestalt psychology in how consumers interpret it as a stimulus. In the design, there is a forward-facing arrow between 'E' and 'X' which follows the figure and ground principle. It has remained captivating as a marketing communication message.
>
> **Source:**
>
> Creative Review (nd) 20. FedEx (1994), www.creativereview.co.uk/fedex-logo/ (accessed 24 August 2022).
>
> **Task**: Explore the Internet as a group and search for another example of the principle of Gestalt psychology applied in marketing.

## SUMMARY

It is often said that beauty lies in the eyes of the beholder. Perception is about how consumers select, organise, and interpret stimuli that they are exposed to from the environment through their sense organs. The attention consumers pay to a stimulus is determined by a number of criteria such as relevance, novelty, pleasantness, size, colour, and how it is positioned. Gestalt psychology has been at the forefront of stimulus interpretation and the principles associated with this include principles of closure, proximity, figure and ground, and similarity. The notion of semiotics, which is about the use of signs and symbols for communicating messages, plays a significant role in perception. The use of digital technology has heightened the relevance of virtual reality, mixed reality, augmented reality, webrooming, and showrooming in consumer perception. The practical application of perception as a topic covers many areas including the use of perceptual maps, product positioning and repositioning, understanding of perceived risks, and how perception is linked to marketing mix elements.

**DIGITAL BOX: VIRTUAL REALITY AT WREN KITCHENS**

Getting a new kitchen is now a big deal. Consumers are not only interested in kitchens at competitive prices but also those that are fit for purpose. This has been the business of Wren Kitchens which is notably the Number 1 kitchen company in the UK. It produces about 2000 kitchens every week to the delight of its growing number of customers. The company has now moved beyond the UK with the objective of creating value for international customers. The process of buying a kitchen can be daunting, beginning with a home visit to take measurements, planning the layout, manufacturing, delivery, and installation. Meanwhile, the use of digital technology has given Wren Kitchens an opportunity to introduce virtual reality as the client and staff work through the plan towards having the desired kitchen in place. It's a fascinating experience for the customer who visualises what will be in the dream kitchen, chooses the style, colours, materials, and equipment and, with the help of a store designer, the new kitchen emerges in a 3D model of the bespoke kitchen. With virtual reality, consumers are able to move things around, add, and remove items from the computer-generated kitchen image which gives the customers a near real-life perception of the new kitchen. It is seen by consumers as a key revolution to kitchen design and production that facilitates transactions and enhances their purchase experience.

**Task:** Choose another business/transaction and explain how virtual reality can be applied to it.

## END OF CHAPTER DISCUSSION QUESTIONS

1. Make a list of ten market offerings and map them to the appropriate senses that they appeal to. Discuss the appropriate marketing strategies that will be useful to the brand managers based on your mapping.
2. Draw a perceptual map for any one physical product and a service offering using relevant dimensions. Assume you are proposing to invest in each of these two markets, and identify the gaps for the new product or service offering in the market that is safe for this investment.
3. What would a company be missing for not adopting virtual reality or augmented reality in this contemporary marketing environment? Webrooming is an important aspect of business in recent times because of the proliferation of the use of the Internet. In view of this, would you suggest to your friend who is contemplating buying a new gas cooker and vacuum cleaner to adopt this approach in these transactions? Give reasons.
4. Assume you have been appointed as the marketing director of a group of companies that sells cars, handbags, mobile phones, confectioneries, and tissue papers. Imagine, from the consumers' viewpoint, the combination of types of consumers' perceived risks which would be related to each of the products. Discuss the implication of these for your marketing communication strategies.
5. Use appropriate examples to discuss the following terms:
    a) Gestalt psychology and consumer behaviour;
    b) Just noticeable difference;

c) Consumer perceived risk in financial markets;
d) Repositioning a salon business from unisex to be gender neutral.

> **Case Study: Product Positioning for Unique Experiences at Nike**
>
> Over the years consumers have come to link Nike to sports, success, and smartness. The popularity of the brand continues to increase and the stark difference between the Nike of today compared to its state at its humble beginnings in 1964, when it was founded by Bill Bowerman and Phil Knight, and 1971 when the name Nike was first adopted, is considerably evident. Even without the name Nike, merely seeing the solid swoosh that communicates the brand of the organisation already resonates with athletes and sports lovers who purchase the firm's various products such as clothing, footwear, and other sports accessories. The formulation and implementation of Nike's marketing strategy are notably successful as shown in the relevant statistics. The revenue for the third quarter of 2022 has increased by 5% from the data recorded for 2021 to $10.9 billion. Similarly, direct sales have increased by 15% on a reported basis while its currency-neutral data increase is 17%. Nike's success story also reflects in its digital sales data which has increased during the year. The assortment of Nike offerings is considerable. In the clothing line, there are tops and T-shirts, jackets, hoodies and sweatshirts, tracksuits, socks, and several other items. In the shoe range, there are some that are noted as lifestyle, running, football, basketball, and many others. In fact, to clearly show its position for an organisation with a focus on sports, it also organises its products on the classification of a sport-by-sport basis. So, when a consumer is interested in sporting wear for tennis, football, golf, yoga, or any other type of sport, they are directly connected to make their shopping experience worthwhile. As shown in its segmentation strategy, the firm has those products specifically designed for kids as compared to others meant for adults. Even among kids, Nike presents products for baby and toddler, younger kids, and older kids.
>
> Nike's presence both online and offline exposes consumers to a superflux of stimuli of athletic clothes, shows, and accessories. This is a perfect blend because consumers are able to visit online and buy later in the stores located in over 170 countries where the company is located, where they can have the opportunity to physically touch the products before concluding the transaction. In several other instances, consumers engage in showrooming in which they first visit the store to speak to staff about the suitability of the product and then buy the product online because of the additional benefits. The marketing communications message of Nike is notably captivating, beginning from the strapline 'Just Do It' which appears on its messages, including those on its social media platforms. Looking back at some of these ad messages shows that Nike carefully plans its messages in terms of exposure, attention, and interpretation. Examples of these messages are '*You can't stop us, One Day, we won't need this Day, Find your Greatness*, and *Dream Crazier.*' In these and other messages, Nike takes and positions these messages clearly and effectively and offers the audience the opportunity to tease out the meanings.

To get attention, Nike is focused on novelty, as it introduces unique products that are uniquely promoted. The company also ensures that its ad messages are pleasant. Over the years, it has promoted its products in various ways including the adoption of celebrity endorsement. Sports personalities like Cristiano Ronaldo, Roger Federer, Serena Williams, and Tiger Woods among many others have been engaged by Nike to endorse its products. This is strategically planned to get the attention of consumers for its various products. Moreover, its products and promotional messages are athletic products specifically targeted at athletes which ensures that the message is relevant to the target segment. In order to be able to secure attention and interpretation of its stimuli, the company adopts the principle of similarity and closure.

Clearly, the brand is an industry leader when compared to competing brands such as Reebok, Adidas, and Under Armour. It enjoys a positive consumer rating in terms of perceived quality. The organisation is notably synonymous with innovation, high quality, and stylish products which indicates that an increase in the price of its products does not specifically repel consumers' interest in those products. So, it has consistent and attractive brand equity. This is not surprising as the organisation invests heavily in research and development, having over 40 researchers dedicated to unravelling new ways to delight their various customers, who are not only sportsmen and women but also ordinary people who have become attracted to its high standard of offerings in the marketplace.

**Sources:**

Firstlawcomic (nd). How many countries has Nike expanded to, first-law-comic.com/how-many-countries-has-nike-expanded-to/ (accessed 22 August 2022).

Nike (2022). Nike, Inc, reports fiscal 2022 third quarter results, March 21. 2022, about.nike.com/en/newsroom/reports/nike-inc-reports-fiscal-2022-third-quarter-results (accessed 19 August 2022).

Robinson, L. (2022). 30 interesting facts about Nike, FACT shop, www.thefactshop.com/fashion-facts/nike-facts/#:~:text=30%20Interesting%20Facts%20About%20Nike%201%20It%20was,at%20Portland%20State%20University.%20…%20More%20items…%20 (accessed 19th August 2022)

Wilson, R. (2020). 5 most inspirational ad campaigns by Nike with powerful messages, www.marketingmind.in/5-most-inspirational-ad-campaigns-by-nike-with-powerful-messages (accessed 22 August 2022).

## CASE STUDY QUESTIONS

1. Draw a positioning map for a widely known brand of sportswear to clearly show the position of Nike with the use of appropriate dimensions;
2. Suggest a new product idea for Nike and how to promote it with the use of novelty, colour, and size for getting the attention of the target audience;

3. Given the increasing popularity of online marketing among consumers and the benefits such as convenience and cost-efficiency, would you advise Nike to be completely online?
4. Based on information from this case study and the one you can see on the company's website, explain how Nike uses semiotics in its marketing activities.

## REFERENCES

Arora, S., & Sahney, S. (2017). Webrooming behaviour: A conceptual framework. *International Journal of Retail & Distribution Management, 45*(7/8), 762–781.

Arora, S., & Sahney, S. (2018). Antecedents to consumers' showrooming behaviour: An integrated TAM-TPB framework. *Journal of Consumer Marketing, 35*(4), 438–450.

Arora, S., Sahney, S., & Parida, R. R. (2022). Drivers of showrooming behaviour: Insights from integrated perspectives. *International Journal of Retail & Distribution Management, 50*(3), 398–413.

Azuma, A. T. (1997). A survey on augmented reality. *Presence, 6*(4), 355–385.

Bae, S., & Lee, T. (2011). Gender differences in consumers' perception of online consumer reviews. *Electronic Commerce Research, 11*(2), 201–214.

Basak, S., Basu, P., Avittathur, B., & Sikdar, S. (2017). A game theoretic analysis of multi-channel retail in the context of showrooming. *Decision Support Systems, 103*(1), 34–45.

Beck, A., Kahl, J., & Liebl, B. (2012). Wissensstandsanalyse zu Verbraucherschutz und Verarbeitung ökologischer Lebensmittel, www.fibl.org/fileadmin/documents/shop/1582-wissensstandsanalyse.pdf (downloaded 18 November 2012).

Bilgihan, A., Barreda, A., Okumus, F., & Nusair, K. (2016). Consumer perception of knowledge-sharing in travel-related online social networks. *Tourism Management, 52*, 287–296.

Borovac Zekan, S., & Zekan, I. (2022, February). Subliminal messages in advertising: do they really work? In *DIEM: Dubrovnik International Economic Meeting, 7*(1), 102–113. Sveučilište u Dubrovniku.

Bourlakis, M., Papagiannidis, S., & Li, F. (2009). Retail spatial evolution: Paving the way from traditional to metaverse retailing. *Electronic Commerce Research, 9*(1–2), 135–148.

Daunt, K. L., & Harris, L. C. (2017). Consumer showrooming: Value co-destruction. *Journal of Retailing and Consumer Services, 38*, 166–176.

Davis, F. D. (1989). Perceived usefulness, perceived ease of use, and user acceptance of information technology. *MIS Quarterly, 13*(4), 319–340.

Ducoffe, R. H. (1996). Advertising value and advertising the web. *Journal of Advertising Research, 36*(5), 21–35.

Farshid, M., Paschen, J., Eriksson, T., & Kietzmann, J. (2018). Go boldly!: Explore augmented reality (AR), virtual reality (VR), and mixed reality (MR) for business. *Business Horizons, 61*(5), 657–663.

Flavian, C., Gurrea, R., & Orús, C. (2016). Choice confidence in the webrooming purchase process: The impact of online positive reviews and the motivation to touch. *Journal of Consumer Behavior, 15*(5), 459–476.

Gensler, S., Neslin, S. A., & Verhoef, P. C. (2017). The showrooming phenomenon: It's more than just about price. *Journal of Interactive Marketing, 38*, 29–43.

Gu, J. Z., & Tayi, G. K. (2016). Consumer pseudo-showrooming and omni-channel product placement strategies. *Management Information Systems Quarterly*, MIS Quarterly *41*(2), 583–606.

Gutiérrez, M., Vexo, F., & Thalmann, D. (2008). *Stepping into Virtual Reality*. London: Springer.

Heitz-Spahn, S. (2013). Cross-channel free-riding consumer behaviour in a multichannel environment: An investigation of shopping motives, sociodemographics and product categories. *Journal of Retailing and Consumer Services*, 20, 570–578. doi: 10.1016/j.jretconser.2013.07.006

Heller, J., Chylinski, M., Ruyter, K. D., Mahr, D., & Keeling, D. I. (2019). Let me imagine that for you: Transforming the retail frontline through augmenting customer mental imagery ability. *Journal of Retailing*, 95(2), 94–114.

Herrero-Crespo, A., Viejo-Fernández, N., Collado-Agudo, J., & Pérez, M. J. S. (2021). Webrooming or showrooming, that is the question: Explaining omnichannel behavioural intention through the technology acceptance model and exploratory behaviour. *Journal of Fashion Marketing and Management: An International Journal*, 26(3), 401–419.

Holz, T., Campbell, A. G., O'Hare, G. M., Stafford, J. W., Martin, A., & Dragone, M. (2011). Mira—mixed reality agents. *International Journal of Human-Computer Studies*, 69(4), 251–268.

Hoyer, W. D., Kroschke, M., Schmitt, B., Kraume, K., & Shankar, V. (2020). Transforming the customer experience through new technologies. *Journal of Interactive Marketing*. https://doi.org/ 10.1016/j.intmar.2020.04.001.

Huang, T. L., & Liao, S. (2015). A model of acceptance of augmented-reality interactive technology: The moderating role of cognitive innovativeness. *Electronic Commerce Research*, 15(2), 269–295.

Interaction Design Foundation (nd). Virtual Reality, Interaction Design Foundation, www.interaction-design.org/literature/topics/virtual-reality (accessed 16 October 2023).

Javornik, A. (2016). 'It's an illusion, but it looks real!' Consumer affective, cognitive and behavioural responses to augmented reality applications. *Journal of Marketing Management*, 32(9–10), 987–1011.

JRNI (2019). What retailers need to know about webrooming & showrooming. Available online at: https://www.jrni.com/blog/webrooming-vs-showrooming (accessed 23 October 2020).

Kempf, D. A. S., & Palan, K. M. (2006). The effects of gender and argument strength on the processing of word-of-mouth communication. *Academy of Marketing Studies Journal*, 10(1), 1–18.

Kim, J., & Forsythe, S. (2008). Adoption of virtual try-on technology for online apparel shopping. *Journal of Interactive Marketing*, 22(2), 45–59.

Kim, T. H., & Choo, H. J. (2021). Augmented reality as a product presentation tool: Focusing on the role of product information and presence in AR. *Fashion and Textiles*, 8(1), 1–23.

Kleinlercher, K., Linzmajer, M., Verhoef, P. C., & Rudolph, T. (2020). Antecedents of webrooming in omnichannel retailing. *Frontiers in Psychology*, 3342.

Lawless, H. T., & Heymann, H. (2010). Sensory Evaluation of Food: Principles and Practices, 2nd edn, New York: Springer. http://dx.doi.org/10.1007/978-1-4419-6488-5

Lee, K. C., & Chung, N. (2008). Empirical analysis of consumer reaction to the virtual reality shopping mall. *Computers in Human Behavior*, 24(1), 88–104.

Lindberg, U., Salomonson, N., Sundström, M., & Wendin, K. (2018). Consumer perception and behavior in the retail foodscape–A study of chilled groceries. *Journal of Retailing and Consumer Services*, 40, 1–7.

Liu, J., Bian, Y., Xi, Y., Zheng, Y., Huang, J., Gai, W., ... & Meng, X. (2022). Evaluating the role of mixed reality in cognitive training of children with ASD: Evidence from a mixed reality aquarium. *International Journal of Human-Computer Studies*, 162, 102815.

Mathwick, C., Malhotra, N., & Rigdon, E. (2001). Experiential value: Conceptualization, measurement and application in the catalog and internet shopping environment. *Journal of Retailing*, 77(1), 51–60.

McLean, G., & Wilson, A. (2019). Shopping in the digital world: Examining customer engagement through augmented reality mobile applications. *Computers in Human Behavior*, 101, 210–224.

Meißner, M., Pfeiffer, J., Peukert, C., Dietrich, H., & Pfeiffer, T. (2020). How virtual reality affects consumer choice. *Journal of Business Research*, *117*, 219–231.

Milgram, P., & Kishino, F. (1994). A taxonomy of mixed reality visual displays. *IEICE Transactions on Information and Systems*, E77-D (12), 1321–1329.

Mugge, R., Dahl, D. W., & Schoormans, J. P. (2018). "What you see, is what you get?" Guidelines for influencing consumers' perceptions of consumer durables through product appearance. *Journal of Product Innovation Management*, *35*(3), 309–329.

Oyman, M., Bal, D., & Ozer, S. (2022). Extending the technology acceptance model to explain how perceived augmented reality affects consumers' perceptions. *Computers in Human Behavior*, *128*, 107127.

Pantano, E., Rese, A., & Baier, D. (2017). Enhancing the online decision-making process by using augmented reality: A two country comparison of youth markets. *Journal of Retailing and Consumer Services*, *38*, 81–95.

Pizzi, G., Scarpi, D., Pichierri, M., & Vannucci, V. (2019). Virtual reality, real reactions?: Comparing consumers' perceptions and shopping orientation across physical and virtual-reality retail stores. *Computers in Human Behavior*, *96*, 1–12.

Plé, L., & Cáceres, R. C. (2010). Not always co-creation: Introducing interactional co-destruction of value in service-dominant logic. *Journal of Services Marketing*, *24*(6), 430–437.

Preece, J., Sharp, H., & Rogers, Y. (2015). *Interaction design – Beyond human-computer interaction*. Chichester: John Wiley & Sons.

Promolta (nd), How To Use Color To Grab Your Audience's Attention, https://blog.promolta.com/how-to-use-color-to-grab-your-audiences-attention/ (accessed, 20th June, 2022).

Qin, H., Peak, D. A., & Prybutok, V. (2021). A virtual market in your pocket: How does mobile augmented reality (MAR) influence consumer decision making? *Journal of Retailing and Consumer Services*, *58*, 102337.

Rejon-Guardia, F., & Luna-Nevarez, C. (2017). Showrooming in consumer electronics retailing: An empirical study. *Journal of Internet Commerce*, *16*(2), 174–201.

Ruppert, B. (2011). New directions in the use of virtual reality for food shopping: Marketing and education perspectives. *Journal of Diabetes Science and Technology*, *5*(2), 315–318.

Schleenbecker, R., & Hamm, U. (2013). Consumers' perception of organic product characteristics. A review. *Appetite*, *71*, 420–429.

Shankar, A., & Jain, S. (2021). Factors affecting luxury consumers' webrooming intention: A moderated-mediation approach. *Journal of Retailing and Consumer Services*, *58*, 102306.

Sijtsema, S. J., Onwezen, M. C., Reinders, M. J., Dagevos, H., Partanen, A., & Meeusen, M. (2016). Consumer perception of bio-based products—An exploratory study in 5 European countries. *NJAS-Wageningen Journal of Life Sciences*, *77*, 61–69.

Smith, K. H., & Rogers, M. (1994). Effectiveness of subliminal messages in television commercials: Two experiments. *Journal of Applied Psychology*, *79*(6), 866.

Solomon, M. R. (2020). *Consumer Behaviour: Buying, Having, and Being*, 13th edn, Essex: Pearson Education Limited.

Statista (2018). Forecast augmented (AR) and virtual reality (VR) market size worldwide from 2016 to 2022 (in billion U.S. dollars), https:// www.statista.com/statistics/591181/global-augmented-virtual-reality-market-size/ (accessed 9 March 2020).

Statista (2016). Share of internet users in the United States who have utilized showrooming and webrooming as of September 2014, www.statista.com/statistics/ 448677/uswebrooming-showrooming-penetration/ (accessed 10 April 2016).

Steuer, J. (1992). Defining virtual reality: Dimensions determining telepresence. *Journal of Communication*, *42*(4), 73–93.

Swahn, J., Mossberg, L., Öström, Å., & Gustafsson, I. B. (2012). Sensory description labels for food affect consumer product choice. *European Journal of Marketing*, 46(11), 1628–1646. http://dx. doi.org/10.1108/03090561211260013

Szmigin, I, & Piacentini, M. (2018). *Consumer Behaviour*. Oxford: Oxford University Press.

Urban, M., & White, C. (1992). Point-counterpoint: A campaign against sublimination perception. *Psychology & Marketing (1986–1998)*, 9(1), 77.

van Herpen, E., van den Broek, E., van Trijp, H. C., & Yu, T. (2016). Can a virtual supermarket bring realism into the lab? Comparing shopping behavior using virtual and pictorial store representations to behavior in a physical store. *Appetite*, 107, 196–207.

van Krevelen, D. W. F., & Poelman, R. (2010). A survey of augmented reality technologies, applications and limitations. *The International Journal of Virtual Reality*, 9(2), 1–20.

Verhoef, P. C., van Ittersum, K., Kannan, P. K., & Inman, J. (2020). Omnichannel retailing: A consumer perspective, in *Handbook of Consumer Psychology*, eds L. Kahle, T. Lowrey, and J. Huber (Cambridge, MA: Academic Press).

wearesocial.com. (2021). Digital 2021, https://wearesocial.com/digital-2021 (accessed 14 April 2021).

Westmattelmann, D., Grotenhermen, J. G., Sprenger, M., Rand, W., & Schewe, G. (2021). Apart we ride together: The motivations behind users of mixed-reality sports. *Journal of Business Research*, 134, 316–328.

www.prnewswire.com. Augmented reality and virtual reality (AR & VR) market size is expected to reach USD 571.42 billion by 2025 | valuates reports, https://www.pr newswire.com/news-releases/augmented-reality-and-virtual-reality-ar–vr-market-si ze-is-expected-to-reach-usd-571-42-billion-by-2025–valuates-reports-301004582. html (accessed 20 October 2020).

# CHAPTER 7

# Impact of Learning and Memory on Consumer Behaviour

................................................

**LEARNING OUTCOMES**

After reading this chapter, you should be able to:

- Define consumer learning;
- Discuss behavioural learning theories;
- Discuss the cognitive learning theory;
- Critically explain and illustrate observational learning;
- Discuss consumer memory and how it works;
- Explain consumer learning in the digital age;
- Explain the 4cs typology of digital consumers and consumer learning.

**INTRODUCTION**

The choices of our goods and services, out of a plethora of options that we have, has a lot to do with learning, especially in the digital age. We buy items like clothes, shoes, laptops, and holiday packages, engage the services of hairdressers and teachers, book gym sessions and transportation services, and pay for numerous other transactions. In some cases, the experiences are very favourable and encourage us to make repeat purchases or even to the extent that we become advocates of such service providers or brands. The multiplier effect of such word-of-mouth communications can be wide-ranging. On the other hand, the expectation and actual experiences are far apart. The gap in these teaches us many things about that product or service. Moreover, in different other contexts, our consumption decisions follow what we see others do, we purposively venture into knowing about specific market offerings so that optimal decisions can be made. All these have something or another to do with our memory as consumers, as the information such as marketing stimuli that we can recall will

DOI: 10.4324/9781003242031-10

be what we can use to make informed decisions. So, the intermingling effects of these in the consumption system and the marketplace in relation to the relevance of digital technology will be our focus in this chapter. We will first begin by having an understanding of consumer learning.

## CONSUMER LEARNING

It is often said that learning is continuous in human life. This is because in most cases it is linked to experience. Consumer behaviour takes place at the intersection of two elements, which are the current consumer behaviour situation and learning history (Foxall, 2017; Almeida et al., 2020). We can simply define learning as a relatively permanent change in one's behaviour that results from experience (Solomon, 2020). Another simple relevant definition that is relatively detailed sees learning as an activity or process involving the acquisition of knowledge or skills either by practising, studying, or through experience (Szmigin and Piacentini, 2020). So, if we look at these definitions, we can logically infer that an individual learns from the 'self' and the environment. The experience of the individual can modify his or her behaviour in the future, which indicates that learning has taken place. Meanwhile, people learn through external stimuli when they observe what happens in the environment. A consumer who has an unpleasant experience with the menu of a restaurant would have learnt to avoid it when the need arises in the future. We will now look at the two commonly discussed broad theories – behavioural learning and cognitive learning.

## BEHAVIOUR LEARNING THEORIES

Behavioural learning is a type of learning that occurs as a result of an individual's interaction with, and response to, external stimuli. So, consumers learn by reacting to marketplace cues such as brands, packaging, prices, advertising messages, and service quality. Two theoretical positions commonly associated with this broad perspective on learning are classical conditioning and operant conditioning. We will now discuss each of these in turn. We can explain **classical conditioning** as what happens when a stimulus that produces a type of response is paired with another that ordinarily does not yield such a response on its own, and after repeated pairing the second stimulus then produces a similar response over time. This theory is a method of associative learning which explains instances where people or animals make connections in relation to the events happening in the environment (Shimp, 1991; Till et al., 2008). This is often traced back to the experiment conducted by a Russian psychologist known as Ivan Pavlov who was interested in studying digestion in animals. In the experiment conducted with dogs, he presented the dogs with food which usually prompts them to salivate. The food is known as the unconditioned stimulus (US) while salivation is the unconditioned response (UR). Meanwhile, he then paired the food with the ringing of a bell which led to the dog salivating. Eventually, after repeated pairing of these two stimuli, the dog ended up salivating to the bell on its own without the food. In this, the bell is known as the conditioned stimulus (CS) while the salivation to the bell without food is known as the conditioned response (CR). The implications of the study of this theory are that it reflects many aspects of the dynamics of human life and specifically explains some aspects of marketplace activities and consumer behaviour. For instance, the pairing of marketplace cues such as products and brands with celebrities in celebrity endorsement deals offers an interesting explanation of classical conditioning learning theory.

Over the years, and in various parts of the world, the use of celebrity endorsement has been a popular marketing communication strategy. The example of Dwayne Johnson endorsing Under Armour, George Clooney's endorsement of Nespresso, and Lionel Messi's endorsement of Pepsi and Huawei, like others, constitute unconditioned stimuli (US) that are paired with the brands they endorse, which then brings about conditioning in consumer behaviour for these items such as interest in the product, purchase of the items, and loyalty to the brand. Existing literature indicates that pleasant images effectively paired with brands could prompt favourable brand attitudes and result in formation of inferential belief (Priluck and Till, 2004; Till et al., 2008). Two core explanations seem to stand out as to why celebrity endorsement is on the increase (Atkin and Block, 1983: Till et al., 2008):

- Celebrities are good and relatively efficient for attracting attention as consumers are inundated with advertising messages;
- Celebrities are perceived to be more trustworthy and entertaining, hence they hold a place in the mind of the consumers.

In a study on classical conditioning and celebrity endorsers, Till et al. (2008) found that when celebrities are appropriately matched with the products being promoted, there is a stronger conditioning effect than if there is a mismatch between celebrities and brands.

From another perspective, businesses that own trusted and tested brands engage in the extension of these brands to new items as the existing brands serve as unconditional stimuli (US), which explains the notion of classical learning theory. It has been reported that 82% of consumers would very likely purchase from brands that they have experienced previously (Renderforest, 2021). Apple products such as iPhone, iPad, and Apple Watch; and Dettol products including Dettol sanitiser, Dettol handwash, and Dettol multi-surface wipes are examples of brand extensions that bring classical conditioning to light.

The key elements of this learning theory and their applications in marketing are noted as follows:

- Repetition: As a repeated pairing of the stimuli was needed in the Pavlovian experiment, repetition of the pairing of the CS and US is also crucial to its application in consumer behaviour. More often than not, celebrity endorsement deals are for a considerable period as consumers engage with the image and the associated marketing communication messages over time. This emphasises the significance of repetition for learning to take place. When brands are promoted through specific advertising messages, to avoid forgetting the message about the market offerings, it is expected that the target audience will be exposed to the message repeatedly in order to remember it and be able to act positively concerning the brand at the stage of decision. Meanwhile, marketers are expected to watch out for **extinction** or **advertising message wear-out** when it gets to the stage when advertising messages start to lose their core value or relevance for attracting customers to products or services. When this is noticed, strategic actions such as making changes to the stimulus could prove very useful in fine-tuning the message to rekindle interest in the message and ultimately in the products.

- Stimulus generalisation: The notion of generalisation is core to the discourse of classical conditioning in that the dog extends the reaction often given to food (salivation) to that of the ringing of the bell. In consumer behaviour, we see a similar principle in operation in many areas including brand extension and family branding. Given the strong positioning of their existing brand offerings, marketers tend to extend the goodwill of the existing offerings to new ones. Businesses such as Virgin, easyJet, Ferrari, and Dyson have demonstrated good examples of successful brand extension in the global marketing environment. In the family branding strategy, businesses like Unilever bring a collection of its products under the same brand to make it easier for consumers to relate to the products and have a unified impression of them. Moreover, as shown in the study of Till et al. (2008), some private-label product items may derive some benefits of stimulus generalisation from the imitation of national brands.

- Stimulus discrimination: In this context, discrimination as an implication of this theory works in the reverse order to generalisation in relation to marketing stimuli. The idea is that if consumers can generalise in the marketplace, it is important for marketers to carefully distinguish their offerings to be sure that the brand equity or goodwill is not encroached upon by competition. For example, marketers of luxury products such as Rolex, Louis Vuitton, and Gucci need to strategically design specific identifiers into their products to deter unscrupulous businesses that may want to sell counterfeit versions of their products. In most cases, the notoriety is achieved through **look-alike packaging**. Several millions of dollars are lost annually by these luxury businesses to the sales of counterfeit products in the marketplace.

## INSTRUMENTAL CONDITIONING

In instrumental conditioning, learning takes place in the form of trial-and-error as the individual learns to perform the behaviour that results in a positive outcome and avoid ones that produce a negative outcome (Solomon, 2020). So, the consequences of action shape and maintain the behaviour (Foxall, 1986; Wells, 2014). Just as Ivan Pavlov's experiment is usually linked to the discourse of classical conditioning, B. F. Skinner, a psychologist whose work is associated with instrumental conditioning, also focused on animals for the explication of his theory. He focused on birds for the study. In the experiment, when the animals exhibited the desired behaviour, they were rewarded with food which serves as positive reinforcement. In the consumer behaviour context, the consumer that has bought a handbag to complement her outfits and is commended for being attractive would have learnt that the brand bought is good and gives her the desired results. This serves as positive reinforcement that will result in repeat purchase and loyalty to the brand. Meanwhile, it is important to also explain the aspect of negative reinforcement which is about taking an action that averts negative consequences. A consumer with an unpleasant skin condition, who tries several brands of antiseptic soaps with no positive results until she finally tries one that gives her the desired improvement to her skin, would have learnt that the last brand tried is the best one having achieved the desired result. This is an example of negative reinforcement. As a way of clearly differentiating these two pathways, we can look at the contention of Schiffman and Kanuk (2010), who indicate that positive reinforcement is about the events that add something to the situation whereas negative reinforcement removes something from the same situation. So, in the latter scenario, the focus is on taking action to prevent a negative consequence. In the consumer behaviour context, most insurance products fit the negative reinforcement scenario. For example, taking a car or home insurance policy is to prevent situations such as being stranded without care after an accident, theft, or any other unfortunate event. More often than not the marketing communication messages associated with insurance products are presented with fear as an emotional appeal to make the audience respond by buying the policies to prevent adverse effects when one suffers loss.

It is important to distinguish negative reinforcement from punishment. This is because the latter is meant to discourage a behaviour whereas negative reinforcement results in addressing an unpleasant outcome. Meanwhile, there is also the notion of extinction to be noted in instrumental conditioning. This refers to a state when the link between the stimuli and the response no longer occurs as the positive outcome anticipated or reinforcement has been removed. A firm noted for offering a good service to consumers would encourage repeat purchases, but when the firm decides to change the composition of its products or services and the new offerings no longer satisfy the consumers, then extinction sets in as the consumers would not be reacting to the products (stimulus) as they used to do before. There is a plethora of areas of consumer behaviour that are amenable to instrumental conditioning. Examples such as loyalty schemes like club cards to compensate frequent purchasers of the firm's products and services show the application of this learning theory.

## REINFORCEMENT SCHEDULES

Having an understanding of reinforcement schedules is an important part of instrumental conditioning. In the consumer behaviour context, marketers need to examine and plan the interval at which reinforcement will be offered in order to be most effective. This varies but the common patterns are continuous, fixed ratio, and variable ratio (Schiffman et al., 2012). As the names suggests, there is no specific termination time for the reinforcement offered in the continuous pattern. For example, a firm that makes free delivery a part of its package of value to its customers would continue to do that irrespective of season or other circumstances. Some high-tech companies offer continuous after-sales installation in addition to selling products of desired quality to the customers, which serves to reinforce the customers, behaviour of purchasing the products. A fixed ratio reinforcement is given at a specific number of responses given by the consumer. For example, a restaurant might offer its customers a free dinner after the purchase of ten meals. With this the customer can plan to earn this reinforcement as the sequence of the reinforcement is known. Meanwhile, a variable ratio reinforcement is random. The irregular reward from gambling makes it a highly relevant example in this case.

## COGNITIVE LEARNING THEORY

While the behavioural learning theories we have discussed so far indicate that behaviour and learning happen automatically, in reality, some learning activities do not follow this pattern. Cognitive learning theory explains the scenario when the behaviour is purposive. In cognitive learning, consumers act as problem-solvers and adopt internal mental processes to reach decisions. In other words, it is about unpacking complexities through mental information processing. Schiffman et al. (2012) show that it is analogous to a computer-information processing scenario in which there will be an input to the processing system leading to an output. With this, the consumer is seen as rational and uses information obtained from various sources in the environment to solve problems. Figure 7.1 shows the typical flow of information processing that depicts cognitive learning theory. The figure is adapted from various sources (Solomon, 2020; Schiffman et al., 2012; Szmigin and Piacentini, 2018) to develop an illustration that combines the explanation of information processing and consumer memory which will be explained later in the chapter. In the figure, the consumers receive marketing stimuli to serve as input into the processing system. The marketing stimuli could be advertising messages, brands, packaging, and information around pricing.

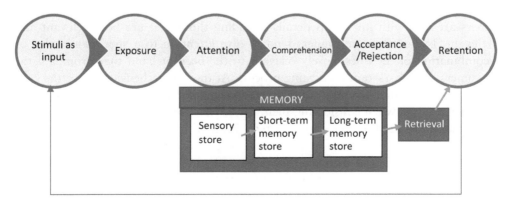

**FIGURE 7.1** Five-stage information processing process and memory

Contrary to the impulsive behaviour explained in behavioural learning, in some circumstances, consumers gather information and process it before arriving at decisions. The obvious examples here are in decisions surrounding the purchase of high-involvement products and services. Selecting the services of a surgeon will be a painstaking task and so will be the process of buying a house. Having an understanding of this is necessary for marketers so that they can design their marketing strategies accordingly. As an example, for a brand to be favoured and selected among products of the same nature, a manufacturer needs to provide adequate information to aid consumers in their selection process in order to come to an informed decision.

## OBSERVATIONAL LEARNING

Observational learning is a change in behaviour that occurs as a result of someone watching others in relation to what they do. Those being observed are known as models as their behaviours are being used as templates. One of the common examples of observational learning is that which takes place between children and their parents. For example, as discussed in Chapter 5, they learn the act of consumption and shopping from their parents and other family members. The relationship that some consumers have with some brands is based on the one they acquire from their parents' choices and interaction in the marketplace (Fournier, 1998). Another is how consumers imitate the consumption pattern of celebrities, which explains why marketers use celebrity endorsement.

## INFORMATION PROCESSING

In Figure 7.1, consumer information processing is preceded by exposure to stimuli through the various sensory organs. As shown so far, we are beginning to see another area showing the link between the chapters of the book as this is a key part of what has been discussed in Chapter 6 on perception. Exposure to stimuli takes place when consumers intentionally seek information towards solving the specific needs to be met. Evidence shows that there could be incidental exposure which prompts implicit learning (Szmigin and Piacentini, 2018). At the stage of exposure to stimuli, consumers are met with numerous details including those that are both relevant and irrelevant. Nonetheless, consumers tend to give attention to a specific stimulus or a combination of the ones closely relevant to the need at hand that prompted the consumers to embark on the learning process. At the comprehension stage, the consumer pays particular attention to details about the stimulus and weighs it up with other alternatives when considering their attributes. The comprehension stage helps the consumer to see how the choice criteria is set to meet the reality in relation to attributes. This will lead the individual to the stage of accepting or rejecting the information available. Going through this process depicts consumer learning and the retention stage involves committing the information gathered and the decision made to memory so that they can be used in the future.

## MEMORY

Memory refers to the systems that comprise the acquisition, sorting, and storing of information to be retrieved for use at a later time. From this definition, it becomes clear that memory is a core aspect of consumer learning and general consumer behaviour. Hence, an understanding of how this works will be very valuable to marketers as they prepare marketing stimuli to compete in the marketplace. The process of how consumer memory works is depicted in Figure 7.1 and consists of:

- Sensory memory;
- Short-term memory;
- Long-term memory.

### Sensory Memory

In sensory memory, the consumers receive information through their senses for a very brief period. So, the storage here is very temporary. There are many examples of this that we experience. The smell of food from a restaurant on your way to a lecture would be momentarily stored in sensory memory, which could be forgotten or could become something that will be retrieved at a later time when considering where and what to take for lunch. Similarly, a glimpse of a pair of shoes for a couple of seconds might stay temporarily with the consumers but could lead to future retrieval of this memory and an eventual decision. There is a high possibility of the consumer forgetting some of what constitutes part of the stimulus, such as forgetting the price on the price tag.

### Short-term Memory

Short-term memory refers to the state in our memory system when information is processed and sorted for a short period of time. Unlike sensory memory which is about receiving information at the initial contact with our senses, in short-term memory the information stays longer, and the role of chunking is very significant at this phase. Chunking here involves bringing the information together in groups with each combination of them being meaningful and easily remembered by the individual. In an article titled 'The magical number seven, plus or minus', Miller (1956) suggests that our short-term memory can handle approximately seven chunks as a fixed limit. While the stance of a fixed number has been criticised (Baddeley, 2001), the notion that consumers process information in short-term memory as chunks remains relatively widely supported. A seminal paper written by Vanhuele and colleagues titled *Consumers' immediate memory for prices* is quite revealing on this subject (Vanhuele et al., 2006). These authors conducted three experiments on unravelling the cognitive mechanics involved in how consumers store prices and engage in their short-term recall. They found that consumers code prices by using three codes which are visual, verbal, and magnitude. Overall, they concluded that consumers' price recall performance is affected by their visual and auditory ability, the speed of their pronunciation, and their price abbreviation habits.

## Long-term Memory

While short-term memory holds information for a brief period of time, long-term memory holds it for a very long time and could even be for life. Ultimately, marketers will be interested in ensuring that their stimuli are registered to this extent in consumers' minds. When they are in the state of deciding on a market offering, information that is in their memory will be recalled and serve as input to the ultimate decision to be made. There are two major types of long-term memory, namely episodic and semantic memory. Our lives are full of episodes of experiences and events such as the birth of a child, a wedding ceremony, purchase of a house, admission to university, graduation, the start of a job, bereavements, and many others so, memories that are linked to these and other similar events are known as **episodic memory**. On the other hand, **semantic memory** relates to general issues such as facts, figures, and places that are not specifically connected to our life events. For example, it has been on record that the late Queen Elizabeth II, who passed away on the 8 September 2022, was the longest serving monarch in British history and that the sitting American President occupies the White House. These are examples of details that remain with us for a long time in the form of semantic memory. Similarly, the euphoria of Christmas celebrations comes around at a specific period of the year which remains as an item in semantic memory.

The key elements that constitute the bedrock of learning are shown in Figure 7.2. Fundamentally, as shown in Figure 7.2, there are four key elements that constitute the backbone of learning. Hence, they are necessary factors for learning to take place. So, for consumers, to embrace the marketing stimuli in the marketplace such as products

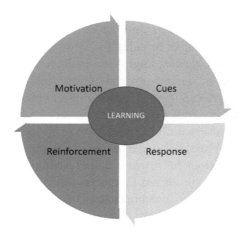

**FIGURE 7.2** Elements of learning

or services offered, their prices, and mode of offering them, these elements are very important. They are:

- Motivation;
- Cues;
- Response;
- Reinforcement.

## Motivation

Meeting consumers' needs has been a fundamental aspect of marketing. So, when consumers have unfulfilled needs to be met, they could be taught that a specific alternative offering would be valuable to address the need. So, the need to be met serves as a prompt or drive for consumer action, which is the explanation behind motivation. Let us look at the example of a consumer's need for an automobile to travel around. This will motivate him or her to become interested in information about these products, brands, the strengths and weaknesses of alternatives, and other details about them so that appropriate choice or choices could be made. The lack of this product serves as the impetus to learn how to use these products and which one to use that solves the current need.

## Cues

While the unmet needs motivate, marketplace cues, which are in the form of marketing stimuli, are needed to stimulate consumers to learn about them. When the consumer with a need for an automobile (mentioned earlier) begins to consider taking steps to buy one, they need information about the brand, prices, availability, and other factors that could form the basis of comparison among other automobiles. These are cues for learning and without them the system is incomplete.

## Response

When consumers are motivated to learn about the marketplace cues, there is a need to have their reactions as to how well these two interact. Consumers respond in different ways. They may respond by buying the product or brand, or have a favourable impression of the product which could be very useful when the consumers want to make a relevant decision in the future.

## Reinforcement

Reinforcement refers to action taken by marketers to encourage the repetition of the response given by the consumer. A primary reinforcement is to ensure that the consumers' actual experience of using the product or service matches or exceeds expectations. Lodging in a hotel that results in satisfaction around the associated services such as meals, lodging, concierge, and facilities like parking, swimming pool, and Internet availability as expected will make the consumers learn that the hotel offers valuable services, which may not only lead to loyalty when a future need arises but could also generate word-of-mouth communication, in which case the customer recommends the hotel to friends, family members, associates, and others.

## RETRIEVAL

The main purpose of storing information in memory is to be able to use it when the need arises. This is especially so as there is always a delay between the time when one is exposed to advertising messages and the time one subsequently makes a choice (Stayman and Batra, 1991). Retrieval is the process of people recovering information stored in their memory. Information about the brands, prices, availability, and many other factors can be retrieved to help consumers at the time of making decisions. Szmigin and Piacentini (2020) indicate three ways this can happen: Recollection, recognition, and relearning. The reconstruction of memory through different narratives and different aspects of memory is the **recollection** such as remembering an encounter with a colleague at a recent birthday party, added to the exposure to the information about the brand on a billboard, or a jingle on the radio. All these added together can aid in the retrieval of vivid details about the market offering. As explained by these authors, when experiencing the product again, we tend to **recognise** it. When we visually come in contact with the product, such as at the till or on the shelf, the encounter aids recognition and retrieval of the details. **Relearning** is about going through the process of acquiring information about the stimuli again when some time has elapsed.

A number of factors are responsible for whether information about a product or service will be retrieved from memory. Some of these are:

**Presentation**: How the marketers present this information can go a long way to determine whether the information will be recalled by the consumers. This covers not only whether the advertising messages are presented before a TV programme begins versus whether they feature during the advertising break in-between programmes, but also the duration of the messages. Similarly, one is likely to recall an ad message that is dramatic rather than one that is not, while those that appear conspicuously in a print media would also be more likely to be recalled than those that do not. In terms of presentation of the stimuli, we can also highlight the relevance of environmental fragrancing which is about using scents in the organisational settings where consumers visit and interact. Using scents is becoming increasingly prevalent in the marketplace such as retail environments, service-oriented business environments, and restaurants (Morrin and Ratneshwar, 2000; 2003). The study of Morrin and Ratneshwar (2003) shows that scents in the environment could influence consumers' behaviour in terms of judgement, decision, and memory. So, perceiving a smell can bring the image of a product, brand, or service to remembrance.

**Situation factors** could also aid recall of the stored message. There are many times you have run into a friend wearing something having information relating to a brand, or something else showing cues related to the product, services, or brand around. These are examples of what could trigger the recall of messages stored in our memory and can then feed into the decision making at the time.

**Personal factors** such as age can also determine how one is able to recall information about products and services. Amer et al. (2018) conducted a study to investigate age differences in memory for meaningful and arbitrary associations. Their study shows that in contrast to the case of the older consumers, younger adults were able to apply strategic retrieval when they had to remember unrealistic prices in the slower, controlled condition.

## LEARNING IN A DIGITAL AGE

As digital technology has changed the ways many things are done in this day and age, this also applies to how we learn in various capacities, including our consumption patterns. One of the notable points emphasised in the use of digital technology is that there are differences in how they are used, especially when our demographic characteristics are considered. In terms of technology adoption, there is a claim that the relationship between age and technology adoption is negative. Hence, the older one gets the less likely he or she will be to quickly or readily adopt technological innovation (Harris et al., 2016). In their study titled 'Consumer preferences for banking technologies by age group', Harris et al. (2016) noted that there is a significant difference between the baby boomers and Generation Y in that the former consider the ability to have a face-to-face talk with a brand representative important, yet this is not a core requirement for Generation Y. So, it is important for us to discuss the notion of a 'digital divide' in online activities.

A distinction is often made between two consumer groups in terms of their knowledge of digital technologies. These are the digital natives and digital immigrants (Hanlon, 2019). In this classification, the digital natives are referred to consumers that are born in the digital era which gives them the opportunity to know a lot about the dynamics of digital technologies. They are versed in the use of several gadgets and clearly associate these to their day-to-day living. On the other hand, the digital immigrants are different in that their births are outside this period and so they lack the depth of understanding of the use of digital technology compared to the digital natives. Apart from the generational divide, the digital divide is also explained in a number of other ways such as using other demographic criteria like gender, education, population size, digital skills, and income (Pérez-Amaral et al., 2021). For example, there is a claim that well-off consumers with economic advantage have more access compared to those in poorer households with a lower level of online access (Chinn and Fairlie, 2006; McDonald and Wren, 2017). When considering competence or gauging digital divides, the gaps can be measured using many services such as e-selling, e-commerce, e-health, e-learning, e-banking, email, e-government social networks, and many others (Pérez-Amaral et al., 2021). Despite the variety of opportunities around digital technology, some consumers are resistant to using them.

From the publication of Ram and Sheth (1989), the following five factors are identified as reasons for the resistance to the use of banking technology:

- Value;
- Risk;
- Tradition;
- Usage;
- Image.

When consumers notice that the value of the new technology is not attractive in relation to competing offerings by gauging the price to pay and the performance of the product, then they tend to resist it. Essentially, the consumers weigh the main risks: Physical risks, performance risks, social risk, and economic risk, and if these are not considered favourable, they are likely to avoid the innovation. Tradition is about the established norms that guide the consumers' action, and they would expect some form of continuity from the new innovation, but when there is a significant shift in how these work, it may result in resistance. As indicated by Ram and Seth (1989), usage resistance occurs when consumers notice that the new technology does not follow their existing routine or is inconsistent with existing practices. More often than not, consumers' choices are driven by image of the product, services, or brand. They are interested in country of origin, or the nature of the industry which the new technology is associated with. These are the issues involved in image as a factor in explaining resistance to new technology.

## THE 4CS OF INTERNET USAGE/USERS

In relation to the discussion of the digital divide, consumers can be categorised or segmented differently in terms of their knowledge and attitude to Internet usage. This typology of the 4c's proposed by Gbadamosi (2021) indicates that we can have consumers that are conservative, while some can be described as circumstantial, while the remaining two groups are identified as centric and contemporary. This is shown in Figure 7.3. In this typology, conservatives are the consumers that are not specifically enthusiastic about digital technology but have a preference for all other plausible alternatives to meeting their consumption needs. They have an aversion for digital technology. Those consumers in the circumstantial segment tend to share some characteristics of the conservatives but are willing to use digital technology only in circumstances when the opportunities to use the Internet for purchases arises. It is worth noting that the circumstantial consumers are not actively searching for the opportunities to use these tools, but interest only becomes kindled at the presence of the occasion that necessitates its use, or makes the usage attractive to them, such as friends and associate members using it and encouraging them to follow suit.

Due to their position in the typology, the centric are noted as such. They are occasionally interested in digital technology and use it to solve some problem and meet their needs. Nevertheless, the fact that they are sporadic users of digital technology

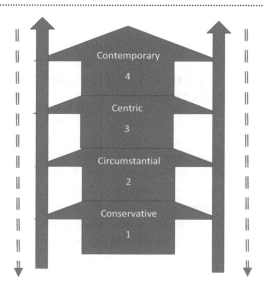

**FIGURE 7.3** 4c's typology of digital consumers

ranks them lower than the contemporary who are ardent users of digital technology in order to meet their day-to-day consumption needs. The contemporary is most likely to be on several social media platforms, active in posting comments, and interacting with posts made by others.

Although this typology was applied to a religious context in Gbadamosi (2021), it has wide-ranging relevance and explication on the relevance of technology to consumption. It is important to stress that these consumers can move from one state to another in terms of their interest in digital technology. For example, consumers noted as conservatives can become circumstantial at some point with the possibility of moving to be in the centric segment and eventually become key users of digital technology (conservative). It can also be argued that various circumstances can cause one to drop in their commitment to digital technology which explains why a dotted arrow is pointing downward. For example, the experience of COVID-19 led to the increase in the use of technology, which indicates that some compelling reasons beyond age could offer an explanation for why this knowledge and interest in the use of digital technology is transient.

It is tempting to quickly conclude that this typology is strictly amenable to age, in which case the conservatives would be seen as old consumers while the contemporary segments are the young consumers. This may not necessarily be so as there may be some old consumers who are very adept in the use of digital technology while some young consumers may not be extremely keen on the use of technology due to several reasons. The cautionary notes also apply to the discussion of the digital divide presented above because the line between the digital native and digital immigrants may be blurry. Hence, those who are noted as digital immigrants may exhibit a very keen interest in digital technology and show great skills in its use while some who are digital natives might not be very keen on digital technology as presented in the postulation.

## HOW DO CHILDREN LEARN THE ACT OF CONSUMPTION? CONSUMER SOCIALISATION THEORIES

Over the years, researchers and marketing practitioners have been preoccupied in knowing how children learn the act of consumption. The fact is that children have needs which cover virtually all aspects of their lives including food, clothing, hairdressing, entertainment, and many others. Details of this are discussed in Chapter 5 under Consumer Socialisation, which addresses how children learn the act of consumption. In this section, building on what has been discussed in Chapter 5, we will be discussing three studies or perspectives on cognitive development, which is about how children grow in relation to consumption of goods and services.

One of the widely read and referenced cognitive development theories is that of Piaget (1952). The perspective suggests four stages of cognitive development, which are:

- Sensorimotor stage (From birth to 2 years);
- Preoperational stage (2–7 years);
- Concrete operational stage (7–11 years);
- Formal operational stage (11 years to adulthood).

Let us look at the second perspective given by McNeal and Yeh (1993). In their postulation, these authors identify five stages of child development in terms of their marketplace and consumption activities. These are:

- The observing (median age of months);
- Making request (median age is 2 years);
- Making selection (median age 3 years and 6 months);
- Making assisted purchases (median age 5 years and 6 months);
- Making independent purchases (approximately 8 years of age).

The third perspective that offers another explanation on cognitive development is the seminal work of John (1999), which is a review of relevant literature on the topic covering 25 years. Three stages highlighted in this perspective are:

- Perceptual stage (ages 3–7);
- Analytical stage (ages 7–11);
- Reflective stage (ages 11–16).

Looking at these perspectives on children's cognitive development, we can see that they all consistently point to the fact that children begin interacting with marketing stimuli from a young age and their understanding of marketplace dynamics continues to improve as they grow towards adulthood.

## ASSOCIATIVE NETWORKS

When storing information from our memory, we tend to use associative networks, which is a network of related items that are linked in a form of pathway showing how each of them is related, and facilitating retrieval of the information when the need arises. The link between some of the elements in the network may be stronger than between others. While this aids recollection of information related to mundane or non-marketing related items, they are clearly amenable to products and services in value-oriented transactions. An example is illustrated below of what may be connected together that will lead to the recollection of many things associated with books including discounts and contemporary issues in marketing.

**FIGURE 7.4** Associative network

> **PAUSE, PLAN, AND PRACTICE: DOVE: A BRAND OF MANY COLOURS**
>
> For several decades, Dove has been positioned at the forefront of beauty products with popularity increasing across various market segments. Meanwhile, the product is a classic example of stimulus generalisation in many ramifications. The brand is seen to be not only easily recognised and easily pronounced by the consumers but also regarded as valuable in addressing their needs. Considering the organisation's product lines, including washing and bathing, skincare, hair care, antiperspirant and deodorant/roll on, the brand Dove resonates with consumers. The idea behind this is simple: When the consumers are in the store considering which beauty cream, hand wash, body wash, or body polish to choose, they will simply remember the brand Dove based on the brand's track record over existing products. The brand has specific products that match different skin colours, yet the quality perception and delivery associated with Dove does not diminish. It has been noted to have championed Real Beauty, and is an advocate of ensuring that people have their self-esteem, as demonstrated in its Dove Self-Esteem Project (DSEP). This makes it widely accepted despite the stiff competition in the market. It has also spread its tentacles to the digital world through Real Virtual Beauty, which is aimed at encouraging women and girls in video games. By and large, the brand is focused on building self-esteem.
>
> **TASKS**
>
> In a group, reflect on various celebrity endorsement deals you are aware of. This could be in the past or currently in operation. Make a list of three or more examples of celebrity and brand matchups that you think give good conditioning in relation to the products, services, or brand advertised and cite examples of others that you think are poorly matched.
>
> Imagine a situation that could make Dove engage in stimulus discrimination. Discuss this scenario and explain how this can be done strategically.

## SUMMARY

Learning takes the form of changing behaviour based on experience. It is broadly explained from two theoretical categorisations – behavioural learning and cognitive learning theories. Behavioural learning theories are of two types, namely classical conditioning and instrumental conditioning. Unlike behavioural theories which involved consumers' response to external stimuli, cognitive learning sees the consumers as active problem solvers who use internal mental processes to arrive at decisions. Consumers' learning is closely linked to memory which varies between sensory memory, short-term memory, and long-term memory. Unlike other types of memory, items stored in long-term memory tend to be retained for a very long time and, in some cases, this could be for life. So, marketers will be interested in how consumers retained cues about their market offerings so that they can be retrieved and recalled to inform their decisions at the appropriate time. Associative networks help in this process. In this digital age, consumers' learning of marketplace cues is being facilitated in various ways by digital technology.

**DIGITAL BOX: CELEBRITY ENDORSEMENT IN A DIGITAL AGE**

Consumers learn in various ways but watching others and engaging in emulative consumption seems to be on the increase in recent times. Children observe their parents, siblings, peers, and others to mould their consumption patterns. However, the rate at which they follow celebrities and use them as models in their purchases is considerable and continues to increase. Purchases such as smartphones, clothes, hairstyling, shoes, and many others indicate the prevalence of observational learning among these young consumers. Meanwhile, one of the recent developments that seem to have heightened this observational learning in relation to celebrity endorsements is the increased availability and use of Internet facilities in various countries. With this, consumers are able to relate with celebrities even at the international level indicating that international superstars in various career fields such as entertainment, sports, fashion, and technology can influence and mould the consumer behaviour of their fans. This is because the world is now closely connected as consumers can readily access information about product endorsements done in several countries as linked together by a network. So, 50 Cent's endorsement of Vitaminwater, Oprah Winfrey's endorsement of Weight Watchers, Taylor Swift and Diet Coke endorsement, as well as Eva Longoria's endorsement of L'Oreal are examples of how marketers formulate a strategy to apply observational learning as facilitated by digital technology.

**QUESTION**

Reflect on and review the information you may have heard on the radio, television, read in the newspapers, or on the Internet about celebrity endorsement deals for luxury products, fast-moving consumer goods, and services. In each of these specific categories, discuss how the influence of the celebrity moulds behaviour of their followers. Does it show a good case of observational learning?

## END OF CHAPTER DISCUSSION QUESTIONS

1. Explain the term classical conditioning learning theory and discuss how it works in relation to the use of celebrity endorsement marketing communication strategies. Cite appropriate examples of celebrity endorsement success stories that support the efficiency of this classical conditioning approach;
2. Although some consumers engage in non-deceptive counterfeiting, some are victims of deceptive counterfeiting as they are affected by stimulus generalisation by buying what seems like the original product but happens to be the replicate offerings. Recommend and discuss sustainable strategies by which authentic brand owners could address the prevailing problem of counterfeiting;
3. Recall four purchases you made that are linked to your episodic memories in your lives. Why do you think this knowledge of your past and the associated purchases remain enduring to you? Based on this, and why you were able to recall them, what advice would you give to marketers of the products or services in these purchases you have made concerning the formulation of appropriate strategies for successful business operations?

4. Critically discuss how observational learning might work concerning children's consumer socialisation with regard to (1) social media usage; (2) healthy eating;
5. Reflect on two or three advertising messages you have been exposed to in any context that you considered to be in extinction or wearing out in their core value and effectiveness. Mention them and discuss the strategies that the advertisers could adopt to revitalise them.

### Case Study: Consumers' Digital Experience at Barclays Bank

Banking, like most other businesses, has changed recently in terms of value co-creation between banks and their customers. The digital presence in banking has moved the threshold of banking transactions in an upward trajectory. This has changed dramatically from what it used to be several years before now. Barclays Bank is clearly among the major banks that are at the forefront of this digital banking in relation to its marketing stimuli, cues detected by the customers, the response they give in relation to these, and how these are reinforced. Any customer of Barclays Bank with access to the Internet has the opportunity of banking from home. Whether the customer is using a laptop, tablet, or mobile phone, he or she does not need to visit a branch of the bank to check balances, make a payment, and enjoy other services. Even depositing a cheque into an account can be done anywhere without reaching the bank, all it takes is simply taking a photo of the cheque on a smartphone and concluding the transaction online. Barclays' mobile app facilitates all of these a great deal. While most of these services are offered by many other competing banks, Barclays does it in a special customer-oriented way that results in a high rate of customer satisfaction. So, when the customer is interested in banking services and products such as mortgages, insurance, loans, or various international financial transactions, Barclays Bank as a brand comes to their memory.

As the bank has many consumer segments registered on its digital banking platform, there are still some who have been accustomed to on-site banking transactions and doing them in the old conventional way. There are many reasons for this but the top two of these are a lack of adequate knowledge of how digital technology would affect their banking transactions and the fear of fraudulent activities. Although Barclays Bank has provided detailed information in various links on how the digital systems work, this consumer segment is still not as enthusiastic as others concerning online banking transactions. However, the number of consumers in this segment is reducing by the day. One of the key reasons for this is the experience of COVID-19 and the lockdown measures introduced by the government, which encouraged the shift in the attitude of some of these consumers in favour of digital banking.

A good number of initiatives have been taken by Barclays Bank concerning consumer education around digital banking. It has what it calls a Digital Confidence Package which provides tools, courses, and sessions for visitors to the website. The package design for children titled Coding and Online Safety for Kids has proved very popular in getting children interested in digital applications. Visitors to the website are directed to various

YouTube link videos showing children-friendly animations and guidance on the digital banking and online safety skills created by the bank. In a related arrangement, the bank also partnered with the BBC through the BBC:micro:bit for the purpose of giving 1 million children a device that will aid their learning of code. This helps significantly in ensuring that consumer socialisation of these children runs brightly and with the right skills to do it in a safe digital environment. There is also the role of the Digital Eagles. These are digital experts that are passionate about helping customers to aid their use of digital tools provided by the banks. The role of a Barclays Digital Eagle is to ensure that customers learn their way to digital banking. This has proved very useful and popular as they are widely available on various social medial platforms such as X, Facebook, LinkedIn, and Instagram to connect with customers.

To support these initiatives, Barclays Bank focuses on improving its digital wings. These encompass the tools and resources that empower customers to move progressively forward from any stage of their digital knowledge. In this, a beginner will be at ease to learn the basics that will aid him or her to approach digital banking from that stage and progressively get better at fully exploring the Internet safely and there are appropriate courses and guidance for those at the intermediate level. Apart from the obvious usefulness of these tools and resources to the customers, their value and popularity are also linked to the fact that these are offered free of charge to consumers. So, the digital experience offered by Barclays creates a lasting positive impression in the mind of consumers which also extends to its various product portfolios and shows that it offers value to its customers.

**Sources**

Barclays Bank (2022). Barclays Q1 2022 Results, home.barclays/investor-relations/reports-and-events/results/barclays-q1-2022-results/ (accessed 10 November 2022).

Barclays Bank (2022). Digital Eagles: Build your digital skills with us, www.barclays.co.uk/digital-confidence/eagles/ (accessed 10 November 2022).

Barclays Bank (2022). Explore Online Banking: Bank from your browser, www.barclays.co.uk/ways-to-bank/online-banking/ (accessed 10 November 2022).

## QUESTIONS

1. Consumer learning in the digital age has changed many things about consumer transactions in the banking industry. Using Barclays Bank as an example, give some examples of the evidence of this change and indicate the impact of these on consumer behaviour and the society;
2. What are the current and other likely future marketing efforts of Barclays that indicate the relevance and application of instrumental learning theory?
3. Discuss some of Barclays' marketing efforts for moving their consumers that typify the conservatives to the threshold of the consumers noted as the 'contemporary' in Gbadamosi's 4c's model of the consumer digital marketing adoption process;

4. Illustrate how repetition and stimulus discrimination might work for Barclays Bank in relation to consumer learning as a topic;
5. How can Barclays use reinforcement concerning its market offerings? Cite specific examples.

## REFERENCES

Almeida, M. I. S, Coelho, R. L. F., Porto, G. B. R. B, & Oliveira, D. S. (2020). Deviances from planned purchases: Consumer learning history and behavior setting implications for consumer spending. *Revista Brasileira de Gestão de Negócios*, 22(2), 331–347.

Amer, T., Giovanello, K. S., Grady, C. L., & Hasher, L. (2018). Age differences in memory for meaningful and arbitrary associations: A memory retrieval account. *Psychology and Aging*, 33(1), 74.

Atkin, C., & Block, M. (1983). Effectiveness of celebrity endorsers. *Journal of Advertising Research*, 23, 57–61.

Baddeley, A. D. (2001). Is working memory still working? *American Psychologist*, 56(11), 851–964.

Chinn, M., & Fairlie, R. (2006). The determinants of the global divide: A cross-country analysis of computer and internet penetration. *Oxford Economic Papers*, 59, 16–44.

Fournier, S. (1998). Consumers and their brands: Developing relationship theory in consumer research. *Journal of Consumer Research*, 24(4), 343–373.

Foxall, G. R. (2010). Accounting for consumer choice: Inter-temporal decision making in behavioural perspective. *Marketing Theory*, 10(4), 315–345.

Gbadamosi, A. (2021). Consumption, religion, and digital marketing in developing countries, in Gbadamosi, A. and Oniku, C. A. (2021) (eds). *Religion and Consumer Behaviour in Developing Nations*, pp. 175–198. London, Cheltenham: Edward Elgar.

Hanlon, A. (2019). *Digital Marketing: Strategic Planning and Integration*. London: Sage.

Harris, M., Cox, K. C., Musgrove, C. F., & Ernstberger, K. W. (2016). Consumer preferences for banking technologies by age groups. *International Journal of Bank Marketing*, 34(4), 587–602.

John, D. (1999). Consumer socialization of children: A retrospective look at twenty-five years of research, *Journal of Consumer Research*, 26(December), 183–213.

McDonald, S., & Wren, C. (2017). Consumer search ability, price dispersion and the digital divide. *Oxford Bulletin of Economics and Statistics*, 79(2), 234–250.

McNeal, J. U., & Yeh, C. (1993). Born to shop. *American Demographics*, 15(6).

Miller, G. A. (1956). The magical number seven, plus or minus two: Some limits on our capacity for processing information. *Psychological Review*, 63(2), 81–97.

Morrin, M., & Ratneshwar, S. (2000). The impact of ambient scent on evaluation, attention, and memory for familiar and unfamiliar brands. *Journal of Business Research*, 49(2), 157–165.

Morrin, M., & Ratneshwar, S. (2003). Does it make sense to use scents to enhance brand memory? *Journal of Marketing Research*, 40(1), 10–25.

Pérez-Amaral, T., Valarezo, A., López, R., & Garín-Muñoz, T. (2021). Digital divides across consumers of internet services in Spain using panel data 2007–2019. Narrowing or not? *Telecommunications Policy*, 45(2), 102093.

Piaget, J. (1952). *The Origins of Intelligence in Children*. New York: International Universities Press.

Priluck, R., & Till, B. D. (2004). The role of contingency awareness, involvement, and need for cognition in attitude formation. *Journal of the Academy of Marketing Science*, 32, 329–344.

Ram, S., & Sheth, J. N. (1989). Consumer resistance to innovations: The marketing problem and its solutions. *Journal of Consumer Marketing*, 6(2), 5–14.

Renderforest (2021), www.renderforest.com/blog/brand-statistics, 55 Branding Statistics for 2021 [Infographic], 21 January 2021 (Accessed 10 November 2022).

Schiffman, L. G., Kanuk, L. L., & Hansen, H. (2012). *Consumer Behaviour: A European Outlook*, 2nd edn, Harlow: Pearson Education Limited.

Schiffman, L. G., Kanuk, L. L., & Wisenblit, J. (2010). *Consumer Behaviour*, 10th edn., New Jersey: Pearson Education Inc.

Shimp, T. A. (1991). Neo-Pavlovian conditioning and its implications for consumer theory and research, in Thomas S. Robertson and Harold H. Kassarjian (eds), *Handbook of Consumer Behavior*, pp. 162–187. Englewood Cliffs, NJ: Prentice Hall.

Solomon, M. R. (2020). *Consumer Behaviour: Buying, Having, and Being*, 13th edn, Essex: Pearson Education Limited.

Stayman, D. M., & Batra, R. (1991). Encoding and retrieval of ad affect in memory. *Journal of Marketing Research*, 28(2), 232–239.

Szmigin, I, & Piacentini, M. (2018). *Consumer Behaviour*. Oxford: Oxford University Press.

Till, B. D., Stanley, S. M., & Priluck, R. (2008). Classical conditioning and celebrity endorsers: An examination of belongingness and resistance to extinction. *Psychology & Marketing*, 25(2), 179–196.

Vanhuele, M., Laurent, G., & Drèeze, X. (2006). Consumers' immediate memory for prices. *Journal of Consumer Research*, 33, 163–172.

Wells, V. K. (2014). Behavioural psychology, marketing and consumer behaviour: A literature review and future research agenda. *Journal of Marketing Management*, 30(11–12), 1119–1158.

# CHAPTER 8

# Attitude Formation and Change in Consumer Behaviour

**LEARNING OUTCOMES**

After reading this chapter, you should be able to:

1. Understand the meaning of attitudes and their characteristics;
2. Discuss the four key functions of consumer attitude;
3. Explain the tricomponent model of attitudes;
4. Critically discuss the multi-attribute model of attitudes;
5. Understand how attitudes are formed;
6. Discuss how marketers can change consumers' attitudes;
7. Understand consumers' attitude in the digital age and the notion of solid consumption.

**INTRODUCTION**

Be it confectionery, shoes, automobiles, movies, holiday packages, or other products, we have our dispositions that explain our stance towards them. Anchoring this with the case of family system could show an interesting pattern. The father in the house may be someone that is often thrilled by action movies, unlike the wife, who could be an enthusiast of travelling, and the children, who have a keen likeness for sports. These are typical examples of attitudes towards things. Over the years, researchers and marketing practitioners have always been interested in consumer attitudes because of their interesting link (or lack of it) to behaviour. As with many other aspects of our lives, digital transformation has an impact on our attitudes. Some consumers' attitudes to shopping have changed significantly in recent times in relation to the surge in Internet usage. COVID-19 has introduced changes to the dynamics of shopping among various consumer segments. The continuous change of consumer

DOI: 10.4324/9781003242031-11

attitude from solid to liquid consumption also emphasises the prevalence of digitalisation and dematerialisation in our consumption. So, attitudes are dynamic. This is the overarching focus of this chapter. We will be defining attitudes and discussing their characteristics, as well as exploring the models and theories that underpin the topic. We will also be discussing the key functions that attitudes play in the lives of the consumer. An in-depth understanding of consumer attitudes is core to marketing strategy formulation, implementation, and evaluation. Accordingly, we will also be examining how consumers form attitudes that they have for the marketplace cues such as products, brands, and marketing communication messages, and how those attitudes can be changed, especially if they are not favourable to the marketers' offerings. Given the significant role of marketing communications to attitude formation and change, we will explore how these are done with reference to digital transformation.

## DEFINING ATTITUDES

The word attitude is very commonly used in relation to our day-to-day activities. We often hear expressions like 'that is her attitude towards travelling', 'my attitude to shopping is doing it just once a week', or 'he has a very bad attitude towards savings'. But what exactly does attitude mean? One of the widely cited definitions given in a seminal paper by Fishbein and Ajzen (1975) defines it as 'a learned predisposition to respond in a consistently favourable or unfavourable manner in relation to some object'. We can also adapt a relatively recent definition of the term by Schiffman et al. (2012) to show consistency in how the term has been defined and applied over the years. So, we can define it as a learned and consistent disposition to behave favourably or unfavourably towards a given objective. It is reasonable to state that attitude plays a significant role in the lives and decisions of consumers covering the way we think, our feelings, and how we behave. We will discuss these three elements in detail at a later stage in this chapter. Put together, we can simply say that attitudes are:

- Goal-oriented;
- Consistent;
- Enduring;
- Learned;
- Evaluative;
- Intensity-oriented;
- Changeable.

When we talk about attitudes, they are related to a goal object. So, attitudes are goal-oriented. The goal object could be a product, service, advertisement, a type of sales promotion offer, or many other things. As an example, Rossiter and Percy (1987; 1997) offer a definition of brand attitude as the evaluation of the brand by a buyer in relation to its expected capacity to deliver on his or her buying motive. Although this is brand specific, it is consistent with the definition given above. Attitudes are not sporadic but consistent. It is expected that an individual will exhibit a frequent disposition towards something for it to be noted as attitudinal. So, when a consumer positively rates a product among others and changes his or her mind on another occasion, such reaction to the stimuli is not enduring and lacks consistency. Hence, one cannot indicate that the individual has a positive attitude towards the product as the initial feelings about the product are not enduring. Meanwhile, consumers learn to react to marketing stimuli in a variety of ways. The disposition to the stimuli is developed over a period of time based on experience and information gathered from various sources such as friends, family members, and colleagues. Attitudes are evaluative as they refer to what an individual makes of the goal object. It is their judgement of that object in relation to many factors. For example, having a disposition that a hotel offers good services comes out of a process of evaluation based on some criteria that the consumer considers valuable. The notion of value is core to defining or explaining attitudes as consumers have positive attitudes towards market offerings that deliver value to them (Babin and Harris, 2018). In their study on the changing attitudes of United States consumers towards humanely raised eggs, meat, and dairy, Spain et al. (2018) noted a high level of concerns for the welfare of farm animals and willingness to pay more for welfare food products. The same research shows that female consumers and the younger respondents in the study have heightened concern for the environment. This is an outcome of their evaluation of the subject.

Attitudes have intensity. There could be varying strengths between consumers' disposition towards a goal object. Prior studies have shown that the attitudes people hold with confidence predict their behaviour better than the ones they doubt, and similar patterns are found concerning attitudes that are decisive vs those that are ambivalent (Glasman and Albarracín, 2006). So, attitudes can vary in terms of strength or intensity. For example, peoples' attitude to sustainability or green consumption vary. While there are many classifications of consumers on this, one commonly cited and widely applied (Ottman and Reilly, 1998; Banytė et al., 2010) sees some consumers as belonging to any of five segments, among them loyal green consumers, less devoted green consumers, and a third segment noted as consumers developing towards green. The remaining two categories in this typology are conservative consumers unwilling to change and those completely unwilling to change. This classification shows the variation in the intensity of attitude towards a goal object as some of the consumers are ardent supporters of sustainability, while some also have a positive attitude to it but not strongly, and the scale of commitment is even worse for some other consumers. Although it was established that attitudes are enduring indicating that such dispositions last for a very long time, they are still subject to change. A consumer that detests a product at some point may eventually regard it as the best among other alternatives, after the marketers have taken some strategic decisions such as modifying the product to suit the taste of the target audience. Putting all these together, the literature indicates that certain types of relationships are considered as important to attitudes, which include the relationship between an evaluation and an attitude object, the one between the attributes of the goal object and how it is evaluated, and the strengths of the links that exist between the attitude object (or goal object) and the attributes or different beliefs (Fazio, 1990; Fishbein and Ajzen, 1975; Monroe and Read, 2008). We will be discussing more on how to change attitudes later in the chapter.

## MODELS OF CONSUMER ATTITUDES

Over the years, explanation of attitudes and their dynamics has been given from different perspectives. This emphasises the complex nature of the phenomenon as a single unifying theory or model is unlikely, but it still remains a significant issue to peoples' lives in various ramifications (Monroe and Read, 2008). There are many unresolved theoretical issues as in the understanding of specific processes and components that make attitudes strong and how each of the components influence this strength (Krosnick et al., 1993; Monroe and Read, 2008). Meanwhile, we will now discuss the various existing and commonly used models of attitudes, which are the following:

- Tricomponent models;
- Hierarchy of effect model;
- Unidimensional model;
- Balanced theory of attitude;
- Multi-attribute model;
- Attitude towards the ad.

## TRICOMPONENT MODEL

The tricomponent model of attitudes sees the functioning of attitudes as based on the interrelationship of their three elements. These elements are easily identified through the acronym ABC with each of the letters standing for the first letter of the elements, which are:

- Affect;
- Behavioural;
- Cognitive.

The affect element is about the feelings towards the goal object. So, an individual can like or dislike a goal object such as a product or service. Meanwhile, the behavioural aspect is about the action that the individual takes based on the feelings he or she has about the item. Cognition is about the beliefs and thoughts that the individual has about it. We can use the example of an automobile. Using the tricomponent model, an individual may exhibit a liking for Toyota cars based on the beliefs he or she has about the brand that it is fuel efficient, comfortable, and reliable. This interaction would then propel the consumer to act by indicating an intention to buy the brand. Clearly, the interaction of the elements work as a system in the form of an individual's embodiment of his or her attitude for the automobile.

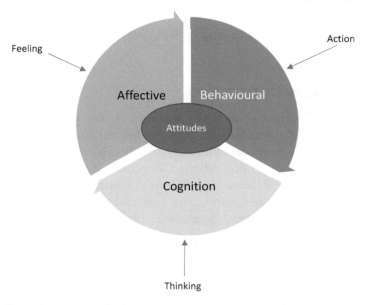

**FIGURE 8.1** Three elements of attitudes

## HIERARCHY OF EFFECT MODEL

While the three elements of attitudes interact, the order in which they take place has been a topic of keen interest over some time as it is significant in consumer behaviour with varying applications. The hierarchy of effect model assumes that consumers go through these stages in a ordered and well-defined form. This is the focus of the hierarchy of effect model. Most of the hierarchy models follow the pattern of cognitive-affective-behavioural sequence. With reference to the explanation given above about what each of the elements stands for, this means that the consumer is believed to first think about the issues around goal objects before exhibiting emotion which could be favourable or unfavourable concerning it, and then making the decision or act in a way consistent with the other elements that come earlier. This standard hierarchy of C-A-B, which simply means think-feel-act, tend to relate to a situation of high-involvement decision making. For example, the purchase of a house, new car, medical services, and several related other market offerings would require extensive thinking and reflection on the choices and the associated information before coming to the stage of showing likeness and preference for any specific one before taking action in favour of it. It assumes that consumers engage in logical decision making. However, as emphasised in previous chapters, especially Chapter 3, this is not the case all of the time. If you reflect on your purchases this year alone, there is a high possibility that some of the decisions taken in these cases are not rational. There are several scenarios when consumers do not engage in any significant thought before buying the product or developing an intention to buy it. While there are many possibilities, we will example three of these commonly discussed as shown in Figure 8.2.

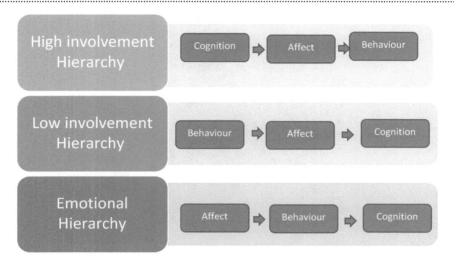

**FIGURE 8.2** Hierarchy of effects

In addition to the high-involvement hierarchy, the figure shows the low-involvement and emotional hierarchies. In the low-involvement hierarchy, consumers act first before developing affection for the product, while developing thoughts and beliefs about the product comes last. Consumers buying candy, bottled water, or salt are likely to buy first without having a preference and then evaluating them after the purchase as they are low-involvement items. As the risks associated with the purchase are very low, consumers can simply act on impulse in choosing the low-ticket items. After the evaluation, a belief could be formed about the choices made. The emotional hierarchy begins with affect followed by behaviour before beliefs about the chosen market offerings are made. Imagine buying gifts for a lover, emotional hierarchy in which the affect begins the process is likely to apply. So, it will follow the 'like-do—think' scenario.

## BALANCED THEORY

We have made reference to the balanced theory of Heider (1946) in Chapter 5 while discussing group dynamics. Essentially, the theory states that an individual would seek to ensure a balance between himself, his attitude towards an object, and the attitude of another person to whom he or she is connected for that object. If these elements are not balanced, there will be tension and the individual would try to resolve the inconsistencies in some way. This is illustrated in Figure 8.3. Imagine your best friend has a positive attitude towards regularly having lunch at a restaurant close to your school. You will feel an imbalance in the system if this is not a place you like to have your meal for some reason. Then the balance theory indicates that you would not like the disharmony to continue without resolution. Hence, steps will be taken to ensure balance among the three elements, which are you and your perception about eating

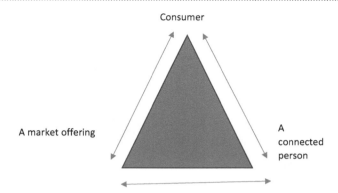

**FIGURE 8.3** Balanced theory

at the restaurant, the restaurant and the associated services, and your friend's attitude to eating at this restaurant. Resolving this imbalance could be done in a number of ways. For example, given your strength of association with your friend, you might hold that the restaurant is not really bad as whatever the misgiving you have about it is negligible and you will then change your attitude to eating at the place. You may even try to convince your friend to change his or her attitude towards the place by providing information that he or she does not know in order to achieve a balance. The example of celebrity endorsement could be used here also. One of the key points brand sponsors examine and scrutinise is the possibility of the celebrity endorser getting into public relation trouble as this can also be very damaging for their brands. In the triad relationship, fans of the celebrity are expected to hold a positive attitude towards the brand the celebrity endorses. However, with the principle of balanced theory, if any atrocity is later associated with the celebrity, the fans are most likely to change their stance and disfavour the brand as they frown at what the celebrity may have done.

## MULTI-ATTRIBUTE MODELS

The multi-attribute model of attitudes indicates that attitudes are more complex than they seem as our interest in the attitude object could be conceptualised into component parts. Essentially, the argument underpinning this model is that consumers' attitudes towards a product, brand, or service consists of three elements, which are the attributes of these market offerings, their beliefs concerning the degree to which the product, services, or brand possess these attributes, and the degree of importance they attach to the attributes, which is also known as the evaluation of the attitude object.

One of the widely acknowledged multi-attribute models that captures this is that of Fishbein and Azjen (1975), popularly known as the Fishbein model of attitude. It measures attitude in relation to three elements, which are noted as:

- Salient beliefs;
- Object-attributes;
- Evaluation.

In their publication, Fishbein and Azjen (1975) present this in terms of a formula as follows:

$$A = \sum B_{ijk} I_{ik}$$

where:

$i$ = attribute or product characteristic,
$j$ = brand,
$k$ = consumer or respondent,

such that:

$Ajk$ = consumer k's attitude score for brand j,
$Iik$ = the importance weight given attribute $i$ by consumer k, and
$Bijk$ = consumer k's belief as to the extent to which attribute $i$ is offered by brand $j$.

Let us look at an example of a house as an attitude object. Let's assume that Mr and Mrs Henry, a newly-wed couple are considering the purchase of a house and Jennifer Gregory, an estate agent, has offered them information about the possible options available. The options could be properties located in four Boroughs in London which are Greenwich, Westminster, Bexley, and Hackney. With the multi-attribute model, we can consider attributes like closeness to the main transportation stations, price, year of construction of the building, the presence and size of a garden, the quality standard of the local schools, and the rate of crime. There are many other possible factors but let us concentrate on these for illustration purposes. So, with the multi-attribute model, the couple's attitude and choice among these four options would involve considering whether these listed factors (attributes) matter to them, the importance they place on such attributes as a couple, and the belief they have that the specific house option provided by Ms Gregory has those attributes.

From Table 8.1, and in view of the overall attitude of the couple to these choices, the best option for the couple to choose is the property at Greenwich as it has the highest score after the weighing of the specific attributes of consideration. This shows an interesting outlook. For instance, the couple may have their personal car that will make their movements easy, which then suggests that they may not be so keen about the nearness of the house to a local transportation hub. As a young couple, they also attach significance to high closeness to schools as preparation for the arrival of children in the family. This may not be a key attribute of consideration for older couples whose children have finished schooling. So, this is quite revealing and pinpoints the dynamics of the multi-attribute model.

An improvement of the Fishbein model is the **Theory of Reasoned Action (TRA)**. It is an extension of the Fishbein model and indicates the need to mention intention to behave as this is considered potentially crucial and relevant to predicting

**TABLE 8.1** Multi-attribute model and house purchase in Greater London

| Serial number | The product attributes or characteristics (*i*) | Belief (*B*) Greenwich | Westminster | Bexley | Hackney | *I* Importance |
|---|---|---|---|---|---|---|
| 1 | Nearness to transportation | 9 | 9 | 6 | 3 | 2 |
| 2 | Price | 8 | 7 | 9 | 5 | 6 |
| 3 | Year of construction | 3 | 4 | 7 | 8 | 2 |
| 4 | Garden | 6 | 3 | 2 | 3 | 7 |
| 5 | Standard of the local school | 8 | 5 | 3 | 2 | 9 |
| 6 | Crime rate | 8 | 2 | 4 | 2 | 8 |
| **Total attitude score** | | **250** | **208** | **192** | **117** | |

behaviour. According to this model, the attitude of an individual has a positive impact on his behavioural intention (Ajzen and Fishbein, 1980). This is because it is not in all cases that attitude directly leads to behaviour. In some instances, it leads to the intention to act. For instance, sensitising people about the benefits of taking a vaccine can encourage perception that the vaccine is good or indispensable and strengthens the possibility that they will opt to take it, but this does not in itself guarantee that people will take the vaccine (Albarracín et al., 2003; Glasman and Albarracín, 2006).

Moreover, it also stresses another element not featured in the previous model. This is the subjective norm. This is the view or disposition of other people about the case in question. In reality, we would know that decisions on what to do and how to do them are influenced by others such as spouses, other family members, co-workers, and others we are connected to in various ways. The TRA is illustrated in Figure 8.4.

Meanwhile, further improvement has also been added to the TRA in that the assumptions of the theory of reasoned action are too restrictive (Leone et al., 1999). An improvement of this is the **Theory of Planned Behaviour (TBA)** which includes a new element known as Perceived Behaviour Control (PBC), which is a measure of whether the consumer feels that s/he has control over the behaviour to be taken or not. According to Ajzen (1991), for the intention to be a predictor of behaviour, it will be in a situation where the person has a significant degree of volitional control over that behaviour but when this is not the case, then the individual's perceived behaviour control should be independently and additionally predictive of behaviour (Kautonen et al., 2013). This is shown in Figure 8.5 as illustrated.

The perceived behavioural control encapsulates factors that may intervene between when a person decided to do something and getting to actually do it. For example, in a consumer's attitude towards buying a fair-trade product, subjective norm can

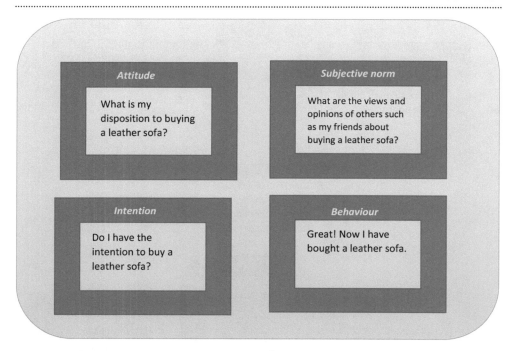

**FIGURE 8.4** Elements of the Theory of Reasoned Action (TRA) model and illustrative questions

produce a strong intention to buy it but, if the consumer realises that the amount he has could not cover this item, then unaffordability of the item indicates that he will most likely buy the ones that could be accommodated by available resources. This is the key relevance of perceived behavioural control as pinpointed in this model. So, ultimately, the weighting of the consumers' attitudes, subjective norms, and perceived behavioural control are added to yield the measure of behavioural intention to perform the act (Szmigin and Piacentini 2022).

## ATTITUDE TOWARDS THE AD

Attitude towards the ad simply explains the process of consumer attitude to marketing communications designed for the products. In this model, it is stated that if there is an understanding of the disposition of the consumer to an advertisement (ad) designed for a product, one can make some form of prediction about their attitudes towards the ad in that the attitude to the ad will influence his or her attitude to the product, service, or brand. This is shown in Figure 8.6.

## DOES ATTITUDE PREDICT BEHAVIOUR?

One question that still lingers is whether attitude predicts consumers' behaviour. As seen from our previous discussion in this chapter so far, including that of the discussion of the hierarchy of effects, there are some circumstances when attitude does

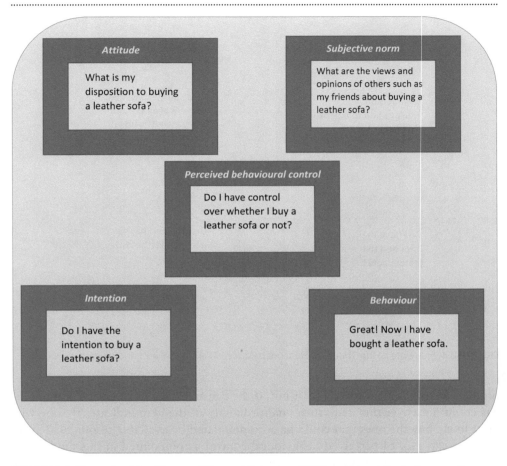

**FIGURE 8.5** Elements of the Theory of Planned Behaviour (TPB) model and illustrative questions

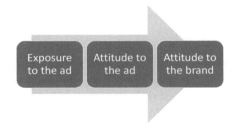

**FIGURE 8.6** Attitude towards the ad model
**Source**: Adapted from Schiffman et al. (2010) & Edell & Burke (1987).

not predict behaviour. So, this question can then be reframed as presented by Hoyer et al. (2018) as 'when do attitudes predict behaviour?' The article of Glasman and Albarracín (2006) that centres on forming attitudes that predict behaviour classifies these factors into two broad processes, which are:

**Attitude accessibility**: Easy-to-retrieve attitudes tend to predict behaviour;
**Attitude stability**: The stability of information connected to the attitudes strengthens the attitude-behaviour order.

Meanwhile, a closely related but more detailed perspective on circumstances leading to when attitudes predict behaviour is given by Hoyer et al. (2018). According to them, some interesting circumstances when attitudes actually predict behaviour are:

- When the consumer has the knowledge and experience of the object;
- When the consumers' involvement in the attitude object is high;
- If the attitude is accessible;
- When the consumer is emotionally attached to the attitude object;
- When the attitude confidence is strong;
- When consumers are involved in analysing reasons for the preference of the attitude object;
- When the attitude is very specific about the behaviour to be predicted;
- When the situational or intervening factors do not prevent the performance of a behaviour;
- When normative factors such as the influence of friends encourage it;
- When the consumer's personality factors are consistent with the attitude-behaviour order.

## HOW ARE ATTITUDES FORMED?

Given the significance of attitudes to consumer behaviour, marketers and researchers are interested in how we form them. One of the primary sources of our attitudes is the knowledge acquired through learning. A good number of studies have confirmed that knowledge is crucial to attitude development. For instance, Park and Sohn (2018) found that knowledge is significant to facilitating how consumers develop green purchase behaviour. And prior to this study, other authors such as Schultz (2002) and Alba and Hutchinson (2000) have found a similar pattern of the relevance of knowledge to attitude formation in relation to consumption and information processing for alternative evaluation in consumer decision-making scenarios.

We mentioned learning as a key characteristic of attitudes earlier. As consumers begin at the very early stage of life and gradually grow into full adult consumers, they learn attitudes towards certain brands, products, and services. Some of these issues are discussed in consumer socialisation in Chapter 5. Children relate with others not only in the family but also at schools and religious settings as well as recreational parks, to pick up attitudes to products and brands from these sources. Even in adulthood, you probably will relate to the fact that some of the products and brands that you are now keenly interested in today were products of influences of others such as celebrities, peers, priests, and partners. Schiffman et al. (2012) show that apart from learning, we can also understand attitude formation by exploring the sources of influences and the influence of personality. Consumers also form attitudes based on their values. This has been established in the academic literature. For example, it has been shown that materialistic values could be negatively linked to environmental-friendly attitudes and behaviour (Hurst et al., 2013; Carey et al., 2019). This is clearly linked to a claim in the literature that nations whose citizens attach high priority to free-market capitalism tend to have a higher level of $CO_2$ emissions (Kasser, 2011; Carey et al., 2019). These findings point to the key relevance of consumer value in forming attitudes towards something.

Apart from the social influences from others, our life experiences are highlighted as a key source of influence. When we use a product, we note the experience, which could eventually make us loyal to the brand or resent it consistently. The various marketing communication tools can be the stimuli that pattern our attitude towards a market offering. The sophistication introduced through the development of technology now makes it easier for marketers to target products to specific consumer segments. This culminates in attitude formation among the target segments. Popy and Bappy (2022) studied attitude of consumers towards social media reviews and their intention to visit a restaurant. They found that consumers' attitudes towards social media reviews could be influenced positively by their perceived ease of use and perceived usefulness of social media reviews. As explained by Schiffman et al. (2010), the personality of an individual will be linked to attitude formation. So, traits like charming, cheerful, friendliness, and patience are more likely to develop an attitude for products that will be different from the ones embraced by individuals with traits such as obnoxious, naughty, and mischievous.

## CHANGING CONSUMERS' ATTITUDES

Although attitudes are enduring, they can still be changed. So, when consumers have unfavourable attitudes towards a product, service, or brand of an organisation, some strategies can be applied to twist consumers' attitudes in favour of these stimuli. We will look at some of the factors as presented by Schiffman and Wisenblit (2019):

- Changing the basic motivation function;
- Linking the market offerings to a desirable group, causes, and events;
- Modifying consumer beliefs of the market offerings of the competitors;
- Altering components of the multi-attribute models;
- Resolving conflicting attitudes.

As shown later in this chapter, attitudes play different functions, and this can vary with different consumer segments. Hence, the key desire of consumers driving their attitudes towards a product might be ego-defensive, utilitarian, knowledge, or value-expressive functions. It is important for marketers to gain insight into the underlying key motivation function that the target market desire in a product and ensure a match between this and what the product offers. In many cases, the information about what the product offers that is fundamental to the consumer may not be clearly communicated, doing this effectively could change consumers' attitudes to the product. As consumers, we are socially connected in various ways and crave associations. Our attitudes to something such as products and services can be changed if such an object is linked to desirable groups. Many youths have decided not to have anything to do with some products because they are associated with the seniors or elderly consumers. Efforts from the marketers to clearly link the products to young consumers, such as having young models in the ad, could change their attitude to the products. The notion of celebrity endorsement also fits in this explanation. Several celebrities have millions of followers on their social media sites. So, it is expected that when products or services are linked to them, the attitudes of their followers to the products are likely to be kindled positively. The meanings associated with some events are so desirable to some segments to the extent that it could change their stance to market offerings. There have been many rumours about the poor green credentials of some companies, in some cases it is alleged that some are involved in greenwashing. Such can prompt negative attitudes to their companies, brands, and their products. However, when such an organisation changes and links their activities to special causes that support the environment, sponsor eco-friendly events, or champion similar events, consumers' attitudes to the organisation can be changed.

As the marketplace is characterised by competition in this day and age, consumers are inundated with options of what to buy. Holiday packages, hotel accommodation, consultancy services, entertainment, clothing and fashion, and several other offerings demonstrate an increasing level of competition between firms. In most cases, consumers' attitudes and interests in these offerings are mutually exclusive such that a positive attitude shown in one means the alternatives are ignored. Sometimes, an item may be ignored because the weaknesses in the alternative offering chosen by the consumers are not clearly highlighted. So, comparative advertising showing the relative strengths of a product or service to competing offerings can change consumers' attitudes towards those offerings. For example, in the automobile market, consumers with unfavourable attitudes to an expensive brand on the ground of price could be convinced to change this attitude by making them note the weaknesses of cheaper cars in the form of high maintenance costs and low symbolism and status-symbol projection.

As we mentioned earlier, multi-attribute models strip a goal object such as a product or service into different attributes that make it what it is, and consumers tend to place more value on some attributes over others in their decision making. As marketers continue to engage in research to know consumers' needs and priorities, the understanding of which attributes appeal more to specific segments will become clearer and they can then adjust by focusing more on what matters to the target group to earn a favourable attitude to their offerings. Hence, altering the structure of existing attributes can change consumers' attitudes. There is a range of possibilities for addressing this. According to Schiffman et al. (2012), marketers can choose to change brand beliefs, change the relative evaluation of the attributes, change overall brand ratings, or add new attributes. A classic example of this is the popular documentary directed by Morgan Spurlock titled *Super Size Me*, aired in 2004, which pinpointed the unhealthy nature of the Supersize meals from McDonald's, which the director ate for one whole month in a social experiment that led him to gain around 25 pounds in weight. This affected the UK sales of the brand, which dropped significantly, but the organisation reacted by introducing healthier options like salad to their menu and phasing out the Supersize options (Clark, 2021).

There are cases when consumers' attitudes can be conflicting. When the attitude to the brand is formed based on attitude towards something else, a thoroughly clarified marketing communication from the marketers to resolve this conflict can go a long way to change attitude towards the brand.

## THE FUNCTIONAL THEORY OF ATTITUDE

Katz (1960) came up with the functional theory of attitudes. The view holds that the main reason why consumers have attitudes is because of the function they serve to the individual.

The **utilitarian function** of attitudes is about the reward or punishment associated with the experience of buying or using the products. So, consumers would develop a favourable attitude to a product or brand that gives them rewards, while they would be unfriendly towards any product or service that does not provide the satisfaction expected. Attitudes can also serve the function of protecting people's self-image to overcome their feeling of insecurity and sense of inadequacy or lack of self-confidence. So, products and services that offer reassurance for consumers' self-confidence and remove self-doubt will attract their favourable attitudes. This is the **ego-defensive function** of attitudes. Meanwhile, the **value-expressive** function indicates that attitudes help consumers to express their values. As explained by Szmigin and Piacentini (2022), it is about consumers using products and services to project some aspect of their lives rather than using them to hide them. The **knowledge** function

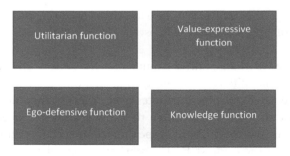

**FIGURE 8.7** Functions of attitudes

indicates that consumers' motivation for forming attitudes is about addressing the need to know, which also brings about order and structure to life. This function ensures consistency. For example, a consumer can develop an attitude to lodge in a particular hotel anytime he is on a trip to the city because of his or her experience in the past. With this, he maintains consistency and would not necessarily need to be bothered about alternatives. Similarly, we can also use the example of a consumer who resolves conflicting choices by choosing the most expensive based on the notion that the most expensive will probably give the most value. However, there are studies which have cautioned that price is not an indication of quality in all cases. One such study involved low-income consumers who indicated that items offered at higher prices are not any better than the alternatives, rather the price difference is due to the popularity of the brand and expensive packaging used by the marketers (Gbadamosi, 2009).

## CONSUMER ATTITUDES IN A DIGITAL AGE

Consumer attitudes are becoming significantly influenced by advancements in technology. Our preferences and choices are now being traced to the impact of technology more than before. Baines (2017) argues that society continues to exhibit remarkable interest and knowledge of technology and its dynamics. Some of the developments in the world of technology that influence marketing include social media communications, virtual reality, neuromarketing, sharing economy, and artificial intelligence (AI). Understandably this is linked to consumer attitudes. In e-commerce, consumer attitudes towards online shopping can be different depending on the associated logistics. This is demonstrated in the article of Wang and Bae (2020) on how to avoid the free shipping pitfall. They note that free shipping which is often linked to e-commerce contributes to the growth of this business format but can also compress the e-retailers' profit margin and ultimately hinder the quality of logistic services. Owing to this, it is suggested that marketers may separate shipping transactions from the main online transaction. However, the study also cautions that this approach can be challenging in that it could affect consumers' attitudes to e-commerce and ultimately lead to cart abandonment. Another concern associated with digital marketing, with implications for consumers' attitudes, is the notion of online privacy as there is a relationship between this and consumer behaviour (Kansal, 2014). One may wonder why privacy concern is upmost in the consumers' mind about digital marketing transactions, the diagram below as adapted from Flaherty (1989) shows the reasons in the form of rights that the consumers are protecting.

Meanwhile, in putting all these together, it is important to note that people's attitude to online transactions vary in relation to so many factors. The study of Sarel and Marmorstein (2003) shows this in relation to online banking services. They reiterate that having an understanding of the consumer adoption of online banking services will also involve acknowledging that people who have already adopted the transactions will be different from potential adopters.

**208** DIGITAL TRANSFORMATION AND PSYCHOLOGICAL BEHAVIOUR

**FIGURE 8.8** Consumers' rights and privacy

## LIQUID CONSUMPTION

The idea of classifying consumption into liquid and solid types is credited to Bardhi and Eckhardt (2017). In this postulation, they indicate that liquid consumption is different from solid consumption in that the former focuses on the ephemeral and places less emphasis on material elements whereas solid consumption is by nature tangible, enduring, and ownership based. This contention is based on the previous work of Bauman (2000; 2007) that metaphorically argues that daily living has changed from being secure and stable to being radically dynamic. In the contention of Bardhi and Eckhardt (2017), we can look at digitalisation as the equivalence of liquid consumption in that it emphasises dematerialisation as consumers have fewer materials in their value-oriented transactions. For instance, digitalisation means that

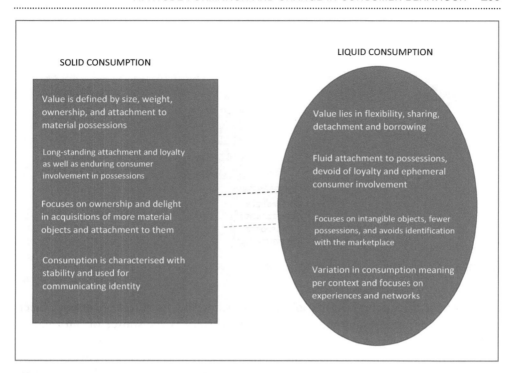

**FIGURE 8.9** Liquid and solid consumption

instead of carrying a burden of physical cash for transactions, consumers' credit or cash cards are being used instead. The ride-sharing transactions and relevant apps are further examples of dematerialisation that characterises liquid consumption. The argument as to whether digitalisation will completely replace traditional transactions still lingers. More often than not, it is often stated and logical to hold that despite the increasing trend of digitalisation in marketing and consumption, some sort of traditional marketing will still remain. In line with this reasoning, Bardhi and Eckhardt (2017) also argue that liquid and solid consumption are two ends of a spectrum and that solid consumption will not completely disappear but will co-exist. The two consumption contexts are shown in Figure 8.9.

## MARKETING COMMUNICATIONS AND CONSUMER ATTITUDES

The impact of marketing communications is significant. A model of this is shown in Figure 8.10. A critical look at each of the elements of this model will show some sort of link they have towards consumer attitudes to market offerings. One of the elements is the **source**. The source of marketing communications is the sender of the message. As expected, consumers weigh the source of the messages received to know the extent to which they could be relied on. Hence, marketers should focus on managing their credibility to be able to influence consumers' attitudes. The credibility of

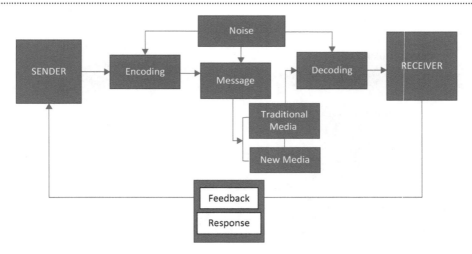

**FIGURE 8.10** Marketing communications model

the source of marketing information is often defined by its trustworthiness, objectivity, and expertise (Solomon 2020). While marketers as the source of information sponsor advertising messages, consumers are often conscious of the extent to which they rely on this. This is because the motive for communications is always known to be for increasing sales and profitability. Meanwhile, word-of-mouth communication, which is the spread of information about the products by consumers to others, such as potential customers, is considered to be more credible as those disseminating the information do not have any commercial-oriented incentive for spreading the information. Moreover, it is also very common for marketers to engage celebrities to endorse their products. Given the expertise of the celebrity and the existing fan base, this strategy tends to be more productive in getting consumers' attitudes to the product or services being advertised or endorsed.

Apart from the source, the message being transmitted is a crucial element of the marketing communication model. Consumers also gauge the credibility of the message received, and according to Hoyer et al. (2018) this is often done through:

- The quality of the argument in the message;
- The nature of the message on whether it is one-sided or two-sided: One-sided message focuses on just the positive side of the product while a two-sided message presents both the negative and positive;
- The type of the message on whether it is a comparative message or not: Compares the product of the organisation with those of the competitor(s) to emphasise the strength of the one marketed by the company.

Moreover, the message's appeal can also be a game changer for consumer attitudes. Based on De Pelscmacker et al. (2010) the two broad classifications of message appeal are:

- Rational appeal: This revolves around offering information that serves as cues for decision making;
- Emotional appeal: This mainly features non-verbal communications and could be in various forms such as fear, humour, fun, music, and eroticism.

Beyond this, consumers are now submerged with a plethora of messages not only from the traditional media like TV and newspapers, but also new media. Most consumers these days are on one social media platform or another. X, YouTube, Facebook, Instagram, and many others now present good opportunities for sharing marketing messages. The relative advantages of these platforms such as low cost and very wide reach make them attractive to marketers.

### PAUSE, PLAN, AND PRACTICE: CHOOSING CONFECTIONERIES: WHY DOES IT MATTER?

Confectioneries are a popular part of life in various societies. They are frequently consumed in different locations such as playfields, amusement parks, homes, and other places of relaxation. Consumers in the United Kingdom spend approximately £1.32 weekly on confectioneries. On the supply side, it is reported that companies producing chocolates and confectioneries made a whopping £4.6 billion in the year 2021. So, it constitutes a big business. As shown in Statistica, the number of Americans who consumed chocolate and other candy in 2020 was 268.09 million and estimated to increase to 275.03 million in the year 2024. While these two countries are just chosen as examples, the popularity of these products is global. Meanwhile, beyond the issue of its high consumption rate, it is interesting that, given its nature that it is cheap and bought very frequently, consumers tend to follow the hierarchy of purchasing the products, before developing emotion and forming cognition, which is typical of the low-involvement hierarchy model of attitude. In some circumstances, that is reminiscent of love and fun, consumers could also apply the emotional hierarchy of 'affect' before behaviour, and then 'cognition'. It is therefore not surprising that retailers are now offering some of these items openly displayed at the till to encourage impulse buying as the purchase process does not involve significant thought as compared to high-involvement products. To the consumers, the monetary, functional, and physical risks are very limited and prepurchase search and alternative evaluation tend to be limited. So, why does it matter? Ultimately, for these products, attitudes do not precede behaviour.

**Sources:**

US population: Consumption of chocolate and other candy in the US, 2011–2024, Statista, Statista Research Department, June 23, 2022, www.statista.com/statistics/283151/us-households-consumption-of-chocolate-and-other-candy-trend/ (accessed 10 February 2023).

Wunsch, N. (2022). Chocolate and sugar confectionary: Turnover of enterprise in the UK 2008–2021, Statista, www.statista.com/statistics/481625/chocolate-and-sugar-confectionary-sales-turnover-united-kingdom-uk/ (accessed 10 February 2023).

**TASKS**

1. In a group, reflect on the content of this mini case and mention three other products that follow low-involvement hierarchy that any member of your group has bought recently. Highlight the reasons for your choice.
2. Select a product or service that fits the high-involvement hierarchy and critically compare it and the purchase process to one of those you mentioned in task 1.

## SUMMARY

Consumer attitudes can be explained by their learned predisposition to consistently respond favourably or unfavourably towards something. Apart from the fact that they are learned and consistent, attitudes are evaluative, enduring, goal-oriented, changeable, and have intensity. Attitudes have three components, namely cognitive, affect, and behavioural, and the ordering of these elements, determine the types of the hierarchy of effects applicable to the scenario. So, there is high-involvement hierarchy in which cognitive (thinking) precedes affect (feeling) which precedes behaviour. This is not always the case, such as in cases of low-involvement hierarchy and emotional hierarchy. Attitudes are also explained through multi-attribute models, in which case an understanding of attitude towards a goal object is based on an understanding of the attitude towards each of the attributes of these market offerings. Attitudes have utilitarian, ego-defensive, knowledge, and value-expressive functions but can be changed. The use of digital technology has deepened the distinction between solid and liquid consumption types. By and large, consumers' attitudes and marketing communications are closely linked, especially in terms of managing the persuasion of consumers about market offerings.

**DIGITAL BOX: THINKING ABOUT A DATING APP?**

The world has gone digital in various ramifications. Consumers' attitudes and behaviour are tuned in various dimensions as a result of this. As people's social needs become triggered, their attention is directed at how these needs can be met. One of the ways technology has helped in this area is through the numerous dating apps available to consumers these days such as Happn, Tinder, Woo, and Try Date. The traditional approach to meeting a potential lover appears too random and remote to many without the use of a dating app. Some have a very negative attitude to using these apps as they consider it weird and desperate to use digital means to find a lover. Some even think it is hard to know the person through this means, as the information provided could be vague it could take longer to determine the person's true identity, and it can also be time-consuming. So, many do not have a positive attitude to using dating apps. Despite the stigma attached to dating apps, some consumers believe that they give users what they want per the time, they boost confidence thereby showing the ego-defensive function of attitude, and they allow the transition from 'texting' to 'talking' more smoothly. Understandably, the app developers would want to encourage more people to 'get it on' digitally, but it may be very challenging convincing the 'naysayers to think positively of these apps'.

**Source**

Sekar, A. (2016). The pros and cons of dating apps. Society, 19, May 20, 2016, www.society19.com/pros-cons-dating-apps/#:~:text=Pros%201%201.%20Apps%20let%20you%20get%20exactly,...%205%205.%20Different%20strokes%20for%20different%20folks.

**QUESTIONS**

1. How can the app developers change consumers' attitude to be in favour of these products?
2. How can a multi-attribute model be applied by consumers to find lovers using the app?

## END OF CHAPTER DISCUSSION QUESTIONS

1. Reflect on any two of your purchases made within the past two years and share experiences to explain which of the hierarchies of effects they follow (i.e. high, low, or emotional). Discuss the implication of this for how the marketers involved can plan their marketing strategies;
2. Discuss and illustrate the relevance of Heider's (1946) balanced theory with the choice of higher education institution or clothing. Discuss the relevance of social media in both scenarios;
3. Critically explain the multi-attribute model and replicate what is in Table 8.1 with another scenario and hypothetical figures and explain the implication of this for marketing strategies for the sale of the chosen product or service;
4. A marketer of an in-house stereo system that has been in business for ten years suddenly noticed that consumers now have a negative attitude towards the products as became evident in the dwindling sales figures. Discuss how this firm can change the attitude of its target market to positively be in favour of this product/brand;
5. Some consumers have a positive attitude to the environment and the notion of sustainability but do not support this with behaviour such as buying eco-friendly products. (a) Discuss this in terms of the ABC elements of attitudes. (b) To ensure that consumers act consistently with the attitude, which of the marketing communication appeals between rational and emotional would you recommend and why?

## Case Study: Campaigning to Curb Obesity – Is the World Losing the Battle?

Although some of cases of obesity are genetic, several others have been identified as attitudinal as they are enduring, consistent, and reflect evaluation of alternatives leading to the choices made. The increasing rate of obesity all over the world has become a worrisome phenomenon, it is noticeable in every segment of society including children. For example, 25% of school-aged children in New South Wales, a state in Australia, is either overweight or obese. In England, the number of women who are obese rose from 21% to 29% of the population during the period 2000–2019 while 63% of UK adults have more than a healthy weight. Similarly, 73% of the Mexican population are reported to be overweight while about one-third of adults in the United States is obese. This is a challenge in global consumerism and communicates something significant about consumer attitudes, lifestyles, and socio-cultural dynamics. In the available record from the 2019 study of the Global Burden of Disease (GBD), it is shown that over 583,000 deaths in European Union (EU) countries are related to issues of obesity. These are worrying statistics in many ramifications.

Over the years, stakeholders have identified many causes of this problem. Some commentators have pointed accusing fingers at marketers of varying sizes, including SMEs and multinationals, that they are not doing enough in terms of their market offerings offered to the consumers. They are expected to be at the forefront of campaigning to curb obesity as part of their strategic approach to practising societal marketing concepts. A deeper investigation into it reveals a litany of other causal factors such as having obese parents, sleep deprivation, weight gain in early childhood, maternal smoking in pregnancy, sedentary lifestyle, and poor socioeconomic status among others. These can be broadly classified as behavioural and environmental factors. When using the lens of the behaviour, consumers that are obese are noted to have an eating pattern that accommodates unhealthy food items and consume more food quantity than their body would normally require. The behaviour explanation also relates to their lack of physical exercise that could have helped to moderate their body metabolism in relation to the diet consumed. So, it is significantly linked to attitudes and decisions made by the consumers and their interaction with marketplace stimuli. As all these become a habit, the challenge lingers on, which begs the question: 'Is the world winning or losing the battle against obesity?'

In the physical sense, some of the signs that children are obese include when they wear clothes much bigger than those meant for their age, if their daily time spent watching television is more than three hours, if they consume takeaway meals more than two times a week, if they are always hungry and looking for food, if they are much bigger than their classmates in school, and if they eat adult portions of food or more in their family. The concerns raised by people are closely connected to the risk associated with it. Nutritionists have linked it to diseases such as Type 2 diabetes, high blood pressure, gastro-oesophageal reflux disease (GORD), cardiovascular disease, sleep apnoea, and mental health problems. Hence, there has been a clamour for a solution. Given what we know about the causes of this problem, the solutions often recommended are for consumers who are obese to change their eating habits. This will include changing attitudes towards food and reviewing the consumption of high-energy foods and drinks. To reduce obesity, further steps often recommended include limiting alcohol consumption and engaging in enough physical activity. Some have argued that the balanced theory of attitudes, through the associations with friends and family members who have interest in healthier diets and physical activities, could be a significant step to solving the obesity problem. Various stakeholders including governments and non-governmental organisations (NGOs) have been on the case of changing consumer attitudes towards achieving the solution. However, while some levels of success have been achieved so far, the statistics are neither clearly promising nor show any significant shift towards overcoming it. Some are claiming that radical approaches, including the use of new media for digital communications, could be the break needed to sensitise consumers to the dangers of this dilemma. It remains to be seen if this will have any impact. In view of the status quo, it is not unreasonable to ask 'is the world winning or losing the battle over obesity?'

**Sources:**

AIHW (2020). Overweight and Obesity among Australian Children and Adolescents, Australian Institute of Health and Welfare, 13th August, 2020, www.aihw.gov.au/reports/overweight-obesity/overweight-obesity-australian-children-adolescents/summary (accessed 16 October 2023).

Department for Health and Social Care (2020). Tackling obesity: Empowering adults and children to live heathier lives. Department for Health and Social Care, Policy Paper, 27 July, 2021, www.gov.uk/government/publications/tackling-obesity-government-strategy/tackling-obesity-empowering-adults-and-children-to-live-healthier-lives (accessed 9 February 2023).

Djordjevic, N. (2021). 36 worrisome global obesity statistics & facts for 2022, medalerthelp.org/blog/obesity-statistics/ (accessed 16 October 2023).

European Commission (2023). Health Promotion and Diseases Prevention Knowledge Gateway, European Commission, 19th September, 2023, knowledge4policy.ec.europa.eu/health-promotion-knowledge-gateway/obesity_en (accessed 17 October 2023).

Healthdirect (nd). Obesity, www.healthdirect.gov.au/obesity (accessed 11 February 2023).

NHS (nd). Obesity, www.nhs.uk/conditions/obesity/ (accessed 8 February 2023).

## QUESTIONS

1. Is it in the interest of the multinational companies to campaign to change consumer attitudes against unhealthy diets? Justify your position.
2. What line of action would you recommend for changing consumers' attitude in favour of healthy living? In the case of using marketing communication tools for

reaching the target audience, which of the two broad appeals (rational or emotional) would you recommend should underpin the communisation strategy?
3. Critically demonstrate the relevance of the multi-attribute model to the attitudes from the content of this case study;
4. How can social media be used to curb obesity or reduce its global rate?
5. Explain the notion of balanced theory of attitudes in the context of how it is used in case studies.

## REFERENCES

Ajzen, I. (1991). Theory of planned behaviour. *Organizational Behavior and Human Decision Processes*, 50(2), December, 179–211.

Alba, J. W., & Hutchinson, J. W. (2000). Knowledge calibration: What consumers know and what they think they know. *Journal of Consumer Research*, 27, 123–156. https://doi.org/cmh8tj

Albarracín, D., McNatt, P. S., Klein, C. T. F., Ho, R. M., Mitchell, A. L., & Kumkale, G. T. (2003). Persuasive communications to change actions: An analysis of behavioral and cognitive impact in HIV prevention. *Health Psychology*, 22, 166–177.

Arora, S., Singha, K., & Sahney, S. (2017). Understanding consumers' showrooming behaviour: Extending the theory of planned behaviour. *Asia Pacific Journal of Marketing and Logistics*, 29(2): 409–431.

Babin, B. J., & Harris, E. J. (2018). *CB8*. Boston: Cengage Learning.

Baines, P. R. (2017). Technological impacts on market attitudes and behaviors. *Psychology & Marketing*, 34(4), 351–355.

Banytė, J., Brazionienė, L., & Gadeikienė, A. (2010). Investigation of green consumer profile: A case of Lithuanian market of eco-friendly food products. *Economics & Management*, 15, 374–383.

Bardhi, F., & Eckhardt, G. M. (2017). Liquid consumption. *Journal of Consumer Research*, 44(3), 582–597.

Bauman, Z. (2000). *Liquid Modernity*. Cambridge, UK: Polity.

Bauman, Z. (2007). *Liquid Times: Living in an Age of Uncertainty*. Cambridge, UK: Polity.

Carey, M., White, E. J., McMahon, M., & O'Sullivan, L. W. (2019). Using personas to exploit environmental attitudes and behaviour in sustainable product design. *Applied Ergonomics*, 78, 97–109.

Clark, M. (2021). 11 Organizations with Negative Brand Images and How They Overcame It, http://etactics.com/blog/organizations-with-negative-brand-images#Samsung (accessed 17 October 2023).

De Pelsmacker, P., Geuens, M., & van den Berg, J. (2010). *Marketing Communications: A European Perspective*, 4th edn., Harlow: Pearson Education Limited.

Edell, J. A., & Burke, M. C. (1987). The power of feelings in understanding advertising effects. *Journal of Consumer Research*, 14(3), 421–433.

Fazio, R. H. (1990). Multiple processes by which attitudes guide behavior: The MODE model as an integrative framework, in M. P. Zanna (ed.), *Advances in Experimental Social Psychology*, Vol. 23, pp. 75–109. San Diego, CA: Academic Press.

Fishbein, M., & Ajzen, I. (1975). *Belief, Attitude, Intention, and Behavior: An Introduction to Theory and Research*. Reading, MA: Addison-Wesley.

Flaherty, D. H. (1989). *Protecting Privacy in Surveillance Societies*, p. 8. Chapel Hill, NC: University of North Carolina Press.

Gbadamosi, A. (2009). Cognitive dissonance: The implicit explication in low-income consumers' shopping behaviour for 'low-involvement' grocery products. *International Journal of Retail and Distribution Management*, 37(12), 1077–1095.

Glasman, L. R., & Albarracín, D. (2006). Forming attitudes that predict future behavior: A meta-analysis of the attitude-behavior relation. *Psychological Bulletin, 132*(5), 778.

Hoyer, W. D., MacInnis, D. J., and Pieters, R. (2018), 'Consumer Behaviour', 7th edn, Boston: Cengage Learning.

Hoyer, W. D., MacInnis, D. J., & Pieters, R. (2018). *Consumer Behavior*, 7th edn., Boston: Cengage Learning.

Hurst, M., Dittmar, H., Bond, R., & Kasser, T. (2013). The relationship between materialistic values and environmental attitudes and behaviors: A meta-analysis. *Journal of Environmental Psychology, 36*, 257–269.

Kansal, P. (2014). Online privacy concerns and consumer reactions: Insights for future strategies. *Journal of Indian Business Research, 6*(3), 190–212.

Kasser, T. (2011). Cultural values and the well-being of future generations: A cross-national study. *Journal of Cross Cultural Psychology, 42*(2), 206–215.

Katz, D. (1960). The functional approach to the study of attitudes. *Public Opinion Quarterly, 24*(2), 163–204.

Kautonen, T., Van Gelderen, M., & Tornikoski, E. T. (2013). Predicting entrepreneurial behaviour: A test of the theory of planned behaviour. *Applied Economics, 45*(6), 697–707.

Krosnick, J. A., Boninger, D. S., Chuang, Y. C., & Berent, M. K. (1993). Attitude strength: One construct or many related constructs? *Journal of Personality and Social Psychology, 65*, 1132–1151.

Leone, L., Perugini, M., & Ercolani, A. P. (1999). A comparison of three models of attitude–behavior relationships in the studying behavior domain. *European Journal of Social Psychology, 29*, 161–189.

Monroe, B. M., & Read, S. J. (2008). A general connectionist model of attitude structure and change: The ACS (Attitudes as Constraint Satisfaction) model. *Psychological Review, 115*(3), 733.

Ottman, J. A., & Reilly, W. R. (1998). *Green Marketing: Opportunity for Innovation*, 2nd edn., Hoboken, NJ: Prentice Hall.

Park, J. O., & Sohn, S. H. (2018). The role of knowledge in forming attitudes and behavior toward green purchase. *Social Behavior and Personality: An International Journal, 46*(12), 1937–1953.

Popy, N. N., & Bappy, T. A. (2022). Attitude toward social media reviews and restaurant visit intention: A Bangladeshi perspective. *South Asian Journal of Business Studies, 11*(1), 20–44.

Rossiter, J. R., & Percy, L. (1987). *Advertising and Promotion Management*. New York: McGraw-Hill.

Rossiter, J. R. and Percy, L. (1997). *Advertising Communications and Promotion Management*. New York: McGraw-Hill.

Sarel, D., & Marmorstein, H. (2003). Marketing online banking services: The voice of the customer. *Journal of Financial Services Marketing, 8*, 106–118.

Schiffman, L. G, Kanuk, L. L., & Hansen, H. (2012). *Consumer Behaviour: A European Outlook*, 2nd edn, Essex: Pearson Education Limited.

Schiffman, L. G., Kinauk, L. L., & Wisenblit, J. (2010). *Consumer Behaviour*, 10th edn, New Jersey: Pearson Education Inc.

Schiffman, L. G., & Wisenblit, J. (2019), *Consumer Behaviour*, 12th edn, Harlow: Pearson Education Limited.

Schultz, W. (2002). Getting formal with dopamine and reward. *Neuron, 36*, 241–263.

Solomon, M. R. (2020). *Consumer Behaviour: Buying, Having, and Being*, 13th edn, Essex: Pearson Education Limited.

Spain, C. V., Freund, D., Mohan-Gibbons, H., Meadow, R. G., & Beacham, L. (2018). Are they buying it? United States consumers' changing attitudes toward more humanely raised meat, eggs, and dairy. *Animals, 8*(8), 128.

Szmigin, I., & Piacentini, M. (2022). *Consumer Behaviour*, 3rd edn, Oxford: Oxford University Press.

Wang, L., & Bae, S. (2020). How to avoid the free shipping pitfall? Changing consumer attitudes from the perspective of information interaction. *Electronic Commerce Research and Applications*, *42*, 100996, https://doi.org/10.1016/j.elerap.2020.100996

# CHAPTER 9

# Consumer Motivation

**LEARNING OUTCOMES**

After reading this chapter, you should be able to:

1. Explain how needs, drives, and goals contribute to an understanding of consumer motivation;
2. Discuss the main theories of motivation and their relevance to consumer behaviour;
3. Explain motivational conflicts;
4. Explain consumer panic buying in relation to global pandemics;
5. Critically discuss consumer digital motivation;
6. Explain consumer social motivation.

**INTRODUCTION**

At every stage of life, we are in need of one thing or another. At one level, consumers' needs are basic while at another level, they are complex and advanced. The need of consumers without a TV set makes them drawn to making efforts to search, evaluate alternatives, and eventually own one. However, after some time and with advancement in technology, even when the current TV set still offers the level of service it provides at the time of purchase, the newer technology offers more convenience, entertainment, and symbolic benefits which will uncover another set and levels of need concerning this product. The same applies to automobiles, fashion products, and other products and services. The tension between the current state and the desired state drives the consumers to act to address this gap. As we grow older, change jobs, move to new environments, and experience other changes in life, our motivation for the consumption of goods and services tends to change. Unravelling the various motivational factors which are dynamic is one of the key challenges for

DOI: 10.4324/9781003242031-12

markets. Nevertheless, it is a very rewarding undertaking as it gives them the opportunity to effectively design their marketing strategies to be in tandem with growing and changing consumer needs. In this chapter, we will be discussing this in detail. We will examine the definition of the elements salient to understanding motivation such as needs, goals, and drives, and discuss theories of motivation as well as their key marketing implications. A part of recent experience in the world is the global pandemic, which brings with it panic buying. We will discuss this and the motivation for this purchase behaviour. In view of the development in technology, we will also discuss consumer digital motivation and consumer social motivation for a deeper discussion of the subject.

## CONSUMERS' NEEDS, DRIVES, AND GOALS: AN OVERVIEW OF MOTIVATION

In a simple form, motivation is about the 'why?' of a behaviour. Why does a consumer choose herbal tea over a chocolate drink? Why are some consumers interested in luxury cars instead of a more modest option? In view of this, motivation can be defined as the interaction of factors and processes that propel consumers to act the way they do. From this definition, we can see the relevance of factors like needs, wants, goals, and drive. A need describes a consumer's stage of deprivation indicating there is a gap between the actual and the desired states. The gap, indicating the need, places the consumer in a state of tension and he or she makes effort to reduce or remove it outright. So, the consumer is motivated to close the gap. The result to be achieved in the motivation process is the goal. So, it is reasonable to assume that all consumption acts are geared towards meeting needs and achieving goals. As an example, consumers can experience self-discrepancy. This produces cognitive, affective, and physiological consequences that motivate the consumer to act in a way to solve the problem (Sela and Shiv, 2009; Packard and Wooten, 2013). The study of Mandel et al. (2017) shows that, in such a case, consumers adopt five strategies to address this, which are:

- **Direct resolution**: Acting in a way to resolve the self-discrepancy;
- **Dissociation**: Acting to separate oneself from the goods and services that bring self-discrepancy;
- **Escapism**: Distracting oneself from thoughts associated with self-discrepancy;
- **Symbolic self-completion**: Acting to show mastery on issues that revolve around the self-discrepancy;
- **Fluid compensation**: Behaving in a way as to reinforce a different aspect of one's identity that is separate from the issues associated with self-discrepancy.

To demonstrate consumers' needs and motivation further, we can also look at the study of Fauzia and Gurtino (2020), which revolves around consumer satisfaction and the use of a co-working space café. This study is linked to the increasing rate of technology, which now encourages people to explore alternative work spaces other than their homes and official office spaces, and organisations' demand for more flexible and temporary services than they used to have in the past. In this study, the authors found that those visiting these places are not only driven by the need to work but also to socialise with others.

As shown in the foregoing, consumer needs vary. They are not rigidly associated with the physical elements of an offering but extend to several other aspects of the consumers' lives. We will discuss the variation later in the chapter. An example to demonstrate motivation could be a consumer who noticed that her current car malfunctions, which gives her constant stress. This indicates the existence of the need for a replacement vehicle. Meanwhile, we still need to distinguish between a need and a want. While the need is the gap between a desired state and the actual state, a want refers to specific satisfiers of those needs. In other words, wants refer to specific manifestations of the consumers' motives and are closely connected to a specific goal object (Szmigin and Piacentini, 2022). The need for food and clothing is primary and as specific satisfiers of this need, eating chicken and chips, and wearing skirts and blouses, depict wants as they are specific ways of meeting these needs even though there are other alternatives. The notion of the drive is also fundamental to the discussion of consumer motivation. It is the strength or extent of the tension experienced by the consumer in relation to the need that arose due to the perceived gap. This drive is the determinant of the feeling of urgency at which the consumer will attempt to reduce or solve the issue (Solomon, 2020). If the drive is very strong, then the consumer will be highly motivated to act to solve the need, whereas a low drive indicates a weak motivation strength towards addressing the need.

## THEORIES OF MOTIVATION

There have been many theories of motivation over the years that provide different perspectives on how to understand the construct. Some of these are discussed in relation to consumer behaviour and marketing in this section.

## HENRY MURRAY'S NEED CLASSIFICATION

Henry Murray, a psychologist, provides two types of classification of needs, which are:

- **Biogenic (primary) needs:** Innate needs that are related to our biological nature and linked to survival, such as the need for food, water, and shelter;
- **Psychogenic (secondary) needs:** These are non-biological needs that relate to our personality and are socially acquired, such as need for self-esteem, status, and affiliation.

Murray (1938) prepared a list of around 20 psychogenic needs, which include those that reflect ambition, accomplishment, and prestige, and those related to human power. Others are those related to the affection between people, those needs that revolve around asking and telling (intercourse), and the one indicated as sadomasochistic need (Schiffman et al., 2012). This postulation has attracted interest among various researchers. One of such contributions is the work of Winter (1996), who indicates that among this long list of psychogenic needs, three stand out as fundamental. As illustrated by Steel and König (2006), these needs are:

- **Need for achievement**: This is related to surmounting obstacles;
- **Need for affiliation**: This is about craving intimacy, socialising, and sharing with others;
- **Need for power**: This relates to having strength or prestige, especially in relation to others.

There are many examples of these needs in consumer behaviour. Products such as organisers, and services such as event planning, address the need for achievement to a great extent while provisions of recreation centres, restaurants, and social media apps help to address the need for affiliation. The purchase of luxury items that symbolically communicate status and esteem, such as jewellery and sports cars, tend to address people's need for power.

## HIERARCHY OF NEEDS

Another well-cited and widely applied theory of motivation is that of Abraham Maslow (1943). It argues that human needs are in a hierarchical order of five stages. The perspective indicates that people act to satisfy lower-level needs before seeking to fulfil higher-level needs and when the lower-level needs are satisfied, then the person is driven to pursue and satisfy a new higher-level need. The first of the stages on the hierarchy is the group of basic and physiological needs. They are linked to human survival and include the need for water, food, clothing, and sex. This is shown in Figure 9.1. The second stage covers the safety and security needs that ensure physical safety and stability. The third level covers social needs. Essentially, it is about the

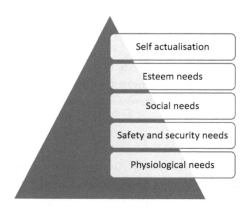

**FIGURE 9.1** Abraham Maslow's Hierarchy of Needs

need to love and be loved such as the need for belonging and affection. As shown in the figure, esteem needs are positioned on the fourth level of the hierarchy and are associated with people's egos. Those motivated to pursue this level of needs are driven to pursue actions such as self-esteem, independence, status, reputation, and recognition. The last stage is known as the self-actualisation level, which covers all the needs to fulfil one's potential.

There are significant consumer behaviour implications of this model. One such area is in the application of segmentation, targeting, and positioning. It is believed that consumers operating at each of the levels would be motivated differently. Marketers targeting consumers that may be operating at each of the levels would choose their strategies appropriately. For a simple illustration, if we look at the broad division between the physiological needs level and those higher-order needs, we can come to see the relevance and focus of strategies for luxury products which are often amenable to higher-order needs such as social and esteem needs. For items such as luxury cars, designer clothes, shoes, and wrist watches that are within conspicuous consumption, the positioning and associated strategies would be different compared to those to be adopted for basic foods such as those found among fast-moving consumer goods. This covers many aspects of the strategies. Consumers buying luxury items such as a Ferrari, yacht, or other luxury items pride themselves in the exclusive distribution strategies adopted by the marketers while intensive-distribution strategies are often adopted for fast-moving consumer goods. A similar explanation of the distinction between these could be made for pricing strategies as those for luxury products, for which the consumers engage in symbolic consumption to communicate their wealth and social class, tend to be different compared to those used for non-status product items.

Despite the popularity of this theory, it has been criticised on some grounds. For instance, it has been argued that, contrary to the claim of Maslow that a lower-level need will have to be met before being motivated to pursue the next higher one, some consumers operating at the physiological level may be motivated to pursue higher-level needs like social needs and/or esteem needs. One of the key reasons why people engage in counterfeiting has been highlighted as self-ambiguity. Hence, some low-income consumers buy to engage in non-deceptive counterfeiting in order to boost their self-esteem. Some scholars argue that Maslow's postulation is not based on empirical work and, as such, would have a limited application (Szmigin and Piacentini, 2022).

## MCCLELLAND'S THREE NEEDS THEORY

Another theory of motivation is the three needs theory proposed by McClelland (1961). In his study of what drives people to act or achieve something, David McClelland argues that humans are motivated to pursue three needs which are:

- Need for achievement;
- Need for affiliation;
- Need for power.

The need for achievement is about accomplishing something. Consistent with this, those strongly motivated in this direction tend to take calculated risks and like individual-based tasks towards achieving their goals. The need for affiliation is about connecting and relating with people. Those with the dominant need for affiliation do not like risk and tend to love belonging to groups, like to maintain good interpersonal relationships, and embrace collaborations in their endeavours (Kovach, 2018). The need for power is about desiring to influence and control others and those having this as dominant in their drive will be very competitive and love winning (MindTools, 2022).

In this postulation, individuals tend to have a specific need(s) more dominant for them, compared to others. This then drives their motivation to act in a way that influences their choices. Symbolic consumption of luxury goods, activities in brand communities, gym membership, and transactions in the games industry are some of the examples of how McLelland's three needs theory are being applied in marketing.

## EQUITY THEORY OF MOTIVATION

J. S. Adams (1963) is credited with the equity theory of motivation. It is about peoples' perception of how fair the outcome of their work is in comparison to the input they invested into it. So, it is about an input vs output comparison as people hold that there is a direct relationship between the two. So, people believe that working hard should result in a commensurate outcome. Similarly, they believe that their output/input ratio should be comparable to others doing similar tasks. Hence, they would expect to get a reward similar to that of another individual that has given similar input or effort to the same task. Logically, if there is a disequilibrium in this, such that the person gets below the perceived point of equity, the individual will perceive inequity and be demotivated. One of the examples of how marketers have been using this theory is in their various rewards programmes. Frequent flyers organised by airlines build some form of equity into the reward to acknowledge that some of the consumers have more transactions than others. Similarly, some telephone companies give special rewards to their customers differently based on the length of the transaction with the companies. For instance, the Sky VIP scheme acknowledges some customers for reward in the various tiers such as Platinum, Gold, and Silver, indicating their years of being with the company and the rewards given to them.

## PANIC BUYING AND GLOBAL PANDEMICS

We have witnessed many unprecedented but noteworthy actions and behaviour during the global pandemic, which have not only affected the health of billions of people but also ravaged the healthcare system and the global economy, and caused great anxiety and fear among many. It was adjudged one of the most substantial challenges that has confronted business and governments in the past 100 years (Hall et al. 2020). Consumer behaviour changed radically in many ways. The chaotic scenes of the consumers' struggle to buy many product items such as tissue papers, sanitisers, eggs, bread, and some fruit items were seen on various national and international television news programmes. The scenes of empty shelves were of concern to numerous consumers. This became heightened by the policies of governments around the world resisting peoples' social interaction and mobility to avoid the spread of the virus. Governments and experts in various countries including the United States, Canada, and United Kingdom warned people not to go out unless it was absolutely necessary and grocery stores reduced their operating hours (Islam et al., 2021). Similarly, online purchases grew significantly. Around the time, online sales of groceries increased by about 43% in a month when compared with the figure reported for the year before (Reuters, 2020; Naeem, 2021).

Consistent with the overarching focus of this chapter, we are still interested in the reasons and drive behind panic buying. As defined in the literature, panic buying is about purchasing an unusually large quantity or unusually varied stock of products as a result of anticipation of a disaster, during the period of disaster, or when there is a suspicion of shortage or increase in price of such products (Yuen et al., 2020; Loxton, 2020). So, it is a form of compulsive consumption (Herjanto et al., 2021). Looking at COVID-19 as a reference point, Razzak and Yousaf (2022) indicate that the pandemic could make some people vulnerable while others will be resilient in terms of how the situation affects their buying behaviour. It is interesting that this study shows that the COVID-19 threat was perceived differently by vulnerable and resilient consumers.

One of the palpable signs we could see, especially at the early stage of the pandemic, is the uncertainty that surrounds consumption, which impacts consumer decisions as exacerbated by the self-isolation rules imposed by governments, as the global challenge continued (Loxton et al., 2020). Just as we discussed the theories of motivation from different perspectives, we will look at some of the factors identified as responsible for such consumption behaviour by various authors. According to Yuen et al. (2020), four factors for panic buying can be identified as:

- Fear of the unknown;
- Social psychology;
- Coping behaviour;
- Perception.

According to these authors, the fear of the unknown reflects in terms of consumers' lack of knowledge of the predicament, and they simply stock the items as a way of providing security. Social psychology is in the form of reactions to rumours, opinions of others, and attitudes of others and communities about the scenario. The perception is about individual consumers' view of a high possibility of contracting the disease, which leads them to engage in panic buying so as to lower the associated risks. Using panic buying as a coping behaviour is borne out of lack of control over the prevailing crises as such purchase serves as some form of stress-relief. In their study on why some consumers bought toilet paper in bulk during the COVID-19 pandemic, Im et al. (2022) found that such panic buying is done as a coping mechanism to navigate through stress conditions such as loneliness and anxiety.

From another perspective (Herjanto et al., 2021), the factors that drive panic buying have been classified into three:

- **Neurological factors**: e.g. depression and anxiety;
- **Situational factors**: supply scarcity;
- **Social factors**: social networking.

This viewpoint is consistent with that of Yuen et al. (2020) in that the reason given for panic buying is not only personal but also social. Meanwhile, in consistency with these, it is also important to note that the scarcity messages that people receive play a critical role in stimulating perceived arousal, which also significantly influences consumers' obsessive and impulsive purchase behaviour (Islam et al., 2021). Many writers have pointed accusing fingers at the media for reporting more infection and mortality cases than they do in relation to cases on people that recover from the sickness, which tends to cause fear that spreads even faster than the pandemic itself (Im et al., 2022). So, the thought about the possibility of death, which is also known as **mortality salience**, served as the driver that prompted overconsumption and increased overindulgence (Campbell et al., 2020; Im et al., 2022).

Another interesting contribution on whether a particular consumer would resort to using the panic purchase to address stress is given to be culture. This is based on the contention that coping with stress is, in some cases, culture related. Im et al. (2022) found that consumers that are from individualist cultures such as the United States believe that personal coping measures to negative emotions such as loneliness, anxiety, and depression are more effective compared to consumers from collectivist cultures such as Koreans, who believe ardently in adopting a social coping mechanism. While the idea of a bandwagon effect leading someone to use panic buying to mitigate stress would not appeal to consumers from individualist cultures, this may well be a personal factor to him or her such as the individual perception of mortality salience.

## MOTIVATIONAL CONFLICTS

There are circumstances when we have motivational conflicts when our needs conflict with one another. The three motivational conflicts are:

- Approach-Approach conflict;
- Avoidance-Approach conflict;
- Avoidance-Avoidance conflict.

In the **Approach-Approach conflict**, the consumer is torn between choosing from two or more desirable alternatives. As we know from fundamental economic principles, financial resources are not infinitely available to us. Hence, this is a very common scenario in that we often have to choose options and forgo others. As an example, when a consumer is faced with buying a car and changing his or her wardrobe, an Approach-Approach motivational conflict is applicable as both scenarios are good but with lack of money, the consumer will have to consider which is needed more using various criteria such as the urgency of the need. Another example could even be the choice between a car that is fuel efficient and another that is not but has Automatic Emergency Braking (AEB).

In the **Avoidance-Approach conflict** scenario, the consumer is confronted with a decision that has both positive and negative outcomes. We can look at the purchase of some luxury SUV cars that have been criticised for being environmentally unfriendly in terms of emissions and environmental pollution as a relevant example. This leaves the consumer in a state of dilemma of owning his or her dream car and coping with the guilt of not being sufficiently protective of the environment and being ostentatious.

The **Avoidance-Avoidance conflict** case presents the circumstances when the consumer must choose from options in which all have undesirable consequences. A consumer who has been planning to book a flight ticket to a destination but suddenly realised that the price has increased significantly will have to choose between paying the new high price or abandoning the journey altogether.

## CONSUMER DIGITAL MOTIVATION

The increase in the use of digital technologies by consumers is now remarkable. Available statistics show that 4.9 billion consumers are Internet users worldwide as of 2021 and the number has risen to 5.2 billion in the year 2022 (Petrosyan, 2023). This implies that about than two-thirds of the global population has access to the Internet with a significant portion of Internet users based in China, the United States, India, Indonesia, and Nigeria. The rise of websites such as Pinterest and YouTube provides consumers with guidance and tutorials on numerous innovative topics (Robson et al., 2019). This indicates that consumption through the Internet has also gone up markedly in recent times. Accordingly, marketers are expected to follow this trend in the digital world and navigate the marketing environment accordingly in terms of the design of the strategy such as its marketing communications. It is therefore understandable that Kannan and Li (2017) claim that digital marketing is now multifaceted, such that it capitalises on all available digital technologies for the purpose of acquiring and retaining customers and influencing their preferences and impacting sales. As students, practitioners, and researchers of consumer behaviour, we are interested in what motivates consumers' consumption via Internet platforms. So, this is about understanding the Internet and external forces that trigger enthusiasm towards digital consumption (Daft, 2014; Tonnette, 2019). In the conventional understanding of motivation, as consumers become aware of their needs and wants, they seek to satiate these by exploring alternatives and choosing the market offerings that best fit their perceived needs (Tonnette, 2019). In exploring the reasons for Internet and digital motivation, we will start with the findings of Robson et al. (2019) in their study, which revolves around consumers' motivation for innovating autonomously in relation to creating new products from old ones. They found that creative consumers are primarily motivated by either of these factors:

- They face a problem;
- They wish to explore the possibilities of products and services offered.

Many times that consumers opt for online shopping, they are doing so to solve a problem they experience. When an old vacuum cleaner suddenly stops working, or there is a party to attend and the current shoes do not fit the occasion, or the children's school stationeries have run out, or any other problem, we notice that our attention is diverted to address this need through the use of Internet facilities. Moreover, the creative consumer intends to explore the possibilities of offerings in the marketplace, which drives them to the Internet space. According to the literature, in either of these two cases, the creative consumers do not have any significant relationship with the brand, or the organisation linked to the source material of their creativity (Berthon et al., 2007; Robson et al., 2019). In a wider context, online purchases have been linked to the need for customers to have access to a wide variety of merchandise and be more flexible in their choices in a more convenient form (Chen and Lin, 2019).

One of the key aspects of e-commerce is electronic word-of-mouth communications (e-WOM). This is about spreading the news about the fitness for purpose and value of a market offering to consumers by other consumers. In the definition given by Jalivand et al. (2010), it is any review that a consumer posts online concerning a market offering that could be informative or recommending with the purpose of guiding a good number of current or potential consumers. Whether in the online platform or in its physical/conventional context, word-of-mouth communication (WOM) is acknowledged to have more credibility than information from marketing sources because they do not have commercial motives. Clearly, it can deter or attract other consumers to the market offerings. It is said that the main reason for 20–50% of all purchase decisions are linked to e-WOM (Bughin et al, 2010). So, this is a considerable motivational factor for brand choices in online transactions. In discussing consumers in relation to eWOM, an emerging terminology that defines their role in the online platform is 'prosumer', which stands for producer-consumer, indicating that they are value co-creators of the online content (Fine et al., 2017). Some examples can be seen in platforms such as Google reviews, TripAdvisor, and Amazon reviews. From this, as these reviews serve as motivational factors for online customers, it is logical for online marketers to be interested in knowing how these prosumers are also motivated to post these contents online. Fine et al. (2017) found that both intrinsic and extrinsic factors motivate these prosumers for writing reviews and the level of the reliability of the service positively influences their decision to engage and write eWOM. In their study, which is focused on social capital, user motivation, and collaborative consumption of online platform services, Kim and Yoon (2021) offer useful definitions of intrinsic and extrinsic motivations. The intrinsic motivations encapsulate factors like fun and enjoyment that emerge from the consumers' inner drive, whereas the extrinsic factors are extraneous rewards like financial gain.

One of the principal motivations for consumers' engagement with digital platforms is the social factor. Millions of consumers are motivated to interact with various brands online as part of their interactions with other consumers. Consumers join social media platforms, follow one another, and are influenced by their following of celebrities on platforms such as Facebook and Instagram. As shown in the figure below, which is adapted from Whiting and William (2013), social interaction is the most prominent of all the factors in why people use social media. The study of Treviño and Pineda Garelli (2019), in their quest to understand motivation for digital moms, found strong support for this. They note that digital mothers' motivation for joining brand pages is to identify with other consumers similar to them and to make them feel part of a group.

## CONSUMER SOCIAL MOTIVATION

Although we have referred to social media in the preceding section as the discussion of digital marketing, consumption, and social media are inexplicably linked, we will be looking at social media in more depth in this section of the chapter. What motivates the consumers in relation to the use of these platforms? This is a valuable and relevant question. Social media is big business as it comes in the form of social networks, media sharing, blogs, microblogs, reviews, and social gaming (Zhang and Mao, 2016). Available statistics show 4.48 billion users as of July 2021, which represents more than double of the figure of 2.07 billion recorded as the number of users for the year 2015 (Dean, 2021). There are many of these in society and many more are being added. Facebook, LinkedIn, Instagram, X, and TikTok are some of the most commonly used among these social media networks.

While some motivational factors have been identified, it is important to also state that these factors can vary among different consumer segments. For example, it has been shown that:

- High-income consumers tend to have more positive attitudes towards social media marketing than others (Akar and Topçu, 2011);
- Young consumers are driven to digital media to test the credibility of online content by following their views of peers (Yu et al., 2022).

One of the key social factors in the online context is brand communities. Many people are passionately committed to some brands. This commitment is exercised in some cases offline and in several other cases online in the form of brand communities. The same question raised throughout this chapter is 'why?'. Three factors that motivate consumers to join these communities are highlighted by Balasubramanian and Mahajan (2001) as:

- Focus-related utility;
- Consumption utility;
- Approval utility.

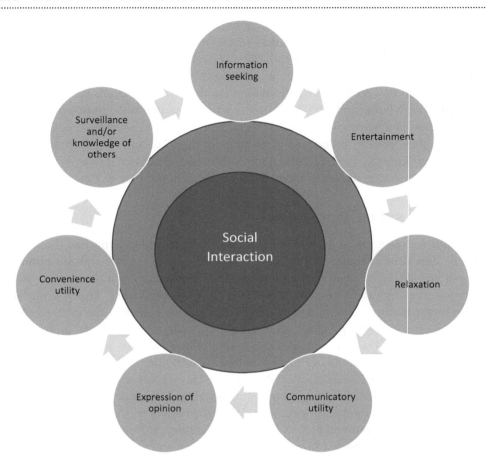

**FIGURE 9.2** Motivation for joining social media
**Source**: Adapted from Whiting and Williams (2013).

The focus-related utility is about joining an online community by adding value in the form of making contributions, while consumption utility is about immediate utilisation of the contribution that has been made by others. Approval utility is the satisfaction that a brand community member gets from the usage and endorsement of the views they express in the community by other users and community members.

Meanwhile, a more elaborate presentation of the most popular motivational factors that lead people to social media usage for the third quarter of the year 2022, as given by Dixon (2023), is shown in Table 9.1. As indicated by the percentage of users, we can see some factors are more popular than others. For instance, it is very common for people to use them to connect with friends and family and this is more popular than using them to connect with and support good causes.

**TABLE 9.1** Most popular reasons for Internet users worldwide to use social media as of 3rd quarter 2022

|    | Reasons for social media usage (worldwide) | Percentage |
|----|---------------------------------------------|------------|
| 1  | Keeping in touch with friends and family    | 47.1       |
| 2  | Filling spare time                          | 36.2       |
| 3  | Reading new stories                         | 34.2       |
| 4  | Finding content (e.g. articles, videos)     | 30.3       |
| 5  | Seeing what's being talked about            | 28.8       |
| 6  | Finding inspiration for things to do and buy| 27.3       |
| 7  | Finding products to purchase                | 25.9       |
| 8  | Sharing and discussing opinions with others | 23.7       |
| 9  | Making new contacts                         | 23.0       |
| 10 | Seeing content for your favourite brands    | 22.7       |
| 11 | Work-related networking and research        | 22.0       |
| 12 | Watching or following sports                | 21.8       |
| 13 | Finding like-minded communities and interest groups | 21.4 |
| 14 | Posting about your life                     | 21.3       |
| 15 | Following celebrities or influencers        | 20.8       |
| 16 | Avoiding missing out on things              | 20.3       |
| 17 | Supporting and connecting with good causes  | 16.1       |

**Source**: (Dixon, 2023)

---

**PAUSE, PLAN, AND PRACTICE: THE MOTIVATION FOR CADBURY CHOCOLATES**

Cadbury has been in the business of producing chocolate for a very long time. The company's website is passionately populated with success stories of the organisation from its inception in the year 1824 to the present date. As a key market player, Cadbury is focused on what motivates people to consume chocolate. Just as there are differences in our taste for other products like cars and fashion products, people buy chocolate for a variety of reasons and knowing this is the bedrock of business success. Some buy chocolate as indulgence, while others buy to share with others as a way of fulfilling their social needs and some use it to show esteem and pride in what they believe in. The company categorises some of these chocolate products under milk, caramel, white or dark, fruity and nutty, biscuit, and others. So, the purchase of Dinky Deckers, Cadbury Roses, Fudge Minis, Cadbury Dairy Milk, or Oreo may have been driven by different needs. Therefore, while some consumers spend to use some of these products to address their biogenic needs, others purchase them with the motivation to address their psychogenic needs.

**Sources**

Cadbury (nd). 1824 John Cadbury opened Bull Street shop, www.cadbury.co.uk/our-story?timeline=1824 (accessed 16 March 2023).

Cadbury (nd). Our products, www.cadbury.co.uk/products (accessed 16 March 2023).

**TASK**

In a group, design a product that will compete with Cadbury's market offerings to be specifically targeted at vegans and high-income earners. Consider the likely needs of these consumer segments and ensure that the product ideas offer what will satisfy them.

## SUMMARY

Consumption is driven by the motivation to fulfil needs. Among the commonly discussed theories of motivation are Henry Murray's need classification, Abraham Maslow's hierarchy of needs, David McClelland's three needs theory, and J. S. Adams' equity theory. It is commonly noted among these theories that consumers' needs vary. For example, consumers can have physiological needs, social needs, esteem needs, need for power, need for achievement, and need for affiliation. Another closely related topic is panic buying, such as the one that characterised the period of the COVID-19 pandemic. The motivation for such purchases has been clarified in various ways. For example, it is stated that it could be neurological, situational, or social in nature. It is important to also note that there can be motivational conflicts of different types. Meanwhile, it is interesting to see that several factors such as information seeking, convenience utility, expression of opinion, communicatory utility, entertainment, and relations motivate the use of social media for consumers.

---

**DIGITAL BOX: CONSUMER DIGITAL MOTIVATION AND THE COVID-19 PANDEMIC**

When the World Health Organization formally recognised the COVID-19 virus as a pandemic on 11 March 2020, there was a significant shift in consumer behaviour as a form of adjustment to cope with the conundrum. One of the most noticeable signs of the change was the panic buying of some essential products for various reasons. However, perhaps a more noticeable change in the society was the astronomical increase in the use of the Internet for shopping and social interaction since governments announced restrictions on movements, including going to retail outlets. The BBC indicated that UK Internet users consumed more than double the level of regular purchases than before the pandemic. While it is very convenient to simply explain what motivated consumers to go online or use the Internet more for consumption as the global pandemic continued, there are more specific reasons.

**Sources**

BBC (2020). UK internet use doubles in 2020 due to pandemic, www.bbc.co.uk/news/technology-55486157 (accessed 17 March 2023).

WHO (2022). Coronavirus Disease (COVID-19) Dashboard, https://covid19.who.int/ (accessed 5 November 2021).

**TASKS**

1. Reflect on your experience as a consumer during the COVID-19 global pandemic. What were the factors that motivated you to use the Internet or use more of it during the early stages of the pandemic? Has the trend changed back to the way it was before the pandemic or remained the same?
2. Considering the main factors that drive people's social media usage, in a group develop an idea for a new social media app and discuss its potential usage for consumers and marketers.

## END OF CHAPTER DISCUSSION QUESTIONS

1. Marketers target consumers with the aim of meeting their needs to ensure that they are satisfied. Using Abraham Maslow's hierarchy of needs, write out a product or service and the brand that are applicable at each of the five levels of the needs. Discuss why these products or services will require different marketing strategies if the firms are to satisfy their target markets.
2. Discuss the application of the J. S. Adams (1963) motivation theory in relation to consumer behaviour in the contexts of insurance and fast-food businesses.
3. Reflect on your participation in panic buying. What were the key driving factors for your action? Compare these experiences with those of another friend or colleague. Upon reflection, would you say the action was warranted or unnecessary? Do you think governments, marketers, and other related parties could have taken steps to prevent or address this?
4. Which social media platform(s) do you belong to? What are the motivating factors that prompted you to join them? How can brand managers use these factors to strengthen the firm's marketing strategy in respect of their brands?
5. Reflect on your purchases to identify those you've bought to fulfil psychogenic (secondary) needs. Were you influenced by e-WOM? What lessons can marketers learn from this?

### Case Study: The Drive for Ferrari Cars

The Ferrari automobile has been a signal of luxury for a long time. As an Italian car manufacturer, this value has been the core aspect of the company since it was founded in 1929 by Enzo Ferrari when the focus was mainly on the production of racing cars. However, in 1947, it became clear that the company had the opportunity for something more, and it was then that the first road car, which was called 125.s, was launched. All over the world, the Ferrari brand offers consumers more than the functional value of the car. Conventionally, consumers are drawn to buying cars for general benefits such as speed, fuel efficiency, comfort, safety, and reliability. These serve as the key motivational factors that drive their brand choices such as Toyota, Mazda, KIA, and Honda. Accordingly, car manufacturers often build these into their cars. However, the drive for the Ferrari brand is more than this. Customers of Ferrari are motivated by the prestige and uniqueness that communicate status symbols beginning with the famous black horse in the company logo. Clearly, it was targeted at fulfilling the consumers' psychogenic needs.

The popularity of the Ferrari F40, which was launched in 1988, was exceptional as Enzo Ferrari himself was the one that led the launch of the car. It is notably a car of elegance and exotic mechanical systems. The consumers using Ferrari see their cars as highly exclusive, fast, and sexy which defines them in a special way beyond the basic level of automobile ownership. They have a quintessential experience which is worth the price. Their focus is on the value rather than the price. For example, the price of

2023 Ferrari 296GTB starts from $342,205 and one of the remarkable tastes of luxury offered by the company is that of the Enzo Ferrari introduced in 2002 to honour the late founder, which costs $1 million. Despite the fact that they made only 400 of these, they became news items all over the world within a short time. Pushing this further, the 2015 Ferrari LaFerrari models, which are sports cars and notably exotic, sell for prices of over $1,420,112, and the 2023 Ferrari Daytona SP3 will require no less than $2,226,935. The consumers of these cars know that in most cases, the Ferrari automobiles cost more than a house, but they consider it appropriate in terms of the value of the brand that these specific cars offer them. What drives the consumers' interest in this brand is not only one aspect of their experience; rather the motivation is more holistic. The interior and exterior parts of Ferrari cars communicate elegance and quality beyond the ordinary. The technical inspections and checks made by Ferrari are excellently done by specialist technicians that are specially trained and the cars need to pass more than 201 of these before they can be adjudged approved. When a Ferrari is tagged as approved by the company, it is associated with many repairs and spare parts warranty as well as Roadside Assistance. The company offers seven years of complimentary service to the customers as one of the key areas of proving excellence in their transactions. Even for cars that are no longer in production, but are offered to buyers as used options, the uniqueness of Ferrari is still something to long for.

It is not surprising to many to later find out that the company made the Guinness Book of World Records on 12 September 2012, as 964 of its cars were collected in one place, at the Silverstone Run in the United Kingdom. The target market consists of affluent consumers as evidenced by the prices charged for various ranges of Ferrari cars. These cars are noted for all the motivation factors associated with mainstream cars but those buying them are also driven by the meaning the brand connotes. It offers them the pride of a high status in society and addresses their need for self-esteem. The news is already well received that Ferrari will be launching its first SUV, the 2024 Purosangue. This is because the market is aware that the company will still maintain its brand sporting ethos, which it has been known for over many decades. Another Ferrari model, the 2024 Ferrari Roma, is described as an elegant car with a new convertible Spider body that offers the buyers a taste of the Ferrari experience.

It is noteworthy that the social needs of Ferrari consumers are being met in several ways. The brand has a very strong and closely connected brand community. The Ferrari Owners Club brings the consumers together to various brand events including launching of new models, where they can express their passion for the brand. The social media presence of the brand on various platforms such as Facebook, X, Instagram, and LinkedIn is considerable. Ferrari owners are having the best experience of the world with their unique taste for quality that is anchored in hedonic motivation where luxury sets the boundary.

**Sources**

Brone.bg (nd). A brief history of Ferrari cars, brone.bg/en/a-brief-history-of-ferrari-cars/ (accessed 24 March 2023).

Ferrari (nd). www.ferrari.com/en-GB (accessed 24 March 2023).

Katsianais, J. (2023). New 2023 Ferrari Roma Spider arrives as luxury drop-top, *Auto Express*, http://www.autoexpress.co.uk/ferrari/roma/358763/new-2023-ferrari-roma-spider-arrives-luxury-drop-top (accessed 19 March 2023).

LivItaly Tour (2017). Ferrari: A brief history of Ferrari, March 1, 2017, www.livitaly.com/ferrari-history/ (accessed 24 March 2023).

## QUESTIONS

1. Discuss the key motivating factors for the purchase of Ferrari cars;
2. Explain the relevance of David McClelland's theory of motivation and draw examples from the case study;
3. Illustrate one of the motivational conflicts with information from the case study;
4. The case emphasises that Ferrari has an affluent target market who have specific motivational factors for buying these luxury cars. Would you recommend that the company target additional consumer segment(s) with different goals for car purchases to increase their customer base and profitability? Give reasons for your standpoint.

## REFERENCES

Adams, J. (1963). Towards an understanding of inequity. *Journal of Abnormal and Social Psychology*, 67, 422–436.

Akar, E., & Topçu, B. (2011). An examination of the factors influencing consumers' attitudes toward social media marketing. *Journal of Internet Commerce*, 10(1), 35–67.

Balasubramanian, S., & Mahajan, V. (2001). The economic leverage of the virtual community. *International Journal of Electronic Commerce*, 5(3), 103–138.

Berthon, P., Pitt, L., McCarthy, I., Kates, S. M. (2007). When customers get clever: Managerial approaches to dealing with creative consumers. *Business Horizons*, 50, 39–47.

Bughin, J., Doogan, J., and Vetvik, O. J. (2010). A new way to measure word-of-mouth marketing. *McKinsey Quarterly*, http://www.mckinsey.com/business-functions/marketing-and-sales/our-insights/a-new-way-to-measure-word-of-mouth-marketing (accessed 08 December 2023).

Campbell, M.C., Inman, J. J., Kirmani, A. & Price, L. L. (2020). In times of trouble: A framework for understanding consumers' responses to threats. *Journal of Consumer Research*, 47(3), 311–326.

Chen, S. C., & Lin, C. P. (2019). Understanding the effect of social media marketing activities: The mediation of social identification, perceived value, and satisfaction. *Technological Forecasting and Social Change*, 140, 22–32.

Daft, R. L. (2014). *Management*. Mason, OH: South-Western, Cengage Learning.

Dean, B. (2021). Social network usage & growth statistics: How many people use social media in 2022?, http://backlinko.com/social-media-users (accessed March 2023).

Dixon, S. (2023). Most popular reasons for internet users worldwide to use social media as of 3rd quarter 2022, Feb 14, 2023, www.statista.com/statistics/715449/social-media-usage-reasons-worldwide/#:~:text=A%20survey%20conducted%20in%20the%20third%20quarter%20of,was%20their%20main%20reason%20for%20using%20online%20networks (accessed 17 March 2023).

Fauzia, A., & Guritno, A. D. (2020). Consumer needs and consumer satisfaction in the creation of co-working space café business concept. In *IOP Conference Series: Earth and Environmental Science, 425* (1), 012032. IOP Publishing.

Fine, M. B., Gironda, J., & Petrescu, M. (2017). Prosumer motivations for electronic word-of-mouth communication behaviors. *Journal of Hospitality and Tourism Technology, 8*(2), 280–295.

Hall, M. C., Prayag, G., Fieger, P., & Dyason, D. (2020). Beyond panic buying: consumption displacement and COVID-19. *Journal of Service Management, 32*(1), 113–128.

Herjanto, H., Amin, M., & Purington, E. F. (2021). Panic buying: The effects of thinking style and situational ambiguity. *Journal of Retailing and Consumer Services, 60*, doi: 10.1016/j.jretconser.2021.102455.

Im, H., Kim, N. L., & Lee, H. K. (2022). Why did (some) consumers buy toilet papers? A cross-cultural examination of panic buying as a maladaptive coping response to COVID-19. *Journal of Consumer Affairs, 56*(1), 391–413.

Islam, T., Pitafi, A. H., Arya, V., Wang, Y., Akhtar, N., Mubarik, S., & Xiaobei, L. (2021). Panic buying in the COVID-19 pandemic: A multi-country examination. *Journal of Retailing and Consumer Services, 59*, 102357.

Jalivand, M. R., Esfahani, S. S., and Samiei, N. (2010). Electronic word-of-mouth: Challenges and opportunities. *Procedia Computer Science, 3*, pp. 42–46.

Jalivand, M. R., Esfahani, S. S., and Samiei, N. (2010). Electronic word-of-mouth: Challenges and opportunities. *Procedia Computer Science, 3*, pp. 42–46.

Kannan, P. K., & Li, H. (2017). Digital marketing: A framework, review and research agenda. *International Journal of Research in Marketing, 34*(1), 22–45.

Kim, E., & Yoon, S. (2021). Social capital, user motivation, and collaborative consumption of online platform services. *Journal of Retailing and Consumer Services, 62*, 102651.

Kovach, M. (2018). A review of classical motivation theories: A study understanding the value of locus of control in Higher Education. *Journal of Interdisciplinary Studies in Education, 7*(1), 34–53.

Loxton, M., Truskett, R., Scarf, B., Sindone, L., Baldry, G., & Zhao, Y. (2020). Consumer behaviour during crises: Preliminary research on how coronavirus has manifested consumer panic buying, herd mentality, changing discretionary spending and the role of the media in influencing behaviour. *Journal of Risk and Financial Management, 13*(8), 166.

Maslow, A. (1943). A theory of human motivation. *Psychological Review, 50*(4), 370–396.

McClelland, D. (1961). *The Achieving Society*. Princeton, NJ: D. Van Nostrand.

MindTools (2022). McClelland's Human Motivation Theory, http://www.mindtools.com/aznjntj/mcclellands-human-motivation-theory (accessed 8 February 2023).

Murray, H. A. (1938). *Explorations in Personality*. New York: Oxford University Press.

Naeem, M. (2021). Do social media platforms develop consumer panic buying during the fear of Covid-19 pandemic. *Journal of Retailing and Consumer Services, 58*, 102226.

Packard, G. M., & Wooten, D. B. (2013). Compensatory knowledge signalling in consumer word-of-mouth. *Journal of Consumer Psychology, 3*(4), 434–450.

Petrosyan, A. (2023). Internet usage worldwide – Statistics & Facts, Statista, January 3rd, 2023, http://www.statista.com/topics/1145/internet-usage-worldwide/#topicOverview (accessed 12 March 2023).

Razzak, A., & Yousaf, S. (2022). Perceived resilience and vulnerability during the pandemic-infused panic buying and the role of COVID conspiracy beliefs. Evidence from Pakistan. *Journal of Global Marketing, 35*(5), 368–383.

Reuters (2020). Coronavirus effect: UK supermarket visits jump by 79 million before lockdown, https://www.indiatoday.in/business/story/coronavirus-eff ect-uk-supermarket-visits-jump-by-79-million-before-lockdown-1661763-202 0-03-31 (accessed 08 December 2023).

Robson, K., Wilson, M., & Pitt, L. (2019). Creating new products from old ones: Consumer motivations for innovating autonomously from firms. *Technovation, 88*, 102075.

Schiffman, L. G, Kanuk, L. L., & Hansen, H. (2012). Consumer Behaviour: A European Outlook, 2nd edn, Essex: Pearson Education Limited.

Sela, A., & Shiv, B. (2009). Unraveling priming: When does the same prime activate a goal versus a trait? *Journal of Consumer Research*, *36*(3), 418–433.

Solomon, M. R. (2020). *Consumer Behaviour: Buying, Having, and Being*, 13th edn, Essex: Pearson Education Limited.

Steel, P., & König, C. J. (2006). Integrating theories of motivation. *Academy of Management Review*, *31*(4), 889–913.

Szmigin, I., & Piacentini, M. (2022). *Consumer Behaviour*, 3rd edn, Oxford: Oxford University Press.

Tonnette, M. (2019). Consumer purchase motivation in digital environments: The effect of intrinsic motivation on banner advertisement effectiveness (Doctoral dissertation of Business Administration, Jacksonville University).

Treviño, T., & Pineda Garelli, J. L. (2019). Understanding digital moms: Motivations to interact with brands on social networking sites. *Qualitative Market Research: An International Journal*, *22*(1), 70–87.

Whiting, A., & Williams, D. (2013). Why people use social media: A uses and gratifications approach. *Qualitative Market Research: An International Journal*, *16*(4), 362–369.

Winter, D. G. (1996). *Personality: Analysis and Interpretation of Lives*. New York: McGraw-Hill.

Yu, F., Wenhao, Q., & Jinghong, Z. (2022). Nexus between consumers' motivations and online purchase intentions of fashion products: A perspective of social media marketing. *Frontiers in Psychology*, *13*.

Yuen, K. F., Xueqin, W., Fei, M., & Li, K. X. (2020). The psychological causes of panic buying following a health crisis. *International Journal of Environmental Research and Public Health*, *17*, 3513.

Zhang, J., & Mao, E. (2016). From online motivations to ad clicks and to behavioral intentions: An empirical study of consumer response to social media advertising. *Psychology & Marketing*, *33*(3), 155–164.

# CHAPTER 10

# Consumer Personality and The Self

## LEARNING OUTCOMES

After reading this chapter, you should be able to:

1. Explain consumer personality and its characteristics;
2. Discuss various theories of personality;
3. Discuss brand personality and its applications;
4. Define consumer self, extended self, and their applications;
5. Discuss consumers' digital self in relation to the prevalent use of social media;
6. Examine the role of lifestyle in consumer behaviour;
7. Analyse consumer values in relation to consumption decisions.

## INTRODUCTION

The marketing environment is replete with events, products, services, brands, and changes such as the COVID-19 pandemic, experiences of the global economic crisis, and the launching of the latest cutting-edge technology by business giants in various sectors of the economy. The prevalence of operations of artificial intelligence (AI) has now moved to a terrain we have not been seeing before. The target of the various successive Conference of the Parties (COP) programmes on environmental sustainability impresses upon all stakeholders, including consumers, to find ways of saving the planet. Options ranging from using electric vehicles, adopting paperless transactions, to recycling and reuse of products continue to surface in the marketplace. We can go on and on in the proliferation of things happening in the marketplace. Similarly, prices of goods and services change upwards and downwards while the mode of distribution and marketing communications are also dynamic showing the latest trends and changes by the day. Meanwhile, it is interesting to note that consumers respond to these differently. The uniqueness with which consumers react to these issues is encapsulated in their personality and self-concept. So, this chapter brings together thoughts on these showing theoretical perspectives on consumer personality and how these are applied to brands in organisational strategic planning. The role of symbolic consumption to address the ever-changing needs of the *Self*, consumer values, and lifestyle are critically discussed in relation to the widespread use of social media. We will begin to unpack these with the discussion of consumer personality.

## AN OVERVIEW OF CONSUMER PERSONALITY AND SELF

### Personality

We will start the discussion of this section with an understanding of personality. Researchers continue to break new ground on consumer personality and the Self. Let us begin with a definition of personality. It can be defined as the collection of unique inner psychological characteristics that pattern a consumer's response to stimuli. To have a deeper level of understanding of this phenomenon, let us direct attention to its characteristics presented by Schiffman et al. (2012), which are:

- It is consistent and enduring;
- It indicates differences between individuals;
- It can change.

Personality shows how people are different from each other. Given that it reflects consumers' uniqueness, it is logical to state that personality indicates differences between them. This explains many things about the preferences of consumers such as product types, colours, sizes, and brands. Interestingly, some personality characteristics develop from childhood and are maintained and continue to show until people's adulthood. This emphasises that it is enduring and consistent. Nonetheless, many circumstances of life such as loss of a job, career changes, bereavement, ill health, and many other factors can change peoples' personalities to some extent. For example, a consistent taste for luxury could suddenly be disrupted by a drain in income that changes consumption patterns.

### Theories of Personality

The commonly discussed theoretical grounds for explaining human personality are highlighted as three, which are:

- Freudian theory;
- Neo-Freudian theory;
- Trait theory.

Let us discuss each of these in turn. The Freudian theory is one of the psychoanalytical theories. The key contention in the psychoanalytical theories is that an individual's personality evolves from the interaction of some unconscious internal elements that work within the mind (Freud, 1959). Freudian theory is specifically about the work of Sigmund Freud, whose perspective emphasises that human personality has a ground explanation from the study of child development stages, identified as:

- Oral (focuses on eating, biting, sucking);
- Anal (usage of the anus for excretion);
- Phallic (awareness of genitals);
- Latent (minimal or no sexual motivation);
- Genital (stage of having sexual intercourse).

According to Freud, these stages contribute to human personality. For example, when any of these stages are not adequately experienced, the individual will exhibit some behavioural pattern linking to these at a later stage in life. Ultimately, Freud indicates that human personality can be explained in relation to three interacting systems in humans, which are:

- Id;
- Ego;
- Superego.

The id element is part of the system that seeks instant gratification or pleasure without giving thought to the circumstances surrounding it or the resultant effect. The superego is about the moral and ethical code of behaviour prescribed by society. Hence, with these in mind, the excesses of the id are checked and moderated. The ego element lies between these two to reconcile their interactions such that appropriate balance can be achieved. It is like the consciousness of the individual playing the role of a negotiator between id and superego. In consumer behaviour, we can look at relating this to **compulsive consumption** in which people engage in excessive gambling, overeating, addictive sexual behaviour, alcoholism, drug use, and many other vices.

## NEO-FREUDIAN THEORY

There are other researchers who are Neo-Freudian that have made contributions on the same subject of personality by extending Sigmund Freud's work using another perspective. Two of these individuals are Karen Horney and Carl Jung. Their approach to a psychoanalytical understanding of personality is that, rather than viewing personality as being determined by inner and biological factors, it is influenced by interpersonal relationships and how they are managed. In the view of Karen Horney, people are known to be in categories of compliant, aggressive, and detached and commonly tagged with the acronym of CAD. Those who are known to be in the compliant category move towards other people while the aggressive are those who move against other people, and the detached are characterised by moving away from others. These personality characteristics have some links to people's consumption behaviour in relation to brand loyalty, the extent of the impact on reference group on consumption, the desire for uniqueness and customisation, and many other factors.

Another Neo-Freudian, Harry Stack Sullivan, argues that people's personalities developed as a result of their desire to decrease anxiety in social relationships. Considering this in relation to consumption will show the relevance of reference groups as a key explanation for their consumption pattern. Gbadamosi's (2015) study of brand personification among teenage ethnic minority groups confirms this postulation as the participants emphasised that the core reason that underlines their consumption is the need for acceptance among their peers.

Carl Jung is another major psychoanalytic theorist but with a different understanding of how human personality develops. He agrees with Freud that personality has some links to the human subconscious mind but extends this further with his stance known as analytical psychology. According to him, people's personality has a considerable link to their collective experiences in relation to past generations. So, from this theoretical sense, the personality dynamics will have to do with memories inherited from past generations such as what they fear and what they value. According to Jung (1959), these memories result in archetypes like those in myths, dreams, and stories (Solomon, 2020). In their way of describing these archetypes, Szmigin and Piacentini (2022) describe them as stable characters which explain basic feelings, ideas, visions, and fantasies that seem stable and frequently re-emerge in relation to different places and times.

## TRAIT THEORY

Unlike the psychoanalytical theories that are focused on the subconscious aspect of life and involve using qualitative methods such as projective techniques and personal observation to explore the deeper inner mind about personality, the trait theory is quantitative. This perspective indicates that people's personality is a composition of some characteristics that define and differentiate them from others. So, a consumer could be noted as aggressive, outgoing, introvert, extrovert, or with other traits. Our interest in understating consumer traits is that they determine consumer choices, and this knowledge is useful to marketers in formulating marketing strategies. So, it is important and relevant to first determine the consumers' personality trait pattern in order to be able to effectively segment on this basis.

Although people tend to share some personality traits such as frugality and ethnocentrism to a great extent, individual consumers tend to have unique characteristics in the ways these traits are combined. For example, a consumer could be an extrovert, highly materialistic, and innovative whereas his friend could also be innovative but frugal and an introvert. This explains the uniqueness of personality. Consumers' traits tend to be enduring but can also change due to various circumstances of life such as age. In this sense, school leavers or young adults may be carefree about money, spending, savings, and transactions but this can gradually change as they grow older and have more responsibilities. Over the years, consumer researchers have identified some relevant personality traits.

A commonly discussed trait-related topic is the 'Big Five' personality trait which has been described as covering the key dimensions of human personality. These are:

- Openness to experience;
- Conscientiousness;
- Extroversion;
- Agreeableness;
- Neuroticism.

As indicated in Solomon (2020), if someone has a high personality trait of openness to experience, then he or she is highly likely to be open to new ideas, things, and processes and tends to be more creative in getting things done. Conscientiousness is about maintaining structures and being organised in order to get things done. Extroversion is about being actively open to people and relationships. When a consumer is noted to be high in extroversion, he or she tends to be assertive, social, and outgoing whereas someone with an agreeableness personality will be less competitive, readily defer to others, and show interest and empathy for others. The neuroticism trait is the degree to which an individual can cope with stress. An individual with a highly neurotic personality would be upset easily, have mood swings, and experience anxiety (Cherry, 2023).

These traits are linked to consumer behaviour in some ways. Solomon (2020) presents a list of several personality traits and their corresponding influence on consumer behaviour. We will take three of these as examples here. According to the author, high personality ranking in the enjoyment of shopping can lead the consumer to spend time searching for products which will ultimately boost their product knowledge. Consumers with a high score in the 'need for uniqueness' personality trait tend to be opinion leaders who function to influence others in terms of marketplace activities, such as offering product information and advice on product suitability. In the example given by this author, when a consumer is high in neuroticism, he or she tends to neither repurchase a product or brand nor complain about their dissatisfaction with it.

## BRAND PERSONALITY

Brand is an important aspect of marketing. It is significant to both the consumer and the marketers. One of the key roles it plays is that it differentiates market offerings from others. From the consumers' viewpoint, they are happy to use it as a point of differentiation in terms of their possessions such as in the ownership of luxury brands in conspicuous consumption. So, brands serve as a good companion to the consumer. We can use this to introduce the notion of brand personality. Let us begin this discussion with the definition of the term provided by Aaker (1997), which presents it as a set of human characteristics linked to a brand. In this, brands are seen to be like humans, possessing human characteristics. The publication of Fournier (1998) is one of the leading brand-as-person metaphor postulations that highlights how consumers relate to brands using three case studies of women to demonstrate the significance of the consumer-brand bonds. We can trace this to the literature on symbolism and Kapferer (1992). The arguments about symbolism indicate that consumers' motivation to buy a product or service goes beyond their functional attributes but also extends to the meanings associated with the purchase (Gbadamosi, 2015). In the work of Kapferer (1992), six elements or facets of brand identity are identified, which are:

- Self-image;
- Culture;
- Physique;
- Reflection;
- Personality;
- Relationship.

Accordingly, the brand personality offers consumers considerable symbolic benefits in relation to the product or service it is attached to (Banerjee, 2016). This explains why there is a link between consumers' personality and their brand preferences. This is considered valuable as marketers are increasingly preoccupied with the search for strategies to create an emotional bond between the consumers and their brand, knowing that such emotional attachment is potentially beneficial in fostering loyalty and marketing success (Park et al., 2010; Malär et al., 2011). Findings suggest that when there is actual self-congruence between the brand and the consumer, it can lead to a high level of emotional brand attachment (Malär et al., 2011). Hence, it is considered an important issue in marketing. For instance, the view that consumers express their identity through the use of brands prompts many marketers to reposition their market offerings from highlighting the functional attributes to focusing how they suit consumers' lifestyles (Chernev et al., 2011).

**FIGURE 10.1** Six elements of brand identity

There are many suggestions in the literature on dimensions of brand personality. One of the widely cited and applied is that of Aaker (1997), who argues that there are five brand personality dimensions, namely:

- Competence;
- Sophistication;
- Sincerity;
- Excitement;
- Ruggedness.

Interestingly, brand personality has been applied very widely to physical products and services. For example, it has been applied to destination brands (Matzler et al, 2016), healthcare branding (Shafiee et al., 2022), and the education sector (Rauschnabel et al., 2016). Six brand personality dimensions are identified for the choice of higher education to be:

- Prestige;
- Lively;
- Sincerity;
- Cosmopolitan;
- Appeal;
- Conscientiousness.

In their study, Rauschnabel et al. (2016) describe the prestige dimension as covering factors such as successful, leading, accepted, and reputable. Factors listed as describing the lively dimension include dynamic, creative, and athletic. Higher education with a sincerity personality is believed to be trustworthy, humane, and fair whereas the cosmopolitan personality dimension is reported to cover factors such as international and networked. The appeal personality dimension of an institution indicates that it is special, attractive, or productive. The conscientiousness personality dimension covers factors like structured, organised, effective, or competent.

Companies continue to use many ways to ensure emotional connection between the consumer and their products and services. One of these is through customisation of the offerings to suit individual personal preferences. Companies like Starbucks,

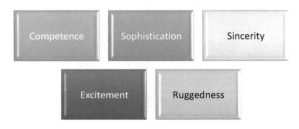

**FIGURE 10.2** Five brand personality dimensions

Coca-Cola, and banks to mention but a few have found this valuable in many ramifications. Customers are able to customise their ringtone, they can determine how their clothes and shoes look, such as the example of Starbucks giving customers the opportunity to create their beverage from numerous alternative combinations (Chernev et al., 2011). We also see a similar pattern in automobile transactions, customised number plates and so on. These are ways by which consumers adopt a self-expressive approach to consumption. This is quite interesting. However, it is important for marketers to be on top of how this is managed through constant monitoring of the efficacy of a particular symbolic package. This is because the idea that consumers can use brands for self-expression is finite as it can reach a saturation level. Chernev et al. (2011) show this in their study by arguing that this is the case because consumers can express their identity through numerous other means other than brands, such as listing television shows or favourite books.

As the rate of Internet usage continues to grow, the relevance of brand personality is also being explored in such avenues as social media usage. Garanti and Kissi (2019) studied how social media brand personality affects customer brand loyalty in the banking industry. Their findings establish that the customer-company relationship developed in relation to the principle of Social Information Processing (SIP) also applies to the individual relationships that people keep. So, maintaining good customer relationships as well as strategic matching with personality can be very rewarding, especially in relation to boosting brand equity and engendering brand loyalty.

## CONSUMER SELF

How do we as consumers define ourselves? What beliefs do we hold about ourselves? How do we evaluate ourselves on some common attributes? These are some of the questions encapsulated in our self-concept. **Self-concept**, which is also known as self-identity or self-image, is someone's summation of his or her thoughts, imagination, and feelings relating to who she or he is (Rosenberg, 1979; Szmigin and Piacentini, 2022). In the complexity of this phenomenon, while an individual may be very pleased with some aspects of herself, other aspects may be regarded as unpleasant and could be what keeps him or her awake at night. So, they become preoccupied with searching for means of expressing and validating their identity (Escalas and Bettman, 2005). The evaluation of self becomes increasingly heightened with the growing use of social media, which makes a comparison between consumers readily available. Let us make a link of this to the notion of **identity** with a definition given by Solomon (2020), which indicates that the term refers to any category label that we as consumers are associated with that is capable of explaining how someone in that category looks, feels, thinks, and acts. So, this aids comparison between consumers at the individual level and in relation to socio-cultural groups. While this is a practice across various age groups, gender categories, marital status, and other identifiable groups, the rate of this among young women is particularly considerable to the extent that they alter their perception of their body shapes after exposure to some television programmes (Myers and Biocca, 1992; Solomon, 2020). Hence, it is closely linked to self-esteem, which is a term that defines how positively an individual thinks of herself. So, a consumer with high self-esteem tends to be more confident about his or her 'self' than another with low self-esteem. At a low level of self-esteem, the consumer will be keen to use consumption to address inadequacies. Logically, this is a continuous process in that we modify some aspects of our lives at some point, compare ourselves with others as we meet new people, move between different cultural systems. This brings us to the discussion of various selves. In its broad form, the consumer has the actual self, which is the current state, whereas the desired state refers to the Self she or he would like to achieve. So, most scholars believe in the agreement that people's self-concept broadly includes their actual self and ideal self (Liu et al., 2010). With exposure to various cues in the environment such as advertising messages and social media posts, consumers are not short of ideas of what they consider to be their ideal selves as they constantly engage in social comparisons. Table 10.1 from Gbadamosi (2020), as adapted from Schiffman et al. (2012) and Solomon (2020), shows various types of consumer selves and the illustration of what they mean.

So, put together, we can claim that we have multiple co-existing narratives of how the Self is constructed in terms of discourse, practice, process, and various reflexivities (Gould, 2010). Now that we have seen that, as consumers, we have different types of selves that suit different circumstances, it is important that we should show interest in discussing consumer self-congruency, which is how consumers perceive the match between their self-image and the image of others such as an influencer (Liberatore and Tascheulin, 2011; Zogaj et al., 2021). Consumers are surrounded by stimuli in the marketing environment which is notably symbolic, and derive and assign meaning to various circumstances and objects such as products and brands which help them to enact various selves. This is known as symbolic interactionism (Solomon, 2020). The understanding of these various selves helps marketers in a number of ways to ensure the fit between the consumers' needs and their offerings. For instance, Zogaj et al. (2021) indicate that social media influencers can drive consumers to perceive credibility in their endorsement of a brand if they match their actual or ideal self. Besides, it has also been argued that consumers tend to choose products or brands that match some of the areas of their selves (Aaker, 1997; Solomon, 2020). It is noted that comparison is made between the image of market offerings such as products, the consumers' self-concept, and the image of a typical consumer of that market offering. This process is known as self-image congruence (Antón et al., 2013; Chouk et al., 2019).

This reasoning is linked to the notion of brand personality discussed earlier, in which brands are considered to have human qualities. Hence, consumers then develop a relationship with brands like we do for humans. The work of Fournier (1998) has been at the forefront of this contention. In this, people develop a relationship with brands for varying reasons. As indicated in the notion of extended self as popularised by Russel Belk (1988) we as consumers are what we consume as we are linked and defined by what we use in terms of goods, services, and brands. So, consumers are

**TABLE 10.1** Consumer self: Illustrations and examples

| | Type of self | Indication | Illustration/Examples |
|---|---|---|---|
| 1 | Actual self | A more realistic view of how one sees himself or herself | This shows the qualities an individual currently has and those s/he lacks |
| 2 | Ideal self | How one would like to see himself or herself | This focuses on achieving the missing qualities |
| 3 | Social self | How the consumers feel other people see them | This emphasises one's consciousness of others and their impression of his or her current state |
| 4 | Ideal social self | How consumers would like to be seen by others | This closely explains consumers' drive towards the fulfilment of social needs |
| 5 | Digital self | How one sees himself or herself or is seen by others in the digital social media platforms such as Facebook and Instagram | Updating online presence with desirable photos |
| 6 | Extended self | The external objects that consumers use as part of their identities | Possessions like clothing, cars, furniture, and homes that form part of the people's identities |
| 7 | Collective self | Circumstance in which one's identity is defined in relation to, and emerges from, a social group to a great extent | Unlike in individualistic cultural contexts, consumers from collectivist cultures tend to focus more on collective self. An example of this is *umbutu* which is a word that has its root in South Africa to mean that an individual does not exist in a vacuum, but is so known because he or she belongs to a group or community |

able to make a link. In a 1999 publication of Keller, the case of Pepsi was cited in which the drinking of Pepsi cola will enable the consumers to restore their vitality (Keller, 1999; Hamadneh et al., 2021).

The notion of the extended self – highlighted in Table 10.1 – has a further analytic sub-division and/or levels to its understanding and application to consumers. This extended self is one of the lines of discourse in consumer research that shows the expressive and the fragmented aspect of consumer self (Stone et al., 2017). Using the participants of their study as the basis, Stone et al. (2017) state that if consumers were to hold a mirror individually, they would perceive themselves in different ways as some would see a lack of their extended self, while it would be vaguely discernible to others. According to Belk (1988), we can have it at different levels such as:

- Individual level;
- Family level;
- Community level;
- Group level.

At the individual level, consumers are seen to be preoccupied with using their possessions such as cars and fashion items to define and communicate who they are. To create a form of identity for others to see, consumers use the purchase of these items as deemed applicable to each. As consumers we create, maintain, and communicate identity at the family level in which case it is about those items that show collective ownership as a family. For example, children in a home would be proud to introduce their friends to the set of furniture they have at home or the family private healthcare and insurance plan, which could communicate their level of affluence to others. In some other cases, people's selves/identities are determined by where they live. It is very common that when a consumer mentions where s/he lives people can figure out his or her identity. For example, living in ghettos will most likely communicate something different about an individual compared to living in central urban areas of a city. This explains why some consumers relocate to other cities and neighbourhoods to communicate identities or alter their previously known identity. This is a notion of community-level extended self. In this postulation, the extended self at the group level shows who an individual is in relation to the group to which he or she belongs. We have discussed various groups in Chapter 5. Each of these has implications for how the individual defines himself or herself. The saying that says 'tell me your friend and I will define who you are' applies here. So, we now see why someone who has been in a group previously may be working very hard to dissociate himself or herself from the group because of their values and interests. Conversely, people make several efforts to join some groups as they help them to feel more positive about themselves.

## DIGITAL SELF AND SOCIAL MEDIA

As indicated in Table 10.1, the notion of self-concept is linked to consumers' Internet activities and transactions. Most issues in life are online in one form or another these days. This is especially so as social media is notably ubiquitous as a marketing tool that shows how consumers interact virtually in the marketplace. Consumers are connected on platforms such as Instagram, LinkedIn, Facebook, X, and TikTok and project their selves. The number of global Internet users as of January 2023 is given as 5.16 billion, representing around 64.4% of the world population. Interestingly, 4.76 billion of these Internet users are users of various social media (Petrosyan, 2023). This is a considerable figure that cannot be ignored in terms of scale and significance.

These social media platforms have their unique values to the users and their relative strengths guide them on which to use or which combination to adopt. For example, while LinkedIn is often associated with professional and career communications among the relevant communities, gaming and other forms of entertainment would be better on Facebook than in the former (LinkedIn). The users of social media cut across various consumer segments – young, old, men, women, and lesbian, gay, bisexual, and transgender (LGBT). Social interactions connect family members, people from various clubs, members of religious circles, political parties, and several others. This is not surprising as humans are social beings in that our interpersonal relationships constitute a key aspect of our lives covering our perception, and the way we understand and act (Chang et al., 2018). It is not unexpected that some social media platforms would appeal to different market segments than others. It is very common for users, especially young women, to become conscious of images of beautiful, young women on Instagram which leads to their own body dissatisfaction and consequent negative mood (Livingston et al., 2020). In many cases, those images are edited and staged and do not reflect reality, but these consumers still use them as the basis for comparison in relation to their own images (Paraskeva et al., 2017). In a study connecting ethnicity, postmodernism, and celebrity culture in relation to how women engage in symbolic consumption, Gbadamosi (2019) found that social trends in society constitute pressure on women consumers. This is noted as linked to the acceptable living standards, mode of appearance, and dressing codes prescribed that they think they must follow to match up, in some cases, with the trending celebrity culture. Most of these interactions, observations, and activities now take place online in the form of blogs and social media platforms.

As consumers are interested in their ideal selves, they continue to associate with others considered significant. They take photos with others and share them on social media platforms. In some cases, they modify and fine-tune the photos they have online to give the desired projects of their identity to others who access their images. As reported by Chang et al. (2018), as young women continue to carefully choose and edit their profile pictures, it constitutes some form of self-identification and self-empowerment. Apart from these, the notion of self-branding is also connected to self-concept and social media activities. In self-branding, the consumers develop their public image to be distinctive for the purpose of having cultural capital and/or commercial gain (Khamis et al., 2017).

## LIFESTYLE AND CONSUMER SELF

As consumers, we spend our time and money differently. Some consumers focus their attention on fishing for fun, while others are preoccupied with gaming and many others are ardent lovers of sport and devote their time to it. These are some of the examples that if brought together, could reflect our lifestyle, which is fundamentally distinct and measured or defined as covering consumers' activities, interests, and opinions. People tend to engage in activities on a day-to-day basis such as shopping, work, and hobbies as well as having interests such as fashion, family, and home and have opinions about issues such as politics and social issues (Chouk et al., 2019). They give a pattern of the definition of who an individual is. In his seminal publication on how lifestyle segmentation can be applied, Plummer (1974: 33) indicates that lifestyle in relation to life cycle segmentation focuses on measuring the following about people's activities in relation to:

- The way people spend their time;
- What they have an interest in, which they consider important within their immediate environment;

- Their opinions in the form of how they view themselves and their surroundings;
- The basic characteristics that define them such as education, lifestyle, where they live, and income.

Szmigin and Piacentini (2022) present a good illustration of the term by positioning it in relation to personality. According to them, while personality covers internal characteristics that define an individual, his or her lifestyles can be explained as how his or her life is manifested externally. So, marketers are interested in consumers' lifestyles as they could be useful in segmenting the market to ensure that the products and services being offered are of a good fit for the target consumers and that the accompanying strategies are appropriate. For instance, the study of Axsen et al. (2012) notes that consumers may reject pro-environmental technology (PET) such as solar panels, electric vehicles, and green electricity programmes if there is an inconsistency between the technology and the consumers' lifestyle.

People can be of the same age, are in the same country, and have a different lifestyle, hence the explanation offered by lifestyle goes beyond demographic segmentation. In the work of Plummer (1974), lifestyle segmentation can be applied as shown in Table 10.2.

Prior to this publication, a related study set the background for this discussion to claim that a demographic dynamic in itself will be insufficient to offer a clear explanation of consumption behaviour but having a lifestyle implication will give a clear picture (Wells and Tigert, 1971).

Meanwhile, a pattern of lifestyle could also be markedly common at the country level. For instance, it has been shown that Japanese women are more home-focused compared to US-based women (Onkvisit and Shaw, 2008).

Some consumer segments have been identified by various scholars over the years. Let us examine some of these as examples. Axsen et al. (2012) studied consumer lifestyle practices in relation to pro-environmental technology. In this study, they identify five clusters in relation to environmental and tech-oriented lifestyles, openness to lifestyle change, and green attitudes. These are:

**TABLE 10.2** Lifestyle segmentation

| ACTIVITIES | INTERESTS | OPINIONS | DEMOGRAPHICS |
|---|---|---|---|
| Work | Family | Themselves | Age |
| Hobbies | Home | Social issues | Education |
| Social events | Job | Politics | Income |
| Vacation | Community | Business | Occupation |
| Entertainment | Recreation | Economics | Family size |
| Club membership | Fashion | Education | Dwelling |
| Community | Food | Products | Geography |
| Shopping | Media | Future | City size |
| Sports | Achievement | Culture | Stage in life cycle |

**Source**: Plummer (1974: 34)

- Engaged;
- Aspiring;
- Low-tech;
- Traditional;
- Techies.

The first three segments are pro-environment in varying forms in terms of their attitudes, while the last two are non-green consumers. The 'engaged' participate actively in technology-oriented and pro-environmental lifestyles and are still open to change, indicating that they are liminal; whereas the engagement of the 'aspiring green' in pro-environmental practices and interest shown in technology are relatively less than those of the engaged but they are also liminal. Those described as 'low-tech green' consumers are not only less engaged in technology-oriented practices but have the lowest rate of openness to change (liminal) when compared to the other two green categories. Meanwhile, the 'traditionalists' are consumers that have the lowest level of interest in pro-environmental technology (PET) and have a low score on liminality compared to the 'techies', who are also low on attitudes concerning pro-environmental issues but are interested in technology-oriented practices. It is important to indicate that the interest shown in technology by the 'techies' is more likely to be on the technology rather than pro-environmental issues per se.

The Gherasim and Gherasim's (2021) report about consumer classification presented by RISC Research Agency, involving the population of 12 European countries in relation to their lifestyle, produces the following segments:

- Traditionalists;
- Individuals connected to the home;
- Rationalists;
- Pleasure lovers;
- Fighters;
- Trend creators.

Traditionalists are consumers whose focus is on tradition and culture, and place value on education as well as the economic and social conditions in their own country. The segment identified as connected to the home are closely connected to their childhood and origin, cherish warm relationships with other people but are not so keen on material security. As indicated in this schema, the rationalists are risk-takers and adept in technology and science and actively pursue self-expression, and can cope with unexpected situations. The focus of pleasure lovers is on emotional and sensual experiences and they show a preference for hierarchically unstructured settings and informality. While the fighters are preoccupied with organising their own lives, the trend creators, who tend to be more individualistic than fighters, focus on spontaneity.

## VALUE AND CONSUMER BEHAVIOUR

Values are important to consumer behaviour, marketing analysts, and practitioners. Let us start this section by first defining the term. We can define values as what individuals hold dearly because they believe that such issues are preferable to their opposing alternatives. This is consistent with an early definition given by Rokeach (1973), who argues that a value refers to an enduring belief held by someone that a mode of demeanour or an end-state of existence is desirable to an opposing mode of conduct or end-state of existence. In view of this definition, we can link the discussion to an individual, a cultural system, a nation, global level, or other contexts. When considering from the legal standpoint, Antaki (2020) describes values as being the groundwork of ethics and, as they become more noticed and embraced, it is an indication of the transformation of the good, not only as what is worthy of being desired but also into something that we pose for ourselves. One view that seems to bring all these together is that of Schiffman et al. (2012), who indicate that values, when compared to other beliefs, are:

- Not tied to specific circumstances or objects;
- Relatively few in number;
- Enduring;
- Broadly accepted by members of a society;
- Guide culturally appropriate behaviour.

Going by the claim of Islam and Chandrasekaran (2019), values are generally universal in nature but vary per culture in terms of their relative importance. As an example of the universal nature of values, we would all agree that being comfortable is preferable to the opposite end but the extent to which individuals and cultures pursue this can vary. It is therefore logical that significant consumption decisions this day and age are closely linked to some goal-related values. In their study, which focuses on religiosity, values, and consumer behaviour, Islam and Chandrasekaran (2019) found that consumers who are more religious tend to be less likely to be brand conscious and novelty-fashion conscious. These authors explain that this finding could be based on the fact that being brand conscious is highly linked to consumption of pricey items, which is often inconsistent with the values of religious people. To emphasise the point we mentioned earlier about the relevance of values to different contexts, Karami et al. (2017) identified 20 values which are considered to be influencing consumption in Iran. They eventually fine-tuned and subsumed these to seven dimensions, which are:

- Cosmopolitanism;
- Convenience;
- Youthfulness;
- Innovation;
- Faithfulness;

- Partiality;
- Other-directedness.

Cosmopolitanism will cover issues such as being fashionable and going after brands that have a global reputation, whereas innovation is about purchasing innovative products and pursuing new models of already used brands. The youthfulness dimension focuses on buying items like fitness products, food supplements, cleansing lotions, and anti-aging facial creams, while being high in convenience would be evident in the purchase of such products as microwave ovens, fryers, food processors, MP4 players, and electrical tea makers, while faithfulness is about showing interest in religious-oriented products such as halal foods, religious entertainment, and clothing. Other directedness is about caring about other peoples' ideas or the ideas of family members in buying products such as apparel and wrist watches. The partiality dimension is about the individual buying preferred products without having to afford free choice. For example, the person would be loyal to the brands she or he is using already.

---

**PAUSE, PLAN, AND PRACTICE: IKEA: THE HOME FOR THE CONSUMERS' EXTENDED SELF**

Increasing evidence continues to show that the goal of consumption transcends the functional benefits of the products. Consumers communicate their status by what they acquire. The Swedish firm IKEA has realised this in how it addresses the needs of its various consumers. The retailer knows that a lot has changed since it was founded in the 1940s. A significant number of consumers believe that 'we are what we own'. When people visit homes, they pay attention to the furniture. So, consumers are keen to make a good impression of these situations through the use of their furniture sets. With experience that covers several decades, IKEA ensures that its furniture sufficiently fills the symbolic needs of its customers. This is not only in living rooms; IKEA customers are also equipped to do impression management with their furniture for the kitchen, garden, bedrooms, and other places. The sparkling kitchen cabinets, elegant worktops, and immaculate and fitting sofas are some of the examples of how the firm helps consumers realise their dreams and create identity. The accompanying services, from the point when the consumers are merely contemplating the purchase, visiting the store or exploring online, to doing the measurement, placing the orders, and receiving them, are noteworthy as all are geared towards increasing the self-esteem of the customers.

**QUESTION**

Using Belk's notion of extended self, discuss ways of demonstrating extended self that relates to students and young adults. Which strategy do you think businesses can put in place that can directly target this consumer segment?

**Sources:**

IKEA (nd). What's new in the IKEA range, www.ikea.com/gb/en/new/ (accessed 29 April 2023).

## SUMMARY

Personality is about the uniqueness of an individual. Essentially, the theories guiding the discourse of this phenomenon are categorised into three, namely Freudian, Neo-Freudian, and Trait theories. The Freudian theory championed by Sigmund Freud indicates that human personality is determined by three interacting inner and biological systems which are id, ego, and superego. Neo-Freudian indicates that human personality is determined by people's interpersonal relationships. Unlike the other two theories, Trait theory indicates that human personality is a composition of some characteristics that define and differentiate them from others. It is also said that brands are like humans as they have personalities and this influences how consumers interact and relate to them. Consumers' self-concept is also linked to personality and with the increasing use of social media, the notion of consumers' digital self is also applicable as they project themselves online towards achieving their ideal selves. It is relevant to also stress that consumers' lifestyles and values are core to the explanation of their personality and consumption.

### DIGITAL BOX: THE PERSONALITY OF RED BULL

Brands are essential parts of our lives these days. Simply searching for items online, driving on the highways, visiting the shopping mall, and several other contacts and exposures we have will bring us in contact with various global brands. Not only brands of physical products for clothes, foods, and automobiles but also services such as banks, hotels, and consultancy services. The reality these days is that these brands 'speak' and 'care' like humans. The symbolic aspect of brands indicates that they are more closely connected to consumers through their personalities. Some would wonder, how can brands, inanimate objects, have personalities? But one would need to consider the example of 'Red Bull', the energy drink that has been associated with sports and physical energy activities over the years. It is considered to be a brand that resonates with excitement. This personality trait is a form of relationship boost between the brand and the lovers of sports as well as young and vibrant consumers. As an example, the excitement that followed the victory of Andrey Rublev in the Red Bull Bassline, a regular tennis tournament in Madrid, Spain on 25 April 2023, clearly indicates what the brand is known for and its personality – Excitement!

### TASK

With this information about Red Bull as a guide, select four other global brands and go online to search details about what the brand stands for, and come up with its personality. Compare these four brands based on the details gathered from their website. Report what you noticed about them and their personality. Is there any reason for you to suggest that the brand owner should consider changing the personality of any of them? If yes, what should the new personality be and why?

**Sources:**

Red Bull (2023). Red Bull Bassline, 25 April 2023, www.redbull.com/int-en/events/red-bull-bassline (accessed 29 April 2023).

The Upwork Team (nd). Brand personality: Dimensions, elements, and examples, The Upwork Team, Sales and Marketing, 4 February 2023, www.upwork.com/resources/brand-personality (accessed 29 April 2023).

## END OF CHAPTER DISCUSSION QUESTIONS

1. To what extent would you agree that consumer personality is best explained by Freudian Theory?
2. Seeing that there is a difference between the consumers' actual self and ideal self, discuss whether the strategy of celebrity endorsement by marketers is justified.
3. A brand distinguishes the market offerings of the firm from those offered by competitors while brand personality refers to a set of human features linked to a brand. Identify some popular brands and what you think are their personalities. Discuss why this personality match-up between the brands and the consumers encourages their consumption.
4. With the continued increase in the use of social media, consumers' digital self is becoming more recognised and relevant. Discuss how these can be an input to marketing strategy.
5. Karami et al. (2017) identified seven values as influencing consumer behaviour as listed below:
   - Cosmopolitanism;
   - Convenience;
   - Youthfulness;
   - Innovation;
   - Faithfulness;
   - Partiality;
   - Other-directedness.

   Which of these apply to you as a consumer? Discuss how marketers can tune their strategy to emphasise consumers' values of cosmopolitanism, convenience, and youthfulness.

### Case Study: Extending the Self on Social Media

With around 4 billion consumers on one social media platform or another, the consumption and business world has changed profoundly in recent times. We have experienced an unprecedented level of social interactions that take place on Facebook, WhatsApp, LinkedIn, Instagram, X, and others as social networking sites. Consumers share news related to politics, education, religion, health, marketing, and a myriad of other subjects. It has formed a major part of consumers' lives. Broadband search indicates that, on average, consumers spend about 2 hours 27 minutes every day on social networking sites and the figure is considerably more for specific countries. So, it is a big deal for both consumers and marketers. Notably, the use of social media varies among consumers. While some devote significant aspects of their lives to it, and even use it to transact business with others in the form of consumer-to-consumer (C2C) transactions, others are occasional users that explore the opportunities to meet and interact with others. These interactions on the social media platform tend to show the personality of the users. In the contents and comments they share, one would see that some are aggressive in their approach to issues while others are compliants who simply yield to the position of others on the topics under discussion. Although they are also on social media, another consumer category on social media has a detached personality. Apart from being sparing users of the platform, their main interest on social media is simply checking the updates of others without any active comment or interaction with them. Fundamentally, these social media networking sites are fun and easy to use. Some of those that are extremely committed to using them appear to be addicted, showing the excessive operation of id in their psychoanalytic personality system. Whichever category the consumers fall into, evidence shows that they demonstrate their extended self on these digital platforms. In a process that is similar to most social media, upon the creation of an account on Instagram, which was launched in 2010, users will have their specific profiles and news feeds through which they can see the updates of other users. Typically, users post their photos and videos about their updates like their latest purchases such as clothes, shoes, cars, houses, and many others on the platform and their followers would then be able to see and interact with the content. This has been seen as a very good opportunity for consumers to communicate their '*self*' to followers and boost their self-esteem in various ways.

While LinkedIn is seen to be related more to professional issues, users also find it a useful platform for communicating their successes around careers, promotions, and changes to statuses which are aspects that offer some explanation around the users' self-concept.

When the consumer notices a difference between their actual and ideal selves, many efforts are expended to work towards bridging the gap such as editing their updates and contents in various ways to suit the need of showing a desired self. An interesting twist on this is that even some users of the platforms that are so desperate to boost their self-esteem, but without the means to acquire the materials, tend to result in 'faking it' by taking photos and videos with other people's possessions to present them as if they are theirs.

These social media platforms reveal a lot about people's values and lifestyles. The photos, videos, and comments show how they spend their time and money revealing where they focus their attention, and what are their interests and opinions. Since these also have a lot to do with showing their personality, and the personality of the brands they consume or would like to consume, global brand managers now have dedicated strategies and resources for social media. Many consumers, including celebrities with numerous followers on various social media platforms such as Cristiano Ronaldo, Rihanna, Beyonce, and Justin Bieber to mention but a few, communicate with their fans through this and endorse brands. As consumers create and communicate their identities on social media and use these platforms to project their extended selves, the possibilities for marketers to co-create value with them are endless.

**Sources**

Broadband Search (nd). Average daily times spent on social media (latest 2023 data), www.broadbandsearch.net/blog/average-daily-time-on-social-media#:~:text=On%20average%2C%20people%20spend%20147%20minutes%2C%20or%20two,hours%20and%20twenty-seven%20minutes%2C%20on%20social%20media%20daily. (accessed 30 April 2023).

Moreau, E. (2022). What is Instagram and why should you be using it?, 9 April 2022, www.lifewire.com/what-is-instagram-3486316 (accessed 30 April 2023).

## QUESTIONS

1. Discuss the four levels of extended self proposed by Belk (1988) in relation to the content of this case study;
2. Explain how the CAD theory of personality by Karen Horney is discussed in this case study. Do you agree with this view? Justify your viewpoint;
3. It is indicated in the case study that at a level, the id element of the psychoanalytic personality system of a user of social media can work disproportionally. How can the interaction of the id, ego, and superego moderate this process?
4. To what extent would you agree that the Big Five personality trait is applicable in the digital context.

## REFERENCES

Aaker, J. L. (1997). Dimensions of brand personality. *Journal of Marketing Research*, 34(3), 347–356.
Antaki, M. (2020). Values. *McGill Law Journal*, 66: *Revue de droit de McGill*, 169–172.
Antón, C., Camarero, C., & Rodríguez, J. (2013). Usefulness, enjoyment, and self-image congruence: The adoption of e-book readers. *Psychology & Marketing*, 30(4), 372–384.
Axsen, J., TyreeHageman, J., & Lentz, A. (2012). Lifestyle practices and pro-environmental technology. *Ecological Economics*, 82, 64–74.
Banerjee, S. (2016). Influence of consumer personality, brand personality, and corporate personality on brand preference: An empirical investigation of interaction effect. *Asia Pacific Journal of Marketing and Logistics*, 28(2).
Belk, R. W. (1988). Possessions and the extended self. *Journal of Consumer Research*, 15(2), 139–168.

Chang, J., Ren, H., & Yang, Q. (2018). A virtual gender asylum? The social media profile picture, young Chinese women's self-empowerment, and the emergence of a Chinese digital feminism. *International Journal of Cultural Studies*, 21(3), 325–340.

Chernev, A., Hamilton, R., & Gal, D. (2011). Competing for consumer identity: Limits to self-expression and the perils of lifestyle branding. *Journal of Marketing*, 75(3), 66–82.

Cherry, K. (2023). What are the Big 5 personality traits? Openness, conscientiousness, extraversion, agreeableness, and neuroticism, *Verywell mind*, March 11, 2023, www.verywellmind.com/the-big-five-personality-dimensions-2795422 (accessed 13 April 2023).

Chouk, I., & Mani, Z. (2019). Factors for and against resistance to smart services: Role of consumer lifestyle and ecosystem related variables. *Journal of Services Marketing*, 33(4), 449–462.

Escalas, J. E., & Bettman, J. R. (2005). Self-construal reference groups and brand meaning. *Journal of Consumer Research*, 32, 378–389.

Fournier, S. (1998). Consumers and their brands: Developing relationship theory in consumer research. *Journal of Consumer Research*, 24(4), 343–373.

Freud, S. (1959). *Collected Papers*, vols I–V, New York: Basic Books.

Garanti, Z., & Kissi, P. S. (2019). The effects of social media brand personality on brand loyalty in the Latvian banking industry: The mediating role of brand equity. *International Journal of Bank Marketing*, 37(6), 1480–1503.

Gbadamosi, A. (2015). Brand personification and symbolic consumption among ethnic teenage consumers: An empirical study. *Journal of Brand Management*, 22(9), 737–759.

Gbadamosi, A. (2019). Postmodernism, ethnicity, and celebrity culture in women's symbolic consumption. *International Journal of Market Research*, DOI: 10.1177/1470785319868363.

Gbadamosi, A. (2020). Buyer behaviour in the 21st century: Implications for SME marketing, in Nwankwo, S. and Gbadamosi, A. (2020) (eds) *Entrepreneurship Marketing: Principles and Practice of SME Marketing*, 2nd edn, pp. 72–96. Oxfordshire: Routledge.

Gherasim, D., & Gherasim, A. (2021). Lifestyle and buying behavior. *Economy Transdisciplinarity Cognition*, 21(1), 27–33.

Gould, S. J. (2010). To thine own self(ves) be true: Reflexive insights for etic theory from consumers emic constructions of the self. *Consumption, Markets and Culture*, 13(2, June), 181–219.

Hamadneh, S., Hassan, J., Alshurideh, M., Al Kurdi, B., & Aburayya, A. (2021). The effect of brand personality on consumer self-identity: The moderation effect of cultural orientations among British and Chinese consumers. *Journal of Legal, Ethical and Regulatory Issues*, 24, 1–14.

Islam, T., & Chandrasekaran, U. (2019). Religiosity, values and consumer behaviour: A study of young Indian Muslim consumers. *Journal of Consumer Marketing*, 36, 7948–7961.

Jung, C. G. (1959). The archetypes and the collective unconscious, in Read, H. Fordham, M. and Adler, G. (eds), *Collected Works*, Vol. 9, Part I, Princeton, NJ: Princeton University Press.

Kapferer, J. N. (1992). *Strategic Brand Management*. New York: The Free Press.

Karami, M., Olfati, O., & Dubinsky, A. J. (2017). Key cultural values underlying consumers' buying behaviour: A study in an Iranian context. *Journal of Islamic Marketing*, 8(2), 289–308.

Keller, K. L. (1999). Managing brands for the long run: Brand reinforcement and revitalization strategies. *California Management Review*, 41(3), 102–124.

Khamis, S., Ang, L., & Welling, R. (2017). Self-branding, 'micro-celebrity' and the rise of social media influencers. *Celebrity Studies*, 8(2), 191–208.

Liberatore, A., & Tscheulin, D. K. (2011). Persönlichkeitsübereinstimmungen zwischen Marke und Konsument: Stand der empirischen Selbstkongruenzforschung und verbleibende Investigationsdirektiven. *Journal of Business Economics*, 81(5), 587–618.

Liu, S., Lu, Y., Liang, Q., & Wei, E. (2010). Moderating effect of cultural values on decision making of gift-giving from a perspective of self-congruity theory: An empirical study from Chinese context. *Journal of Consumer Marketing*, 27(7), 604–614.

Livingston, J., Holland, E., & Fardouly, J. (2020). Exposing digital posing: The effect of social media self-disclaimer captions on women's body dissatisfaction, mood, and impressions of the user. *Body Image*, 32, 150–154.

Malär, L., Krohmer, H., Hoyer, W. D., & Nyffenegger, B. (2011). Emotional brand attachment and brand personality: The relative importance of the actual and the ideal self. *Journal of Marketing*, 75(4), 35–52.

Matzler, K., Strobl, A., Stokburger-Sauer, N., Bobovnicky, A., & Bauer, F. (2016). Brand personality and culture: The role of cultural differences on the impact of brand personality perceptions on tourists' visit intentions. *Tourism Management*, 52, 507–520.

Myers, P. N., & Biocca, F. A. (1992). The elastic body image: The effect of television advertising and programming on body image distortions in young women. *Journal of Communication*, 42(3), 108–133.

Onkvisit, S., & Shaw, J. (2008). *International Marketing: Strategy and Theory*, 5th edn, London: Routledge.

Paraskeva, N., Lewis-Smith, H., & Diedrichs, P. C. (2017). Consumer opinion on social policy approaches to promoting positive body image: Airbrushed media images and disclaimer labels. *Journal of Health Psychology*, 22, 164–175. http://dx.doi.org/10.1177/1359105315597052.

Park, C. W., Macinnis, D. J., Priester, J., Eisingerich, A. B., & Iacobucci, D. (2010). Brand attachment and brand attitude strength: Conceptual and empirical differentiation of two critical brand equity drivers. *Journal of Marketing*, 74(6), 1–17.

Petrosyan, A. (2023). Worldwide digital population 2023. *Statista*, April 3, 2023, www.statista.com/statistics/617136/digital-population-worldwide/ (accessed 17 April 2023).

Plummer, J. T. (1974). The concept and application of life style segmentation: The combination of two useful concepts provides a unique and important view of the market. *Journal of Marketing*, 38(1), 33–37.

Rauschnabel, P. A., Krey, N., Babin, B. J., & Ivens, B. S. (2016). Brand management in higher education: The university brand personality scale. *Journal of Business Research*, 69(8), 3077–3086.

Rokeach, M. (1973). *The Nature of Human Values*. New York: Free Press.

Rosenberg, M. (1979). *Conceiving the Self*. New York: Basic Books.

Schiffman, L. G, Kanuk, L. L., & Hansen, H. (2012). *Consumer Behaviour: A European Outlook*, 2nd edn, Essex: Pearson Education Limited.

Schiffman, L. G., Wisenblit, J., & Kumar, S. R. (2018). *Consumer Behaviour*, 12th edn, Harlow: Pearson Education Limited.

Shafiee, R., Ansari, F., & Mahjob, H. (2022). Physicians' brand personality: Building brand personality scale. *Services Marketing Quarterly*, 43(1), 48–66.

Solomon, M. R. (2020). *Consumer Behaviour: Buying, Having, and Being*, 13th edn, Essex: Pearson Education Limited.

Stone, T., Gould, S. J., & Szabó-Douat, T. (2017). "Am I as extended as you say I am?" Consumer's emic perspectives on the extended self. *Marketing Theory*, 17(4), 559–577.

Szmigin, I., & Piacentini, M. (2022). *Consumer Behaviour*, 3rd edn, Oxford: Oxford University Press.

Wells, W. D., & Tigert, D. J. (1971). Activities, interests and opinions. *Journal of Advertising Research*, 11(4), 27–35.

Zogaj, A., Tscheulin, D. K., & Olk, S. (2021). Benefits of matching consumers' personality: Creating perceived trustworthiness via actual self-congruence and perceived competence via ideal self-congruence. *Psychology & Marketing*, 38(3), 416–430.

**PART 4**

# EXPLORING CREATIVITY AND INNOVATION IN HOW TECHNOLOGY IMPACTS CONSUMER BEHAVIOUR

# CHAPTER 11

# Technology, Diffusion of Innovation, and Consumer Behaviour

## LEARNING OBJECTIVES

After reading this chapter, you should be able to:

- Explain developments in the use of technology and consumer behaviour;
- Discuss how innovation is linked to marketing;
- Discuss the diffusion of innovation and factors influencing it;
- Discuss resistance to innovation;
- Explain consumer behaviour in relation to the product life cycle;
- Discuss the emerging trend in social media.

## INTRODUCTION

Evidently, we now live in a world characterised by technology. Our homes, workplaces, schools, religious places, and virtually every other aspect of our day-to-day living feature the introduction of one new technological invention or another. You are probably reading this book in its e-form or will do that at some point soon, using mobile gadgets, looking at monitoring your blood and oxygen rate on smartwatches, or asking artificial intelligence tools like Google Assistant what the condition of the weather will be in your holiday destination tomorrow to know the level of preparation to have. All of these are examples of how digital transformation has become a reality. In some cases, we develop cold feet as consumers when we hear of new ways of doing things. Among the reasons for this, are the thoughts of the complexity of the new processes, whether they will offer value that supersedes the benefits of the existing ones, and whether they will be compatible to address the needs which occupy the mind. Similarly, the question of whether one could try the new technology on a limited basis before becoming fully committed to it is a consideration for new inventions. Within all these, the notion of generation divide in

DOI: 10.4324/9781003242031-15

the use of technology among consumer segments is noteworthy. Interestingly, it is becoming apparent that children lend some support to their parents to help them find their feet in embracing these new processes that are changing the dynamics of living. So, it is understandable that the rate of adoption of the new technological tools is different among consumer segments in society, some are more enthusiastic than others and at different stages of the product life cycle. Increasing evidence suggests that there is a link between these and how the information about new products or services spreads among consumers, which is known as diffusion of innovation. The advent of social media and the increasing rate of its usage has dramatically changed the rate at which this is done. In view of this, we will be discussing technology, markets, and consumption, and the link between innovation and marketing as well as diffusion of innovation. We will also be discussing the product life cycle as well as the trend in social media in relation to consumer behaviour. We will start by examining interactions of the rise of technology and consumer behaviour.

## TECHNOLOGY, MARKETS, AND CONSUMPTION

There has been a significant increase in the rate of technological development in recent times. Media opportunities have increased drastically, and media consumption has also markedly changed upward over the years. As we have noted in several chapters of this book, it is difficult to explain this change in usage of technology without some form of mention of the COVID-19 pandemic, which has redefined and fine-tuned our way of life. The lockdown measures introduced by governments meant that transportation systems were restricted and came to a standstill in some countries and contexts. So, technology came to the centre stage of consumption in various ways, such as online purchases and social media usage for interactions. At the time of writing this book, the number of Internet users in the world is over 5 billion (Petrosyan, 2023a). Contemporary consumers, especially Generation X, are now socially connected, more pragmatic, and notably multitasking in the digital environment (Schiffman et al., 2008). The digital opportunity does not only introduce consumers to convenience but also demonstrates resilience as a medium of communication, education, and entertainment (Lissitsa and Cohen, 2018). Using 2020 figures, it has been noted that an average Internet user spends not less than 145 minutes online daily, whereas the duration is even longer in many cases, such as in the United States where they spend 24 hours on a weekly basis online, which is the highest weekly usage (World Population Review, 2023). Apart from other factors responsible for this surge in Internet usage, the availability and high usage of smartphones has been shown to be a significant factor in this as their use grew by 268 million from 2021 to 2022 (World Population Review, 2023). To cite further specific examples, China is noted as the country with the highest number of Internet users at around 1.05 billion (Petrosyan, 2023a), while Western countries, such as the United States and the United Kingdom, have more than 90% Internet penetration rates (World Population Review, 2023). Moreover, there are interesting dynamics about gender and Internet usage. Although in some places such as in the Americas, the proportions of male and female Internet users are equal at 83%, there are disparities in several other places, like in Africa where 45% of men have online access compared to 34% of women, and Arab states where the male digital population is 75% compared to that of women at 65% (Petrosyan, 2023b). The increasing use of digital technology permeates virtually every aspect of our lives, including for religious purposes, where adherents of various religions adopt it to foster relationships and uphold the tenets of their religious values (Gbadamosi and Oniku, 2021).

This is a remarkable development. Being innovative has now become a panacea for firms' competitive advantage and survival in the marketplace as they find the market more volatile. The Internet is now regarded as a fully-fledged distribution channel indicating that marketers will be compelled to deal with the associated complexity, especially with regards to online information exchanges (Grant et al., 2013). Statistically, there is a vibrant youth population embracing technology in their consumption practices. For instance, 70% of this population is connected to the Internet in one form or another while about 94% of the consumers aged 15 to 24 in developed countries use the Internet for various transactions, and those having access in developing countries is approximately 67% (International Telecommunication Union, 2017).

From a broader perspective, information and communication technology (ICT), in the form of innovation and Internet usage, has introduced structural changes that prompt economic growth in various ways (Haldar et al., 2023). Increasing evidence also shows that consumers are becoming exposed to different products and services as businesses are pressured to become innovative. They also have access to a considerable depth of information such as online reviews provided by other customers. Clearly, product development is becoming the rule of the day as firms are inspired by the consumers, competitors, external opportunities, and threats. They use it as a form of competitive advantage addressing issues such as quality, speed, and capabilities (Kamboj and Rahman, 2017). Consumers of all ages are seeking ways to be convenient, save costs, and have more value in their transactions. An example of this is the quest for businesses to think of alternative products and processes to preserve the environment. So, more consumers become more knowledgeable about sustainability, are sensitive to think beyond the immediate gratification of only meeting their needs conventionally, and demand eco-innovation from firms to minimise harm to the environment. Studies are showing that the more a business focuses on green product innovation, the more positive an impact this has on their performance indicators such as sales, profitability, and credibility in the society (Lin et al., 2013). In the automobile world, consumers are seeking fuel economy, easy and cost-efficient car maintenance. Accordingly, we are now beginning to see intense competition regarding electric cars and hybrid cars from car manufacturers, emphasising that they are focused on supporting consumers to use fewer natural resources. Business organisations now focus on encouraging their customers to switch to email messages, and using various apps instead of printing several pages of papers, while most books are now being provided to readers in e-form. Meanwhile, it is interesting that if this competition from businesses is not well managed, the positive impact achieved may be less significant than expected. For example, it is stated that while the positive impacts of ICT on the economy are achieved through technological efficiency, the increasing electricity consumption by the ICT system could have a harmful effect on the environment (Haldar et al., 2023). Another interesting cautionary note about the advent and use of technology in consumer behaviour is noted by Talpau (2014), who indicates that transaction of goods offered online could have the limitation of the consumers' inability to touch, taste, and smell them, which prompts marketers to offer visitors to their websites the opportunity to zoom out and in for a more visible display of the items. Despite these and other limitations, technology has increasingly become the cornerstone of consumption and marketing transactions in the contemporary marketing system.

## DIFFUSION OF INNOVATION

Organisations of various types and sizes are becoming more innovative in recent times as they introduce new products and services into the marketplace to meet the ever-growing needs of the consumer. The successful operation of these businesses in the competitive marketing environment is linked to offering innovative products and services that create and deliver value to the customers. To be innovative means creating new ideas, practices, and objects, or reinventing these so that they are considered new by the unit of adoption (Roger, 1995; Walker et al., 2011). To explain innovation in greater depth, let us see five sources of innovation which are teased out of Schumpeter (1934) as revisited by Deakins and Freel (2003). Based on this perspective, innovation can result from these:

- Introduction of a new product or significant improvement to the ones currently in the market;
- Opening a new market;
- Introduction of a new method of production;
- Discovering a new source of supply of raw materials or half-manufactured product;
- Creation of a new type of industrial organisation.

Since consumers experience these innovations in different ways, we will now look at their various types for clarity purposes. Broadly speaking, we have three types of innovation which are:

- Continuous innovation;
- Dynamically continuous innovation;
- Discontinuous innovation.

Continuous innovation is about extending the usage advantage of existing products by making little changes to them in the new version. So, it is not about creating something radically different yet there is a bit of difference between the old and the new

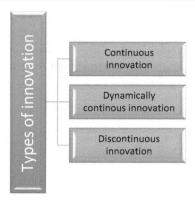

**FIGURE 11.1** Three types of innovation

one introduced. While they may argue against this, some changes that we see in the mobile phone market fit this scenario. Some of the phones are differentiated from their old version by the way of size, others simply increase how long the battery can last before one recharges the phone. But it is fair to indicate that the level of creativity and innovation vary between these firms. Dynamically continuous innovation involves introducing technology that has a marked effect on our consumption behavioural pattern as consumers but is still not radically new. The MP3 is a good example in this regard. While the old way of making music and entertainment is still possible, MP3 brought a considerable change to this through its digital format that compresses a huge amount of data to relatively good audio quality and opened an opportunity for people to download, stream, and listen to these audio materials that is of a higher standard than what was in place before (British Library Learning, nd). A discontinuous innovation is the creation of something radically different from what we have known before, so much so that it has disruptive effects on how we handle things. We can see this in the examples of the Internet and aeroplanes. Looking at how these discontinuous inventions work, one would wonder how humans were coping with their lives without them prior to their introduction. They brought considerable ease and changes to communications, entertainment, purchase transactions, and transportation among many other things.

Discussion of transactions in marketing involves not only physical products but also services as they are presented to deliver value to the customer. Accordingly, in an existing body of literature (Osborne, 1998; Walker et al., 2002), there is a discussion of innovation of service offerings. In this schema, the service-oriented organisations such as banks, insurance companies, hotels, and consultancy services firms, the possibilities for innovation are:

- Offering new services to new users;
- Providing existing services to a new user segment;
- Offering new services to existing customers.

Another form of innovation as identified by Edquist et al. (2001) is process innovation, which is about making changes to organisational members, which affects the structures, procedures, roles, rules, and communications both within the organisation and between the organisation and the environment. Consistent with this, three types of process innovation can be identified:

- Marketisation innovation;
- Organisational innovation;
- Technological innovation.

If we pull together perspectives from Edquist et al. (2001), Schilling (2005), and Damanpour (1987) we can explain these innovation types as follows. Marketisation is about modifying operating systems and processes for the purpose of increasing the effectiveness and efficiency associated with creating and delivering services to users. Organisational innovation is about changes adopted concerning the strategy and structure and administrative processes of the establishment, whereas technological innovations relate to changes in the physical environment, organisational communications, and techniques.

When innovation becomes available, it is imperative that people become aware of it towards adopting it to meet their needs. Individuals adopt different innovations and spread the information to others at different rates, while some innovations adopted become abandoned at some point and others are never adopted (Greenhalgh et al., 2004). We can see some common examples among SMEs that introduce many products and processes into the marketplace but, for various reasons, some of these inventions die before they become a commercial success. Rogers (1962) is consistently acknowledged for developing the diffusion of innovation (DOI) theory. In this postulation, Rogers' focus is on how the new invention gains momentum and spread in the marketplace to different social systems. So, in this, we tend to have these different consumers (adopters) of the innovation:

- Innovators;
- Early adopters;
- Early majority;
- Late majority;
- Laggard.

Based on Rogers (1995), innovators are the first set of consumers to adopt the new invention and they constitute a small proportion of the market given as approximately 2.5%. These consumers are enthusiastic about technology and keen to be the first to own new high-tech products. The early adopters are relatively more than the innovators in number (about 13.5%). They are known as lovers of technology, have social status, and adopt new social technologies ahead of most people. The early majority constitute 34% of the population and tend to love technology that gives incremental and predictive improvements compared to the currently existing

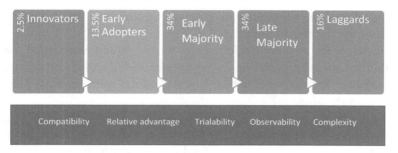

**FIGURE 11.2** Diffusion of innovation (category of adopters)
**Source**: Adapted from Rogers, E. M. (1995). Diffusion of Innovations: modifications of a model for telecommunications. *Die diffusion von innovationen in der telekommunikation*, 25–38.

technology. They are price sensitive, and do not like to take risks but buy new products that conform to their lifestyle. Statistically, they constitute 34% of the population. The late majority is given as the same proportion of the population as that of the early majority but they are characteristically different. They are conservative, hold on to tradition, and are cautious of new technology. Their fear of high-tech means that they tend to buy these items only when forced to do so. The last group to adopt an innovation is the laggards, who tend to be older consumers and are sceptical of technology. They are given as 16% of the population.

Looking at this discussion, based on Rogers (1983), it becomes clear that there are four elements that are associated with the diffusion of innovation. These are:

- An innovation that is perceived by consumers as new;
- The channels of communication;
- Time;
- A social system.

It is important to show that, while this discussion of the topic and Figure 11.2 on diffusion of innovation show the five categories as adoption of different groups in the population, in reality, there are some who may not adopt the product. These people are known as non-adopters. Meanwhile, irrespective of when the product is introduced, there are some cases when some people would eschew the functionality of technology (Bruland, 1995).

## FACTORS INFLUENCING DIFFUSION OF INNOVATION

Whether an innovation will diffuse properly and be a commercial success is a function of many factors, which are identified by Roges (1983) as below:

- **Relative Advantage:** Does the innovation have a clear advantage such as in effectiveness and cost-saving over existing technology?

- **Compatibility:** Does the new product reflect the values, norms, experiences, and lifestyle of the potential adopters?
- **Complexity:** Is the new innovation simple to understand and easy to use?
- **Trialability:** Can the potential users experiment with the usage on a limited basis?
- **Observability:** Are the benefits of the new products noticeable or clearly visible to the potential adopters?

These explanations are presented in the form of questions here indicating that the new products tend to be more easily adopted if the answers to these questions are in the affirmative. This is especially so as the adopters would want to reduce the risk and have the desired value in the transactions.

## INVENTION ADOPTION PROCESS

Be it a mobile phone, electric vehicle, lawn mower, or a new book like this you are reading, consumers move through stages before they eventually adopt it. According to Schiffman and Kanuk (2012) these are listed as follows:

- Awareness;
- Interest;
- Evaluation;
- Trial;
- Adoption.

It is important to be aware that inventions exist in the first place before consumers can take any action towards acquiring them. After being exposed to, and becoming aware of, the products, consumers can then show an interest that will trigger the need to know more and a search for information related to them. The information obtained from sources such as the Internet and word-of-mouth communication gauges whether the new products fit all the criteria we have highlighted including complexity, relative advantage, and observability. The positive outcome of the evaluation is expected to trigger action to buy a limited quantity or trial purchase. If there is a pleasant experience at the trial stage, it is highly logical to expect consumers to adopt it and, on the flip side, an unfavourable experience at this trial stage can make them reject it.

## WHY WOULD CONSUMERS RESIST INNOVATION?

Much as the inventors would like all their innovations to be adopted, over the years, there have been many unsuccessful attempts. For so many reasons, people tend to resist some innovations. Let us look at some notable examples in the business world. Harley-Davidson is a widely-known brand. The company's history dates as far back as 1903, and the company has been noted for the business of motorcycles, which resonates with its target market. The motorcycles designed and produced by

Harley-Davidson transcend mere engineering efficiency as the brand positions itself as a lifestyle brand that emphasises emotion, adventure, and freedom for the customers. However, while this brand and its success persist, the extension of the brand to perfume in 1996 met with consumers' resistance. The perfume, branded 'Hot Road', was unpopular among customers as female riders of Harley-Davidson bikes felt that the positioning of the brand as 'masculine' was stereotypical. Besides, the customers felt the new invention was not of clear fit for their desired product portfolio of the organisation (Ahmad, 2021). The Evian Water Bra is another invention that did not survive the volatile marketing environment. It was not considered as valuable by the consumers as the organisation thought. In the automobile market, the case of the Ford Pinto still lingers in the memory of many. Ford introduced it as an iconic car that was within a reasonable budget. Nonetheless, the safety record of the car concerning the fuel tank was not great. There were numerous reported cases of its flawed fuel system and fires in the 1970s (Armstrong, 2022). The company had to recall it and discontinue the making of the car.

Earlier, we highlighted some factors that could influence the adoption of innovation. Logically, if these are not adhered to or managed effectively, consumers can resist the new market offerings. For instance, if the consumers do not think that the invention offers something substantial over what they currently have in the market, there is a high likelihood of resistance to the new innovation (relative advantage). Resistance to innovation could also come when the new product is considered too complex to understand and use, and when it is not considered compatible with the current need and values of the target market. The marketers may have devoted significant resources to a particular idea in turning it into a product introduced to the market. However, this would mean little or nothing to the consumers if all these do not translate into bridging the gap between their current and desired states (compatibility). Other factors raised as questions earlier, namely observability and trialability, also apply to why there could be resistance to the innovation. Just as emphasised in the examples given, the degree of perceived risks such as physical risk, financial risk, functional risk, and social risk is a key factor as to whether an innovation will be resisted.

When a new product is introduced into the market, it is important for marketers to use appropriate marketing communications to ensure that the target market is aware of the invention. Marketing communications has been the bedrock of marketing for a long time. When the value of a product is not properly communicated to the target market, it could lead to resistance. A related point lies in the choice of messages, medium of communication, and the amount of money devoted to doing it among many other factors. For instance, the use of digital technology such as social media is proving to be cost-effective, very quick, and more accessible to many these days. Not adopting these could mar the success of the products. We will also need to link this to another major factor that could cause resistance – culture. This is especially important from the viewpoint of global marketers that target multiple countries. A product that is well embraced in a cultural context could be resisted in another cultural system. For example, while several cultural systems such as the United States or the United Kingdom had no issue with the Pepsi slogan 'Come alive with the Pepsi generation', the catchphrase was interpreted and perceived differently in the Chinese market to mean 'Pepsi will bring your ancestors back', which sounds awkward (Rachi, 2016). Similarly, there was controversy around the brand of Toyota Fiera, in that the word 'Fiera' connotes 'ugly old woman' in the Puerto Rico context (Rachi, 2016; Sesztak, 2018). This explains why marketers often consider the notion of launching new products in different countries as strategic. They are expected to gauge whether a simple adaptation strategy would be necessary, or standardisation would still give them the needed success. Standardisation is about employing the same strategy adopted to sell the product in one country in other countries the firm is moving to without any change, whereas adaptation involves fine-tuning the strategy to fit into the new cultural system. If an adaptation strategy is needed and standardisation is used instead, then there is a high likelihood of resistance to such innovation.

Essentially, the marketer can adapt the product, price, place, and promotion strategy to fit the new system. Meanwhile, it could also be that neither standardisation nor adaptation would fit the system directly, then completely developing something bespoke for that cultural context may be the only applicable strategic option. By and large, the firm would need to check the financial implications to be sure that the anticipated proceeds of creating an entirely new product or service is worth the investment.

## INNOVATION AND CONSUMERS' VALUE CO-CREATION ROLES

As seen so far from the discussion of innovation, it is a big deal. Apart from the technical and technological requirements, it is imperative that the product or service innovation satisfies the needs of the consumer in order to gain adoption. The contemporary marketing and consumption system now realises that consumers of today are no longer passive in the value system of organisation. They are expected to be actively involved in how businesses develop new products and services so that such outputs will fit the need effectively. This is one of the key points that differentiate marketing orientation from selling orientation in that consumers' needs are known and incorporated into the marketing system in the former while the latter is about aggressively promoting what has been produced with the hope of convincing the market that the offerings will be a good fit to satisfy needs. The significant improvement in the world of technology, such as the ubiquity of social media, even strengthens consumers' role in value co-creation as it encourages expeditious communication and interaction between firms and consumers as they exchange content through social networking sites. A typical new product development process begins with idea generation. At this stage, the firm is expected to be open to new ideas from various stakeholders including consumers. Great ideas of what could be the new product, and improvements needed to existing ones, can come from consumers. Hence, there is great value in co-creation. In their article titled 'consumer co-creation in new product development', Hoyer et al. (2010) highlight the following potential benefits associated with co-creation:

- Given the input of the consumers, the innovation will likely be of good fit to meet their needs;
- Collecting ideas from consumers through social media is cheap and relatively faster than if they are to be gathered through conventional means;
- The strategy of co-creation strengthens the relationship consumers have with the organisation;
- The products or services that result from innovation will likely have higher demand from consumers because of their involvement in creating it, which also communicates some sense of belonging in the process.

## EMERGING TRENDS IN SOCIAL MEDIA

Social media is a big deal these days. Originally, it was designed as a set of leisure tools whereby family members and friends could relate, connect, and share information with one another, but has now grown into a significant aspect of businesses as marketers continue to explore relationships with their customers through the tools (Benson et al., 2015). Banks, supermarkets, educational institutions, automobile organisations, and many other businesses connect with their customers on one social media platform or another. Examples of these social networking sites include X (formerly Twitter), Facebook, Instagram, LinkedIn, and Pinterest to mention but a few. All evidence around us now shows that businesses are becoming more strategic in managing social media. Similarly, social media organisations also continue to be innovative and follow the trend in the dynamic business environment. All news media are awash with the changes made by the new Twitter owner Elon Musk, especially the announcement of the appointment on 12 May 2023 of a new CEO, Linda Yaccarino, and the rebranding of the platform as X. Prior to this, the Facebook boss, Mark Zuckerberg, announced the change of the name of Facebook to Meta in October, 2021 as a key strategic effort to rebrand the organisation. Taking a cue from the literature (Kaplan and Haenlein, 2010), social media could be classified into six types as follows:

- Content communities: This is about sharing media content among users who are in a virtual community – e.g. YouTube and Flickr;
- Social networking sites: This involves using applications that allow connection with others and sharing content such as video and audio files, after creating personal information profiles – e.g. LinkedIn and Facebook;
- Collective projects: This allows many end-users to jointly and simultaneously create content thereby giving room for a better result than if it had been done by an individual – e.g. Wikipedia;
- Blogs and micro-blogging – e.g. it is about presenting date-stamped entries to visitors of the site in chronological order which now comes in a variety of media forms such as video e.g. X and Blogger;

- Multiplayer online role-playing games: This is about creating a virtual social presence in which case the people on it use personalised avatars relating with others as they would do in real-life scenarios, and users are to follow strict rules in relation to a massively multiplayer online role-playing game (MMORPG) – e.g. World of Warcraft;
- Virtual social worlds: This involves users operating as avatars and relating to others in a three-dimensional virtual environment but without any strict rules applicable in the virtual gaming world – e.g. Second Life.

This is a very detailed and useful breakdown of social media classification by looking at factors like social media presence, media richness, self-presentation, and self-disclosure. Meanwhile, another useful perspective indicates that we can look at social media from two interrelated areas: The social interaction by people who are social actors networking, and the communication and content sharing part (Wasserman and Faust, 1994; Benson et al., 2015).

## MOTIVATION FOR SOCIAL MEDIA PARTICIPATION

Another area of interesting discussion is identifying why people belong to one social media platform or another. We can see that the level of engagement with social media tends to vary with individuals and segments. The literature has indicated some of the common motivational factors that prompt consumers to join a social network platform. While there is much scholarship work on this, we will look at the example given by Tuten and Solomon (2018) which is fairly comprehensive. They refer to these as impulses and are mainly:

- Affinity impulse;
- Contact comfort/immediacy impulse;
- Personal utility impulse;
- Altruistic impulse;
- Validation impulse;
- Curiosity;
- Impulse.

**Affinity impulse** is about joining social media to show a connection or relationship with others. There are many people such as old school friends, and members of associations we used to belong to or are still affiliated to, whom we would ordinarily not have the opportunity to relate with as frequently if not for social media. **Contact comfort/immediacy impulse** is about satisfying the urge and need to relate with someone and, in some cases, these are considered important. Experiences show that we as consumers crave social connections. The experience of the COVID-19 global pandemic is a good example as people needed one another for consolation, succour, and stability. The **personal utility impulse** emphasises that people join social media networks for personal reasons such as entertainment, need for information and clarification, and incentive seeking. **Altruistic impulse** is about joining to be part of a community to ease an ongoing pain in society. It is about social causes such as charity activities to help those affected by world catastrophes like earthquakes, flooding, fire incidents, and the like. In similar form, it could also be about standing up to unscrupulous businesses to get them to change their course of action. **Validation impulse** is about self-lifting such as craving to be liked and to impress others. It is not uncommon to see social media users these days post materials for the purpose of recording a significant number of reactions of 'like' and directly soliciting for this is very rampant. According to Tuten and Solomon (2018) some social media users are prompted to join and use the platform to acquire new knowledge about an issue and to follow specific individuals such as celebrities to check their profiles and explore their updates. This is the curiosity impulse.

## CLASSIFYING SOCIAL MEDIA USERS

Although the number of social media users keeps increasing, the rate and extent of its usage vary among consumers. One of the many classifications given on this is linked to Forrester's research that used the term 'technographic' to describe the characteristics of consumers in relation to their digital lives and how they relate with brands (Forrester, nd; Tuten and Solomon, 2018). From this, four segments of social media users are identified and ranked as the following:

- Social stars;
- Social savvies;
- Social snackers;
- Social skippers.

The social stars are regular users of social media with the highest ranking of usage. They are so active that they demand interaction from the brands in relation to social media. While the social savvies are also good users of social media, they rather expect businesses to relate with them through social media. The snackers neither seek social interactions from companies nor shy away from them. Nonetheless, they appreciate social interactions with brands. The social skippers are ranked the least among the four in terms of their usage of social media and hardly use the tools to relate with businesses, but prefer to use other means of reaching out to companies such as directly in-store or via email.

## SOCIAL MEDIA LIVE STREAM, USER STORIES, AND CONSUMER DECISIONS

Social media tools come in various forms. Looking at social media live and user stories as a specific form is a valuable addition to the segment of this chapter. Given that it works differently, generating live stream and user story content has become very popular among consumers. It has changed the dynamics of how consumers interact in the social media system. This is the focus of the publication by Fletcher and Gbadamosi (2022) which offers a conceptual framework that indicates the specific dynamics and how this works to influence consumer behaviour. Although the authors acknowledge the existing decision models that have been developed for conventional consumer decision processes as discussed in Chapter 3, with reference to existing work on this such as Nicosia (1966); Engel et al. (1968); Darley et al. (2010); Osei and Abenyin (2016); they developed a new framework that depicts the specific nature of social media live stream and user stories. According to Fletcher and Gbadamosi (2022), the framework brings these factors together comprehensively. For instance, there is a reference to factors influencing consumers' social media interactions, such as:

- Engagement;
- Intention;
- Decision;
- Evaluation.

In this perspective, the engagement factor or customer engagement (CE) is about how stakeholders interact in online brand communities, especially in relation to brands, individuals, and customer-brand relationships. In live streaming, the consumer intention is considered to be part of the decision process not only in terms of purchase intention but in relation to engaging with the online community, like doing online live demonstration activities such as unboxing videos and demonstrating a product's use. The decision to engage with the community, such as with videos and the decision to purchase, are both embedded under 'decision' as a factor influencing live social media interactions. Evaluation is about the opportunity for consumers to gauge their experience against pre-purchase expectations. It has been stated that live videos can give a real face to the reviewers of the products thereby breaking the anonymity of society and enhancing trustworthiness (Hajli, 2014). As demonstrated in the framework (Fletcher and Gbadamosi, 2022), the overall themes to consider are:

- Community motives;
- Credibility development;
- Competitive analysis;
- Information search; and
- Knowledge and opinion sharing.

So, by and large, for live-streaming social media content in the form of live video and user stories, the consumers/social media users are aided in their decisions through knowledge and opinion sharing at the pre-purchase phase. This knowledge and these opinions emerged from the actions of the experienced consumers during their post-purchase phase.

## INNOVATION AND MARKETING

With the complexity of the marketing environment and the dynamic nature of the associated factors, it is imperative for marketers to be innovative. Consumers' appetite for something new continues to grow. As an example, the quest for eco products is growing. For instance, generating green electricity from renewable sources like solar and wind is considered beneficial to the consumers and good for the environment. Ozaki (2011), in a study on what makes consumers sign up to green electricity, found that the motivation for purchase is more than usability, functionality, or cost but the meaning of this purchase to them such as image, values, mores, and how it reflects their identity. Innovations are also seen in several other areas apart from automobiles. Fashion items are appearing in the market, communication systems, and several other areas that demonstrate that businesses are engaging in research to fill gaps in the ever-increasing needs of consumers.

Meanwhile, innovation and marketing are becoming increasingly linked and transcend the technological platform that dominates the discussion in this chapter. In fact, there is a phenomenon acknowledged as marketing innovation. It is defined as implementing new marketing methods which entails changing product packaging or design, pricing, placement, or promotion (OECD, 2005; D'Attoma and Ieva, 2020). So, it is relevant for us to explore an interesting classification in innovation and marketing as highlighted in the work of Purchase and Valery (2020) who note that we have technological innovation and non-technological innovation. According to them, technological innovations cover developing new products or services whereas non-technological innovation covers issues such as inventions around introducing new pricing methods, modes, and channels of distribution, how to promote the market offerings in a new way such as using integrated marketing communications (IMCs), changes around the brand, and changes to the design of the product and packaging without changing the product's use and functioning. It is therefore very relevant for marketers to manage the systematic combination of technological and non-technological innovations to know how to achieve success in delighting consumers with their market offerings. This is because the relationship may not be straightforward if it is not well researched and managed. For example, an interesting finding from the publication of D'Attoma and Ieva (2020) shows that when a firm undertakes a technological innovation, developing marketing innovations may not play a significant role towards innovation success and failure. However, when the marketing innovation types are disentangled, the authors found that product design relates positively to innovation success. In this context, innovation success refers to having turnover that directly emanates from introducing technological innovation while innovation failure is abandoning innovation before launching to the market (Mothe and Nguyen, 2010; Tranekjer, 2017).

## PRODUCT LIFE CYCLE (PLC) AND CONSUMER BEHAVIOUR

The easiest metaphor to use for describing the notion of the product life cycle (PLC) is that it is like us, humans. As people are born, so we have new products introduced into the marketplace. As typical of humans, we grow, become mature, and die at some stage. Similarly, after introduction, products grow, become mature, and reach the decline stage. For products, each of these phases is determined by sales and profits generated. So, essentially, it is the consumers' response to marketing stimuli that determines the life cycle of a product. Understandably, the marketing strategies adopted by the firm are a major part of the triggers of such behaviour.

Consumer behaviour can vary at each of the stages. As we have discussed earlier, there can be resistance to innovation. Hence, it is possible that a product can even fail during the introduction stage. Although the innovators in Figure 11.2 of Rogers (1995) are usually enthusiastic about new products at the early stage, a significant number of consumers might be sceptical of the value of the products in terms of how they solve problems. Marketers are also aware of the challenge to win consumers over at this early stage, which explains why they invest significantly into marketing communications to encourage adoption. Nonetheless, it is important to note that new products should meet the criteria guiding customers in the adoption process such as their ability to offer relative advantage and compatibility to solving existing problems, rather than merely focusing on using marketing communications to promote products that are not needed. At the growth stage, sales and profits increase, which is an indication of wider acceptance of the product by the consumers. However, these sales and profits peaked at maturity. This is partly because competition would have been attracted at the growth stage. At the decline stage, the consumers are looking for something new to spice up their consumption and transaction in terms of new products or modification of the existing offerings. Firms explore these strategic alternatives in such a way that will give optimal benefit to them and the consumers.

It is important to note that the duration of the products in each of these phases varies. While a product might quickly move from introduction to growth, another could take a significantly longer time to make the transition.

**PAUSE, PLAN, AND PRACTICE: CONSUMERS AND THEIR SMARTPHONES**

Communication with mobile telephones began several years ago and has developed gradually over time. The advent of smartphones has raised this to a whole new level. It has become clear to inventors over the years that consumers' needs around communication transcend simply calling and receiving calls and text messages, which are typical utilities associated with the old generation of mobile phones. With smartphones, consumers can do multiple things and achieve relevant goals. Compared to their preceding versions, smartphones offer consumers the opportunity of a touchscreen interface and functions like a computer. They have several other features including a web browser, camera, extra storage space, and high-density display. It is therefore understandable why they have now become a key aspect of consumers' lives these days. Characteristically, they function with the use of applications commonly known as apps through which consumers are able to execute many things. There are numerous apps available for consumers to download and use on their mobile phones such as organiser, calendar, social media apps, and apps from various companies. While several factors determine consumers' choice of mobile phones, a key influence on the choice is the operating systems that accompany them. This is because these are fundamental to determining the smooth experience consumers have on smartphones. Two commonly used are the Android and iOS from Google and Apple, respectively. Given that they are multi-functional, smartphones have revolutionised the way consumers live their lives. To consumers with smartphones, there are no dull moments. They offer numerous possibilities for communication, entertainment, education, relationships, religion, and a host of other things. It is tempting to claim that smartphones make smart people.

**TASKS**

1. Discuss four ways smartphones are useful to you as a consumer. In a group of 3 or 4, compare your answers with other members of the group. Can you see a pattern emerging from this? Explain the implication of the differences and similarities in usefulness discussed by your group.
2. Using the points discussed under the diffusion of innovation, why do you think smartphones are so popular?

**Sources**

Benson, V., Saridakis, G., Tennakoon, H., & Ezingeard, J. N. (2015). The role of security notices and online consumer behaviour: An empirical study of social networking users. *International Journal of Human-Computer Studies*, *80*, 36–44.

Darley, W. K., Blankson, C., & Luethge, D. J. (2010). Toward an integrated framework for online consumer behavior and decision-making process: A review. *Psychology & Marketing*, *27*(2), 94–116. https://doi.org/10.1002/mar.20322

Engel, J. F., Kollat, D. T., & Blackwell, R. D. (1968). *Consumer Behavior*. Hinsdale, IL: Dryden Press.

Fletcher, K. A., & Gbadamosi, A. (2022). Examining social media live stream's influence on the consumer decision-making: A thematic analysis. *Electronic Commerce Research*, https://doi.org/10.1007/s10660-022-09623-y

Gbadamosi, A. (2021). Consumption, religion, and digital marketing in developing countries, in Gbadamosi, A. and Oniku, C. A. (2021) (eds), *Religion and Consumer Behaviour in Developing Nations*, pp. 175–198. London, Cheltenham: Edward Elgar.

Grant, R., Clarke, R. J., & Kyriazis, E. (2013). Modelling real-time online information needs: A new research approach for complex consumer behaviour. *Journal of Marketing Management*, *29*(7–8), 950–972.

Hajli, M. N. (2014). A study of the impact of social media on consumers. *International Journal of Market Research*, *56*(3), 387–404, https://doi.org/10.2501/IJMR-2014-025.

Haldar, A., Sucharita, S., Dash, D. P., Sethi, N., & Padhan, P. C. (2023). The effects of ICT, electricity consumption, innovation and renewable power generation on economic growth: An income level analysis for the emerging economies. *Journal of Cleaner Production*, *384*, 135607.

Hiley, C. What are smartphones?, Uswitch, 20 September 2022, http://uswitch.com/mobiles/guides/what-are-smartphones/ (accessed 15 May 2023).

Hoyer, W. D., Chandy, R., Dorotic, M., Krafft, M., & Singh, S. S. (2010). Consumer cocreation in new product development. *Journal of Service Research*, *13*(3), 283–296.

Kamboj, S., & Rahman, Z. (2017). Market orientation, marketing capabilities and sustainable innovation: The mediating role of sustainable consumption and competitive advantage. *Management Research Review*.

Kaplan, A.M., & Haenlein, M. (2010). Users of the world, unite! The challenges and opportunities of social media. *Business Horizons*, *53*(1), 59–68.

Kleinman, Z., & Vallance, C. (2023). Geoffrey Hinton warns of danger as he quits Google. BBC, 2 May 2023, http://www.bbc.co.uk/news/world-us-canada-65452940 (accessed 11 May 2023).

Lin, R. J., Tan, K. H., & Geng, Y. (2013). Market demand, green product innovation, and firm performance: Evidence from Vietnam motorcycle industry. *Journal of Cleaner Production, 40*, 101–107.

Metz, A., & Walker-Todd, A. (nd). The best phone 2023: Top smartphones to consider buying, TechRadar, www.techradar.com/uk/news/best-phone (accessed 15 May 2023).

Nicosia, F. N. (1966). *Consumer Decision Processes*. New York: Prentice Hall.

Osei, B. A., & Abenyin, A. N. (2016). Applying the Engell–Kollat–Blackwell model in understanding international tourists' use of social media for travel decision to Ghana. *Information Technology & Tourism*, *16*(3), 265–284. https://doi.org/10.1007/s40558-016-0055-2.

Ozaki, R. (2011). Adopting sustainable innovation: What makes consumers sign up to green electricity? *Business Strategy and the Environment*, *20*(1), 1–17.

Rogers, E. M. (1995). Diffusion of Innovations: Modifications of a model for telecommunications. *Die diffusion von innovationen in der telekommunikation*, 25–38.

Schiffman, L. G., Kanuk, L. L., & Hansen, H. (2012). *Consumer Behaviour: A European Outlook*, 2nd edn, Essex: Pearson Education Limited.

Schiffman, L. G., & Wisenblit, J. (2019). *Consumer Behaviour*, 12th edn, Harlow: Pearson Education Limited.

Solomon, M. R. (2020). *Consumer Behaviour: Buying, Having, and Being*, 13th edn, Essex: Pearson Education Limited.

Szmigin, I., & Piacentini, M. (2022). *Consumer Behaviour*, 3rd edn, Oxford: Oxford University Press.

Talpau, A. (2014). The marketing mix in the online environment. *Bulletin of the Transilvania University of Brasov. Economic Sciences. Series V*, *7*(2), 53.

Tuten, T. L., & Solomon, M. R. (2018). *Social Media Marketing*, 3rd edn, London: Sage.

Walker, R. M., Avellaneda, C. N., & Berry, F. S. (2011). Exploring the diffusion of innovation among high and low innovative localities: A test of the Berry and Berry model. *Public Management Review*, *13*(1), 95–125.

Wasserman, S., & Faust, K. (1994). *Social Network Analysis: Methods and Applications*. Cambridge and New York: Cambridge University Press.

## SUMMARY

Consumers' interest in technology-oriented products has increased in recent times as around 5 billion people are connected to the Internet in one form or another. Although the proportion of young consumers using technology, including social media, is more than that of older consumers, the number of the latter using the Internet has also increased recently. Innovation varies in terms of the extent of how radical the new process is to the existing systems. Hence, there are continuous, dynamically continuous, and discontinuous innovation types. Irrespective of the type of innovation, there has to be a spread of the news about the innovation for it to be adopted. One of the enduring theories that addresses this is the diffusion of innovation theory of Rogers (1962) which identifies adopters' categories to be innovators, early adopters, early majority, late majority, and laggards. When adopting new innovation, consumers' decisions are influenced by relative advantage, compatibility, complexity, trialability, and observability. Hence, it is possible that consumers would resist innovation especially when it is not deemed to be valuable. This explains why some organisations engage in value co-creation with the consumers, thereby ensuring that the consumers are involved in the development of new innovation.

---

**DIGITAL BOX: ARTIFICIAL INTELLIGENCE, MARKETING, AND CONTROVERSIES**

Artificial intelligence (AI) has introduced a new level of technological innovation to the world in an unprecedented form. Given its functionality and scope of application, it is regarded as an extremely powerful technology. It has relevance in education, marketing, the health sector, construction and engineering, and a host of other areas. There is a plethora of examples of AI all around us as consumers including facial recognition systems and Google Assistant. Its operations have brought significant automation to our processes and paved the way for comfort and efficiency in many ramifications. However, there have been concerns raised about this phenomenon in relation to its potential to foster ill practices. This reservation has been in the news globally over the years but a more recent news item in May 2023 indicates that Geoffrey Hinton, who is also known as 'AI godfather' working for Google, has quit the organisation. He then raised one of the strongest criticisms of this technology and specifically warned of the associated danger that AI may soon be more intelligent than humans. Obviously, this can have devastating consequences. Some commentators are citing examples of how there are issues concerning social media misuse even though it has many positive roles, implying that things could get out of hand if not properly managed. So, the debate is still ongoing as to whether artificial intelligence is helpful or destructive.

**TASKS**

1. In two groups, with each holding one of the two opposing perspectives on artificial intelligence and considering future possibilities on AI, debate whether it is helpful or descriptive;
2. Reflecting on the current situation of the market environment, project the likely developments in artificial intelligence in the next ten years and give reasons why you think this is applicable.

**END OF CHAPTER DISCUSSION QUESTIONS**

1) Which technology is commonly used by consumers of your generation? List them and explain how they have changed the consumption pattern of this consumer segment compared to ten years before now. What are the key motivating factors? What advertising strategy would you recommend to engender positive responses from those in this generation that are not yet enthusiastic about technology?

2) Present two pieces of evidence of discontinuous innovation in the global marketing environment in recent times. Why do you consider them to be in this category? Working in a group of 2 or 3, develop new ideas of discontinuous innovation and recommend which strategies to adopt to make it a commercial success.

3) Check the Internet or reflect on your experience of a failed innovation. From this information, which of the factors influencing the diffusion of innovation would you say was violated? What lessons can inventors learn from this?

4) Social media has improved the way of life of most people in recent times as many more consumers are joining by the day and existing users are joining new platforms in addition to those they are currently linked to. In view of this, in a flashback highlight why you joined the latest social media platform you are connected to. Which of the categories cited in the chapter, based on Forrester (nd) and Tuten and Solomon (2018) in terms of your relationship with brands do you belong? Are you among social stars, social savvies, social snackers, or social skippers?

5) A UK-based firm has developed a new product that has been widely hailed as a clear case of the successful innovation of the year. The business success has now indicated that the firm should seriously consider taking it abroad to serve international markets with some African countries and the Middle East as the first phase of the rollout of the product. The investor is concerned as to whether to use an adaptation or standardisation strategy. What do you advise on this?

### Case Study: Samsung: How Technology Rules the World

Samsung is one of the leading innovative organisations in the world. It is known as a major manufacturer of several products including home appliances, mobile devices, televisions and AV, and computing. The company prides itself on its image as an organisation dedicated to excellence and creation of human-driven experiences. Its logo is part of the communication of the excellence the company stands for. In 2005, the newly redesigned logo of 'Samsung' with special spacing and height was introduced to improve its visibility. To Samsung, the new logo, the sleek lettermark, is about expressing a contemporary feel and look. This resonates with its customers all over the world as the company has one product or another for different consumer segments. Its refrigerator is a sought-after technology among consumers as they offer them easy access to refreshingly cold water at an impressively fast rate. Some even offer opportunities like autofill pitcher, purified water, Power Freeze to provide a dynamic experience of the refrigerator in relation to food preservation. The focus of the company is to offer customers a relative advantage over what they are already using. The same dedication to top quality characterises Samsung manufacturing in respect of other home appliances such as washing machines, cooking appliances, vacuum cleaners, and dishwashers. Despite the plethora of products in Samsung's portfolio, it is focused on turning new ideas into products.

During May 2023, the company launched the Samsung TV Plus mobile app, which is a vertical video experience. Through this, consumers would be able to scroll through their preferred short video which is meant for use on mobile devices. With the app, Galaxy users would have instant access to more than 100 free channels. So, this is good news as it gives people in 24 countries free TV content or entertainment. The electronic products market was dazed in May 2023 when Samsung Electronics Co. introduced another surprise new addition to the market – the UI 5 watch. This is about improving people's health by helping them to monitor their sleep patterns to allow them to adjust where and when necessary. In this technological breakthrough, three issues emphasised are building healthy habits, getting customers to understand sleep patterns, and offering a sleep-friendly environment.

In the same month the company announced the launch of the KMC-W, also known as Samsung Kiosk, which is a self-service display to help retailers maximise sales. This contactless technology has proved popular among Samsung customers because it introduces convenience into transactions, facilitates drive-through, self-ordering, bill payments, and a host of other areas. This device is compatible with vending machines, external cameras, and ID/passport scanners. It is known to be high-performance power. The excitement of Hoon Chung, the Executive Vice President of Visual Display Business for Samsung Electronics cannot be hidden as he indicates that the device accelerates business in a wide variety of areas including travel, food and beverages, and healthcare.

In its strategy, given that each has its own benefits, Samsung is focused on introducing not only continuous innovation and dynamically continuous innovation but also discontinuous innovation that strategically revolutionises how the technology markets live. They show this in the areas of home entertainment, mobile devices, home appliances, and others. Something interesting about the company is that despite the available resources that could be invested to reintroduce its products at the decline stage, the company sometimes allows a product at this stage of the product life-cycle to be phased out to give room for new inventions. Examples are in many of the product mixes of the company including telephones and televisions. The Galaxy fold, released in 2019, became popular soon after release but later lost its stay in the market as consumers became underwhelmed and consider that it cost more than the quality. A similar fate was recorded concerning Galaxy Note 7, which was launched in August 2016 and considered stylishly good with a big screen and good camera, but was later reported as overheating and considered a safety hazard.

Although the company also supplies laptops, the consumers seem to know it more for smartphones. So, efforts are being made to boost this product line to match the popularity of their other key products that have been successful over the years.

Meanwhile, to encourage the diffusion of their innovations, Samsung adopts several methods. The company knows that the innovators among the product adopters are few, so they ensure that these people are kept informed of their products early enough to give them a good start before the early adopters, early majority, late majority, and the laggards adopt the products. It has a very strong social media presence on many platforms including X, Facebook, Instagram, and Snapchat which have been pivotal to its product launches over the years.

**Sources**

Samsung (2023). Samsung news room UK, http://news.samsung.com/uk/latest/page/2 (accessed 25 May 2023).

Tanta, R. (2022). Samsung failures: List of failed products of Samsung, http://startuptalky.com/samsung-failed-products/, Start-up talky, February 7, 2022 (accessed 25 May 2023).

## QUESTIONS

1. Consider a product idea you could recommend to Samsung to produce and release next year. Describe this and explain why you think it will be a commercial success.
2. How can Samsung adopt value co-creation in its new product development? Illustrate with a seasoned and contemporary example.
3. To what extent can culture influence the planning of Samsung in its new global product development strategy?
4. Select two examples of Samsung products, and discuss how social media platforms could be used to aid product diffusion.

## REFERENCES

Ahmad, Z. (2021). The failure of Harley Davidson perfumes: Hot Road Catalogue – How could they have done a better job?, http://zaemalahmad95.medium.com/the-failure-of-harley-davidson-perfumes-hot-road-catalogue-how-could-they-have-done-a-better-55004badff3a (accessed 18 October 2023).

Armstrong, S. (2022). The horrifying story behind the Ford Pinto, *Hot Cars*, 11 December 2022, http://www.hotcars.com/horrifying-story-behind-ford-pinto/ (accessed 12 May 2022).

Benson, V., Saridakis, G., Tennakoon, H., & Ezingeard, J. N. (2015). The role of security notices and online consumer behaviour: An empirical study of social networking users. *International Journal of Human-Computer Studies*, *80*, 36–44.

British Library Learning (nd). From Phonautographs to MP3: A history recording formats', ww.bl.uk/history-of-recorded-sound/articles/timeline-of-formats (accessed 8 May 2023).

Bruland, K. (1995). Patterns of resistance to new technologies in Scandinavia: An historical perspective, in Bauer, M. (ed.), *Resistance to New Technology: Nuclear Power, Information Technology and Biotechnology*. Cambridge, UK: Cambridge University Press.

Damanpour, F. (1987). The adoption of technological, administrative, and ancillary innovations: Impact of organizational factors. *Journal of Management*, 13(4), 675–688.

Darley, W. K., Blankson, C., & Luethge, D. J. (2010). Toward an integrated framework for online consumer behavior and decision-making process: A review. *Psychology & Marketing*, 27(2), 94–116. https://doi.org/10.1002/mar.20322

Deakins, D., & Freel, M. (2003). *Entrepreneurship and Small Firms*. Berkshire, UK: McGraw-Hill Education.

Edquist, C., Hommen, L., & McKelvey, M. D. (2001). *Innovation and Employment: Process Versus Product Innovation*. Cheltenham: Edward Elgar.

Engel, J. F., Kollat, D. T., & Blackwell, R. D. (1968). *Consumer Behavior*. Hinsdale, IL: Dryden Press.

Fletcher, K. A., & Gbadamosi, A. (2022). Examining social media live stream's influence on the consumer decision-making: A thematic analysis. *Electron Commerce Research*, 1–31. https://doi.org/10.1007/s10660-022-09623-y

Ganglmair-Wooliscroft, A., & Wooliscroft, B. (2016). Diffusion of innovation: The case of ethical tourism behavior. *Journal of Business Research*, 69(8), 2711–2720.

Gbadamosi, A., & Oniku, A. C. (2021). Consumption, religion, and digital marketing in developing countries, in Gbadamosi, A. and Oniku, A. C. (eds), *Religion and Consumer Behaviour in Developing Nations*, pp. 175–198. London, Cheltenham: Edward Elgar.

Grant, R., Clarke, R. J., & Kyriazis, E. (2013). Modelling real-time online information needs: A new research approach for complex consumer behaviour. *Journal of Marketing Management*, 29(7–8), 950–972.

Greenhalgh, T., Robert, G., Macfarlane, F., Bate, P., & Kyriakidou, O. (2004). Diffusion of innovations in service organizations: Systematic review and recommendations. *The Milbank Quarterly*, 82(4), 581–629.

Hajli, M. N. (2014). A study of the impact of social media on consumers. *International Journal of Market Research*, 56(3), 387–404. https://doi.org/10.2501/IJMR-2014-025.

Haldar, A., Sucharita, S., Dash, D. P., Sethi, N., & Padhan, P. C. (2023). The effects of ICT, electricity consumption, innovation and renewable power generation on economic growth: An income level analysis for the emerging economies. *Journal of Cleaner Production*, 384, 135607.

Hoyer, W. D., Chandy, R., Dorotic, M., Krafft, M., & Singh, S. S. (2010). Consumer cocreation in new product development. *Journal of Service Research*, 13(3), 283–296.

International Telecommunications Union (2017). www.itu.int/en/ITU-D/Statistics/ Documents/facts/ICTFactsFigures2017.pdf (accessed 19 September 2020).

Kamboj, S., & Rahman, Z. (2017). Market orientation, marketing capabilities and sustainable innovation: The mediating role of sustainable consumption and competitive advantage. *Management Research Review* Emerald Group Publishing Limited, 40(6), 698–724, June.

Kaplan, A. M., & Haenlein, M. (2010). Users of the world, unite! The challenges and opportunities of social media. *Business Horizons*, 53(1), 59–68.

Lin, R. J., Tan, K. H., & Geng, Y. (2013). Market demand, green product innovation, and firm performance: Evidence from Vietnam motorcycle industry. *Journal of Cleaner Production*, 40, 101–107.

Lissitsa, S., & Cohen, O. R. (2018). The Decade of Online Shopping in the Jewish Ultra-Orthodox Community. *Journal of Media and Religion*, 17(2), 74–89.

Nicosia, F. N. (1966). *Consumer Decision Processes: Marketing and Advertising Implications*. Upper Saddle River, NJ: Prentice Hall.

Osborne, S. (1998). *Voluntary Organizations and Innovation in Public Services*. London: Routledge.

Osei, B. A. & Abenyin, A. N. (2016). Applying the Engell–Kollat–Blackwell model in understanding international tourists' use of social media for travel decision to Ghana. *Information Technology & Tourism*, 16(3), 265–284. https://doi.org/10.1007/s40558-016-0055-2.

Ozaki, R. (2011). Adopting sustainable innovation: What makes consumers sign up to green electricity? *Business Strategy and the Environment*, 20(1), 1–17.

Petrosyan, A. (2023a). Countries with the highest number of internet users, *Statista*, Feb 23, 2023, http://www.statista.com/statistics/262966/number-of-internet-users-in-selected-countries/ (accessed 5 May 2023).

Petrosyan, A. (2023b). Global internet usage rate 2022, by gender and region, *Statista*, Jan 31, 2023, http://www.statista.com/statistics/491387/gender-distribution-of-internet-users-region/ (accessed 5 May 2023).

Purchase, S. & Volery, T. (2020). Marketing innovation: A systematic review. *Journal of Marketing Management*, 36(9–10), 763–793. doi: 10.1080/0267257X.2020.1774631

Rachi, C. (2016). 13 times cultural differences resulted in hilarious brand fails, Indiatimes, June 19, 2016, http://www.indiatimes.com/culture/13-times-cultural-differences-resulted-in-hilarious-brand-fails-255968.html (accessed 18 October 2023).

Rogers, E. M. (1976). New product adoption and diffusion. *Journal of Consumer Research*, 2(4), 290–301.

Rogers, E. M. (1995). *Diffusion of Innovations*, 4th edn, New York: The Free Press.

Rogers, E. M. (1995). Diffusion of Innovations: Modifications of a model for telecommunications. *Die diffusion von innovationen in der telekommunikation*, 25–38.

Rogers, Everett M. (1962). *Diffusion of Innovations*. Free Press of Glencoe: Macmillan Company.

Rogers, Everett M. (1983). *Diffusion of Innovations*, 3rd edn, New York: Free Press.

Schiffman, L. G, Kanuk, L. L., & Hansen, H. (2012). *Consumer Behaviour: A European Outlook*, 2nd edn, Essex: Pearson Education Limited.

Schiffman, L. G. and Wisenblit, J. (2019). *Consumer Behaviour*, 12th edn, Harlow: Pearson Education Limited.

Schilling, M. A. (2005). *Strategic Management of Technological Innovation*. New York: McGraw Hill.

Schumpeter, J. (1934). *The Theory of Economic Development*. Cambridge, MA: Harvard University Press.

Sesztak, Z. (2018). 10+ offensive car names failures, LinkedIn October 15, 2018, http://www.linkedin.com/pulse/10-offensive-car-name-failures-zsolt-sesztak/ (accessed 18 October 2023).

Solomon, M. R. (2020). *Consumer Behaviour: Buying, Having, and Being*, 13th edn, Essex: Pearson Education Limited.

Szmigin, I., & Piacentini, M. (2022). *Consumer Behaviour*, 3rd edn, Oxford: Oxford University Press.

Talpau, A. (2014). The marketing mix in the online environment. *Bulletin of the Transilvania University of Brasov. Economic Sciences. Series V*, 7(2), 53.

Tuten, T. L., & Solomon, M. R. (2018). *Social Media Marketing*, 3rd edn, London: Sage.

Walker, R. M., Avellaneda, C. N., & Berry, F. S. (2011). Exploring the diffusion of innovation among high and low innovative localities: A test of the Berry and Berry model. *Public Management Review*, 13(1), 95–125.

Wasserman, S., & Faust, K. (1994). *Social Network Analysis: Methods and Applications* (Vol. 8). Cambridge: Cambridge University Press.

World Population Review (2023). http://worldpopulationreview.com/country-rankings/internet-users-by-country (accessed 5 May 2023).

Zurcher, A. (2023). AI: How 'freaked out' should we be?, http://www.bbc.co.uk/news/world-us-canada-64967627 (accessed 9 May 2023).

# CHAPTER 12

# Contemporary Consumer Research

**LEARNING OUTCOME**

After reading this chapter, you should be able to:

- Explain the need for consumer research;
- Discuss the issues associated with setting the stage for consumer research;
- Discuss perspectives on consumer research: Interpretivism and positivism;
- Present a critical analysis of the consumer research process in a digital age;
- Discuss various data collection methods and instruments and how they are aided by technology;
- Discuss contemporary data analysis and interpretation methods often used in consumer research;
- Explain the notion of netnography and how it facilitates data management in a digital age;
- Critically discuss Neuromarketing and its role in consumer research;
- Explain the importance of Big Data in consumer research;
- Discuss ethical issues in consumer research.

## INTRODUCTION

As we have seen from the beginning of this book until this stage, consumer behaviour is a complex phenomenon. On a personal note, irrespective of your class, position, role, nationality, marital status, and other descriptors, imagine how you decide on what you buy for personal consumption and how you decide on what to buy as gifts for others on occasions like Fathers' Day, Mothers' Day, Valentine's Day, birthday, wedding day, and other momentous events. You have on many occasions changed your mind due to various reasons and factors. The way you do this in recent times has changed due to technology in comparison to how it was done several years ago. You now have a plethora of options available to you from various sources all over the world. In view of this, marketers also have a greater need to have insight into the dynamics of the decisions you and other consumers being targeted make. This brings in the significant role of consumer research in this contemporary era. It is important to stress here that as you read this chapter, it would seem as if consumer research and marketing research are being used synonymously. That is not the intention. More often than not, consumer research is explained as a part of marketing research. In view of this, the processes adopted for the latter are understandably applicable to the former, which explains why the content of this chapter will be swaying between the mention of marketing research and consumer research. Meanwhile, from another perspective, it is noteworthy that the core focus of marketing is the consumer. So, most of the discussion about marketing revolves around customer value as the customer is the king who dictates the direction of affairs through their transactions and activities with the organisation. Accordingly, in this chapter, we will be looking at the activities involved in conducting consumer research and its processes as well as how digital transformation has influenced how they are done. Although you may have got an idea of this from this introduction, let us start with a deeper discussion of the need for consumer research.

## THE NEED FOR CONSUMER RESEARCH

What we have established throughout this book is that technology has changed consumption over the years, our needs have grown significantly and still continue to grow. This dynamic nature of consumer needs is a big challenge for businesses, and they need adequate knowledge of this in order to be able to formulate, implement, and monitor their marketing strategies. So, consumer research is essential for business success. We can define consumer research as collecting, recording, and analysing data relating to consumption with regards to products and/or services in the marketplace. So, why are we interested in this? We can look at the core interrelated reasons for this, especially from the marketers' viewpoint, as:

- Knowing the needs and wants of the target market;
- Uncovering marketplace opportunities that can be explored;
- Minimising strategic risks.

Fashion items, automobiles, communications, and a plethora of several areas of consumers' lives have seen dramatic changes in terms of how consumers' needs are met. Marketers' investment in research into a consumer's changing needs will put them in a better position to be able to know changes in the taste of the consumers and the appropriate market offerings to use to match these growing needs. Despite the complexity of the marketing environment, it has numerous opportunities for marketers around consumption and transactions. Continuous research will reveal these to businesses for effective planning towards exploring these opportunities. This has to do with the relevance of what is called a marketing information system (MIS), which brings together a set of procedures and people for gauging the information need of the organisation, developing this information, and aiding the decision-maker in acting on the information to create and validate actionable customer and marketing insights (Armstrong and Kotler, 2013). This shows a holistic system integrating internal data of the organisation, marketing intelligence, and consumer research that interrelates continuously to help marketers in their decision making in order to create value for their customers. Marketing intelligence refers to everyday information relating to the marketing environment that helps marketers in their decision about the necessary changes to the firms' existing marketing plans (Gbadamosi and Padya, 2013). For marketing intelligence, data can come from various sources including customers, suppliers of syndicated data, sales representatives, and others. Meanwhile, when marketers engage in consumer research, risks that could cause devastating outcomes to the business can be minimised as the data obtained would be a significant input to strategic decisions, including resource allocation, to create and deliver value to the consumers.

## SETTING THE STAGE FOR CONSUMER RESEARCH

The journey of consumer research as a process begins long before the actual data collection and number crunching that we always see. In some cases, organisations conduct their research in-house. In this case, they have staff members dedicated to conducting consumer research. They tend to work as a department within the larger organisation structure. So, they work as a subsystem that serves as the interface between the company and the customers for the purpose of creating and delivering value as well as engaging the customers to be a part of the value co-creation system.

From a different perspective, organisations commission the project of marketing research to other organisations working as consultants to handle the process and report to the organisation on its findings to serve as input for their marketing decisions. It is not uncommon for businesses like supermarkets, banks, hotels, utility companies, and automobile firms, to mention but a few, to have gotten in touch after completing transactions to want to gauge consumers' level of satisfaction and to get suggestions on the strategic direction for the organisation. Examples of these agencies operating internationally include YouGov, which provides marketing data for brands, media, and agencies, SIS International with its headquarters in New York, and Ipsos, which has been providing valuable data to industry giants that constitute its clients since 1975 (Indeed, 2023). It is reasonable to wonder why an organisation will commit such an important task to an agency, rather than doing it in-house. There are many reasons for this, but the most common ones are lack of skills and experience to handle the marketing research activities, lack of the needed time to get it done effectively, and the desire to employ an independent and neutral body to handle the tasks involved more objectively (Gbadamosi and Pandya, 2013).

With the arrangement to involve a marketing research consultant, some formalities such as exchanging contracts, terms and conditions, presenting the marketing research brief, and marketing research proposal are involved. There are no hard and fast rules about these as they can vary between companies and specific transactions. Nonetheless, we will be looking at these because they tend to be common among many transactions these days.

## CONSUMER RESEARCH BRIEF

One of the most common documents or pieces of information that a client gives to his or her lawyer is the brief on the case. This will empower the lawyer to know how to address the case presented by the client and which approach to adopt. When a firm commissions its consumer research activities to an outside firm, it is imperative that the agency handling the project receives a brief from the company to give them access to necessary information that will aid their role in the project. Although there may be some differences, depending on the companies involved, the essential elements of a marketing research brief are listed below:

- Introduction;
- Background details;
- Statement of the problem;
- Objectives of the study;
- The proposed scope and case of the project;
- The proposed timetable for the completion of the project and delivery of the report.

Let us look at what will be under each of the segments. Like any document, an introduction provides information on what the document stands for and highlights what readers should expect to read in the full document. The background details are essential aspects of the company that will be relevant to the research project at hand. Given that the company doing the research is not an insider, giving as much information as useful at this stage could be very significant to the outcome of the research. As the world has gone digital these days, some of these details could be obtained online by the agency but providing it directly by the firm commissioning the project would add credibility to the validity of the information being supplied. Some of the points to highlight in the background could be the following:

- When the product or brand that is being researched was launched;
- The critical moments and events about the brand since its launch;
- The sales and profit records showing the trends;
- The competing products/brands;
- The market share of the company's brand when compared to competing alternatives;
- The consumers' perception and attitude towards the product/brand.

The statement of the problem is another vital part of this document. You'll probably recall that your doctor will always ask to know why you have invited or visited him or her. How well you describe the ailment will greatly help to support his or her knowledge in determining what tests to conduct, and what recommendations will be given to you to address the ongoing illness. This is similar to the case between companies commissioning the research project (the client) and the agency accepting the brief. To define the problem clearly, it may be useful getting many staff members and departments involved. For example, salespeople in the organisation relate frequently with the consumers and would have access to what they are saying and feeling about the product or brand. Hence, seeking their contribution to defining the problem will be of great value to the project. Similarly, the line manager of the product in question is expected to have a deeper level of knowledge of the problem and would be a great contributor to the document. In fact, it may be a useful approach to organise a brainstorming session for the relevant key staff member to discuss the problem.

When the problem is well defined, then objectives can be teased out from it indicating what the company considers to be germane to solving the problem. It is about what the company thinks is the direction of travel for the agency handling the problem. This helps in streamlining the budget and managing the time for the project. The same reason applies to why there is a need to specify the scope and scale of the project. Essentially, this is driven by the nature of the problem, but it is important to still note the trade-off involved. While a large-scale project will not only be extensive and sophisticated, it will also offer detailed findings with wide-ranging applications, the small-scale project will be less time-consuming and cost-efficient also. It is important to indicate the timescale of the project. A project without a timescale can take forever as there is no indication of when the report is to be submitted. Moreover, it is common for companies to time the report of such research projects to sync in with important events such as opening a new investment pathway, launching a new product, pending decision on a product at the decline stage of the product lifecycle, and extending to an international market.

## CONSUMER RESEARCH PROPOSAL

As a response to the research brief given by the company, the marketing research agency will also submit a research proposal to detail what will be done and how it prepares to address the problem highlighted in the research brief. While there may be some differences in what to include in a proposal, it is very common to have the following segments in a research proposal to be submitted by agencies to their clients:

- Introduction and background of the study;
- Research problem;
- Objective of the study;
- Research questions/hypotheses;
- Significance of the study;

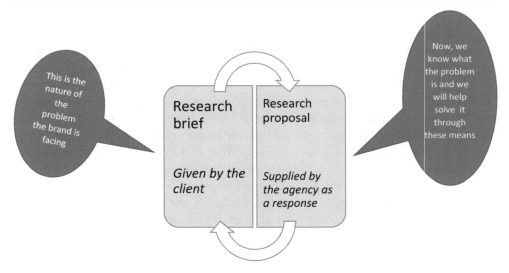

**FIGURE 12.1** Research brief and proposal

- Research methodology;
- Timetable of the study;
- Budgeting the project;
- Terms and conditions of the contract.

The introduction and background of the study provide information to show that the agency understands the issues raised in the brief presented by the client. In most cases, this is a quick gaze into what the proposal contains. It will show what to expect when reading the full proposal. The research problem is stated to ensure that there is a meeting point in the impression had by both the client and the agency in relation to the problem to be solved. If it is well stated, then the findings will be seen to be properly targeted to the issue at hand. Conversely, if it is ill-stated, then the research project may not be hitting the target. In the same way as indicated in the research brief, the research objectives are teased out from the research problem as an indication of what the study is poised to achieve. For clarity, these objectives could also be presented in question form to show consistency in the understanding of the problem at hand. How well a problem is addressed is also significantly linked to the methodology adopted. The method proposed to be used to solve the problem will be discussed in the proposal. Issues such as the population of the study, the sample design, the data collection methods, how the sample will be drawn, and the justification of these would be expected in the proposal. An idea of the justification of the budget will also be gained from the approach indicated to be used. A timetable is also added to this proposal. This tends to be a more realistic one compared to the one indicated in the brief as the agency is the one who will conduct the research and has considered the issues involved in the study. A budget in the proposal shows the financial commitment expected concerning the project. This is also linked to the terms and conditions in the proposal. More often than not, issues such as the percentage of the budget to be paid before, during, and after the project has been executed as well as the copyright rights around the document to be produced in respect of the project will be covered in the terms and conditions.

Given the development in the technology sector, the activities involved in setting the scene for consumer research have changed significantly. Developments such as the use of the Internet has facilitated how the parties develop the contents of the research brief and proposal. Issues such as meeting to discuss issues, signing documents, and asking for and providing clarifications can now be done in more expeditious ways reflecting digital transformation in how firms handle consumer research in this day and age.

## PERSPECTIVES AND PARADIGMS ON CONSUMER RESEARCH

In a case that is reminiscent of building a house, it is important to understand the layout of the foundation. This understanding will help one in knowing what structure to put on it and how to achieve the desired output. So, it is important to know the foundational principles that underpin how the study will be conducted. In a broad sense, the term paradigm can be defined as a basic set of beliefs that guide what we do whether on everyday garden variety or action taken in relation to a disciplined inquiry (Guba, 1990). So, from this, we can infer that as we have paradigms for other phenomena, there are paradigms for consumer research, and these paradigms have assumptions that are followed which differentiate one from another. The literature evidence on this (Morgan, 1979; Collis and Hussey, 2003) suggests that we can have three levels at which the term paradigm is often used including in the consumer research context which is the focus of this chapter. According to them, these levels are:

**A philosophical level**: This is about using it to reflect the beliefs about the world;
**A social level**: This relates to using it to offer guidelines conducting how the consumer researcher should conduct his or her activities;
**A technical level**: This concerns the usage type for specifying the technique and methods that are ideal for the research.

If we strip the term paradigm down to its elements, from the perspective of Denzin and Lincoln (1998), it comprises:

- Ontology;
- Epistemology;
- Methodology.

In looking at each of these one after the other we will see how interrelated they are to giving a clear indication of the focus of the consumer researcher. Ontology is about the essence and very nature of things in the social world (Mason, 2002). So, it addresses the question of whether social entities can be considered as objective entities, in which case they have a reality that is external to the social actors, or whether they should be deemed to be social constructions built up from the viewpoint and action of social actors (Bryman, 2001). The second element, epistemology, relates to addressing the question of whether the social world can and should be studied with the use of the same principles, ethos, and procedures consistent with those of natural sciences (Bryman, 2001). So, if stated differently, epistemology is about answering the questions 'How do we know the world?' (Denzin & Lincoln, 1998) and 'What is the nature of the relationship between the researcher and those being studied (researched)?' (Hussey and Hussey, 1997). Methodology, which is the third element, is concerned about the issue of how the consumer researchers gain knowledge about the world (Denzin & Lincoln, 1998).

Following these, we will now look at the two main paradigms that guide consumer research and their assumptions. Authors like Solomon (2020) and Marshall (2023) and many others identify these two paradigms as positivism and interpretivism. The positivism paradigm holds that there is an objective and single truth and that the world is rational and that the present, past, and future are clearly defined (Solomon, 2020). On the other hand, interpretivism holds that human behaviour occurs within the context of the complex social world and it emphasises the focal relevance of consumers' subjective experience which should be taken into consideration in research. Table 12.1 provides a detailed depiction of the differences between these paradigms.

It is not unreasonable to ask at this stage which of these two paradigms should guide consumer researchers in their quest to unpack issues about consumer behaviour.

**TABLE 12.1** A summary of positivist and phenomenological paradigms

|  | **Positivism paradigm** | **Phenomenological paradigm** |
|---|---|---|
| **Basic beliefs** | The world is external and objective | The world is socially constructed and subjective |
|  | The observer is independent | The observer is a party to what is being observed |
|  | Science is value-free | Science is driven by human interest |
| **The researcher should** | Focus on facts | Focus on meanings |
|  | Locate causality between variables | Try to understand what is happening |
|  | Formulate and test hypotheses (deductive approach) | Construct theories and models from the data (inductive approach) |
| **Methods include** | Operationalising concepts so that they can be measured | Using multiple methods to establish different views of a phenomenon |
|  | Using large samples from which to generalise to the population | Using small samples researched in depth or over time |
|  | Quantitative methods | Qualitative methods |

**Source**: Gray (2004, p. 22) as adapted from Easterby-Smith et al. (1991, p. 27)

It is tempting to conclude that one is better than the other. The debate is not unusual. However, the choice of which to use should be based on the appropriateness of each in terms of the specific objectives, nature of the study, and the circumstances around the study to be done being the key determining factors. This is because each has its own strengths and weaknesses and exploring these in light of what the study is focused on achieving should be a key action for consumer researchers. By now, it is clear that while these two main paradigms are the two extreme ends of a continuum, there are different possible variations that lie within them. This is especially useful when considering how to address the weaknesses of the methodological stance adopted. Like most other authors, Marshall (2023) argues that both paradigms are valid for marketing research. So, researchers will have to be guided by the circumstances of their research in making the choice. This distinction will be illustrated further in the chapter, especially as we examine how the use of technology has impacted the activities of consumer researchers in recent times.

## THE MARKETING RESEARCH PROCESS IN A DIGITAL AGE

This segment presents the stages involved in conducting marketing research. It is called the digital marketing process because each of the stages is significantly impacted by the use of technology which has changed the approach adopted over the years. The five main stages are given in Figure 12.2, and it shows that all of these stages and activities are conducted within a wider technological context.

## DEFINITION OF PROBLEM AND RESEARCH OBJECTIVES

The research process begins with defining the problem in clear terms. The problem can be from any aspect of the organisation, marketing mix elements, and external factors from outside the organisation or a combination of these. Issues about consumer perception and attitudes towards the product and services of the organisation could be combined in relation to external factors like the impact of COVID-19 and

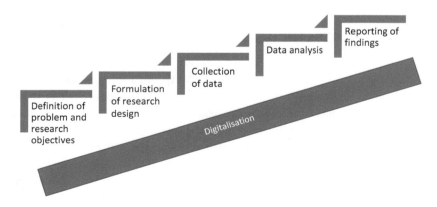

**FIGURE 12.2** The marketing research process in a digital age

the global economic crisis that affects energy prices, changes in interest rates, shortage of specific inputs, changes in consumer taste, shift in the socio-cultural environment, and several other factors. The problem may relate more to specific marketing mix elements such as reduced sales or market share, consumers' negative attitude to the products, packaging, marketing communication messages, and pricing. Logically, a well-defined problem should give the consumer researchers ideas of the research objectives. In defining the research objectives, the focus of the researcher should be why the study is necessary and what will be delivered. For example, research objectives could be:

- To gauge the consumers' perception of a new market offering such as a service, or product;
- To determine the likely effectiveness of a proposed new marketing communications method;
- To examine consumers' perception of a planned distribution strategy for specific products;
- To determine the appropriate pricing strategy in respect of a specific product item or line;
- To determine the optimum combination of marketing mix elements necessary to drive or increase repeat purchase of a specific product;
- To explore consumers' perception of the positioning of the market offerings of the organisation in comparison to competitors.

The use of the Internet has opened numerous possibilities of how the internally provided research problem can be fine-tuned with information from various other sources. More often, communication tools like MS Team, Zoom, and Skype are becoming increasingly popular for holding meetings, which could be very valuable for brainstorming especially when members are not in immediate proximity to one another. Although there are some cases when meeting in-person is preferred, the cost-efficiency and convenience associated with virtual meetings make this approach very valuable for research activities.

## FORMULATION OF RESEARCH DESIGN

Digital transformation has influenced businesses in how they formulate their research design. Since the data collection, analysis of data, and reporting of findings have been influenced by digitalisation, as discussed later in the chapter, it is reasonable to see how the discussion of digital processes feeds into the research design. This is because research design is a blueprint of how the research will be conducted towards the realising of the stated objectives. This is the stage where the researcher indicates specific information on how to collect and analyse the data, where the data will come from, the sampling plan, methods for contacting the likely respondents, and the research instruments that will be used. Let us now look at the three types of research design.

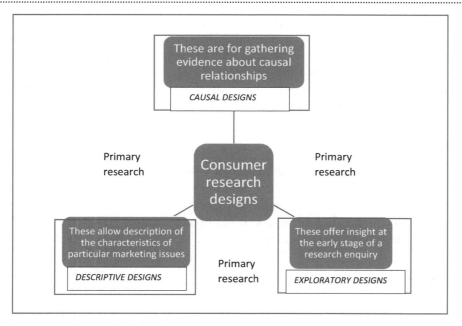

**FIGURE 12.3** Types of research design

As shown in Figure 12.3, the three types of research designs are:

- Exploratory research design;
- Descriptive research design;
- Causal research design.

Exploratory research design is focused on identifying the real nature of the research before the extensive study is conducted. So, it is usually done as the initial step in the process of a marketing research project. It tends to be qualitative rather than quantitative in nature with commonly used methods such as focus group discussion, in-depth interviews, secondary data analysis, case analysis, word association exercise, and other projective techniques. They are often useful for clarifying concepts, gathering background information, and formulating hypotheses to be tested at a later time.

Essentially, descriptive research design focuses on identifying characteristics of the issue around marketing in relation to the research objectives. For example, it addresses issues such as knowing the quantity of a specific product sold and how many customers purchase a specific brand within a given period. Consumers' attitudes, behaviour, and preferences as well as demographic factors like gender, marital status, and age are covered in this type of research design. In doing this, the consumer researcher has the option of designing the study to be either cross-sectional or longitudinal. While longitudinal studies involve collecting data from a fixed sample of the population at different times and measuring this repeatedly, cross-sectional studies involve taking the sample of the population of interest for a study only once.

Unlike the other two design types, the causal research design is about examining if one variable results in a change in another. It is basically about collecting evidence concerning cause-and-effect relationships. For example, one might use it to know the impact of a 50% increase in advertising budget on consumers' purchase of a particular brand. In this case, the advertising budget is the independent variable while the sales figure for the specific brand will be the dependent variable.

## DATA SOURCES

Essentially, data sources can be classified as either primary or secondary. Primary data is collected from primary sources and is new data that is collected in particular to achieve the objective of the current research. Conversely, secondary data comes from secondary sources indicating that it has been previously collected and used but is now considered useful to the current research.

### Secondary Data

As shown in Figure 12.3, we have internal and external secondary data sources as shown in the examples given. One may wonder why consumer researchers would

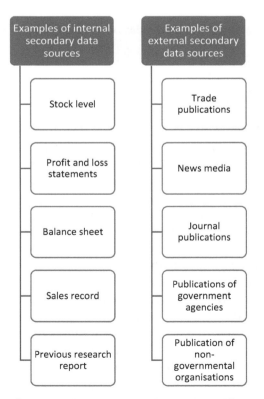

**FIGURE 12.4** Examples of internal and external secondary sources of data

settle for secondary sources of data instead of primary sources. It solves the problem at hand more quickly than if primary data is to be used. So, it saves time. Besides, it is less expensive to conduct as the data is already in existence. Meanwhile, it also has the limitation of not being as specifically relevant to the research at hand as if the primary sources had been used. Besides, there is also the difficulty in ascertaining the validity or quality of the data.

The increasing use of digital technology has widened opportunities for sources of secondary data. Consumer researchers find Internet search engines very useful tools for various types of secondary data such as data from blogs and online institutional data.

## Primary Data

The common sources of collecting primary data are observations, surveys, and experimentation. Observational studies involve carefully and attentively watching consumers and/or objects in order to be able to have an understanding of the circumstances and how they operate in relation to the context of the study. Observing people in the real act is an interesting phenomenon, especially because of the great depth of information that can be garnered through the process. There are many examples of how this method is being applied these days. Shopping malls, supermarkets, reception areas in business premises, banking hall activities, buses, train stations, and several other contexts are all examples of cases amenable to observational studies. Table 12.2 shows the common types of observational studies in consumer research.

**TABLE 12.2** Types of observational studies

| | Type of observation | Description |
|---|---|---|
| 1 | *Participant observation* | The consumer researcher acts as a co-participant in the actions he or she is observing. |
| 2 | *Non-participant observation* | The researcher observes the people in a setting without taking part in the activities and events being observed. |
| 3 | *Open observation* | The people being observed are aware that they are being observed. |
| 4 | *Disguised observation* | The people under observation are not aware that they are being observed. |
| 5 | *Structured observation* | A structured observation entails having an already prepared questionnaire-like form to record the actions of those being observed. |
| 6 | *Unstructured observation* | The marketing researcher observing the people simply makes notes of things that happen at the setting being observed without having any particular format for it. |
| 7 | *Equipment-based observation* | This involves using equipment such as cameras and other audio-visual equipment to record events at the setting being observed. |

**Source**: Gbadamosi and Padya (2013)

This specific benefit of the observational study lies in the fact that the researcher has access to real data rather than relying on the comments given by the participants in respect of the focus of the study (McDaniel and Gates, 1998). On the other hand, it has a limitation, as it may not be effective to reveal consumers' motives and attitudes behind the behaviour exhibited. As we have mentioned in Chapter 8 and shown in Gbadamosi (2019) consumers' attitudes and behaviour may not be consistent. As indicated in No 7 in the table, technology-based observational studies are now on the increase these days compared to several decades ago.

## SURVEY

Surveys involve gathering information about people's opinions, perceptions, attitudes, preferences, knowledge, and buying behaviour. Characteristically, it is about communicating with the chosen target respondents representing the population for the purpose of gathering relevant data. The most commonly used techniques are person-administered questionnaires, mail/self-administered questionnaires, individual interviews, telephone interviews, and focus group discussions. As mentioned earlier, while discussing consumer research paradigms, a combination of these can be used, especially when time and budget permit and the strategy will result in having more diverse target respondents.

## EXPERIMENTATION

Experimentation is about finding out the effect of a change in the independent variable (I) on the dependent variable (D) after manipulating the former. In marketing research, researchers are always looking for three pieces of evidence to establish that a causal relationship exists between these two variables in the research context. These are highlighted in the form of questions below:

- **Concomitant variation:** What is the degree to which $I$ and $D$ happen together in the manner predicted?
- **The time order of the occurrence of the changes:** Did $I$ occur before $D$ or did both happen simultaneously?
- **Elimination of other possible causal factors:** Have other likely causal factors been eliminated?

Let us illustrate these pieces of evidence with the example of expenditure on sales promotion targeted to a consumer segment and their purchase of the product. In this case, for us to conclude that sales promotion expenditure (independent variable 1) is the cause of purchases made by the specific consumer segment, then we would not expect there to be a significant increase in the purchase of these target consumers when the sales promotion has not been activated. This is the key issue in concomitant variation. In this given scenario, for the time order of occurrence, the increase in the purchase of the consumer segment will have to be preceded by the increase in spending on sales promotion tools, or both of them will have to happen at the same time. For the third condition (elimination of other possible causal factors), it is important to acknowledge that many other factors can lead those consumers to buy more, other than that promotion. These could be factors such as the sudden lack of supply of competing offerings, the introduction of new distribution outlets by the company, rumours of likely future shortages of the product in question that can make consumers engage in panic buying, such as was the case during the COVID-19 global pandemic, and many others. So, the third piece of evidence is about showing that these likely other factors have been controlled to be sure that the increased spending in sales promotion is the only cause of the increase in purchase of this product by the consumer segment.

## QUALITATIVE VS QUANTITATIVE CONSUMER RESEARCH DATA

Taking a cue from Table 12.2, which shows qualitative studies as falling under interpretivism, and quantitative data coming from the positivism paradigm, we will now look at the commonly used methods for collecting each of these data categories. The major difference between the two data types lies in the fact that while qualitative data uses small samples, focuses on verbal data, and is usually flexible, the quantitative involves the use of numeric data, often gathered from large samples, and is relatively less flexible than the quantitative approach. We will now look at the commonly discussed qualitative methods which are *in-depth interviews*, *focus group discussion*, and *ethnography*.

## IN-DEPTH INTERVIEW

Saunders et al. (2023) explain an in-depth interview as a purposive conversation that takes place between the interviewer, who asks clear and concise questions, and the interviewee, who is willing to listen to these carefully and respond to them accordingly. Usually, it starts with the interviewer building rapport with the participant to ease them into answering the questions on the subject-matter. Since in-depth interview is about probing to unpack issues around the topic, the questions often used and the approach for raising them are flexible. It is expected that the consumer researcher will skilfully listen to the interviewees and raise the correct questions at the right time during the interview. To avoid or minimise the interviewer's bias during the interview, the researcher is expected to avoid influencing the direction of the response of the participants.

## ETHNOGRAPHY

Ethnography is a data collection method often used in anthropology for having an in-depth understanding of people's culture as well as the dynamics of their social systems. As we have mentioned in Chapter 4, culture plays a very significant role in how we consume, why we do it, and how often we do it. Ethnographers often have prolonged engagement with the people of interest in their natural and cultural settings. This often involves living with them for a considerable period of time during the period of the study, visiting them if considered necessary for uncovering the details needed, and making notes on the findings concerning the objective of the study. Digitalisation has introduced netnography as a data collection tool in qualitative studies, but it will be discussed separately on its own later in the chapter.

## FOCUS GROUP DISCUSSION

Some people are often shy or intimidated during the one-to-one in-depth interviews. Participating in a group discussion in which ideas can be shared with others can encourage such individuals to participate. Hence, in consumer research, focus group discussion involves bringing a group of consumers together at a convenient and safe place to discuss the focus of the study. Technology has added many options to how this data collection is being adopted. For example, this can be tape-recorded, audio-taped, or conducted virtually through systems such as MS Teams, Zoom, Skype, and others. Since the focus is to draw out points, feelings, and themes from the discussion, it often involves having a trained and skilled moderator who will need to be directing the focus of the discussion on the subject at hand through some prepared guide questions. One recurring question on this is 'How many participants are expected in a focus group discussion?' Table 12.3 shows a collation of authors and the diversity of their opinions on this.

In deciding on how many participants, the focus should be on ensuring that the discussion is productive. Hence, there is no hard and fast rule about it but it is important to note that when the group is too large, it may not be conducive for the productive and natural discussion expected, and if the participants are too few, the motivation and energy for having a valuable session may be lacking (Burns and Bush, 1998; Bernard, 2000). However, it is important to state that most consumer researchers tend to use focus group participants of between six and twelve in number.

**TABLE 12.3** Different views on focus group composition

| Suggested number | Authors/year of publication |
| --- | --- |
| *as few as two and as many as twelve* | Wilkinson (2004) |
| *between six and ten* | Zikmund (1997); Kotler et al., (1999); Tonkiss (2004) |
| *between six and twelve* | Bernard (2000); Malhotra and Birks (2003), Welman et al., (2005) |
| *between six and nine participants* | Denscombe (1998) |
| *between seven and ten participants* | Marshall and Rossman (1999) |
| *between eight and twelve participants* | Myers (1986); Tull and Hawkins (1987); Burns and Bush (1998); May (2001); Robson (2002) |

**Source**: Adapted from Gbadamosi (2009)

**FIGURE 12.5** The attributes of a good focus group moderator

The role of a moderator of a focus group discussion is critical as it can go a long way to determine the type of data that will emerge from the process. Figure 12.5 below shows the key attributes of a focus group moderator as adapted from the literature (Churchill, 1996). In the observation of Cronin (2003), it is common to have a few individuals in the focus group discussion that might want to dominate the discussion while others may be shy and reluctant to make contributions. The role of the moderator should help him or her to ensure adequate participation and moderate the discussion to avoid unnecessary domination of the exercise by one or more participants.

## SAMPLING PLAN

In marketing research, a population refers to all conceivable individuals or elements of the phenomenon that we intend to conclude about. For reasons such as limited funds, the need to save time, the impracticability of studying the entire population of interest, and the similarities of the members of the population in terms of their attributes, researchers tend to engage in sampling. By definition, a sample is a subset or small part of the population that is chosen to represent the entire population. The process of doing this is known as sampling. From a broad perspective, there are two types of sampling that a researcher can do. These are shown in Figure 12.6

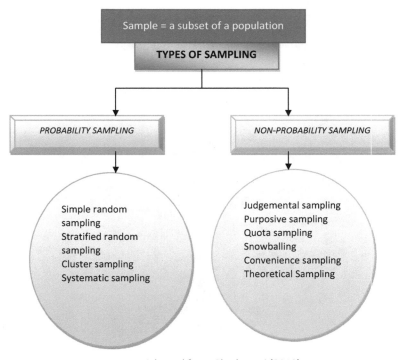

**FIGURE 12.6** Sampling methods
**Source**: Adapted from Gbadamosi (2010).

as adapted from Gbadamosi (2010). The difference between the two broad categories is that in probability sampling every individual element has a non-zero and known chance of selection. So, the chosen sample is a representative cross-section of the population of interest. On the other hand, in non-probability sampling, the sample is selected such that the process is based on human judgement, and not based on probability. Table 12.4 shows the types of each of these two broad sampling methods.

## RESEARCH INSTRUMENT

All the plans and steps we have been discussing will be of minimal value without a good research instrument, as the researcher needs this to collect the needed data from the target respondents. If we follow the classification given by Armstrong and Kotler (2006), they can be classified into mechanical devices and questionnaires. One example of mechanical devices is the people meter which is used for tracking TV viewing habits or the radio programmes that one listens to. This is an example of how technology aids data collection for effective decision making in recent times. The second type, the questionnaire, is a document featuring a collation of questions

**TABLE 12.4** Different types of samples in consumer research

| | **PROBABILITY SAMPLING** | |
|---|---|---|
| 1 | Simple random sampling | All members of the population must be known and numbered, and a sample is drawn such that every member of the population has a known and equal chance of being selected. |
| 2 | Systematic sampling | Choosing every nth element within a numbered population such that a fixed skip interval is observed. For example, every tenth element of a numbered population is made to be in the sample. |
| 3 | Stratified sampling | All conceivable elements (the population) are first divided into different identifiable units (known as strata) and probability sampling is done in each of the strata. |
| 4 | Cluster sampling | The population is separated into clusters and a random sample of the clusters is done. Data can then be collected from all members of the selected clusters (one-stage cluster sampling) or from some members of the selected clusters in some random ways (two-stage sampling). Cluster sampling is different from stratified sampling in that the former involves selecting the groups (clusters) whereas the latter involves selecting elements within the groups (strata). |

| | **NON-PROBABILITY SAMPLING** | |
|---|---|---|
| a. | Convenience sampling | Selecting elements to constitute the sample in a way and manner that is convenient to the researchers. This saves time, is easy to adopt, and is cost-effective but the process is rather subjective. |
| b. | Judgement sampling | This involves relying on one's experience as a researcher to select the elements of a sample. |
| c. | Quota sampling | Adhering to a quota in the sample selection such as ensuring a specific number of certain demographic characteristics of interest such as gender, age, and income feature as members of the sample. |
| d. | Snowballing | Getting in touch with people in the population to be studied, requesting them to recommend additional participants who could provide the needed data. Given that the person recommending other sample members is likely to be known by them, it can strengthen the authenticity and integrity of the researcher. |
| e. | Theoretical sampling | Selecting people to be interviewed on the basis of how likely they have what it takes to give information that will contribute to the theory being developed. Accordingly, the sampling is done in the field based on the pattern of the data rather than being predetermined before the beginning of the study. To an extent, this can also be called purposive sampling. |

designed to help the researcher tease out the data needed from the target respondents. To design a questionnaire, researchers often start with planning before formulating the questions, and checking to be sure the ordering and the length are appropriate for the study and the target respondents. More often than not, they pretest it so that necessary changes can be made before they do a full-blown distribution of the questionnaire. Table 12.5 shows examples of very commonly used questions in a questionnaire and other data collection methods.

**TABLE 12.5** Various types of questions for consumer research questionnaires

| Question Type | Illustrations |
|---|---|
| (1) *Dichotomous Questions:* Having Two Answer Options | Do you own a smartphone? (a) Yes (b) No |
| (2) *Multiple Choice Questions* | Which of the following factors motivated you to buy your Lexus car? (a) Prestige (b) Fuel efficiency (c) Price (d) Warranties (e) Reliability (f) Other (please specify)_____ |
| (3) *Likert Scale* | My participation in social media platforms such as Instagram, Facebook, and X motivates me to buy clothes and shoes. Strongly Disagree (1) Disagree (2) Uncertain (3) Agree (4) Strongly agree (5) |
| (4) *Semantic Differential* | My experience of reading the book *Consumer Behaviour and Digital Transformation* has shown that it is:<br><br>Comprehensive 1 2 3 4 5 6 7 Superficial<br>Educative 1 2 3 4 5 6 7 Uninformative<br>Contemporary 1 2 3 4 5 6 7 Traditional<br>Interesting 1 2 3 4 5 6 7 Boring |
| (5) *Rate Items* | How important would you rate the following factors in influencing your selection of hotels?<br><br>　　　　　　　　　　　　　　　Very Important　　Not Important<br>Opinion of family & friends　　1 2 3 4　　5 6 7<br>Price　　　　　　　　　　　　1 2 3 4　　5 6 7<br>Nearness to city centre　　　　1 2 3 4　　5 6 7<br>Brand name　　　　　　　　　1 2 3 4　　5 6 7<br>Special offers　　　　　　　　1 2 3 4　　5 6 7<br>Online reviews　　　　　　　　1 2 3 4　　5 6 7<br>Facilities offered　　　　　　　1 2 3 4　　5 6 7 |
| (6) *Ranking Scales* | Please rank the following factors that can influence your purchase of a house from the most important to the least important with 1 = most important, 2 = second most important, 3 = third most important, and 4 = least important<br>Nearness to good school　　Nearness to public transportation<br>Nearness to city centre　　Price |
| (7) *Staple Scales* | Please use the following scales to describe the Louis Vuitton bag based on your experience of using it. Choose a positive (+) number for words that you consider to give its description perfectly. The more accurate the given description is in your thought, the greater the plus number you should select. Conversely, choose a negative (-) number for descriptors you think do not describe the bag. The less accurate you think the word is in portraying the feature, the greater the minus number you should choose: |

**TABLE 12.5** (Continued)

| Question Type | Illustrations |
|---|---|

|  | 5 | 5 | 5 |
|---|---|---|---|
|  | 4 | 4 | 4 |
|  | 3 | 3 | 3 |
|  | 2 | 2 | 2 |
|  | 1 | 1 | 1 |
|  | Elegant | Prestigious | Spacious |
|  | -1 | -1 | -1 |
|  | -2 | -2 | -2 |
|  | -3 | -3 | -3 |
|  | -4 | -4 | -4 |
|  | -5 | -5 | -5 |

(8) *Unstructured Questions* — Why do you prefer online shopping for clothing to visiting the store for the same transaction?

(9) *Sentence Completion* — (a) The main reason why I buy Brand X body lotion is_____

(10) *Word Association Method* — Write the first word that comes to your mind at the hearing of the following words:

Artificial intelligence_____

Consumer behaviour_____

COVID-19_____

e-Book_____

Walmart_____

—

(11) *Story Completion* — Please read the following passage and complete the story.
The ten of them are students at the same university and their consumption pattern is interesting, especially when explored in relation to their lifestyle _____

(12) *Lists Methods* — Explore the shopping list of Joseph, Grace, and Margaret and describe each of them in relation to the products they have bought.

| **Joseph** | **Grace** | **Margaret** |
|---|---|---|
| DIY tools | Laundry detergents | Pineapple |
| Shaving foam | School uniform | Olive oil |
| Cereal | Stationeries | Salad dressing |

(13) *Thematic Apperception Test* — The researcher presents a picture to the subjects, who are then asked to write or tell a story about the picture and indicate their thoughts on what is happening in it.

(14) *Rorschach Ink Blot Test* — Ink blots are shown to the subjects, after which the researcher will ask them to tell them what they think they look like. In the form presented to them, the stimulus is incomplete and as the subjects attempt to make sense of the scenario, they will be giving the researcher very useful information.

(*Continued*)

**TABLE 12.5** (Continued)

| Question Type | Illustrations |
|---|---|
| (15) *Picture Completion Method* | In this, the consumer researchers display a picture to the respondents showing them characters in it making statements; they then ask the respondents to respond to the statement shown to have been made by the characters. In some cases, the consumer researchers could offer sketches and cartoons of people in a conversation in a given setting to the respondents and ask them to fill the empty spaces in the cartoon as a response to the messages of the person in the picture. |

## DATA COLLECTION

You may have noticed that a significant part of this chapter has focused on the first two stages in the consumer research process (see Figure 12.2). Having defined the research problem and objectives and formulated an appropriate blueprint for achieving it (research design), it is now the stage to put all the highlighted activities and tasks into action. A well-articulated research design does not turn to the solution needed in itself if the elements of the plan are not implemented. The stage of data collection is when the consumer researchers contact the target respondents to collect the data. By doing this, they are implementing the appropriate sampling plan, administering questionnaires, conducting interviews, moderating the focus group discussion, doing the observation, conducting the consumer research experiment, implementing the research budget, or other applicable research activities.

## DATA ANALYSIS

Whatever route is adopted for the study, be it interpretivism or positivism or any variations of these, researchers are bound to have voluminous raw data from the field. This could be in the form of numerous copies of the completed questionnaire, several pages of interview transcripts, multiple pages of field notes taken from observational studies, or piles of data collected from social media platforms. All of these amount to nothing in these forms if they are not analysed. So, at this stage of data analysis, the consumer researchers look for patterns, put things in tabular form for coherent presentation, and explore relationships and themes. We will now look at data analysis in both quantitative and qualitative forms briefly.

### Quantitative Analysis

Having collected the quantitative data, transforming them from raw data to what many stakeholders can relate to is a major task with huge significance. Essentially, the process at this stage involves some tasks which include the following:

- **Editing**: Checking the questionnaire collected to be sure they are filled in appropriately and demonstrate consistency;

- **Coding:** Allocating numerical values to the information provided by respondents such that they are made ready for computer processing;
- **Data entry:** Entering data into the applicable computer software programme such as MS Excel, Statistical Package for Social Science (SPSS), Statistical Analysis System (SAS).

These three activities help the consumer researcher to get the data into the form fit for the analysis. Hence, they are important to the quality of the output that emerges from the research process. The focus will be on how the data will be presented to ensure that the research objectives are achieved and those who use the document understand what they mean. So, tables, graphs, charts, and explanatory notes will be very relevant to convey the messages at this stage to raise the communication beyond the technical details that served as a means of teasing the findings out from the raw data.

## Qualitative Data Analysis

As indicated earlier, the data collected in qualitative form can be from in-depth interview, focus groups discussion, observational notes, and data from ethnographic studies. Just as there is a need to reduce the data collected in quantitative form to usable form, there is also a need for the consumer researcher to analyse qualitative data collected. Usually, there is a need to transcribe the qualitative data into texts that can be analysed further. From this, researchers engage in coding, which can be done in different ways such as line-by-line, in sentence form, or even on the basis of paragraph by paragraph. Although there are various qualitative data analysis methods, Figure 12.7, which is developed based on the work of Strauss and Corbin (1998), shows an example of different types of coding in the grounded theory methodological stance.

Looking at the explanation of *theoretical sampling* which is often used for grounded theory as given in Table 12.4, the data collection and analysis are closely connected (Glaser and Straus, 1967). This analytical process involves searching for common themes and patterns in the documents, transcripts, and field notes. It is important to stress that this process is expected to begin during the early stages of data collection in the field and will continue to a stage known as *theoretical saturation* which is the stage where the researcher stops the data collection because there are no more new ideas to be added by the inclusion of another interview (Strauss and Corbin, 1998). In bringing the analysis together, the method involves three related coding types known as open coding, axial coding, and selective coding. These codings are facilitated by the principle of constant comparison for the purpose of identifying differences and similarities between the themes. Open coding begins the process and, at that stage, data will be broken down to events, ideas, acts, and discrete incidents. As shown in the figure, the focus here is on conceptualising, discovering categories, and developing them in relation to their properties and dimensions. After this, the next stage is to relate those categories to sub-categories in terms of their properties and dimensions, which is called axial coding. Following the axial coding is the third

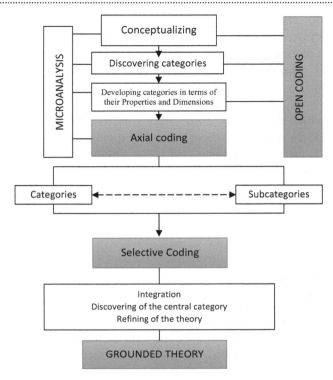

**FIGURE 12.7** Grounded theory data analysis process

level of coding known as selective coding and it is about developing paradigmatic constructs, delineating patterns and relationships, and specifying such relationships (Spiggel, 1994).

## PRESENTATION OF FINDINGS

At the commencement of the research process, the expectation is that the findings of the study will be used by the organisations' decision-makers for strategy formulation. This is the role that this last stage of the research process plays. The researchers will have to make the findings available to the relevant people in a language they will understand. Accordingly, when preparing the final report, the researchers will need to know who will read the report and how the message of the report can be tailored to them. In some cases, tables, graphs, charts, and diagrams will be needed to make the findings clear and comprehensive. There may be different audiences for this final report and translating the language to suit different groups or giving verbatim quotes from the study participants would make the report valuable. Although there may be little variations in the outline and content of the final report depending on the specific circumstances of the research, the report to be written will most likely have the following segments as shown in Figure 12.8.

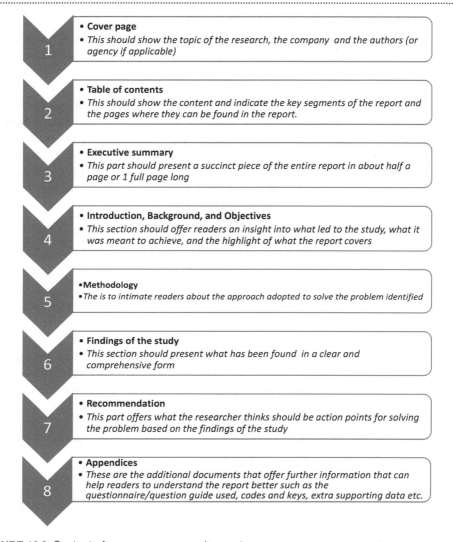

**FIGURE 12.8** Content of a consumer research report

## NETNOGRAPHY IN CONSUMER RESEARCH

One of the key themes that runs through this book is that consumers of today are interacting more with technology and exploring computer-mediated communications in their day-to-day transactions. Accordingly, among the changes to marketing research in recent times is the increase in avenues for collecting data digitally. Netnography is the equivalent of ethnography conducted in the digital context. As indicated by Kozinets (2002), as consumers debate and discuss in online communities, it is of paramount importance that those researching relevant topics also have ethical and rigorous methodological procedures in place for collecting and analysing the data in this challenging and novel context. What has been established is that ethnography is often known as the anthropological method and commonly used in cultural studies, sociology, consumer research, and many other social science contexts, which involves observation and participation in specific cultural arenas and is characterised by acknowledgement and adoption of researcher reflexivity (Kozinets, 2002). We can explain netnography as a written account that emerges from the study of culture and commodities, which emanates from the communication that takes place on the Internet in which the fieldwork and the textual interpretation follow the techniques and tradition of cultural anthropology (Kozinets, 1998). Given that it is amenable to collecting and managing the depth of data collection and analysis in an online setting, it has been a popular choice for consumer research in various contexts such as tourism, retailing, and several others. Essentially, it is about teasing out relevant information from online settings such as user-generated content like online reviews, and the 'electronic word of mouse' (Mkono and Markwell, 2014). This popularity is not surprising as the methodology addresses complex phenomena, excels in storytelling, and aids marketing researchers in the development of relevant themes from the viewpoint of the consumers (Rageh et al., 2013; Thanh and Kirova, 2018). In the way it works, it can be used as a sole method for inquiry or be used in combination with other methods both online or offline (Costello et al., 2017). Characteristically, the method is also useful for content analysis, long-term embedded research, and unobtrusive observation in online communities (Quinton and Wilson, 2016; Lugosi and Quinton, 2018). These characteristics are seen in the study of Kozinets (2002) about the activities of coffee drinkers in their online interactions discussing issues such as home-brewing, decaffeinated drinking, and home-roasting in relation to Starbucks products, where the study shows online activities including social and communal relationships and several others that transcend these.

In application, the steps often adopted for the study to achieve qualitative rigour as suggested by Kozinets (2002) are highlighted below:

- **Entrée:** This first stage is about setting the relevant research questions that the study focuses on as well as identifying and learning about the individuals and online fora to approach and explore for the research;
- **Data collection and analysis:** This is about copying data from the computer-mediated communications of the members of the forum and being mindful of the data inscribed into the communication as part of the process of observing the community;
- **Providing trustworthy interpretation:** Making sense of the data and the interactions of the members of the online forum in a trustworthy manner;
- **Conducting ethical research:** This is an inclusive aspect of the research in terms of what it covers. It is about focusing on issues such as full disclosure of the researcher's intention, confidentiality, anonymity, and informed consent;
- **Member checks:** The focus on this is about soliciting comments from some or all of the members of the forum on the findings of the study to be sure that they reflect the investigated dynamics of the forum.

## BIG DATA IN CONTEMPORARY MARKETING RESEARCH: AN OVERVIEW

As the use of technology in business increases in terms of scale and significance, the impact of the development is wide-ranging. This also gives businesses opportunities and access to unprecedented volumes of data in various ways. The Internet has opened up new forms of data to marketers. Data about consumers come from a variety of sources such as social media and in the form of Internet of Things (IoT) multimedia. In the explanation given by Akhtar et al. (2017), Internet of Things covers those devices with network connectivity and the ability to not only send but also receive data associated with other connected objects, which has developed as one of the key technologies in recent times. So, with this opening, let us turn to the subject of Big Data. The term has been explained as the set of data and technology that accesses, integrates, and reports all accessible data through filtering, correlating, and reporting insights that could not have been achieved through past data technology systems (APICS, 2012; Kude et al., 2017). To make it clearer, let us look at another definition of the term. It is defined as the '… artefact of human individual as well as collective intelligence generated and shared mainly through the technological environment, where virtually anything and everything can be documented, measured, and captured digitally, and in so doing transformed into data' (Sivarajah et al., 2017: 263). Another way to have a deeper understanding of Big Data is to look at the differences it has in comparison to traditional data. Essentially, these are identified by Laney (2001) as the following 3Vs:

- Volume;
- Variety;
- Velocity.

According to relevant literature (Fan and Bifet, 2013; Amado et al., 2018), two more distinguishing factors have been added to these three, making a total of five. So, the additional two are:

- Variability;
- Value.

In terms of components and layers, Mysore et al. (2013) indicates that Big Data has four layers, which are:

- **Big Data sources:** Various channels from which the data emerge;
- **Data messaging and store:** The layer about acquisition and storage of the data;
- **Analysis:** The layer where the extraction of data and insights takes place;
- **Consumption:** The usage of the analysis of the layer results.

Clearly, Big Data (BD) is not only getting bigger but also becoming increasingly acknowledged. Focusing on it has been regarded as a very rewarding undertaking for marketers in many ramifications. It is noted as useful for supporting decision making in relation to answering some key issues such as knowing the most suitable product for a specific market, what communication channel to use to advertise to them, how to advertise such market offerings, at what price, and many others (Amado et al., 2018). Another set of examples of the use of Big Data is listed by Paas (2019): It can help in relation to retention models, supporting the design of customer segmentation, prospect selection for marketing, campaign, and credit scoring models. In a view that stresses most of these benefits, Orenga-Roglá and Chalmeta (2016) add that, in the context of social CRM, Big Data offers marketers competitive intelligence, commercial recommendations, routing of customer interactions over any channel, 360° customer view, predictive models of trend, and automated categorisation. To sum it together, it can help firms to achieve new levels of efficiency in how marketing orientation is managed (Zhang and Song, 2022).

## NEUROMARKETING AND THE CONTEMPORARY CONSUMER RESEARCH

Conducting research by soliciting for information from the consumers is very common in marketing research. However, there has been a critical look at the effectiveness of this in recent times. Sometimes, participants may not be as forthcoming or truthful as necessary for the study. To what extent can we rely on information provided by respondents on the type of product or brand they claim to use, the frequency of purchase, or the specific factors that influenced the purchase decisions? Neuromarketing has been described as a key approach to addressing this limitation. It is about using neuroimaging, psychological, and physiological tools for recording the neutral correlates of consumer behaviour in relation to market stimuli such as prices, advertisements, packaging, or brands (Alsharif et al., 2021). In another somewhat similar definition, it is described as using non-invasive brain signal recording technology for directly collecting information such as consumers' feedback on marketing stimuli like packaging, advertising messages, and brands, instead of the conventional or traditional investigation methods (Rawnaque et al., 2020; Zhu et al., 2022). The term, which was introduced in 2002 by Ale Smidts (Hussein 2019; Chi, 20 et al., 2022), is formed as a combination of the words neuroscience and marketing. While neuroscience is about the study of the brain dynamics, marketing is about creating, delivering, or co-creating value with the customer, which is expected to ultimately lead to their satisfaction, and profitability for the firm. Now let us look at how it works. Essentially, the neuromarketing tools can be classified into three as indicated by Lim (2018), as shown below:

Those that record neural activity inside the brain:

- Electroencephalography (EEG);
- Magneto-encephalography (MEG);
- Steady state topography (SST);
- Functional magnetic resonance imaging (fMRI);
- Positron emission tomography (PET).

Those that record neural activity outside the brain:

- Electroencephalography (EEG);
- Eye tracking (ET);
- Skin conductance (SC);
- Facial electromyography (fEMG).

Those that manipulate neural activity:

- Transcranial magnetic stimulation (TMS);
- Neurotransmitter (NT).

Neuromarketing as a tool has grown in popularity in recent times. Studies have shown that EEG and fMRI are the most commonly used in neuromarketing studies (Aisharif et al., 2021). Meyerding and Mehlhose (2020) describe it as decoding a shopper's brain and indicate that it is valuable to marketing research in that it offers an understanding of the underlying processes that result in consumer purchase behaviour. According to them, it can be a guide to the design of the product in relation to the labels and brands. It has also been shown to be useful for the design of effective pricing strategies, especially in the service business (Fugate, 2008). On the other hand, it has to be said that it is a relatively more expensive approach compared to traditional marketing research approaches. In relation to this, it is also important to note that it relies on relatively small samples such the commonly used sample of six to ten participants for fMRI experiments (Meyerding and Mehlhose, 2020). Despite the increasing popularity of the research approach, it has raised some ethical questions which remain points of debate in the literature. For example, it has been argued that the method could give insight and access to the unconscious mind of the participants, resulting in manipulating their purchase behaviour thereby raising the issues of privacy in the consumer research ethic context (Hussein, 2019). So, critics feel that it could be used to target and exploit vulnerable consumers such as economically disadvantaged consumers, children, and the elderly (Hussein, 2019). In that sense, strengthening the appropriate regulatory frameworks on this and similar marketing activities could help to normalise or minimise potential ethical problems.

## ETHICS AND CONSUMER RESEARCH

Generally, the notion of ethics is about what is right and wrong in a given scenario. So, there are ethical issues associated with virtually all phenomena including consumer research. When considering all the data collection and management tools, methods, and processes we have discussed in this chapter, it is imperative to also consider the ethical issues that underpin them. It is about being sensitive to the rights of others, especially in human sciences where people relate to one another (Bulmer, 2003); in this case consumer researchers are studying consumers who are participants in their studies. The challenge associated with doing this becomes even wider in scope as technology increases the opportunity for data collection using different approaches such as we discussed in neuromarketing. Figure 12.9 presents a sketch of the commonly discussed ethical issues in consumer research as teased out from Fontana and Frey (1998), Robson (2002), and Marshall (2023).

As shown in the figure, when conducting research, participants would expect the researchers to be open about the focus of the study rather than being deceived into participating in what they did not prepare for. This is closely linked to the need to adhere to informed consent and ensuring that they participate voluntarily such that they can withdraw from the process at any stage. To volunteer as participants in a study, be it experiment, observation, survey, or in any other way, it is expected that the respondents will be protected from all conceivable harm such as physical or emotional harm. Apart from the need to treat them courteously, participants are also entitled to their privacy and should have their identity protected as expected in relation to the study at hand. The danger of reporting data collected inaccurately can be huge. So, it is an ethical requirement that the researcher should use all means possible to ensure the accuracy of the data collected to avoid misleading the stakeholders. As with several other sectors where there are regulatory bodies that focus on maintaining ethical standards in the profession or sector like the medical profession, pharmaceutical profession, and advertising practitioners, there are some regulatory bodies that focus on getting marketing researchers to adhere to these and other relevant ethical guidelines for their research. An example of this is the Marketing Research Society (MRS), which is widely acknowledged for this role.

**FIGURE 12.9** Common ethical issues in consumer research

### PAUSE, PLAN, AND PRACTICE: HILTON, SOCIAL MEDIA, AND CONSUMER RESEARCH

Hilton is one of the world's leading organisations in the hospitality business. It operates in over 120 countries and offers more than 7000 hotels from which its target market can choose. It has recorded many success stories. While the organisation is focused on excellent customer service with creating value for them and making them loyal to the brand, its effort in research cannot be discounted in this package. The effort of the company for obtaining data is noticeable, especially in relation to the use of contemporary methods such as 'social listening'. The organisation examines comments given by people about the brand and its services on social media from X (formerly Twitter), which is the most popular platform used for discussing the brand, to Facebook, YouTube, and others. This is an acknowledgement that social media is now a big mode of communication among their target consumers. Some of those who comment about the brands would be showing photographs of the beautiful rooms where they stayed, while others comment about their experiences. Nonetheless, while there are more positive comments than negative ones, the organisation also does not ignore the latter category in that it reviews, analyses, and uses them to improve its services and ensure customer loyalty.

#### Sources

Bredava, A. (2018). Case study: How Hilton uses social media listening to win customers, *Awario*, http://awario.com/blog/hilton-social-media-case-study/ (accessed 26 June 2023).

Hilton (nd), Join Hilton Honors and get up to 3,000 Bonus Points on your next two stays, www.hilton.com/en/?WT.mc_id=zINDA0EMEA1MB2PSH3GGL4INTCRB5dkt6MULTIBR7_121127646_1003528_p7954679738&&ads_rl=7695469998&&&&gclsrc=3p.ds&&msclkid=5ac16bf648f110e9e2220e4c7f10bfc6&gclid=5ac16bf648f110e9e2220e4c7f10bfc6&gclsrc=3p.ds (accessed, 31st January, 2024).

Naeringavisen (nd). How many rooms does Hilton have?, http://næringsavisen.no/nyu-langone/how-many-rooms-does-hilton-have (accessed 26 June 2023).

#### QUESTIONS

As Hilton continues to do 'social listening', what ethical issues do you think the organisation should take into consideration? Would this be different if the focus is on the traditional data collection method?

## SUMMARY

Consumer behaviour is a complex and interesting phenomenon. Hence, it is important for marketers to have a good understanding of how it works. Doing this will mean that the needs and wants of the target market can be known and more effectively managed. Before commissioning a marketing research project, a firm would need to decide and check the trade-off of whether to handle the research itself as a company or pay for the services of a research agency to do it for them. If the latter approach is adopted, then there is a need for both the firm and the agency to exchange relevant information. While the firm commissioning the consumer research gives a research brief to the agency, the latter responds by providing the research proposal. Since consumer behaviour is being significantly influenced by technology, accordingly, all the stages involved in conducting consumer research have also been significantly impacted by digitalisation. Meanwhile, more contemporary issues in consumer research such as Big Data, neuromarketing, and ethnography, are now more relevant to conducting various studies and they have also widened the scope of consumer research ethics as well.

---

**DIGITAL BOX: SURVEYMONKEY FOR CONSUMER RESEARCH DATA COLLECTION**

To business organisations, charities, students, and other categories of consumer researchers, SurveyMonkey has been a highly regarded data collection solution over the years. They know that having the research problem and objectives well-defined will provide the needed solution to addressing them. Data collection is a critical and invaluable aspect of the research process. With the popularity of the survey data collection approach, SurveyMonkey offers researchers the opportunity to collect survey data in a flexible and non-complicated form. The target respondents may be in any continent of the world; digitalisation now means that such respondents can be reached for data collection online which could be by email, weblinks, or embedded on the website of the sponsor of the research at an incredible speed. As indicated by the company on its website, it asks over 25 million questions daily. By implication, these are efforts towards creating value for the consumers because answers to these questions will serve as input to strategic formulation in the sponsoring organisation towards satisfying the customers. Its operations over the past two decades of providing solutions to research of different types have been lauded among academics and practitioners. While it is managed by Momentive as an organisation, many researchers all over the world where it is being used including New York, Berlin, London, Canada, and Australia, are more aware of SurveyMonkey as a brand. The organisation is so proud of its achievements of offering user-friendly survey questions to the over 17 million active users and more than 345,000 organisations. The possibilities of having this in many languages, billions of questions managed over the years, and the creation of exceptional experience in research for various stakeholders globally are just examples of many ways SurveyMonkey and digitalisation have positively changed the dynamics of consumer research.

**Source**

Create free surveys and forms online in minutes, SurveyMonkey: http://www.surveymonkey.co.uk/?ut_source=sem_lp&ut_source2=sem&ut_source3=header (accessed 26 June 2023).

**QUESTION/TASK**

1. Design ten questions related to consumer attitude and behaviour concerning any product or service of your choice and send them through SurveyMonkey to ten of your friends or classmates;
2. Discuss the difference between this approach and the traditional method of doing survey research. What are the similarities and differences?

## END OF CHAPTER DISCUSSION QUESTIONS

1. Assume you have been approached with a consumer research brief indicating that sales and profit figures of a new body lotion launched onto the market a decade ago have reduced for the third time in a row. A preliminary investigation indicates that consumers' attitudes to this product are no longer favourable. Develop a research proposal showing the key elements including objectives, methodology, and significance of the study;
2. Assume you have been invited to a debate club where some speakers have argued that the following pairs of data simply refer to the same thing with no difference between them. As a marketing student with good knowledge of marketing and consumer research terminologies, present your case to debunk this position:
   a) Ethnography and netnography;
   b) Big Data and primary data;
   c) Marketing research brief and marketing research proposal;
   d) Cluster sampling and purposive sampling;
   e) Structured observation and unstructured observation.
3. The increase in the use of digital technology has impacted many aspects of marketing including consumer research. Discuss.
4. Select a consumer behaviour related topic for research and design a questionnaire to use for the data collection phase of the research. Ensure that you have a total of 25 questions which should be allocated as follows:
   a. Respondents' characteristics (5);
   b. Multiple-choice questions (5);
   c. Likert Scale questions (5);
   d. Dichotomous scale (5);
   e. Open-ended questions (5).
5. The notion of ethics in consumer research has never been considered more serious than now, especially in the collection and use of primary data. In view of this discuss the key ethical issues to be considered by a marketing researcher who has decided to use neuromarketing in the test of a new soft drink to be launched the next Summer.

### Case Study: Big Data and Consumer Research in British Supermarkets

Supermarkets are generally known for their critical role in the retail business. In the United Kingdom (UK), supermarkets like Morrisons, ASDA, Sainsbury's, and Tesco are household names because of the roles they play daily in creating value for various segments of the British market, especially in relation to the sales of grocery items. In reflection back to 2021, a figure of around £211.9 billion was reported as the total market value of grocery retailing in the UK. This is projected to increase to about £241 billion by the year 2027. These are significant figures which show that consumers have turned back to shopping and have a 'big basket' again after the global pandemic that affected most aspects of lives including shopping. Evidence shows that about 46.5% of these grocery sales for the year 2022 came from just supermarkets or large-format stores. Whether the market is segmented on the basis of demography, geography, consumption behavioural pattern, or psychography, there are some inherent complexities associated with the operations of the supermarkets. In one form or another, consumers that visit supermarkets either offline or online are looking for laundry and cleaning products, toiletries and beauty products, fruits and vegetables, dairy products, and meat and poultry items to mention but a few, to satisfy their needs. Meanwhile, meeting the needs of this heterogenous market is a challenge but very rewarding when it is handled effectively. Among the challenges are the level of diversity that characterises the consumers in the country, and the volume of data to handle and manage to be able to serve the nation as a community. Moreover, several products sold in the supermarkets become spoilt quickly, hence, if not managed properly, can result in significant losses.

Supermarkets work with various other organisations in order to be able to create value for their customers. The flow of data linked to supermarkets that relates to operating and satisfying their customers does not just begin from the organisation, it is linked to various other actors and stakeholders in the business network. A clear example is the data connecting the various suppliers of the products and services to the organisations. There are local and international suppliers like farmers producing and supplying the items needed by supermarkets to meet the needs of their customers. It is imperative for these supermarkets to keep track of their activities and transactions with these suppliers in all ramifications. Data relating to order processing, delivery, and many others are crucial to the efficiency and smooth running of these retailing organisations. Meanwhile, the bulk of data lies in customer-facing operations. The supermarkets need to keep track of their stock levels, order processing, transportation interactions, and warehousing activities. This will help in many ways, especially in the handling of perishable items. It will be relevant to minimise waste as records show that around 1.3 billion tonnes of food become wasted every year at the global level. Although the core aspects of the supermarkets are groceries, many of them are now adding more product lines such as financial services like insurance products, clothing, and many others. The more of these they add, the more the volume, variety, and velocity of the data that are needed by the organisations in order to carefully manage and inform their decisions. These are big issues that involve Big Data. So, Big Data analysis can help offer insights into managing these products into profitability.

Opportunities associated with digital processes have opened numerous other sources of data to these supermarkets. Some of the consumers of the products offered by them are already adept with the use of technology and gradually embracing online grocery shopping. Their online transactions and activities are being recorded so that they can form part of the inputs to the decision of the supermarkets. In a similar view, some of the consumers are following the supermarkets on social media such as Facebook, Instagram, and YouTube. Data such as social media posts, comments, and likes of these in relation to their brands are part of the data that feed into their decisions to ensure that provisions are made appropriately. Data from the self-service system, loyalty cards, and other areas add to enrich their data system. These can give insights into customer buying preferences as well as patterns and frequency of purchase. Hence, Big Data Analytics (BDA) can help supermarkets to build and manage customer loyalty and is of great value to stakeholders in order to meet their dynamic needs and reduce waste.

**Sources**

Bedford, E. (2022). United Kingdom: Grocery retail market value 2020–2027, by channel, Sep 28, 2022, http://www.statista.com/statistics/295656/grocery-retail-market-value-by-channel-in-the-united-kingdom-uk/ (accessed 30 June 2023).

Carroll, N. (2022). UK supermarkets market report, http://store.mintel.com/report/uk-supermarkets-market-report (accessed 30 June 2023).

ONS (2021). Retail sales: Great Britain: December, 2021, http://www.ons.gov.uk/businessindustryandtrade/retailindustry/bulletins/retailsales/December2021 (accessed 30 June 2023).

Quantzig (2021). How are Big Data supermarkets revolutionizing the shopping experience?, November, 2021, http://www.quantzig.com/blog/big-data-can-supermarkets/ (accessed 30 June 2023).

## QUESTIONS

1. Explain why Big Data Analytics (BDA) is considered useful to British supermarkets;
2. List some examples of secondary data that can help supermarkets as they focus on customer-centred operations;
3. Assume one of the leading UK supermarkets has approached you to conduct primary research into dwindling consumer attitudes towards its brands. Which of the possible research designs would you use and why?
4. Do you think adopting online data collection exclusively can give rich and valuable data for research to determine UK consumers' supermarket preferences?

## REFERENCES

Akhtar, P., Khan, Z., Tarba, S., & Jayawickrama, U. (2017). The Internet of Things, dynamic data and information processing capabilities, and operational agility. *Technological Forecasting and Social Change*, 136, 307–316.

Alsharif, A. H., Md Salleh, N. Z., Baharun, R., & Rami Hashem E, A. (2021). Neuromarketing research in the last five years: A bibliometric analysis. *Cogent Business & Management*, 8(1), 1978620.

Amado, A., Cortez, P., Rita, P., & Moro, S. (2018). Research trends on Big Data in marketing: A text mining and topic modeling-based literature analysis. *European Research on Management and Business Economics*, 24(1), 1–7.

APICS (2012). APICS 2012 big data insights and innovations executive summary, available at: http://www.apics.org/docs/industry-content/apics-2012-big-data-executive-summary.pdf?sfvrsn=0/ (accessed 4 December 2014).

Bernard, H. R. (2000). *'Social Research Methods', Qualitative and Quantitative Approaches*, p. 502, London: Sage Publication Limited.

Bryman, A. (2001). Social Research Methods, pp. 224–264. New York: Oxford University Press.

Bulmer, M. (2003). The ethics of social research, in Gilbert, N. (ed.) *Researching Social Life*, 2nd edn., pp. 45–57, London: Sage Publications Ltd.

Burns, A. C. and Bush, R. F. (1998). *Marketing Research*, 2nd edn, p. 209. Upper Saddle River, NJ: Prentice Hall, Inc.

Chi, A. (2022). A brief history of neuromarketing, Boonmind, http://www.boonmind.com/a-brief-history-of-neuromarketing/ (accessed 15 June 2023).

Churchill, Jr., G. A., & Iacobucci, D. (2005). *Marketing Research: Methodological Foundation*, 9th edn, Ohio: South-Western.

Collis, J., & Hussey, R. (2003). *Business Research: A Practical Guide for Undergraduate and Postgraduate Students*, 2nd edn, pp. 46–47, New York: Palgrave Macmillan.

Costello, L., McDermott, M. L., & Wallace, R. (2017). Netnography: Range of practices, misperceptions, and missed opportunities. *International Journal of Qualitative Methods*, 16(1), 1609406917700647.

Cronin, A. (2003). Focus groups, in Gilbert, N. (ed.) *Researching Social Life*, 2nd edn., pp. 164–167, London: Sage Publication Ltd.

Denscombe, M. (1998). *The Good Research Guide for Small-scale Social Research Projects*. Buckingham: Open University Press.

Denzin, N. K., & Lincoln, Y. S. (1998). Major paradigms and perspectives, in Denzin, N. K., and Lincoln, Y. S. (eds) *The Landscape of Qualitative Research: Theories and Issues*, pp. 185–193, Thousand Oaks, CA: Sage Publications Inc.

Easterby-Smith, M., Thorpe, R., & Lowe, A. (1991). *Management Research: An Introduction*. London: Sage.

Fan, W., & Bifet, A. (2013). Mining Big Data: Current status, and forecast to the future. ACM sIGKDD Explorations Newsletter, 14(2), 1–5.

Fontana, A., & Frey, J. H. (1998). Interviewing: The Art of Science, in Denzin, N. and Lincoln, Y. S. (eds) *Collecting and Interpreting Qualitative Materials*. Thousand Oaks, CA: Sage Publications, Inc.

Fugate, D. L. (2008). Marketing services more effectively with neuromarketing research: A look into the future. *Journal of Services Marketing*, 22(2), 170–173.

Gbadamosi, A. (2009). Cognitive dissonance: The implicit explication in low-income consumers' shopping behaviour for 'low-involvement' grocery products. *International Journal of Retail and Distribution Management*, 37(12), 1077–1095.

Gbadamosi, A. (2010). *Low-income Consumer Behaviour: A Contextual Focus on Women and Low-involvement Grocery Products*. Germany: LAP LAMBERT Academic Publishing.

Gbadamosi, A. (2019). Ethics and sustainable marketing, in Gbadamosi, A. (ed.) *Contemporary Issues in Marketing*, pp. 185–218, London: SAGE.

Gbadamosi, A., and Pandya, K. V. (2013), Managing marketing information for value creation, in Gbadamosi, A., Bathgate, I., and Nwankwo, S. (eds), *Principles of Marketing: A Value-based Approach*, pp. 104–138. Basingstoke: Palgrave Macmillan.

Glaser, B. G., & Strauss, A. L. (1967). *The Discovery of Grounded Theory*. Chicago: Aldine Publishing.

Gray, D. E. (2004). *Doing Research in the Real World*. London: Sage Publications Ltd.

Guba, E. G. (1990). *The Paradigm Dialog*, p. 17. Newbury Park: Sage Publications, Ltd.

Hussein, N. H. (2019). Neuromarketing, in Gbadamosi, A. (ed.) *Contemporary Issues in Marketing*, pp. 96–117, London: SAGE.

Hussey, J., & Hussey, R. (1997). *Business Research: A Practical Guide for Undergraduate and Postgraduate Students*. London: Macmillan Press Ltd.

Indeed (2023). 14 national and international market research companies, 22 May 2023, http://uk.indeed.com/career-advice/finding-a-job/market-research-companies#:~:text= 14%20examples%20of%20market%20research%20companies%20for%20employment,...%208%208.%20Acumen%20Fieldwork%20...%20More%20items (accessed 29 May 2023).

Kotler, P. (2003). *Marketing Management*, 11th edn, pp. 132–133, Upper Saddle River, NJ: Pearson Education, Inc.

Kotler, P., & Armstrong, G. (2006). *Principles of Marketing*, 11th edn, pp. 100–101, Upper Saddle River, NJ: Pearson Education, Inc.

Kotler, P., Armstrong, G., Saunders, J., & Wong, V. (1999). *Principles of Marketing: Second European Edition*, p. 317, London: Prentice-Hall Europe.

Kozinets, R. V. (1998). On netnography: Initial reflections on consumer research investigations of cyberculture, in Alba, J., & Hutchinson, W. (eds), *Advances in Consumer Research*, Vol. 25, pp. 366–371. Provo, UT: Association for Consumer Research.

Kozinets, R. V. (2002). The field behind the screen: Using netnography for marketing research in online communities. *Journal of Marketing Research*, 39(1), 61–72.

Kude, T., Hoehle, H., & Sykes, T. A. (2017). Big data breaches and customer compensation strategies: Personality traits and social influence as antecedents of perceived compensation. *International Journal of Operations & Production Management*, 37(1), 56–74.

Laney, D. (2001). 3D data management: Controlling data volume, velocity and variety. META Group Research Note, 6, 70–73.

Lim, W. M. (2018). Demystifying neuromarketing. *Journal of Business Research*, 91, 205–220.

Lugosi, P., & Quinton, S. (2018). More-than-human netnography. *Journal of Marketing Management*, 34(3–4), 287–313.

Malhotra, N. K., & Birks, D. F. (2003). *Marketing Research: An Applied Approach*, 2nd European edn, pp. 183–184, 218, 468, Essex: Pearson Education Limited.

Marshall, A. (2023). *Marketing Research: A Managerial Approach*. London: SAGE.

Marshall, C., & Rossman, G. B. (1999). *Designing Qualitative Research*, 3rd edn, London: Sage Publications, Inc.

Mason, J. (2002). *Qualitative Researching*, 2nd edn, p. 25, London: Sage Publications Ltd.

May, T. (2001). *Social Research: Issues, Methods and Process*, 3rd edn, Buckingham: Open University Press.

McDaniel, C., & Gates, R. (1998). *Marketing Research Essentials*, pp. 5–10, 179, Ohio: South Western College Publishing.

Meyerding, S. G., & Mehlhose, C. M. (2020). Can neuromarketing add value to the traditional marketing research? An exemplary experiment with functional near-infrared spectroscopy (fNIRS). *Journal of Business Research*, 107, Issue C, 172–185.

Mkono, M., & Markwell, K. (2014). The application of netnography in tourism studies. *Annals of Tourism Research*, 48, 289–291.

Morgan, G. (1979). Response to Mintzberg. *Administrative Science Quarterly*, 24(1), 137–139.

Myers, J. H. (1986). *Marketing*. Singapore: McGraw-Hill.

Mysore, D., Khupat, S., & Jain, S. (2013). Big Data architecture and patterns. Part 3: Understanding the architectural layers of a big data solution, developerWorks. IBM, http://www.ibm.com/developerworks/library/bd-archpatterns3/ (accessed 11 December 2023).

Orenga-Roglá, S., & Chalmeta, R. (2016). Social customer relationship management: Taking advantage of Web 2.0 and Big Data technologies. *SpringerPlus*, 5(1), 1462.

Paas, L. (2019). Marketing research education in the Big Data era. *International Journal of Market Research*, 61(3), 233–235.

Quinton, S., & Wilson, D. (2016). Tensions and ties in social media networks: Towards a model of understanding business relationship development and business performance enhancement through the use of LinkedIn. *Industrial Marketing Management*, 54, 15–24. doi:10.1016/j. indmarman.2015.12.001

Rageh, A., Melewar, T. C., & Woodside, A. G. (2013). Using netnography research method to reveal the underlying dimensions of the customer/tourist experience. *Qualitative Market Research: An International Journal*, 16(2), 126–149.

Rawnaque, F. S., Rahman, K. M., Anwar, S. F., Vaidyanathan, R., Chau, T., Sarker, F., et al. (2020). Technological advancements and opportunities in neuromarketing: A systematic review. *Brain Informatics*, 7, 1–19.

Robson, C. (2002). *Real Word Research: A Resource for Social Scientists and Practitioner-Researchers*, 2nd edn, Massachusetts: Blackwell Publishers Inc.

Saunders, M. N. K., Lewis, P., & Thornhill, A. (2023). *Research Methods for Business Students*, 9th edn. Harlow: Pearson Education Ltd.

Sivarajah, U., Kamal, M. M., Irani, Z., & Weerakkody, V. (2017). Critical analysis of Big Data challenges and analytical methods. *Journal of Business Research*, 70, 263–286.

Solomon, M. R. (2020), *Consumer Behaviour: Buying, Having, and Being*, 13th edn,: Essex: Pearson Education Limited.

Spiggle, S. (1994). Analysis and interpretation of qualitative data in consumer research. *Journal of Consumer Research*, 21(3), 491–503.

Strauss, A., & Corbin, J. (1998). *Basics of Qualitative Research – Techniques and Procedure for Developing Grounded Theory*. Thousand Oaks, CA: Sage Publications.

Thanh, T. V., & Kirova, V. (2018). Wine tourism experience: A netnography study. *Journal of Business Research*, 83, 30–37.

Tonkiss, F. (2004). Using focus groups, in Seale, C. (ed.), pp. 193–206, *Researching Society and Culture*. London: Sage Publications Ltd.

Tull, D. S., & Hawkins, D. I. (1987). *Marketing Research: Measurement and Method*, 4th edn, New York: Macmillan Publishing Company.

Welman, C., Kruger, F., & Mitchell, B. (2005) *Research Methodology*, 3rd edn, Southern Africa: Oxford University Press.

Wilkinson, S. (2004). Focus group research, in Silverman, D. (ed.) pp. 177–199, *Qualitative Research, Method and Practice*, London: Sage Publications.

Zhang, H., & Song, M. (2022). How Big Data analytics, AI, and social media marketing research boost market orientation. *Research-Technology Management*, 65(2), 64–70.

Zhu, Z., Jin, Y., Su, Y., Jia, K., Lin, C. L., & Liu, X. (2022). Bibliometric-based evaluation of the neuromarketing research trend: 2010–2021. *Frontiers in Psychology*, 13, 872468.

Zikmund, W. G. (1997). *Exploring Marketing Research*, 6th edn, pp. 428–429, Fort Worth, TX: The Dryden Press.

# CHAPTER 13

# Consumer Behaviour and Technology

## A Look into the Future

### LEARNING OUTCOME

After reading this chapter, you should be able to:

- Explore the future of technology and consumer behaviour;
- Discuss the role of artificial intelligence and the associated emerging thought;
- Discuss customer segmentation, targeting, and positioning;
- Discuss consumer personas and its relevance in consumption;
- Explain the role of consumer demographics and webographics in consumption.

### INTRODUCTION

The fact that the world is immersed in technology is now a widely held view. Looking back 20 years ago to what we do now as consumers will reveal a radical change in the pattern of living. From the moment we wake up in the morning to the last minute before going to bed, we encounter technology in one form or another. Although in varying ways, consumers of various segments interact with technology. We often hear of Generation Y, X, Z, and Alpha, and others as well as voice recognition, touch screen face recognition devices, and many more. The past, present, and the predicted future of consumption are changing. This development does not take place in isolation, every factor and force in the marketing environment is dynamic. It is now crystal clear that we have not seen the end of development in the world of artificial intelligence (AI). To succeed in delighting them in the turbulent marketing environment, it is imperative for marketers to do a thorough customer analysis. As the scope of consumers' needs expands, the notion of segmentation, targeting, and positioning (STP) will be a relevant strategic tool. As the conventional application of this tool offers some level of solution to the marketing world, some more contemporary focus

DOI: 10.4324/9781003242031-17

of meeting needs will continue to emerge. An understanding of consumers' personas with relevance to their characteristics such as demographics and webographics is considered germane. It is expected that this will be a key antecedent to consumer trust and loyalty, which is a bedrock of successful marketplace dynamics. Our focus in this concluding chapter is to look at the interaction of these elements in relation to the role of technology in the future of the consumption system.

## THE FUTURE OF TECHNOLOGY AND CONSUMER BEHAVIOUR

The marketing environment is very dynamic with changes experienced continuously in several aspects. One of the most obvious of these is the changes in the use and experience of technology in consumption. The process of digital transformation for organisations consisting of three stages, as given by Perkin and Abraham (2017), involves:

- Legacy;
- Enabling;
- Naturalising.

At the legacy stage, the thought revolves around checking which of the conventional ideas and processes will be kept and which will be jettisoned. When an organisation is at the stage of enabling, the focus has changed in that the organisation has made a shift in mindset around resources, strategy, processes, and culture towards the new approach, but efforts are underway for maintaining these new elements. In the naturalising stage, the organisation has fully embraced digital transformation and has tuned in to the changing environment evident in its culture and operations. Given this schema, it is logical to indicate that the stage at which an organisation operates will most likely vary. However, given the pace at which consumers' demands are changing in in favour of consumption within a digital context, any organisation that delays action in their transition to digital space may be unable to satisfy the customers due to changing tastes and does so at its own peril. Times are changing, consumption patterns are shifting as technology becomes pervasive. As indicated by Khoa (2020), banking transactions have developed in various ways including the use of ATMs and online transactions, and these have constituted new added value for consumers.

Let us look at one of the common technological innovations in marketing and consumption, self-service technology (SST). One clear benefit of this is that consumers are able to be actively involved in the service they experience (Robertson et al., 2012). As good as they look and sound to the consumption experience, there are cases of failures where things may have gone contrary to expectations. As in the mainstream service marketing literature, when things go wrong with SST, it is expected that a service recovery will be put in place. Over the years, there have been two relevant guarantees that are often offered as solutions to this context (Wirtz et al., 2000; Van Looy et al., 2003: Robertson et al., 2012). These are:

- Unconditional guarantees;
- Attribute-specific guarantees.

When the service provider offers unconditional guarantees, it means that the consumer can evoke this in relation to the core service offerings involved in the transaction when there is a gap between their expectation and actual experience. The scope of what is covered in the attribute-specific guarantee is rather narrow in that it only relates to a specific attribute of the services or a combination of some of them rather than covering the core services being provided by the firm. As shown by Robertson et al. (2012), the attribute-specific type of guarantee is the one commonly applied for SST. They suggest that the easier it is for consumers to make claims in respect of the guarantees given concerning SST, the better or more delighted the consumers will be in the form. Imagine there is a guarantee that if the vending machine could not serve you within five minutes after applying the correct and appropriate payment, you would be entitled to a full refund and a free drink. To perceive procedural justice in this, the process for claiming these should not be frustrating. Otherwise, the dissatisfaction would not be deemed to have been addressed. Robertson et al. (2012) cite the example of online banking in which banks could ensure that an incorrect statement reported could be immediately corrected, especially since one of the key benefits of SST is time saving for the consumer. However, if the consumer had to keep calling bank staff members several times before an issue was addressed, then the consumer would not perceive procedural justice.

## SERVICE ROBOTS

To tease out a definition of robot from the perspective of Wirtz et al. (2018), then we can define it as a system-based autonomous and adaptable interface that does a number of things with the customer including communication, interaction, and delivering of services. We now see robots welcoming customers in the banking halls and prompting them to take steps that will help to address the needs that brought them to the bank in the first place. Through this, the number of employees at work will be reduced as others can then focus on more human-facing services. Retailing environments, restaurants, and many other service-oriented organisations have been using robots to create value for their customers. This is especially so, as using them has been considered efficient in terms of speed of service and cost-saving (Ameen et al., 2021). As we see in places where they are being used, some look like humans while others look simply like machines. While there may be some form of symbolic implication for how these robots look in the service environment, the expectation is most likely to be around the delivery of the core service for which they are intended.

## WEARABLE TECHNOLOGY

Another way in which technology has moved forward, and continues to play a significant role in our day-to-day living, is in wearable technology. This works in such a way that sensors and transmission chips are embedded into items that consumers wear so that they have communication processing capabilities (Jung et al., 2016; Yasar and Wigmore, 2022). There are many examples of these in the marketplace today. Smartwatches, smart clothing, smart glasses, and smart jewellery are examples of these technological devices. Available statistics show that the approximate number of people using wearable devices globally as of 2022 is 1.1 billion, which is a significant increase when compared to the 929 million indicated for the previous year (Laricchia, 2023). The competition around smartwatches between technological giants like Samsung, Apple, and Google is very clear, with improvements introduced in one form or another on how to create value for the consumer in a better way. Another indicator attesting to the popularity of these devices can be seen from the projected sales figures for smartwatches, which is expected to increase by 37.41% between 2023 and 2027. This projected increase is a total of $16.8 billion USD (Statista Research Department, 2023). Essentially, the watches are designed to monitor some health conditions that could be very helpful to the owners. They track things like heart rates and levels of physical activity, thereby providing insight into the fitness of people at work and improving their productivity. Although, like any other technology type, there may be some concerns around consumer privacy and safety in the use of wearable technology, these seem not to be very compelling as shown in the various available data indicating their popularity. It is not unexpected that many more of these will be added through innovation in the coming years.

## ARTIFICIAL INTELLIGENCE AND MARKETING

There is a plethora of artificial intelligence (AI) technological tools in society today and the number still continues to grow. The popularity of these tools and the rate at which they were adopted became significantly noticeable during the COVID-19 pandemic with several restrictions that were introduced into the marketing environment by various governments all over the world. So, technology came to the rescue to a great extent, even among some people who were initially sceptical of using technology. There is a report that investment in Generative AI has increased significantly to $2.1bn, representing an increase of 425% since 2020 (Pennington, 2023), and the United Kingdom announced an investment into the development of AI worth a whopping £54 million (Pike, 2023). It has also been noted that the adoption of AI has increased markedly among businesses by 270% and its global market is anticipated to be worth around $267 billion by the year 2027 (Lin, 2020; Mogaji and Nguyen, 2022). We see evidence of these on a daily basis in the operations of firms like Spotify, Google, and Rare Carat through their adoption of AI-based platforms such as Google Assistant and Amazon Lex (Vlačić et al., 2021). It was reported that the term artificial intelligence was introduced by a group of authors (McCarthy et al., 1955) decades ago. It can be defined as a technology-enabled system for evaluating real-time service scenarios involving the use of data obtained from digital or physical resources to offer alternative solutions and personalised recommendation to the customers' enquiries or problems (Xu et al., 2020; Gołąb-Andrzejak, 2023). We can compress this definition to another given by McCarthy et al. (1955) which is succinct but rather broad in scope. According to them, AI refers to a machine that behaves in a manner that could be described as intelligent, as if it was a human being. So, AI tools tend to emulate human beings in terms of their capabilities and operations. It helps the marketing system in a variety of ways. It assists the consumer in their purchase processes and decision making and aids the effort of the marketer in monitoring and analysing the behaviour of the consumer, thereby improving their efficiency and effectiveness (Gołąb-Andrzejak, 2023). In highlighting further benefits of AI in marketing to the consumers, Mustak et al. (2021) indicate that it offers them innovative breakthroughs, decreased costs, opportunities for expanded human creativity and ingenuity, and more diverse service channels. Moreover, it helps in dynamic pricing, entering chatbot, programmatic ad targeting, sales forecasting, speech recognition, and understanding customer preferences among many other things (Mehta et al., 2022). With these various examples, it is reasonable for us to claim that AI has become a very powerful tool that helps in reducing risks and costs and enhancing reliability and consistency in various marketing transactions (Hermann, 2022).

Let us look at AI classification for further understanding of how it works, as given by Mehta et al. (2022) based on their review of relevant literature:

- Virtualisation: This category consists of tools that allow consumers to digitally enjoy products or services that are not available in physical form.
- Self-service: These allow consumers to be able to enjoy services without having any interaction with business representatives such as employees. Examples include vending machines, automated teller machines (ATMs), and self-service machines at airports and supermarkets;
- Sensory-enabled: These operate to target consumers' five senses of smell, sight, sound, taste, and touch. An example cited by Mehta et al. (2022), with reference to Mayor and Moynihan (2021), is the AI tool that detects the smell from an oven and switches it off before the food gets burnt and detects gas leakage;
- Image interactivity technology: These give the consumers the opportunity to indicate their preferences to the marketers so that the latter can give them customised products, services, or experiences.

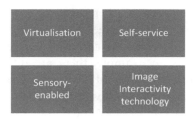

**FIGURE 13.1** Classification of artificial intelligence (AI)

There are a good number of ways artificial intelligence is used in digital marketing. The two are becoming inextricably linked. Some good examples of these are listed in Gołąb-Andrzejak (2023: 399) as follows:

- AI-powered chatbots (smarter versions of chatbots);
- Content generation (generating user-engaging and human-like content);
- Content curation (searching for more popular content and managing the dissemination);
- Email marketing campaigns (creating effective personalised email marketing campaigns);
- E-commerce (offering suitable solutions and an intelligent data management approach);
- Online advertising (programmatic advertising);
- Personalised user experience (data-based personalisation);
- Predictive analysis (predicts future actions of customers);
- Web designing (new possibilities for website design and re-design);
- Voice search optimisation (optimising websites for voice search and increasing site traffic).

As useful as AI is considered to be in many contexts, its acceptance for solving life issues as explained above is yet to appeal to some consumers. There have been some areas of reservation among some critics. The concern about consumers' personal privacy and data protection has been raised in that data may be collected without the informed consent of users, AI might draw data from people directly or indirectly, and data breaches could have devastating consequences for the victims (Hermann, 2022). There is also another concern that the more AI tools in operation, the more we are motivated to consume more such as the ease of having a personalised marketing mix leading to over consumption that is not environmentally friendly (Hermann, 2022). Some public commentators are even cautioning on the use of AI on the grounds that it may bring devastating consequences to humanity. What is clear is that there are arguments on both sides of the divide about using it. However, it is interesting to note that studies have found a positive correlation between consumer attitudes and the adoption of AI (Rezaei et al., 2020; Mehta et al., 2022).

## STP AND CONSUMER DEMOGRAPHICS

Fundamentally, consumer markets are heterogeneous. This is even more so as we have the proliferation of technology usage. They are characterised by a high level of diversity in terms of their tastes, choices, and preferences. If we take the consumer automobile market as an example, there are different brands, makes, and model variations that depict the level of diversity. The preference of customers for Mini Coopers is inconsistent with those of the users of Range Rovers in terms of size and other functions while the taste of those using Lamborghini is different from those of the users of Toyota, especially in terms of income. A similar level of diversity characterises several other products and services such as fashion products, food items, financial services, hotels, holiday packages/destinations, electrical and electronic products, and entertainment. In view of this, the notion of segmentation, targeting, and positioning (STP) is considered relevant and necessary. Segmentation simply refers to dividing the total market, which is heterogeneous, into small homogeneous units in terms of how their needs can be met. Marketers achieve this by adopting various criteria such that each segment can be seen to be different from the other for efficient and effective management. The criteria commonly used by firms that constitute the bases for segmentation are:

- Demography;
- Geography;
- Behaviour;
- Psychography.

Demographic segmentation involves using customer characteristics or variables such as age, marital status, life cycle, income, gender, occupation, and ethnicity to identify segments from a broad market. Geographic segmentation is location-based and involves dividing the market into geographic units such as regions, states, nations, and cities. In behavioural segmentation, the buyers are identified in terms of their actions and response towards the products or services, such as knowledge about the products, attitudes towards them, and the rate at which they use them. Psychographic segmentation covers a number of variables to identify the consumers. These include consumers' characteristics like traits, social class, and lifestyle (Kotler et al., 2023). Hence, it uses peoples' activities, interests, and opinions (AIO), which we have discussed in Chapter 10.

Now that we know the criteria for dividing the market into segments, it is important to note that it is not all segmentation efforts that can be deemed effective. Let us now highlight the conditions to be met for effective market segmentation as indicated consistently in most marketing textbooks, including Kotler et al. (2023). These are listed as follows:

- The market segments must be **measurable** in terms of variables such as size and the consumers' purchasing power (Measurability);
- It is expected that the number of people that constitute the market segment will be **substantial** to ensure the firm's profitability (Substantiality);
- The segment should be **discrete** from others such that it can respond differently to different marketing strategies (Differentiation);
- The market segments should be such that can be **reached** and served effectively (Accessibility);
- It is expected that the segments should be such that can be **amenable** to a specific marketing programme (Actionable).

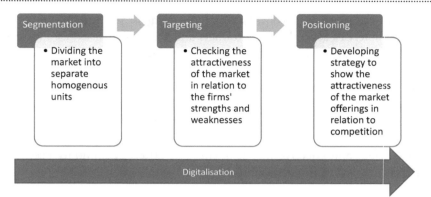

**FIGURE 13.2** Segmentation, targeting, and positioning (STP)

Having performed the segmentation, the targeting stage is about weighing the attractiveness of each of the segments in relation to the firm's strengths and weaknesses towards choosing which and how many to choose to serve with the appropriate market offerings. This can lead firms to pursue any combination of undifferentiated marketing, differentiated marketing, concentrated (niche) marketing, or individual/customised marketing. Positioning is about strategising to influence the way specific consumer segments perceive the firm's market offerings in relation to competitive offerings.

Clearly, segmentation, targeting, and positioning (STP) is an important topic in marketing and consumer behaviour. However, the focus in this section is not really about having an exhaustive discussion of this topic but about using it as a background to the discussion of consumer demographics and how these are influencing consumption and reflecting the future of technology in marketing. So, we will now switch back to consumer demographics.

Consumer demographics serve as a guide to many aspects of consumption and the corresponding strategic actions of the firm. For example, Josiassen et al. (2011) focused on three of these demographic characteristics for studying consumers' willingness to buy and their ethnocentric tendencies. These are age, income, and gender. They found that young consumers have a higher tendency to be ethnocentric than older consumers. This study also shows that female consumers have a tendency to buy on the basis of the principle of ethnocentrism more so than men. However, they could not see any discriminating impact on the purchase in relation to income. Accordingly, it is expected that managers will use this knowledge in their segmentation, targeting, and positioning strategies of their market offerings. On a slightly different subject, Rahim et al. (2017) studied electronic word of mouth, consumer demographics, and purchase intention to purchase green products. They reported some interesting findings. According to them, female consumers tend to have the intention to buy green products as they tend to be more knowledgeable about green products and their benefits to consumers. Meanwhile, it is understood from early studies, such as Promotosh and Sajedul (2011), that higher education level of consumers propels them to purchase green products. However, in a more recent study, Rahim et al. (2017) show that consumers' income, age, occupation, and education do not indicate any significant differences in their green purchase intention. One would wonder why part of these findings is contradictory to an early study. Rahim et al. (2017) suggest that it is highly likely this is related to the increasing popularity and acceptance of green products in the Malaysian context in which the study was conducted. Notably, this study shows that e-WOM plays a significant role in these dynamics. Clearly, it is relevant to stress that digital transformation seems to be changing the way customer demographics influence consumer behaviour.

In a study about consumers' demographic factors and loyalty towards fast food chains, Srivastava (2015) found that men and women have similar opinions about these offerings whereas consumers aged 19–25 demonstrate more interest in this type of food, unlike those aged over 50 years who are not as enthusiastic about it. The results also distinguish between undergraduate and postgraduate students in that the former is more interested in it compared to the latter student category. Some other findings around demographical factors are stated, including income. This point also features in the publication of Cleveland et al. (2011) where it is shown that high-income earners tend to be more prone to buying luxury and status-enhancing products. This is not out of place in that the resources at their disposal indicate that they can afford such items.

Looking at consumer demographics in relation to the use of technology more closely is quite revealing. Although the consideration of factors such as risk, perceived usefulness, convenience, bargain hunting, and attitude would play a part in the consumers' consideration of using it, engaging in mobile shopping has increased greatly in recent times. Those who are without a mobile device are probably considering getting one soon. In their paper titled 'Mobile shopping intensity', Hou and Elliott (2021) found that young consumers engage more in mobile shopping than their older consumer counterparts while male consumers spend more online than female consumers. As shown in Chapter 11, young people tend to be early adopters of new technology such as mobile devices that encourage mobile shopping. Meanwhile, this study also shows that consumers' income levels and education motivate significant engagement in mobile shopping.

Meanwhile, moving beyond the basic demographic factors, there have been several attempts to provide a market segmentation breakdown of consumers in relation to their online transactions or engagements. Let us look at two of these in this chapter as given in the extant literature (Hill et al., 2013; Pandey and Chawla, 2018; Gbadamosi, 2021). The first one is given by Pandey and Chawla (2018) who identify the following segments in relation to their online clothing shopping activities:

- Disengaged averse online shoppers;
- Adept online shopping optimists;
- Interactive convenience shoppers.

The disengaged averse online shoppers are drawn to shop online mainly to take advantage of offers and deals as well as the availability of varieties concerning clothing sizes. They exhibit apathy for online clothing purchases and are not loyal to any particular website. The adept online shopping optimists are delighted about shopping online and find it convenient, rationally useful, and trustworthy. They are equipped with an advanced level of technology-oriented skills. Hence, they may be switching from one website to another. Although interactive convenience shoppers have low income, are characterised with e-distrust, and do not have a good level of technological prowess, they do not mind committing a higher amount of money to clothing than the other segments.

As discussed earlier in this chapter, young adolescents and other young consumers are heavy users of the Internet, which also reflects in their online shopping activities. Despite this, there are still further segments (niches) which are noted among adolescents. These segments, as presented by the second online segmentation pattern (Hill et al., 2013), are:

- Internet conquerors;
- Virtual pragmatists;
- Recreational shoppers.

The segment that tops the list is that of the Internet conquerors who devote a significant amount of time to surfing the Internet as they have the highest level of online accessibility among the three groups. In terms of age, they are the oldest of the three. According to the authors, most of these adolescents are opportune to make purchases with permission from their parents (Hill et al., 2013). Those identified as virtual pragmatists have the lowest level of online social motivation and are the youngest of the three segments. Their online accessibility and self-efficacy are low. Meanwhile, the segment identified as recreational shoppers have the highest-ranking with regards to making purchases with their parents' permission and have persistent online shopping interest. This segment lies in between the virtual pragmatists, and the recreational shoppers.

## CONSUMER PERSONA

As discussed above, market segmentation has been a valuable aspect of marketing for a long time in terms of addressing and meeting the needs of the consumers effectively and efficiently. Meanwhile, an attempt to be able to do this even better led to the discussion of consumer persona. A search of the literature (Onel et al., 2018) indicates that the term was introduced by Cooper (1999). Let us begin with the definition given by Pruitt and Adlin (2006). According to them, it refers to the abstractions of groups of consumers in terms of common characteristics or needs they share. It performs a deeper description of the consumer beyond what is commonly done in conventional segment descriptions. It humanises and contextualises a generic abstract consumer (Onel et al., 2018). So, in a way, it is a fictional characterisation of a user developed specifically to depict a user group and often includes a photo, name, background, habits, likes and dislikes, and expectations (LeRouge et al., 2013). We can formulate a hypothetical example as follows:

*Greg is a Bachelor who has just graduated from the university, has a passion for football, does his shopping once a week, and hangs out with friends at a local pub at the weekend with an expectation to be in a full career within the next two years.*

We would look at further examples of personas that have been used or indicated in the literature in various studies. In a study related to sustainable fashion, Kaner and Baruih (2022) came up with four consumer personas, which are:

- Romantic optimists;
- Egocentrics;
- Confused Alecs;
- Gloomies.

Each of these gives a representation of diverse behaviour, attitudes, and demand for these products. We would look at some of the key details the authors presented to describe each of the personas in relation to consumption of sustainable fashion. **Romantic optimists** are driven by an intrinsic motivation to learn more about sustainability issues and hold the belief that every little action towards sustainability helps. With this level of optimism, they can be triggered in favour of buying sustainable fashion through exposure to information about it. **Egocentrics** are driven to consider buying sustainable products if they notice that they will derive material benefits from the transaction. The **Confused Alec** has a reasonable level of education, but is confused by the knowledge they have. The **Gloomy** persona is not optimistic about sustainability, they see the sustainability objective as unattainable. The persona is suspicious about environmental issues and the information offered by the marketers.

Using personas is a useful strategic action in marketing in that it clarifies assumptions made about consumers and allows marketers to extrapolate the information they have gathered to different circumstances (Grudin and Pruitt, 2002). So, adopting the use of personas makes it possible for marketers to identify the needs of the target market very well (Ma and LeRouge, 2007). In their study that covers the use of personas in relation to the development of health technologies for consumers, LeRouge et al. (2013) indicate that the use of personas allows them to be able to engage older adult consumers in the design, gain access to psycho-social and demographic perspectives on health issues in respect to elderly consumers, and capture relevant knowledge for other possible future projects. While this information given here relates specifically to the context of the study, it also does point to the fact that personas have a much higher value in making a thick description of the consumers' needs and how the appropriate market offerings can be targeted to them.

We now know that consumers are linked to, or expectedly identify with, the given personas. Kennedy et al. (2019) studied comparisons of how celebrity and film personas work in terms of influencing consumer judgement. In this study, they found that the use of film personas is preferable to celebrities themselves for advertising the product or service. The rationale for this conclusion is that when celebrities are involved in a scandal or commit any scandal such as drug use, the negative development would most likely affect the brand that is being endorsed by the individual. However, when a film persona is used, it is understood that there is a degree of abstraction in the role played by the celebrities in the film and a rather weak link to the celebrities themselves (Kennedy et al., 2019).

## WEBOGRAPHICS

One of the elements of consumer personas is webographics. As indicated by Hanlon (2022), this is about the study of consumers' Internet usage, the website browser they visited, the duration of time they spend on the Internet, their social media usage, the pattern of times and days they spend on the Internet, which ad or type of ad they like or comment on, and many other related factors. This is especially useful as consumers' online activities keep increasing. A specific example of how consumers are connected to the digital world is that, as of January 2023, Cristiano Ronaldo, a Portuguese footballer, has 539 million followers on Instagram, which makes him the most followed individual on this platform (Dixon, 2023). Consistent with the data collection we discussed in Chapter 12, these webographics data can be available in secondary and primary forms. The secondary data relating to webography are often available from sources such as Google Analytics, and Statista or primary sources such as observation and interviews (Hanlon, 2022).

Google Analytics has been widely noted as being good for finding out patterns of consumers' interaction with a firm's website so that the appropriate content can be developed and targeted to the right people. So, to check demographics of website users, the following steps have been recommended (Akhtar, 2023):

- Installation of MonsterInsights and connecting to Google Analytics;
- Enabling demographics reports in MonsterInsights;
- Enabling demographics reporting in Google Analytics;
- Viewing the demographics reports.

Statistical evidence shows some common data concerning website usage. It is reported that the worldwide data of Internet users is in the proportion of 42% female and 58% male (Schneider, 2023). However, it is noted that women comment more on Facebook in comparison to men, while female consumers aged 18–34 engage in the least activity on the platform, compared to those aged 45–54 who are the most engaged among women (Schneider, 2023; Kemp, 2020).

There are differences in what the various consumer segments are looking for online. As an example, the motivation for online visits of consumers aged 25–34 can be gauged by the percentage they represent among those that visit online in particular industries. As given by Schneider (2023) at the global level, in terms of the Arts and Entertainment industry, this age group constitutes 32%, while they are 29% of those who go online for Business and Consumer Services, and those who are there for eCommerce and Shopping are approximately 31% of the website visitors, and the same percentage of 31% visit for News and Media.

You will probably know that you are on different social media platforms compared to those used by your parents or children. That is not unexpected as what constitutes good value to a consumer segment may be different from what others are passionate about. Available data shows some interesting patterns about the popularity of social media and their usage among various consumer segments. For instance, as shown in Schneider (2023), although TikTok is seen to be very popular among young consumers, especially teenagers, the popularity of X (formerly Twitter) is higher among young male audiences, and people aged 25–50 who are educated and pursuing career growth are more attracted to LinkedIn. Meanwhile, as shown in the same publication, while YouTube appeals to all consumer categories, the popularity of Facebook seems to be noticeable among consumers aged 30 and over.

This type of information, and if necessary supported by primary data, will offer strategic direction to firms in terms of how they plan their content to be sure that they are hitting the appropriate target. So, when targeting an elderly couple on the website of a company, the content will probably be different from when the consumer segment are the young female consumers or teenagers.

In a study that explores the website experiences of restaurant customers, Namkung et al. (2007) indicate that, while some information about consumers' online information searches may be available in the general e-commerce literature, it is useful to acquire idiosyncratic behaviour patterns concerning restaurant websites. According to these authors, this is a very valuable task in that consumers could express their experience of using the restaurant through email or bulletin boards. The study emphasises that factors that determine critical web usability include technology, interactivity, information, and design and the way the consumers perceive these vary in relation to their motivation for visiting the website and the time of visiting it. By and large, the study stresses that the customer experience covers not only the usability attribute of the website but the whole experience of visiting the website. Similar or related studies could be done in respect of various other businesses, and sectors such as fashion, consumer electronics, books and stationeries, and home improvements to inform the organisations' decisions with regards to the consumers' digital operations.

## CUSTOMER TRUST AND LOYALTY

As marketing is about creating, delivering, co-creating, and managing customer value, the issue of customer trust and loyalty is very important to business transactions whether it is done online or offline. One of the old definitions of trust given by Rotter (1967) will be used here because of its comprehensive nature. According to him, we can define it as a general expectation in a relationship such that the word of another party can be relied upon by the other. So, as consumers are encouraged through various promotional messages to shop online with the promise that their data will be saved, they expect that such a promise will not be breached. A breach of that is a betrayal of the trust invested into the transaction by the consumers. It is also possible that trust is built upon other related evidence such as in the claim of Khoa (2020), which shows that as more consumers use mobile banking services, the trust in the use of this approach to banking becomes boosted. Another contribution highlights this further by stressing the elements of trust. According to Heffernan et al. (2008), the elements of trust are integrity, credibility, and benevolence. So, we can now see that trust and loyalty are closely linked. That is why it is argued that, in its general form, loyalty is the characteristic of an entity that is linked to attributes such as integrity, honesty, devotion, or allegiance to someone (Krawczyk-Sokołowska and Caputa, 2023). When there is competition, the need to foster loyalty will occupy a central stage in the strategic management of an organisation. Clearly, competition has become more intense as consumers have access to more data through digital opportunities. But consumers' loyalty is not always the same as it sounds. It can be in various forms depending on the intensity. Let us look at the two different classifications of loyalty. The first is given by Casalo et al. (2007) as follows:

- **Apparent (passive) loyalty**: Based on the rational behavioural reaction in the form of repurchasing a product or brand out of different alternatives;
- **Occasional loyalty**: Prompted by circumstances or individual characteristics of the consumer;
- **Real loyalty**: characterised by habit, commitment to engaging in various activities such as supporting the sale and value co-creation.

The second typology that also shows loyalty can vary, which we will examine in this chapter, is that given by Dick and Basu (1994), which identifies four loyalty types or different patronage behaviour. These are:

- No loyalty;
- Spurious loyalty;
- Latent loyalty;
- Loyalty (sustainable loyalty).

In the no loyalty case, the buyer is committed to neither the organisation nor its brand but buys with no identifiable pattern. In the spurious loyalty scenario, the consumers demonstrate high patronage behaviour concerning the brand but the attitude towards the product or service is low. When consumers demonstrate a latent loyalty type, they show a relatively high attitude toward the products or services, but the patronage of the market offering is low. The sustainable loyalty shows a deep-rooted consistent loyalty towards the product or brand as both attitude and patronage are pretty high and are not easily discouraged by marketplace factors (Dick and Basu, 1994; Gbadamosi, 2019).

Although there are slight differences between these two typologies, we are able to see that loyalty is not strait-jacketed and the motivation or level of loyalty vary.

Fundamentally, trust and loyalty of consumers for an organisation or its brands are closely linked to the consumer experience, which is about the view of the consumer concerning the brand in relation to every contact they make with it, which could be face-to-face interaction, or through advertising concerning service quality, or personal care received (Alloza, 2008; Sadek and Mehelmi, 2020). From this, the marketing literature identifies these three behavioural outcomes:

- Brand satisfaction;
- Brand loyalty;
- Brand trust.

We have discussed trust and loyalty earlier but what this has shown us is that both are closely linked to satisfaction. How would a consumer know that he or she is satisfied with the transactions? The basic principle lies in the fact that the consumers have expectations before they approach the transaction system and gauge how well these have been met after the transaction. Satisfaction occurs when this has been met or exceeded. So, consumer expectation is a key benchmark upon which satisfaction is measured.

---

**PAUSE, PLAN, AND PRACTICE: TESCO CLUBCARD AND CUSTOMER LOYALTY**

Tesco, a supermarket giant, has been at the forefront of British supermarkets for a long time. It caters for the needs of millions of customers in various ways, especially in relation to grocery products. The organisation understands that while it is good and necessary to satisfy the needs of the customers, the prevalent competition in that industry indicates that other supermarkets such as ASDA, Morrisons, Lidl, and Sainsburys are in the marketplace vying for the same customers' attention. Hence, it is important to have a strategy in place for ensuring repeat purchase and keeping the customer loyal to the organisation, its brands, and products. This explains why it introduced and continues to maintain its loyalty card – popularly known as Tesco Clubcard. With this card, there are special prices and deals introduced for the members. After registration for the card, the customer continues to earn points on their purchases, and these become considerable over time. Taking this scheme further, Tesco works closely with many other organisations such as Pizza Express, RAC, Virgin Atlantic, and Disney+, called Reward Partners, to ensure that the customers have linked and integrated benefits through which points are earned and used. In the way it works, the customers can view their Clubcard statements online to see how close they are to specific targets and can use the card through the special app created for it. In view of these special benefits, customers with Clubcards see themselves as special and become loyal to the brand.

**Source**

Tesco (nd). Tesco Clubcard, http://secure.tesco.com/clubcard (accessed 29 June 2023).

**QUESTION/TASK**

With reference to the framework of Dick and Basu (1994) discussed in this chapter, do you think Tesco Clubcard can result in sustainable loyalty?

## SUMMARY

The use of technology by consumers has revolutionised the consumption system. The changes we see in terms of consumption as a result of technology will increase even further in the future. For example, the use of artificial intelligence (AI) is now commonplace and keeps increasing. AI is often categorised into virtualisation, self-service, sensory-enabled, and image interactivity technology. They meet consumers' needs in various ways. Given that consumers' needs vary, having an understanding of segmentation, targeting, and positioning (STP) is crucial. The commonly used segmentation criteria are geography, psychography, behaviour, and demography. Emphatically, in consumers' demographics, a variety of consumption patterns are noticeable. Meanwhile, the use of consumer persona, which is an abstraction of consumer groups in terms of their common characteristics, is now becoming more commonly applied for planning to meet consumers' needs. The increasing use of the Internet has also strengthened the use of webographics, which is about understanding consumer behaviour on the Internet in terms of how they use the Internet, at what rate, and many other related issues. This understanding and the study of the pattern of usage of social media will help businesses to be able to manage their customers' loyalty and trust.

---

**DIGITAL BOX: APPLE SELF-SERVICE REPAIRS: A STEP TO SAVE THE FUTURE**

Apple has proved to be a leading organisation in digital transformation over the years. Its products are seen to be a demonstration of cutting-edge technology in one form or another, be it iPhone, iPad, iPod, or any of many others. The organisation has now moved its application of technology to a new level. In its quest to contribute to environmental sustainability, it has now introduced out-of-warranty Apple self-service repairs (on 21 June 2023) for Mac laptop, iPhone, Mac desktop, or Apple display. So, this will reduce waste, encourage reusage of the gadgets, and prolong their lifespan. As planned by Apple, any consumer that has experience of repairing consumer electronics can do it. All they have to do is to follow a process which involves downloading the repair manual, ordering the genuine parts and tools needed to do the repair, do the repair, and return the old part for recycling. The online information available to the consumers doing the repair through the self-service repair store and the use of system configuration, which is a post-repair software that finalises the repair, contribute to enrich the repair experience for the consumers of these Apple products.

**Source**

Apple (nd). Self-service repair, http://support.apple.com/en-gb/self-service-repair (accessed 29 June 2023).

> **QUESTION**
>
> In view of this innovative step taken by Apple, select any other organisation, and suggest a realistic innovative idea it can implement that will benefit some of the stakeholders. Highlight the likely impact of the suggested idea on the consumer experience of the firm.

## END OF CHAPTER DISCUSSION QUESTIONS

1. There has been a significant increase in the demand for wearable technology in recent times. Check online or from personal experience of using these products. Highlight what these products currently offer consumers in terms of benefits and come up with an idea for a new wearable technology that will add value to the consumers above what is currently offered in the market. Explain why you think this new product will be well received by consumers.
2. Select five consumers who could be of any age group but with some knowledge of digital technology. Conduct a webographics study on them to collect information about their Internet activities such as the pattern of times they explore the Internet, the type of content they access when they are online, how many hours/days they spend on the Internet, and many other related factors. Compare these for the five participants and report on the discrepancy. How can this information be useful to marketers for planning purposes?
3. Describe any two or three specific encounters you have had with artificial intelligence (AI) as a consumer. Would you say the encounters were pleasant experiences? What is your opinion about the reservation some commentators have about AI?
4. There is a contention that the use of consumer persona seems more effective than traditional market segmentation. Present your view and justifications for your position.
5. Using relevant examples, such as grocery shopping and hotel accommodation, to discuss and illustrate how repetitive purchase of some products may not necessarily connote consumers' loyalty to the brand.

> ### Case Study: Small is Beautiful: Can Technology be the Missing Link for SMEs in Consumer-focused Marketing?
>
> Small and medium-sized enterprises (SMEs) constitute strategic actors in the marketing environment in most developed and developing countries. Although the definition of this business tends to vary from one society to another, one of the commonly used definitions is that of the European Union (EU), which defines it as a business with less than 250 employees. They are characterised by some limitations such as operating with very limited resources compared to large enterprises, which impacts the extent to which they can explore market opportunities. In most countries of the world, these enterprises

make up not less than 90% of the business organisations producing goods and services to create and deliver value to the consumers. This is an indication of their significant role in employment creation as they create 70% of the available jobs in various sectors. Besides, their size also has positive implications in terms of flexibility in meeting the dynamic consumer needs and the level of closeness they have with their target market which has some links to the loyalty system within the firm. Hence, their small size, which is often seen as a constraint, could have advantages which indicate that small can actually be beautiful. Meanwhile, the prevalent use of technology, which dominates the consumption system these days and, by implication, is expected to reflect in the operations of businesses, continues to grow.

Although there are discrepancies in viewpoints in relation to the discussion of technology these days, one thing that most people would agree on is that digitalisation is multi-faceted. For example, Radio Frequency Identification (RFID) technologies permit near-field communication (NFC) and has been regarded as essential in many ramifications such as inventory tracking and control, while Big Data analytics (BDA) helps in the analysis and management of the huge amount of data coming from these firms. Social media opens businesses to relationships and interactions with their customers, while customer relationship management (CRM) helps them in managing the myriad of relationships they have with stakeholders. The roles of cloud computing and enterprise resource planning (ERP) are also adjudged significant in how these businesses focus on meeting consumers' demands. Clearly opportunities for SMEs in digitalisation for meeting consumers' needs are numerous. Emphatically, available evidence shows that demand for technology-oriented products, such as wearable technology, is increasing, and artificial intelligence (AI) now mimics humans in many real-life scenarios. However, the extent to which small businesses are using them as leverage to create and deliver value for consumers has been a focus of some studies. Opinions are somewhat mixed on this. Some commentators believe that SMEs are increasing their use of technology but some hold that more could still be done for these businesses to be able to continue playing their strategic role in the business community. One of the notable periods to reckon with was the time of the COVID-19 pandemic when the prevalent circumstances then switched most consumers to the Internet for consumption activities. In a study conducted by the World Economic Forum, it was shown that the adoption of technology and integration of digital technology into business increased among SMEs. Nonetheless, the research shows that while 97% of big global organisations were able to increase the adoption of technology to cope with the pandemic, only 23% of SMEs were able to invest in digital resources. This means that these firms still lag in how they embrace the new reality of high technology usage. Accordingly, their potential for addressing emerging consumer needs is being curtailed. As reported in the study conducted in six countries, namely Brazil, South Africa, Azerbaijan, Colombia, Turkey, and Kazakhstan, there is keen interest among SMEs to explore digital technology in their businesses. This survey, which involved 141 SMEs, indicates special interest in AI, the Internet of Things (IoT), and cloud computing.

By all indications, digitalisation will continue to grow and consumers' appetite for related products will also be unabated. They yearn for convenience, cost-saving, and to be topical. So, businesses that will address these needs will have to embrace cutting-edge technology to be able to compete effectively and earn customers' trust and loyalty. So, the increasing pace of technological development may as well aid SMEs in how they satisfy consumers and tilt the narrative from the point of their limitations to how well and enthusiastically they adopt new technology to be able to operate effective consumer-focused marketing. Indeed, small can be beautiful.

**Sources**

Chamberlain, L. (2021). Pandemic drives need for technology adoption among SMEs but barriers remain, http://www.weforum.org/press/2021/12/pandemic-drives-need-for-technology-among-smes-but-barriers-remain (accessed 30 June 2023).

Digital tools and practices: SME access and uptake, http://www.oecd-ilibrary.org/sites/9816a98d-en/index.html?itemId=/content/component/9816a98d-en#:~:text=SMEs%20lag%20in%20digital%20adoption%2C%20in%20all%20technology,invoicing%20or%20social%20media%2C%20or%20in%20selling%20online (accessed 30 June 2023).

OECD iLibrary (nd). Digital tools and practices: SME access and uptake, http://www.oecd-ilibrary.org/sites/9816a98d-en/index.html?itemId=/content/component/9816a98d-en#:~:text=SMEs%20lag%20in%20digital%20adoption%2C%20in%20all%20technology,invoicing%20or%20social%20media%2C%20or%20in%20selling%20online (accessed 21 July 2023).

## QUESTIONS

1. Despite their limitations, the case study indicates that SMEs create and deliver value to consumers in various ways. Based on your opinion and the content of the case, what sort of artificial intelligence–oriented product/service can be provided by these businesses to consumers within a budget that can reasonably be managed by them?
2. To what extent can webographics help SMEs to satisfy the contemporary consumer?
3. The case study indicates that consumers' appetite for convenience, cost-saving, and topical products continues to grow. In view of this, identify any two products that can be offered by SMEs to deliver these criteria and such products will remain relevant in the marketing environment for the next five years;
4. It is reported in the case study that a study conducted in six countries, namely Brazil, South Africa, Azerbaijan, Colombia, Turkey, and Kazakhstan, shows that SMEs have a keen interest in exploring digital technology in their businesses. Nonetheless, it is also reported that less than a quarter of these SMEs were able to invest in digital resources during the COVID-19 lockdowns. In view of

this, identify key stakeholders that can be involved in facilitating how SMEs use cutting-edge technology to serve consumers effectively and what roles each of them will play in this towards showing further that 'Small can actually be beautiful'.

## REFERENCES

Akhtar, A. (2023). How to see the demographics of your website visitors [GA4], 4 January 2023, http://www.monsterinsights.com/how-to-see-the-demographics-of-your-website-users/#:~:text=How%20to%20Check%20Website%20Visitor%20Demographics%20 1%20Step,Analytics%20...%204%20Step%204%3A%20View%20Demographics%20 Reports (accessed 25 June 2023).

Alloza, A. (2008). Brand engagement and brand experience at BBVA, the transformation of a 150-year-old company. *Corporate Reputation Review*, 11(4), 371–379.

Ameen, N., Hosany, S., & Tarhini, A. (2021). Consumer interaction with cutting-edge technologies: Implications for future research. *Computers in Human Behavior*, 120, 106761.

Casalo, L., Flavian, C., & Guinaliu, M. (2007). The impact of participation in virtual brand communities on consumer trust and loyalty: The case of free software. *Online Information Review*, 34(6), 775–792.

Cleveland, M., Papadopoulos, N., & Laroche, M. (2011). Identity, demographics, and consumer behaviors: International market segmentation across product categories. *International Marketing Review*, 28(3), 244–266.

Cooper, A. (1999). *The Inmates are Running the Asylum: Why High-tech Products Drive Us Crazy and How to Restore the Sanity*. Indianapolis: Morgan Kaufmann.

Dick, A. S., & Basu, K. (1994). Customer loyalty: Toward an integrated conceptual framework. *Journal of the Academy of Marketing Science*, 22(2), 99.113.

Dixon, S. (2023). Instagram accounts with the most followers worldwide 2023, 24 Jan 2023, http://www.statista.com/statistics/421169/most-followers-instagram/ (accessed 25 June 2023).

Gbadamosi, A. (2019). Marketing: A paradigm shift. in Gbadamosi, A. (ed.) pp. 3–31, *Contemporary Issues in Marketing*, London: SAGE.

Gbadamosi, A. (2021). Consumption, religion, and digital marketing in developing countries, in Gbadamosi, A. and Oniku, C. A. (2021) (eds), *Religion and Consumer Behaviour in Developing Nations*, pp. 175–198. London, Cheltenham: Edward Elgar.

Gołąb-Andrzejak, E. (2023). AI-powered digital transformation: Tools, benefits and challenges for marketers—Case study of LPP. *Procedia Computer Science*, 219, 397–404.

Grudin, J., & Pruitt, J. (2002). Personas, participatory design and product development: An infrastructure for engagement. PDC Conference Proceedings, 144–152.

Hanlon, A. (2022). *Digital Marketing*, 2nd edn, London: SAGE.

Heffernan, T., O'Neill, G., Travaglione, T., & Droulers, M. (2008). Relationship marketing. *International Journal of Bank Marketing*, 26(3), 183–199.

Hermann, E. (2022). Leveraging artificial intelligence in marketing for social good—An ethical perspective. *Journal of Business Ethics*, 179(1), 43–61.

Hill, W., E., Beatty, S., & Walsh, G. (2013). A segmentation of adolescent online users and shoppers. *Journal of Services Marketing*, 27(5), 347–360.

Hou, J., & Elliott, K. (2021). Mobile shopping intensity: Consumer demographics and motivations. *Journal of Retailing and Consumer Services*, 63, 102741.

Josiassen, A., Assaf, A. G., & Karpen, I. O. (2011). Consumer ethnocentrism and willingness to buy: Analyzing the role of three demographic consumer characteristics. *International Marketing Review*, 28(6), 627–646.

Jung, Y., Kim, S., & Choi, B. (2016). Consumer valuation of the wearables: The case of smartwatches. *Computers in Human Behavior*, 63, 899–905.

Kaner, G., & Baruh, L. (2022). How to speak 'sustainable fashion': Four consumer personas and five criteria for sustainable fashion communication. *International Journal of Fashion Design, Technology and Education*, 15(3), 385–393.

Kemp, S. (2020). Report: Most important data on digital audiences during coronavirus, April 24, 2020, http://thenextweb.com/news/report-most-important-data-on-digital-audiences-during-coronavirus (accessed 25 June 2023).

Kennedy, A., Baxter, S. M., & Ilicic, J. (2019). Celebrity versus film persona endorsements: Examining the effect of celebrity transgressions on consumer judgments. *Psychology & Marketing*, 36(2), 102–112.

Khoa, B. T. (2020). The impact of the personal data disclosure's tradeoff on the trust and attitude loyalty in mobile banking services. *Journal of Promotion Management*, 27(4), 585–608.

Kotler, P., Armstrong, G., & Balasubramanian, S. (2023). *Principles of Marketing*, 19th edn., NJ: Pearson Education Inc.

Krawczyk-Sokołowska, I., & Caputa, W. (2023). Awareness of network security and customer value – The company and customer perspective. *Technological Forecasting and Social Change*, 190, 122430.

Laricchia, F. (2023). Connected wearable devices worldwide 2019–2022, *Statista*, 22 May 2023, http://www.statista.com/statistics/487291/global-connected-wearable-devices/ (accessed 23 June 2023).

LeRouge, C., Ma, J., Sneha, S., & Tolle, K. (2013). User profiles and personas in the design and development of consumer health technologies. *International Journal of Medical Informatics*, 82(11), e251–e268.

Lin, Y. (2020). 10 artificial intelligence statistics you need to know in 2021, https://www.oberlo.com/blog/artificial-intelligence-statistics (accessed 11 December 2023).

Ma, J., & LeRouge, C. (2007). Introducing user profiles and personas into information systems development. AMCIS 2007 Proceedings, 237, 1–12. https://aisel.aisnet.org/cgi/viewcontent.cgi?article=1747&context=amcis2007

Mayor, L. G., & Moynihan, Q. (2021). From tasting food to recalling smells, here's how AI now mimics our senses, *Business Insider*, https://www.Businessinsider.com/olfactory-robot-technology-tech-advancesrevolution-robots-deep-learning-machines-2021-

McCarthy, J., Minsky, M. L., Rochester, N., & Shannon, C. E. (1955). A proposal for the Dartmouth summer research project on artificial intelligence. *AI Magazine*, 27(4), 12–14.

Mehta, P., Jebarajakirthy, C., Maseeh, H. I., Anubha, A., Saha, R., & Dhanda, K. (2022). Artificial intelligence in marketing: A meta-analytic review. *Psychology & Marketing*, 39(11), 2013–2038.

Mogaji, E., & Nguyen, N. P. (2022). Managers' understanding of artificial intelligence in relation to marketing financial services: Insights from a cross-country study. *International Journal of Bank Marketing*, 40(6), 1272–1298.

Mustak, M., Salminen, J., Plé, L., & Wirtz, J. (2021). Artificial intelligence in marketing: Topic modelling, scientometric analysis, and research agenda. *Journal of Business Research*, 124, 389–404.

Namkung, Y., Shin, S. Y., & Yang, I. S. (2007). A grounded theory approach to understanding the website experiences of restaurant customers. *Journal of Foodservice Business Research*, 10(1), 77–99.

Onel, N., Mukherjee, A., Kreidler, N. B., Díaz, E. M., Furchheim, P., Gupta, S., ... & Wang, Q. (2018). Tell me your story and I will tell you who you are: Persona perspective in sustainable consumption. *Psychology & Marketing*, 35(10), 752–765.

Pandey, S., & Chawla, D. (2018). Evolving segments of online clothing buyers: An emerging market study. *Journal of Advances in Management Research*, 15(4), 536–557.

Pennington, C. (2023). Generative AI: The new frontier for VC investment. *Forbes*, January 17, 2023. http://www.forbes.com/sites/columbiabusinessschool/2023/01/17/generative-ai-the-new-frontier-for-vc-investment/?sh=5f51154e519c (accessed 16 June 2023).

Perkin, N., & Abraham, P. (2017). *Building the Agile Business through Digital Transformation*, 1st edn, London: Kogan Page Ltd, https://www.amazon.com/Building-Business-through-Digital-Transformation/dp/0749480394 (accessed 11 December 2023).

Pike, J. (2023). British government announce £54 million investment into the development of trustworthy artificial intelligence. *International Business Week*, 16, June, 2023, http://www.ibtimes.co.uk/british-government-announce-54-million-investment-development-trustworthy-artificial-1716788 (accessed 16 June 2023).

Promotosh, B., & Sajedul, I. M. (2011). Young consumers' purchase intentions of buying green products A study based on the Theory of Planned Behavior. Master Thesis. UMEA University.

Pruitt, J., & Adlin, T. (2006). *The Persona Lifecycle: Keeping People in Mind throughout Product Design*. Amsterdam: Morgan Kaufman.

Rahim, R. A., Sulaiman, Z., Chin, T. A., Arif, M. S. M., & Hamid, M. H. A. (2017, June). E-WOM review adoption: Consumers' demographic profile influence on green purchase intention. In *IOP Conference Series: Materials Science and Engineering*, 215(1), 012020.

Rezaei, R., Safa, L., & Ganjkhanlo, M. M. (2020). Understanding farmers' ecological conservation behavior regarding the use of integrated pest management – An application of the technology acceptance model. *Global Ecology and Conservation*, 22, e00941.

Robertson, N., McQuilken, L., & Kandampully, J. (2012). Consumer complaints and recovery through guaranteeing self-service technology. *Journal of Consumer Behaviour*, 11(1), 21–30.

Rotter, J. B. (1967). A new scale for the management of trust. *Journal of Personality*, 35, 651–665.

Sadek, H., & El Mehelmi, H. (2020). Customer brand engagement impact on brand satisfaction, loyalty, and trust in the online context. Egyptian banking sector. *Journal of Business and Retail Management Research*, 14(3), 22–33.

Schneider, D. (2023). How to use website demographics effectively in your audience analysis, Similarweb Blog, 8 January 2023, http://www.similarweb.com/blog/research/market-research/website-demographics/ (accessed 25 June 2023).

Srivastava, R. K. (2015). How differing demographic factors impact consumers' loyalty towards national or international fast-food chains: A comparative study in emerging markets. *British Food Journal*, 117(4),1354–1376.

Statista Research Department (2023). Revenue of the smartwatches industry worldwide 2018–2027, *Statista*, 1 June 2023, http://www.statista.com/forecasts/1314322/worldwide-revenue-of-smartwatch-market (accessed 23 June 2023).

Van Looy, B., Gemmel, P., & Van Dierdonck, R. (2003). *Services Management: An Integrated Approach*, 2nd edn, Essex: Prentice Hall.

Vlačić, B., Corbo, L., Costa e Silva, S. & Dabić, M. (2021). The evolving role of artificial intelligence in marketing: A review and research agenda. *Journal of Business Research*, 128, 187–203.

Wirtz, J., Kum, D., Lee, K. S. (2000). Should a firm with a reputation for outstanding service quality offer a service guarantee? *Journal of Services Marketing*, 14(6): 502–512.

Wirtz, J., Patterson, P. G., Kunz, W. H., Gruber, T., Lu, V. N., Paluch, S., & Martins, A. (2018). Brave new world: Service robots in the frontline. *Journal of Service Management*, *29*(5), 907–931.

Xu, Yingzi, et al. (2020). AI customer service: Task complexity, problem-solving ability, and usage intention. *Australasian Marketing Journal*, *28*(4), 189–199, doi:10.1016/j.ausmj.2020.03.005.

Yasar, K., & Wignore, I. (2022). Wearable technology. *Tech Target*, May, 2022, http://www.techtarget.com/searchmobilecomputing/definition/wearable-technology (accessed 23 June 2023).

# Index

*Note*: Page numbers followed by b denotes boxes. Page numbers in **bold** denotes tables. Page numbers in *italics* denote figures.

acculturation 84, 86, 103
achievement, need for 222, 223–224
actual self **247**
Adams, J. S. 224
adaptation/standardisation 272
addictive consumption 29, 47
Adidas 165
advertising: attitude towards 201, *202*; consumer involvement 71–73; and consumers' attention 147; extinction (advertising message wear-out) 173; high level of 71
affective decision model **70**, 71
affiliation, need for 222, 223–224
affinity impulse 274
African Traditional Religions (ATR) 97
age, as subculture 101–102
agents, socialisation 120–121
agreeableness 242
AI *see* artificial intelligence (AI)
AliBaba 90
alternatives, evaluation of 19, 63–64
altruistic impulse 274–275
Amazon 228; case study of 22–24; emergence of 22–24; Kindle 22–23
Amazon Lex 328
Amazon Prime 23–24
American Express 21b
American social classes 125

Android 278–279
anthropology 13
anti-brand activity 129
apparent (passive) loyalty 338
Apple 3, 21b, 172, 277, 328; self-service repairs 340b–341b
approach-approach conflict 226–227
approval utility 229, 230
AR *see* augmented reality (AR)
Arab Spring movement 45
Argos 75
ARIT *see* augmented reality interactive technology (ARIT)
artificial intelligence (AI) 42, 61, 207, 238, 325, 342, 343–344; classification 329; defined 329; in digital marketing 330; examples 330; as image interactivity technology 329; investment in 328; and marketing 328–330; and marketing and controversies 281b; self-service 329; sensory-enabled 329; STP and consumer demographics 330–334; virtualisation 329
aspirational group 114
assimilation, culture 86
associative learning 171
associative networks 185
atheism 97
attention: and advertising 147; and colour *147*, 148; and consumer perception

146–148; stimulus 147; strategies for catching 146–147
attitude(s): accessibility 203; balanced theory 197–198; behaviour prediction 201, 203; brand specific 193; campaigning to curb obesity (case study) 214–215; consistent 193; consumer: changing 204–206; in a digital age 207, *208*; marketing communications 209–211; models of 195–201; rights and privacy *208*; defining 193–195; ego-defensive function 206; elements of 195, *196*; formation 203–204; functional theory of 206–207; goal-oriented 193; hierarchy of effect model 196–197; intensity 194; knowledge function 206–207; liquid consumption 208–209; marketing communications model 209–211; overview 192–193; perceived behaviour control (PBC) 200–201; solid consumption 208–209; stability 203; theory of planned behaviour (TBA) model 200–201; theory of reasoned action (TRA) model 199–200, *201*; towards the ad 201, *202*; tricomponent model 195; utilitarian function 206; value-expressive function 206
attitude, multi-attribute models 198–201
attribute-specific guarantees 327
augmented reality (AR) 150–151; and consumer perception 150–151
augmented reality interactive technology (ARIT) 150, 151
augmented virtuality (AV) 152
autism spectrum disorder (ASD) 153
Automatic Emergency Braking (AEB) 227
automobile industry, perceptual map for 157, *158*
avoidance-approach conflict 226, 227
avoidance-avoidance conflict 226, 227

baby boomers 102
Baha'i 97
balanced theory 115; consumer attitudes 197–198
banking technology 182; Barclays Bank, consumers' digital experience at (case study) 188–189; Coding and Online Safety for Kids 188–189; Digital Confidence Package 188
Barclays 3
Barclays Bank, consumers' digital experience at (case study) 188–189

bargaining to resolve family conflicts 117–118
BBC 189
BBC:micro:bit 189
behaviour: and culture 89; defined 4; dysfunctional behavioural pattern 37; prediction, consumer attitudes and 201, 203; subjective culture and social behaviour 91 *see also* consumer behaviour; misbehaviour
behavioural learning 171–173; classical conditioning 171–172; operant conditioning 171; repetition 172–173; stimulus discrimination 173; stimulus generalisation 173 *see also* learning
behavioural segmentation 331
beliefs: and religion 95; *vs.* values 252 *see also* values
Beyonce 257
Bezos, Jeff 22
Bieber, Justin 257
Big Data, in British supermarkets (case study) 319–321
Big Data analytics (BDA) 342
'Big Five' personality traits 242
biogenic (primary) needs 221
blogs 273
Body Shop, The 45
Boots 75
Bottom of the pyramid (BOP) consumers 89, 90
Bowerman, B. 164
brand ambassadors 33–36; Louis Vuitton and BTS in global brand ambassador deal 35; selection criteria 34–36
brand community 126–129; characteristics 128–129; consumer social motivation 229; and digitalisation 127–128; kind of consciousness 128; online brand culture 127–128; rituals and tradition 128; social identification 127; social relationships in 126–127, 128; word-of-mouth communication 127, 128–129
brand identity 243
brand names 70
brand personality 242–245; dimensions 244–245; elements of brand identity 242–243; Internet usage and 245
brands 5, 126–129, 242–245; anti-brand activity 129 *see also* brand community
Breton, T. 49
'Brick-and-mortar' (instore) transactions 7

# INDEX

British Airways 3
British Sociological Association 13
British supermarkets, Big Data and consumer research in (case study) 319–321
Buddhism 97
bullying 40–41 *see also* cyberbullying
business markets 9
Business-to-Business (B2B) transactions 9, 10
Business-to-Consumer (B2C) transactions 8–9, 10
buying, panic: defined 225; factors 225–226; and global pandemics 224–226; neurological factors 226; situational factors 226; social factors 226

Cadbury chocolates, motivation for 231
Candomblé 97
Carrefour 151
case study(ies): Amazon 22–24; Barclays Bank, consumers' digital experience at 188–189; Big Data and consumer research in British supermarkets 319–321; Clubhouse, as hub for valuable conversations 133–134; EU' agenda for SMEs and quest for sustainable consumption (case study) 49–50; extending self on social media 255–257; Ferrari cars, drive for 233–235; McDonalds in the Middle East 107–108; Nike, product positioning for unique experiences at 164–165; Obesity, campaigning to curb 214–215; PayPal and digital transformation in consumer decision-making process 74–76; Samsung, as innovative organisation 282–284; SMEs in consumer-focused marketing (case study) 341–343
celebrity endorsement 172–173, 187b
children: cognitive development 184; as consumers 119–120; learning, act of consumption 184; socialisation, parents' role in 121–122 *see also* family
Christianity 97
Chung, H. 283
classical conditioning 171–173
'Click-and mortar' (online) transactions 7
Clooney, G. 172
Clubhouse, as hub for valuable conversations (case study) 133–134
co-branding strategy 34
cognitive component, social identification 127

cognitive decision-making model 69–70
cognitive development 184
cognitive learning theory 175–176 *see also* learning
Coca-Cola 245
Colgate 3
collective projects 273
collective self 247
collectivism, cultural dimension 90–91
commitment: high-context *vs.* low-context cultures 93, 94; and sacredness 95
communication(s): eWOMs 36, 63; high-context *vs.* low-context cultures 93, 94; marketing 19; 'one-to-many' 68; parents and children 122; peer-group communications 122; unethical marketing 30; WhatsApp, connecting and consuming on 132b; word-of-mouth (WOM) 67, 127, 128–129 *see also* word-of-mouth (WOM) communications
communitas, sacredness and 100
community(ies): brand 126–129; protest 43–45; and religion 95
compatibility 270
compensatory rule 64
competitive advantage 265
complexity 270
compulsive consumption 29, 46, 240
Comte, A. 13
conditioned response (CR) 172
conditioned stimulus (CS) 171–172
confectioneries 211–212
Conference of the Parties (COP) programmes 238
conflicts, motivational 226; approach-approach conflict 226–227; avoidance-approach conflict 226, 227; avoidance-avoidance conflict 226, 227
confrontation, high-context *vs.* low-context cultures 93, 94
Confused Alec 335
conjunctive rule 65
conscientiousness 242
consensus parents 121
*Consideration set* 63
consumer behaviour: boundaries, defining 4–7; concepts, examining 4–7; defined 5; dynamics of 7–11; family dynamics 116–118; and hero-villain 36; interdisciplinary nature 12–15; and marketing ethics 29; and marketing mix, in digital environment 5–7; reference

groups 114–115; and social classes 124–126 *see also* consumer decision-making process; consumer(s); family; marketing
consumer decision-making process: affective decision model 70, 71; cognitive decision model 69–70; consumer involvement 71–73; decision rules 64–66; decision situations 69–71; decision stage 64; in digital age 58–59, 60; and digital transformation 57–58; evaluation of alternatives 63–64; Google as consumers' search engine 73b–74b; habitual decision model 70–71; information search 61–62; mobile shopping 58–59, 60; need recognition 60–61; online shopping 58–59, 60; overview 56–59; PayPal and digital transformation in (case study) 74–76; post-purchase evaluation 66–68; post-purchase phase 57; prepurchase phase 57; purchase phase 57
consumer demographics, STP and 330–334
*consumere* 15
consumer involvement 71–73
consumerism 43–44
*Consumerism in the digital age* (Kucuk) 44
consumer misbehaviour 36–38, 40
consumer persona 334–336
consumer power 19
consumer research: Big Data and consumer research in British supermarkets (case study) 319–321; brief 290–291, 292; data analysis 308–310; data collection 308; data sources 298–300; defined 288; design formulation 296–298; digital marketing process 295; and ethics 315, 316; ethnography 301–302; experimentation 300–301; focus group discussion 302–303; Hilton 317; in-depth interview 301; need for 288–289; netnography in 311–312; and neuromarketing 314–315; objectives 295–296; perspectives and paradigms on 293–295; presentation of findings 310, 311; problem, defining 295–296; proposal 291–293; qualitative vs quantitative data 301; research instrument 304–305, 306–308; sampling plan 303–304, 305; setting stage for 289–290; Surveymonkey, for data collection 318b; surveys 300
consumer(s) 7–8; children as 119–120; and citizen activism 130; defined 4; digital, emergence of 15–18; exploiting disadvantaged 31; green and sustainable consumption 31–33; organisational vs consumer transactions 8–11; rights and privacy 208; rights of, digitalisation and 44; traditional consumption *vs.* consumption in digital age 19–20 *see also* attitude(s); consumer behaviour; consumer decision-making process; learning; marketing; motivation; perception, consumer
'Consumers Bill of Rights' 43–44
consumer self 245–248; community level 247, 248; family level 247, 248; group level 247, 248; illustrations and examples 247; individual level 247, 248; and lifestyle 249–251
*Consumers' immediate memory for prices* (Vanhuele) 177
Consumers International 44
consumer socialisation 120–123, 131, 184
consumer-to-consumer (C2C) transactions 256
consumption 3; addictive 29, 47; compulsive 29, 46; green 31–33; sustainable 31–33; technology, markets and 264–266; traditional *vs.* consumption in digital age 19–20; utility 229, 230
contact comfort/immediacy impulse 274
contactless payments 20b–21b
contamination, sacredness and 95
content communities 273
continuous innovation 266–267
convenience 5, 252, 253
coping behaviour, panic buying and 225
cosmopolitanism 125–126, 252, 253
counterfeiting 29, 38–39
country of origin 70
covariations 70
COVID-19 pandemic 3, 47b–48b, 114, 183, 192, 238, 264, 328, 342; consumer digital motivation and 232b; online grocery shopping 122; and panic buying 224–226; panic buying and 224–226; PayPal (case study) 75; PPE, organisational and personal transactions for 9–10
credibility factor 146
cues, learning 178, 179
culture(s) 83–84; acculturation 84, 86; age 101–102; as arbitrary 88; assimilation 86; behaviour regulation and 89; characterising 85–89; collectivism 90–91; defined 84, 105; digital/digitalisation

84–85; dimensions (Hofstede) 85, 90–91; dynamism 87–88; enculturation 84, 85; enduring nature of 87; geographical subculture 102; global consumer culture (GCC) 89–90; high-context 93–94; individualism 90–91; integration 86; learning 85–86; long-term orientation 91; low-context 93–94; marginalisation 86; masculinity 90; McDonald's in the Middle East (case study) 107–108; models 90–91; movement of cultural meaning 91–93; myths 94; pop 94–95; popular 94–95; power distance 91; as purpose-driven and satisfies needs 88–89; race and ethnic subcultures 103–104; religion and 95–101; religion-based subculture 104; rituals 92–93, 94; separation 86; sex-based subculture 102–103; sharing 86–87; spirituality and 95–101; subcultures 101; subjective culture and social behaviour 91; uncertainty avoidance 91; Valentine's day (as ritual for consumption) 104–105; YouTube and digital transformation of pop culture 106b
customer engagement (CE) 276
customer relationship management (CRM) 342
customer trust/loyalty 337–339
cyberbullying 29, 40–41
cybercrime: increasing rate of 44; in UK 47b–48b

data sources, consumer research 299–300
data analysis, consumer research 308–310; qualitative 309–310; quantitative 308–309
data collection, consumer research 308
data sources, consumer research 298–300; secondary data 298–299
dating app 212b–213b
dealing with new situations, high-context *vs.* low-context cultures 93, 94
decision making 20, 56–57; affective decision model 70, 71; cognitive decision model 69–70; habitual decision model 70–71 *see also* consumer decision-making process
decision rules 64–66 *see also* consumer decision-making process
decision situations (models) 69–71; affective decision model 70, 71; cognitive decision model 69–70; habitual decision model 70–71 *see also* consumer decision-making process
decision stage 64
demographics, consumer, STP and 330–334
demographic segmentation 331
Dettol 172
Dichter, E. 14
diffusion of (DOI) innovation 266–270
digital self 247
digital age/digitalisation 16, 42, 113; Amazon (case study) 22–24; Barclays Bank, consumers' digital experience at (case study) 188–189; brand community 127–128; celebrity endorsement in 187b; consumer attitudes 207, *208*; consumer decision-making process in 58–59, *60*; consumer misbehaviour in 40; consumer motivation and 227–229; consumers' rights and 44; consumption *vs.* traditional consumption 19–20; culture 84–85; information search 62; learning in 181–182; meeting consumers' needs in (case study) 22–24 *see also* Internet; mobile shopping; online shopping; technology
Digital Confidence Package 188
digital consumer, emergence of 15–18
digital culture 84–85
digital divide 181
Digital Eagles, the 189
digital immigrants 18, 87, 181, 183
digital marketing: AI in 330; process 295
digital natives 18, 87, 181, 183–184
digital networked technology (DNT) 89
digital protection 29, 42–43
digital self 248–249
digital technology 116; evolutionary phases 16–18; learning and 181–182
digital transformation 28–29; brand communities 129; consumer decision-making and 57–58; in consumer decision-making process, PayPal and (case study) 74–76; cultural dynamism 88; cultural integration 90; evaluation of alternatives 63–64; family buying roles and 118–120; for organisations 326; of pop cultures, YouTube and 106b
direct resolution 220
disadvantaged consumers, exploiting 31
disclaimant group 114
discontinuous innovation 266, 267
disjunctive rule 65

Disneyland, consumer socialisation at 131
dissociation 220
dissociative/avoidance group 114, 115
distributive misbehaviour 37–38
divestment rituals 92
DNT *see* digital networked technology (DNT)
Dolby Atmos 23
Dove 186
Dove Self-Esteem Project (DSEP) 186
dynamically continuous innovation 266, 267
dynamism, culture 87–88
dysfunctional behavioural pattern 37
Dyson 173

easyJet 173
e-books 88
eco-innovation 265
e-commerce 23, 58, 68, 337
economics 12–13
ecstasy and flow, sacredness and 101
ego 206, 240, 335
electroencephalography (EEG) 14
electronic word-of-mouth communications (eWOMs) 36, 63, 155, 228, 333 *see also* communication(s); word-of-mouth (WOM) communications
emotional appeal 211
emotional component, social identification 127
empathy 41
enculturation 84, 85
enduring involvement 72
enduring nature, of culture 87
Engel-Kollat-Blackwell model 57
enterprise resource planning (ERP) 342
environmentalism 43
episodic memory 178
equity theory of motivation (Adams) 224
escapism 220
e-service 66
ethics: consumer research and 315, 316; marketing 29; unethical marketing communications 30; unethical pricing 29–30 *see also* marketing ethics
ethnicity: and religion 104; subculture 103–104 *see also* religion(s)
ethnocentrism 332
ethnography, consumer research and 301–302
eurobarometer survey 49

European Commission 49
European Green Deal 49–50
European Union (EU) 214, 341; agenda for SMEs and quest for sustainable consumption (case study) 49–50
evaluation of alternatives 19, 63–64
evaluative component, social identification 127
event-related potential (ERP) 14
*Evoke set* 63
exchange rituals 92
exended self 247
experimentation, consumer research 300–301
exposure: consumer perception 144–146; selectivity theory 145–146
extended family 116–117
extended self: IKEA as home for consumers' 253; on social media (case study) 255–257
extinction (advertising message wear-out) 173
extroversion 242
eye-tracking 14

Facebook 7, 23, 40, 113, 133, 189, 229, 248, 255, 273, 337
faithfulness 252, 253
family 116–118; buying roles, digital transformation and 118–120; conflicts, approaches for resolving 117–118; connecting and consuming on WhatsApp 132b; and consumer socialisation 120–123; and contemporary consumer behaviour 116–118; extended 116–117; FLC model 123–124; nuclear 116; of orientation 117; of procreation 117; stem 116, 117
family life cycle (FLC) 123–124
fear of the unknown, panic buying and 225
Federer, R. 165
FedEx 162
feminine traits 90
Ferrari 173
Ferrari, E. 233–235
Ferrari cars, drive for (case study) 233–235
five senses, consumer perception 144–145
FLC *see* family life cycle (FLC)
Flickr 273
fluid compensation 220
Focus group, consumer research 302–303
Focus-related utility 229, 230

Ford 271
Formal group 114
4Cs of Internet usage/users 182–184
fraud 37
Freud, S. 14, 240
Freudian theory 239–240; child development stages 240; ego 240; id 240; superego 240
'From Culture to Smart Culture' 84–85
functional magnetic resonance imaging (fMRI) 14
functional risk 160–161
functional theory, of attitude 206–207

Gbadamosi, A. 31, 32, 70, 86, 88, 90, 96, 103–104, 119, 121, 182, 183, 185, 241, 249, 276, 300
GCC *see* global consumer culture (GCC)
Generation Alpha 325
Generation X 102, 264, 325
Generation Y 102, 325
Generation Z 102, 325
geographical subcultures 102
geographic segmentation 331
geography 15
Gestalt psychology 148–149, 162
global consumer culture (GCC) 89–90
globalisation: global consumer culture 89–90; global users, Internet (2005-2022) 16–18; Louis Vuitton and BTS in global brand ambassador deal 35
global pandemics *see* COVID-19 pandemic
gloomy persona 335
Google 21b, 61, 228, 277, 328; as consumers' search engine 73–74, 73b–74b; overview 73
Google Analytics 336
Google Assistant 263, 281b, 328
government 8
grandparents 122 *see also* family
Green Deal (EU) 49–50
green marketing 31–33 *see also* sustainable marketing
greenwashing 33
groom rituals 92
guarantees 327
Gucci 3, 56, 173

habitual decision-making model 70–71
Happn 212
Harley-Davidson 270–271

hierarchy of effect model, attitude 196–197
hierarchy of needs (Maslow's) 61, 222–223
hierophany 95
high-context cultures 93–94, 107 *see also* culture(s)
high-income consumers 229
high-pressure selling 30
Hilton 317
Hinduism 97
Hinton, G. 281b
history 14–15
Honda 157
Horney, K. 240
Huawei 172

id, 240
ideal self 247
ideal social self 247
identity 245; cues, displaying 116 *see also* self-identity
IKEA 151, 253
image interactivity technology, AI as 329
impression management theory 115
in-depth interview, consumer research 301
individualism, cultural dimension 90–91
informal group 114
information access 19
information and communication technologies (ICTs) 40–41, 265–266 *see also* technology
information processing 176; process stages, memory and 175–176
information search 61–62; commercial sources 61; digitalisation 62; non-commercial 61–62; online/offline 62
infotainment 146
in-group 114
innovation 252, 253; adaptation/ standardisation, figure 272; consumers (adopters) 268–269; and consumer's value co-creation roles 272–273; continuous 266–267; diffusion of (DOI) 266–269; discontinuous 266, 267; dynamically continuous 266, 267; eco-innovation 265; emerging trends in social media 273–274; factors influencing diffusion of 269–270; invention adoption process 270; and marketing 276–277; marketisation 268; non-technological 277; organisational 268; process 268; resistance to 270–272; Samsung, as innovative organisation

(case study) 282–284; sources of 266; technological 268, 277; types of 266–267; and value co-creation 272–273
Instagram 18, 23, 40, 113, 189, 229, 248, 249, 255, 273
instrumental conditioning 173–174
integrated marketing communications (IMCs) 277
integration, culture 86
interactional misbehaviour 37
Interaction Design Foundation 151
interaction(s): social media 276; strategies 116; VR system 152
International Chambers of Commerce 38
internationalisation 42
international marketing 31
Interne: global users (2005-2022) 16–18; social media, global users 231 *see also* digital age/digitalisation
Internet 16, 42, 62, 90, 145, 149, 264; Barclays Bank, consumers' digital experience at (case study) 188–189; brand personality 245; and consumer motivation 227–229; 4Cs of usage/users 182–184; marketing activities 122–123; penetration rates 264–265; self-concept 248
Internet conquerors 334
Internet of Things (IoT) 10, 146, 342
interpretation, consumer perception and 144, 148
instrument, consumer research 304–305, 306–308
invention adoption process 270–272
involvement: degree of 160; enduring 72; response 72; situation 72 *see also* consumer involvement
iOS 277
Islam 98

Jainism 98
Jehovah's Witnesses 98
JND *see* just noticeable difference (JND)
Johnson, D. 172
*Journal of Applied Psychology* 157
Judaism 98
Jung, C. 240, 241
just noticeable difference (JND) 156

Kennedy, J. F. 43
Kindle 22–23
Knight, P. 164

knowledge function, attitude 206–207
kratophany 95

Laissez-faire parents 121
Lamborghini 56, 330–331
Landor Associate 162
learning: associative 171; behavioural 171–173; children, act of consumption 184; cognitive learning theory 175–176; consumer 171; consumer socialisation theories 184; cues *178*, 179; culture 85–86; defined 171; in a digital age 181–182; elements of 178–180; and 4Cs of Internet usage/users 182–184; information processing 176; instrumental conditioning 173–174; motivation *178*, 179; observational 176; reinforcement 174–175, *178*, 179–180; response *178*, 179 *see also* memory
Lego 129
lesbian, gay, bisexual, and transgender (LGBT) 248
lexicographic rule 65
Lexus 157
life-cycle theory 13
lifestyle: and consumer self 249–251; segmentation 250–251
LinkedIn 7, 189, 229, 248, 255, 256, 273, 337
liquid consumption 208–209
live stream, social media 275–276
logistic companies, perceptual map for 157, *159*
long-term memory 178–179
long-term orientation 91
look-alike packaging 173
L'Oreal 45
Louis Vuitton 173
low-context cultures 93–94, 107 *see also* culture(s)
lower (working) class 125
loyalty 337–339; apparent (passive) 338; occasional 338; real 338; Tesco clubcard 339

MAR *see* mobile augmented reality (MAR)
marginalisation, culture 86
marketers 7, 8
marketing 5; and AI 281b; AI and 328–330; brand community 126–129; consumer-focused, SMEs and (case study) 341–343;

contemporary 4–5; customer trust and loyalty 337–339; green 31–33; high-pressure selling 30; and innovation 276–277; international 31; Internet 122–123; social media 122–123; sustainable 31–33 *see also* consumer behaviour; consumer(s); digital marketing; marketing ethics
marketing application, of consumer perception 157–158; marketing mix 161–162; perceived risk 159–161; perceptual map 157–158, *159*; positioning and repositioning 157–158
marketing communications **19**, 30
marketing communications model, consumer attitudes 209–211
marketing ethics 29; addictive consumption 47; brand ambassadors 33–36; compulsive consumption 46; consumerism 43–44; consumer misbehaviour 36–38, 40; counterfeiting 38–39; cyberbullying 40–41; cybercrime in UK 47b–48b; digital protection and security 42–43; environmentalism 43; EU's agenda for SMEs and quest for sustainable consumption (case study) 49–50; exploiting disadvantaged consumers 31; green marketing and sustainable consumption 31–33; greenwashing and sustainable consumption 33; hero-villain and consumer behaviour 36; high-pressure selling 30; international marketing 31; marketing research 30–31; protest communities 43–45; trolling 45–46; unethical communications 30; unethical pricing 29–30 *see also* ethics
marketing mix: and consumer behaviour, in digital environment 5–7; ethics 29; and perception 161–162
marketing-oriented stimuli 145
marketing research 30–31; Big Data in 313–314
marketisation innovation 268
market(s) 264–266; business 9
masculinity 90
Maslow, A. 61, 222–223
Maslow's hierarchy of needs 61, 222–223
maximiser 66
McClelland, D. 223–224
McDonalds 88; in the Middle East (case study) 107–108

memory: associative networks 185; defined 177; episodic 178; information processing process stages 175–176; long-term 178–179; retrieval 180–181; semantic 178; sensory 177; short-term 177–178 *see also* learning
Messi, L. 172
micro-blogging 273
Microsoft 23
middle-class 124–125, 126
Middle East, McDonalds in (case study) 107–108
Mini Coopers 330
misbehaviour, consumer 36–38; in digital age 40; distributive 37–38; interactional 37; procedural 37 *see also* behaviour
mixed reality (MR) 152–153
mobile augmented reality (MAR) 150
mobile health (m-health) technology 16
mobile shopping 58–59, *60 see also* digital age/digitalisation; online shopping
mobile telecommunications 90
Money Supermarket 62
mormonism **99**
mortality salience 226
motivation: for Cadbury chocolates 231; consumer: digital 227–229; digital motivation and COVID-19 pandemic 232b; needs, drives, and goals 220–221; social 229–230, **231**; defined 220; digitalisation and 227–229; direct resolution 220; dissociation 220; equity theory of 224; escapism 220; Ferrari cars, drive for (case study) 233–235; fluid compensation 220; and Henry Murray's need classification 221–222; and hierarchy of needs (Maslow's) 222–223; for joining social media 229–230, **231**; in learning *178*, *179*; and McClelland's three needs theory 223–224; motivational conflicts 226; approach-approach conflict 226–227; avoidance-approach conflict 226, 227; avoidance-avoidance conflict 226, 227; overview 220–221; panic buying and global pandemics 224–226; for social media participation 274–275; symbolic self-completion 220; theories 221–224 *see also* need(s)
movement of cultural meaning 91–93 *see also* culture(s)
MR *see* mixed reality (MR)

multi-attribute models, attitude 198–201
multiculturalism 89, 103 *see also* culture(s)
multiplayer online role-playing games (MMORPG) 274
Murray, H. 221–222
Musk, E. 133, 273
mystery, sacredness and 100
myths: and culture 94; defined 94; and sacredness 100

National Crime Agency (NCA) 48b
navigation, VR system 152
near-field communication (NFC) 21b, 342
need recognition 61–61
need(s) 5, **19**; for achievement 222, 223–224; for affiliation 222, 223–224; biogenic (primary) 221; Henry Murray classification of 221–222; higher-order 223; lower-level 223; for power 222, 223–224; psychogenic (secondary) 221; and purpose-driven culture 88–89; *vs.* want 221 *see also* motivation
negative reviews 67–68
negative word-of-mouth (WOM) communications 129
Neo-Freudian theory 240–241
Nespresso 172
Netflix 75
netnography, in consumer research 311–312
networks, associative 185
neurological factors, panic buying 226
neuromarketing 14; and consumer research 314–315
neuroscience 14
neuroticism 46, 242
Nike 45, 75, 185; product positioning for unique experiences at (case study) 164–165
Nissan 157
non-compensatory rule 64, 65; conjunctive rule 65; disjunctive rule 65; lexicographic rule 65
non-deceptive counterfeiting 39
non-government organisations (NGOs) 8
Novelty, adopting 147, 165
nuclear family 116

obesity, campaigning to curb (case study) 214–215
objectification, sacredness and 95
observability 270

observational learning 176 *see also* learning
occasional loyalty 338
OCR *see* online customer review (OCR)
Office of National Statistics (ONS) 40, 47
omni-shoppers 153
online brand culture 127–128 *see also* brand community
online customer review (OCR) 63, 65, 67
online shopping 65; consumer decision-making process 58–59, 60, 65–66; showrooming 153–154 *see also* consumer decision-making process; digital age/digitalisation; mobile shopping
openness to experience 242
operant conditioning 171
opinion leaders 129–131; characteristics 130–131; in social networks 129, 130; WOM communications 130
opposition to profane, sacredness and 95
Oracle 23
organisational innovation 268
organisation(s): distinguishing factors of organisational purchases 10, **11**; organisational and personal transactions for COVID-19 PPE 9–10; organisational vs consumer transactions 8–11
other-directedness 253
out-group 114–115

packaging style 71
paganism **99**
panic buying: defined 225; factors 225–226; and global pandemics 224–226; neurological factors 226; situational factors 226; social factors 226
parents: consensus 121; Laissez-faire 121; pluralistic 121; protective 121; role in children's socialisation 121–122 *see also* family
partiality 253
Pavlov, I. 171, 173
payment(s), contactless 20b–21b
PayPal (case study) 74–76
PBC *see* perceived behaviour control (PBC)
peer-group communications 122
Pepsi 172, 246–247, 271–272
perceived behaviour control (PBC) 200–201
perceived risk, consumer perception and 159–161; functional risk 160–161; psychological risk 161; social risk 160; time risk 161

perception, consumer: attention 144, 146–148; augmented reality (AR) 150–151; concepts 144–148; defined 144; exposure 144–146; five senses: sight 144; smell 144, 145; sound 144–145; taste 144; touch 144; Gestalt psychology 148–149; interpretation 144, 148; marketing application of 157–158; and marketing mix 161–162; and mixed reality (MR) 152–153; Nike, product positioning for unique experiences at (case study) 164–165; overview 143–144; and panic buying 225; perceived risk 159–161; semiotics 150; sensation 144; sensory threshold 156–157; and showrooming 153–155; subliminal 156; and virtual reality 151–152; and webrooming 155
perceptual map 157–158; for automobile industry 157, *158*; for logistic companies 157, *159*
permanent income model 13
persona, consumer 334–336
personal factor, memory retrieval 181
Personal Identity Number (PIN) 21b
personality 239; brand 242–245; defined 239; Freudian theory 239–240; Neo-Freudian theory 240–241; Red Bull 254b–255b; theories 239–242; trait theory 241–242 *see also* self
personal protective equipment (PPE): COVID-19, organisational and personal transactions for 9–10
personal transactions, for COVID-19 PPE 9–10
personal utility impulse 274
persuasion to resolve family conflicts 117–118
PIN *see* Personal Identity Number (PIN)
Pinterest 227, 273
pluralistic parents 121
politics, to resolve family conflicts 117, 118
pop cultures 94–95; digital transformation of, YouTube and 106b *see also* culture(s)
positioning map, consumer perception and 157–158; Nike (case study) 164–165
positive reviews 67–68
positron emission tomography (PET) 14
possession rituals 92
post-purchase evaluation 20, 66–68
power, need for 222, 223–224
power distance 91

PPE *see* personal protective equipment (PPE)
preferences 5
presentation, memory retrieval 180
price(s) **20**, 71; unethical pricing 29–30
primary (biogenic) needs 221
principle of closure 149
principle of proximity 149
principle of similarity 148
Privacy Calculus Theory (PCT) 43
problem-solving, to resolve family conflicts 117, 118
procedural misbehaviour 37
process innovation 268
product life cycle (PLC) 277–278
pro-environmental technology (PET) 250, 251
protective parents 121
protest communities 43–45
pseudoshowrooming 153, 155
psychogenic (secondary) needs 221
psychographic segmentation 331
psychological risk 161
psychology 14
purpose-driven culture 88–89

race, subculture 103–104
radio frequency identification (RFID) 21b, 342
Ramsey, G. 147
Range Rovers 330
Rare Carat 328
Rastafari **99**
rational appeal 211
real loyalty 338
Red Bull, personality 254b–255b
recognise 180
recollection 180
recreational shoppers 334
Reebok 165
reference groups 114–115; defined 114; social identity theory 115–116; types of **114**
reinforcement 174–175, *178*, 179–180
relative advantage 269
relearning 180
*Religion and Consumer Behaviour in Developing Nations* (Gbadamosi) 96
religion(s): African Traditional Religions (ATR) **97**; Atheism **97**; Baha'i **97**; and beliefs 95; Buddhism **97**; Candomblé **97**; Christianity **97**; and community 95;

and culture 95–101, **97–100**; defined 95; dynamics **97–100**; and ethnicity 104; Hinduism **97**; Islam **98**; Jainism **98**; Jehovah's Witnesses **98**; Judaism **98**; Mormonism **99**; Paganism **99**; Rastafari **99**; and rituals 95; sacredness, properties 95–101; Santeria **99**; Shinto **100**; Sikhism **100**; Spiritualism **100**; subcultures based on **97–100**, 104; Taoism **100**; Unitarianism **100**; and values 95; Zoroastrianism **100**
rental agreements 20
repositioning, consumer perception and 157–158
research: consumer: marketing 30–31 *see also* consumer research
resistance to innovation 270–272
response, learning *178*, 179
response involvement 72
responsibility, high-context *vs.* low-context cultures 93, 94
retrieval, memory 180–181
reverse socialisation 120
reviews 67; negative/positive 67–68; online 67–68; word-of-mouth 67
Rihanna 147, 257
RISC Research Agency 251
risk-benefit analysis 43
risk(s) 182; functional 160–161; perceived 159–161; psychological 161; social 160; time 161
rituals: and brand community 128; and culture 92–93, 94; and religion 95; and sacredness 95; Valentine's Day as ritual for consumption 104–105 *see also* religion(s)
robots, service 327
Rolex 56, 173
romantic optimists 335
Ronaldo, C. 147, 165, 257, 336

sacredness: and consumer categories 101; properties 95–101 *see also* religion(s)
sacrifice, sacredness and 95
sales-personal factors, showrooming 154
sampling plan, consumer research 303–304, *304*, **305**
Samsung 328; as innovative organisation (case study) 282–284
Samsung Kiosk 283
Santeria **99**
satisfaction 5

satisficers 66
Savage, M. 125
Schulman, D. 75
search 19; information 61–62
secondary (psychogenic) needs 221
security 29; and digital protection 42–43
segmentation: behavioural 331; defined 331; demographic 331; geographic 331; psychographic 331
segmentation, targeting, and positioning (STP) 325; and consumer demographics 330–334; defined 331
selective interaction 115
selectivity theory 145–146
self 239, 245–248; extending, on social media (case study) 255–257 *see also* consumer self; digital self; personality
self-brand connection (SBR) 115
self-concept 39, 115, 161, 245–248
self-esteem 39, 41, 46, 186, 246
self-identity 245
self-image 245
selflessness 90
self-ordering system 107
self-reliance 90
self-service repairs (Apple) 340b–341b
self-service technologies (SSTs) 7, 326–327
self-verification 115–116; displaying identity cues 116; interaction strategies 116; selective interaction 115
selling, high-pressure 30
semantic memory 178
semiotics 150
sensory memory 177
sensory threshold 156–157
separation, culture 86
service robots 327
sex-based subculture 102–103
sharing, of culture 86–87
Shinto **100**
shoplifting 37
short-term memory 177–178
showrooming 164; consumer motivation for 153–154, *154*; and consumer perception 153–155, *154*; pseudoshowrooming 153, 155; sales-personal factors 154; store-related factors 154
siblings 121, 122 *see also* family
sight, in consumer perception 144
Sikhism *100*
silent generation 102

SIP *see* Social Information Processing (SIP)
situational factors, panic buying 226
situation factors, memory retrieval 180–181
situation involvement 72
situations, decision *see* decision situations (models)
Skinner, B. F. 173
small and medium-sized enterprises (SMEs) 341; in consumer-focused marketing (case study) 341–343; EU' agenda for, sustainable consumption and (case study) 49–50
smartphones 264, 278–280; usage 264
smell, in consumer perception 144, 145
SMEs *see* small and medium-sized enterprises (SMEs)
Snapchat 23
snobbism 126
social behaviour, subjective culture and 91
social class(es): classifications 125–126; and consumer behaviour 124–126; and cosmopolitanism 125–126; and income 126; lower or working class 125; middle-class 124–125
social exclusion 126
social factors, panic buying 226
social groups 132; Clubhouse, as hub for valuable conversations (case study) 133–134; WhatsApp, connecting and consuming on 132b
social identification 127
social identity theory 115–116
Social Information Processing (SIP) 245
socialisation: agents 120–121; children, parents' role in 121–122; consumer 120–123, 131; consumer socialisation theories 184; and selectivity theory 145–146; young consumers 120–121
social media 18, 23, 113–114; affinity impulse 274; altruistic impulse 274–275; classifying users 275; connecting and consuming on WhatsApp 132b; contact comfort/immediacy impulse 274; and digital self 248–249; emerging trends in 273–274; extending the self on (case study) 255–257; global users **231**; interactions 276; live stream, user stories, and consumer decisions 275–276; marketing activities 122–123; motivation for joining 229–230, **231**; participation, motivation for 274–275; personal utility impulse 274; validation impulse 274, 275 *see also specific* entries
social networking sites 273
social networks 126, 129; Clubhouse, as hub for valuable conversations (case study) 133–134; opinion leaders in 129, 130; WhatsApp, connecting and consuming on 132b *see also* social class(es)
social orientation, high-context *vs.* low-context cultures 93–94
social psychology, panic buying and 225
social relationships, in brand community 126–127, 128
social risk 160
social savvies 275
social self **247**
social skippers 275
social snackers 275
social stars 275
society: classification 124–126; defined 124 *see also* social class(es)
sociology 13–14
solid consumption 208–209
sound, in consumer perception 144
spiritualism **100**
spirituality: and culture 95–101 *see also* religion(s)
Spotify 328
SST *see* self-service technology (SST)
stakeholders 8 *see also specific* entries
standardisation/adaptation 272
Starbucks 45, 129, 244, 245
stem family 116, 117
stereotypical male traits 90
stimulus: attention 147; behavioural learning 173; conditioned (CS) 171–172; unconditioned (US) 171, 172
store-related factors, showrooming 154
stores 70
stories, social media 275–276
STP *see* segmentation, targeting, and positioning (STP)
subcultures 101; age 101–102; geographical 102; race and ethnic 103–104; religion-based **97–100**, 104; sex-based 102–103 *see also* culture(s)
subjective culture, social behaviour and 91
subliminal perception 156
Sullivan, Harry Stack 241
superego, Freudian theory 240

**362** INDEX

supermarkets, British, Big Data and consumer research in (case study) 319–321
Surveymonkey, for data collection 318b
surveys, consumer research 300
sustainability: green marketing and sustainable consumption 31–33; greenwashing 33
sustainable consumption: EU' agenda for SMEs and quest for (case study) 49–50; green marketing 31–33; and greenwashing 33
sustainable marketing 31–33 *see also* green marketing
symbolic interactionism 246
symbolic self-completion 220
symbolism 243

tacit knowledge, transmission of 126
Taoism **100**
taste perception 144
TBA model *see* theory of planned behaviour (TBA) model
technological innovation 268
technology 41, 150, 264–266, 325–343; augmented reality (AR) 150–151; cyberbullying 29, 40–41; developments 150; digital, evolutionary phases 16–18; digital protection and security 42–43; future of 326–327; Samsung, as innovative organisation (case study) 282–284; service robots 327; showrooming 153–155; SMEs in consumer-focused marketing (case study) 341–343; STP and consumer demographics 330–334; wearable 327–328 *see also* artificial intelligence (AI); digital age/digitalisation
Tesco Clubcard, customer loyalty and 339
theory of planned behaviour (TBA) model 200–201
theory of reasoned action (TRA) model 199–200, *201*
three needs theory (McClelland) 223–224
TikTok 229, 248, 337
time risk 161
Tinder 113, 212
touch, in consumer perception 144
Toyota 331
Toyota Fiera 272
traditional consumption *vs.* consumption in digital age **19–20**
traditions: and brand community 128 *see also* rituals

trait theory 241–242
TRA model *see* theory of reasoned action (TRA) model
transaction(s) 3; B2B 9, 10; B2C 8–9, 10; organisational and personal, for COVID-19 PPE 9–10; organisational vs consumer 8–11
transmission of tacit knowledge 126
trialability 270
tricomponent model, attitude 195
TripAdvisor 62, 228
trolling 45–46
trust 337–339
Try Date 212
Twitter 7, 18, 23, 40, 113, 189, 229, 248, 255, 273, 337

uncertainty avoidance 91
unconditional guarantees 327
unconditioned response (UR) 171
unconditioned stimulus (US) 171, 172
Under Armour 165, 172
unethical marketing communications 30
unethical pricing 29–30
Unilever 173
unitarianism **100**
United Airline 129
United Arab Emirates (UAE) 88
United Kingdom, cybercrime in 47b–48b
upper-class 124, 125–126
utilitarian function, attitude 206

Valentine's Day, as ritual for consumption 104–105
validation impulse 274, 275
value co-creation, innovation and 272–273
value co-destruction 154–155
value-expressive function, attitude 206
value-oriented transactions 3
value(s) 252–253; *vs.* beliefs 252; defined 5, 252; dimensions 252–253; and religion 95 *see also* beliefs
Virgin 173
Virgin Mobile 148–149
virtualisation, AI 329
virtual pragmatists 334
virtual reality (VR): and consumer perception 151–152; interaction 152; navigation 152; online competitive advantage 152; at Wren Kitchens 163b
virtual self 16
virtual social worlds 274

Visa 21b
Volkswagen 29, 157

wants 5; *vs.* need 221
wearable technology 327–328
Weber's law 156
webographics 336–337
webrooming 66, 155
WhatsApp 132b, 255
Williams, S. 165
Winfrey, O. 133
Woo 212
Woods, T. 165
word-of-mouth (WOM) communications 67, 170, 228; in brand community 127, 128–129; Clubhouse, as hub for valuable conversations (case study) 133–134; electronic WOM (eWOMs) 36, 63, 155; negative 129; and opinion leaders 130; WhatsApp, connecting and consuming on 132b *see also* communication(s)
World Health Organization (WHO) 9, 232b
Wren Kitchens, virtual reality at 163b

Xbox 129

Yaccarino, L. 273
young consumers 229, 334; socialisation 120–121
youthfulness 252, 253
YouTube 7, 18, 23, 40, 95, 106b, 129, 189, 227, 273, 337

Zoopla 62, 69
Zoroastrianism **100**
Zuckerberg, M. 133, 273

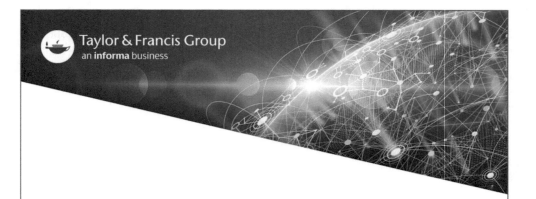

# Taylor & Francis eBooks

www.taylorfrancis.com

A single destination for eBooks from Taylor & Francis with increased functionality and an improved user experience to meet the needs of our customers.

90,000+ eBooks of award-winning academic content in Humanities, Social Science, Science, Technology, Engineering, and Medical written by a global network of editors and authors.

## TAYLOR & FRANCIS EBOOKS OFFERS:

- A streamlined experience for our library customers
- A single point of discovery for all of our eBook content
- Improved search and discovery of content at both book and chapter level

## REQUEST A FREE TRIAL
support@taylorfrancis.com